How Places Make Us

FIELDWORK ENCOUNTERS AND DISCOVERIES

A series edited by Robert Emerson and Jack Katz

How Places Make Us

Novel LBQ Identities in Four Small Cities

JAPONICA BROWN-SARACINO

The University of Chicago Press
Chicago and London

The University of Chicago Press, Chicago 60637
The University of Chicago Press, Ltd., London
© 2018 by The University of Chicago
All rights reserved. No part of this book may be used or reproduced in any manner whatsoever without written permission, except in the case of brief quotations in critical articles and reviews. For more information, contact the University of Chicago Press, 1427 East 60th Street, Chicago, IL 60637.
Published 2018
Printed in the United States of America

27 26 25 24 23 22 21 20 19 18   1 2 3 4 5

ISBN-13: 978-0-226-36111-6 (cloth)
ISBN-13: 978-0-226-36125-3 (paper)
ISBN-13: 978-0-226-36139-0 (e-book)
DOI: 10.7208/chicago/9780226361390.001.0001

Library of Congress Cataloging-in-Publication Data
Names: Brown-Saracino, Japonica, author.
Title: How places make us : novel LBQ identities in four small cities / Japonica Brown-Saracino.
Other titles: Fieldwork encounters and discoveries.
Description: Chicago ; London : The University of Chicago Press, 2018. | Series: Fieldwork encounters and discoveries
Identifiers: LCCN 2017019114 | ISBN 9780226361116 (cloth : alk. paper) | ISBN 9780226361253 (pbk : alk. paper) | ISBN 9780226361390 (e-book)
Subjects: LCSH: Gays—New York (State)—Ithaca. | Gays—California—San Luis Obispo. | Gays—Maine—Portland. | Gays—Massachusetts—Greenfield.
Classification: LCC HQ76.3.U5 B765 2018 | DDC 306.76/60974771—dc23
LC record available at https://lccn.loc.gov/2017019114

For Lida

CONTENTS

When Sam—a petite, tattooed woman in her early thirties with a degree from an Ivy League university—decided to move from Boston, Massachusetts, to Portland, Maine, for graduate school, she knew her new daily life would be significantly different than the bustle of her twenty-something world in Boston; but what she didn't anticipate was how her very sense of self would change.[1]

On moving, she found that the cities share a number of traits: a cityscape marked by antique homes and proximity to water, and pockets of both gentrification and poverty. However, something unexpected occurred after her move. After years of thinking of herself as lesbian, as a woman who loved other women but who did not devote much thought to what kind of a lesbian she might be, she came to think about and speak of herself as "stone butch." Not only did the way she thought about herself change, but her ties—and the basis on which she forged them—changed, too. She cofounded an online and off-line meet-up group for butch individuals, which, via bowling nights, dance parties, and conversation over coffee, celebrated the diverse forms butch identity can take—spanning the gamut from the "tea-drinking-fairy-butch" to the "preggers butch" to the "survivor butch"— and immersed herself in a network of individuals committed to polyamory.[2]

Sam could not put her finger on the source of her personal transformation, but she was certain that it had occurred. She also noted that those around her in Portland approached identity and difference in a manner distinct from that which she had found in other small, Northeastern cities. In Portland, like Sam many celebrated very specific lesbian, bisexual, and/or queer (LBQ) identities, like stone butch, high femme, or queer punk. Sitting on the back patio of her rental in Portland's Munjoy Hill neighborhood she said, "[In Boston] there's like a *different kind of queer* . . . I couldn't really escape being around, like, student groups and there's always kind of like an 'outy' feeling . . . that feels different than, like, queer here." In Portland, she said, "there's more opportunity for people to feel welcome even if they have sort of a particularized identity."

This book charts the stories and experiences of just over one hundred seventy individuals whom I formally interviewed and the many others I observed who identify as LBQ. All are residents of four small, politically progressive US cities: Ithaca, New York, San Luis Obispo, California, Portland, Maine, and Greenfield, Massachusetts. Like Sam, most are highly educated, white and mobile individuals, who moved to these cities sometime in the decade before I met them. Moreover, like Sam, nearly all have found that in these new places, they felt a shift both in how they relate to those around them (gay and straight alike) and in how they understood themselves and the group to which they belonged.

Taken alone, Sam's personal transformation is not particularly surprising. Indeed, the notion that identities change on moving will surprise few. We have long associated relocation with reinvention of the self: for example, the pioneer who started anew in California in the 1850s or the immigrant who traversed an ocean to find new economic possibilities in nineteenth-century New York City.

However, at heart this book challenges an assumption most of us share about such transformations: that transformation is either an individual process (the wanted man from Connecticut who reinvents himself as a law-abiding citizen in San Francisco or the frantic executive who takes up yoga and meditation and becomes a calmer, more "centered" person) *or* that it is universal (the seemingly standard process of assimilation for all nineteenth-century European immigrants). Considering Sam's personal transformation alongside that of many other LBQ individuals rules out individual-level explanations for her transformation, such as life stage, or personality, as well as broadscale or more universal explanations, such as far-reaching changes across American identity politics.

It also challenges an even more fundamental assumption: the belief that, beyond the basic groups we belong to based on our race, class, and sex, we, as individuals, are the ones who change who we are and the group to whom we belong. Even though we know that each of us is growing and changing all the time, most of us hold onto the notion of an essential self—a core identity that is who we *really* are, regardless of where we live, what job we have, or where we go to school. This book troubles this assumption by revealing how places make us.

Why is this the case? As we will see, Sam's transformation was city specific. That is, if she had moved to a different city—even another very similar city—the way she thinks about herself as a sexual minority, and the way she relates to both other LBQ individuals and her heterosexual neighbors, would be different. Despite the fact that the four cities I studied share many traits, and that the people I spoke with and whom I observed who moved to these places are themselves quite similar, on moving without meaning to and without even fully recognizing that they are doing so, LBQ migrants craft a sense of self that corresponds with their new home. That is, their new cities call out new ways of relating to those around them and therefore new ways of thinking about their sexual identity and difference and, ultimately, a different sense of who one is. As a result, there is, in Sam's words, a *"different kind of queer"* in each of the four similar cities I studied.

Consider that shortly after Sam left Boston for Portland, another woman—Lisa—left Northampton for Ithaca, New York. While in Northampton, Lisa thought of herself as lesbian and occasionally described herself to friends as "butch." Once in Ithaca, Lisa found that she rarely considered herself "lesbian" or "butch," although she suspects that throughout her adult life most have read her as a "big old dyke." While she remains with her female partner, in Ithaca the story she tells herself about who she is has shifted. She increasingly thinks of herself as carpenter and gardener. Just as Sam wonders how she became resolutely "stone butch" and enmeshed in a world of butch-femme polyamory, Lisa wonders when "lesbian" stopped being the defining facet of her self and how she came to spend evenings beside heterosexual men in a working-class bar. In fact, Lisa wasn't very happy with her personal transformation; she did not feel entirely at home in the person she had become in Ithaca, and yet, despite this discomfort, in her new context she found that she couldn't be any other version of herself.

The personal transformations of these two women, taken together with the many other individuals I interviewed, affirm Sam's notion that what it is to be lesbian, or bisexual, or queer, varies from city to city.[3] Indeed, this book reveals what I call a *sexual identity culture* that is distinct in each city; in other words, we will find that sexual identity and even our basic notions of difference are shaped by the city in which we live. Despite the fact that the LBQ residents I encountered across the cities share many demographic and cultural traits, their approaches to sexual identity politics and to ties with other LBQ individuals and heterosexual residents vary markedly by city. Specifically, by suggesting that their sexual identity cultures vary by city, I mean that the way they talk about or describe themselves varies by city, as do their coming out practices and even whether they prioritize being "out" and "proud," the degree to which they seek to build ties with heterosexuals, and their attitudes about contemporary LGBTQI (lesbian, gay, bisexual, transgender, queer, and intersex) politics and issues, such as marriage equality and transgender rights.[4]

Scholars write about small group cultures, and even about particular *sexual cultures* (Irvine 1994; Hennen 2008). I use "sexual identity culture" to capture something different. The identity cultures I describe are not as broad or diffuse as city-spanning or even international leather or bear subcultures that scholars refer to as constituting "sexual cultures" (Hennen 2008). They also are not as narrow as the "idioculture"—shared customs, habits, and beliefs—that takes shape among members of a Little League baseball team (Fine 1979). Instead, an identity culture is geographically specific, composed of those who share a defining demographic trait, and spans multiple friendship or institutional groups.[5] For instance, in Portland, Maine, identity culture unites LBQ residents who belong to broader reaching sexual cultures, such as femmes, butches, or gender-queer individuals; they share a similar sensibility about what it means to be LBQ. In this sense, an identity culture provides a geographically specific way of conceptualizing, relating to, and talking about a facet of the self that is shared by members of distinct friendship and demographic groups.

It would be impossible to overemphasize the degree to which informants' sexual identities and ways of relating to their neighbors vary by city. In Ithaca, New York, which is home to Cornell University and Ithaca College, most, like Lisa, think of themselves as being "post-identity politics," downplaying the centrality of sexual identity to their self-understandings and celebrating ties predicated on shared politics, beliefs, and practices, rather than on sexual identity. In San Luis Obispo, on California's Central Coast, most identity as "lesbian" and surround themselves with others who share that same identity. In Portland, Maine's most populous city, many, like Sam, emphasize the import of sexual identity for their self-understandings, celebrating hyphenated sexual identities, such as "stone butch" and "queer-punk." Finally, in Greenfield, a former-factory town located in the verdant northwestern corner of Massachusetts, longstanding residents identify as "lesbian feminists" and cultivate lesbian-only networks centered in neighboring Northampton, otherwise known as "Lesbianville, USA" (Forsyth 1999). However, in contrast to the other cities where sexual identity cultures span migration waves, newcomers to Greenfield think of themselves differently. Much like those in Ithaca, new residents emphasize facets of the self other than sexual identity, like being members of the local co-op and taking classes at the YMCA.

The existence of city-specific identity cultures presents two interrelated puzzles. First, within any given city, there is enough variation—in age, income, education level, and the like—that we would assume (and current research predicts) an equally large variation in sexual identity. But why, then, do LBQ residents *within* each of our four cities articulate similar orientations to sexual identity (setting Greenfield's migration waves aside for a moment)? Second, from the opposite perspective, our four cities are quite similar, sharing many ecological traits. Why, then, do sexual identity cultures vary so markedly *between* these four cities?

The solution to these puzzles is that sexual identity cultures are different in each city because each city is distinctive. That is, sexual identities are responsive to city ecology; they respond to abundance and acceptance, place narratives, and socioscape, or the demographic and cultural character of the local population, particularly of LBQ residents. Despite their similar profiles, we will see that the cities have subtly distinct local ecologies that shape what it feels like to be a sexual minority, such as the degree to which one feels accepted, how many other LBQ individuals one encounters in her daily rounds (i.e., the abundance of LBQ residents) and, in general terms, what those individuals are like, or how often one hears refrains about how their new city embraces difference. The local ecology, in turn, impacts how one "does" LBQ in that place—how a person relates to other LBQ individuals and heterosexuals and how she thinks about her sexual identity and difference. We take for granted the fact that we, as humans, are fundamentally social creatures. But what we will see here is that "social" is not sufficient by itself; we are also fundamentally *local* creatures. Even on a matter as intimate as sexual identity, each of us is a part of a community; each of us is created by and contributes to a collective answer to some of life's foundational questions: Who am I? How should I relate to those around me?

In an age of globalization and corporatization, how do we explain our deep-set feeling that places maintain distinctive personalities?[6] When I step foot in a Target in exurban New Hampshire why do I immediately recognize, despite the store's unwaveringly uniform layout, that I am decidedly *not* in exurban Massachusetts or Rhode Island? How is it that the bodies around me, perhaps wearing clothes available at any Target, look different from those in another place? Why is it that in one Target three individuals boldly cut me in line and in a Target in a different city a woman hesitates to move her cart past my own on as we negotiate a narrow aisle? This book provides a method for answering such questions by identifying *how* places make us, specifically how they shape how we think about ourselves and interact with others. Indeed, while this book takes LBQ individuals as its case, it also introduces the very real possibility that, to varying degrees, places make all of us; that the way one "does" professor, doctor, plumber, or stay-at-home-mom is different in Santa Fe than in Denver, and that what it feels like to be single or married varies between Tampa and Tallahassee.

The existence of place-specific sexual identities matters for how we think about sexuality, and about identities more generally, but it is also consequential for how we think about place. The variations that we'll explore reveal the durability and the power of differences between one place and the next, and our sensitivity to subtle ecological differences.

The Enduring Influence of City Ecology

The existence of city-specific sexual identities challenges how, in the current era, we tend to think about place. Despite the experience I describe above in Target, common wisdom tells us that places have become less distinct. Downtowns have been "Disneyfied."[7] On certain shopping streets, or in certain tourist districts, one cannot be certain whether one is standing in Baltimore or Boston, or San Francisco or New York. Street names and housing styles are the same in exurban Illinois and Connecticut. You can get toothpaste at thousands of Duane Reades across the country and withdraw cash from a zillion chain banks. And needless to say, Starbucks is pretty much everywhere. More and more often, I suspect, as we wait for our lattes, we experience the increasingly familiar disorientation borne of briefly forgetting precisely where one is.

The list goes on. Mass communication threatens distinctive local accents. With the click of a button one can purchase the same pair of pants a friend wears one thousand miles away. That encroaching sense of sameness has even filtered down to the pockets of people who have for so long seemed so utterly distinct or removed from mainstream America. The backbone of Harlem, 125th Street, now features the same chain restaurants and big-box department stores that you can find in any mall in the middle of the country.[8] And in the realm of queer culture, some worry that one of our greatest achievements of recent decades—the increasing acceptance and equality of gays and lesbians—is having the unintended effect of reducing the distinctive character of gay and lesbian neighborhoods.[9]

This book challenges all of that, as well as a closely related assumption: that as places lose their distinction, we do, too. Even in the face of globalization and other homogenizing forces, we shall see how and why places and the people who call them home remain distinctive.

Our anxiety that places are becoming less and less distinct is partially rooted in the largely unspoken and untested assumption that such distinction is consequential because places shape the character of their residents.[10] By this logic, distinctive places produce distinctive people. Many of us appreciate heterogeneous human characters, even as we sometimes make light of or even deride them. We want the Maine fishing village, complete with "real" Mainers whose character is inseparable from the brutal winters, the remote landscape, and the tendency for people to only say the minimum amount necessary in any given conversation. We want the Wyoming ranch complete with rustic, sun-hardened cowboy. We complain, when we visit Manhattan, that the streets are filled with more Midwestern tourists than native New Yorkers.

While this book challenges the notion that place distinctions are fading, it affirms our sense, however vague, that place shapes character. We will see, again and again, that places *make* us; they shape the deeply personal and intimate realms of self-understanding and how we relate to those around us. In this sense, this is a book about the persistence of city cultures and about the crucial role they play in maintaining human distinction.

Of course, even if we hope that our vacation destinations abound with distinctive characters, or appreciate, from afar, that an aunt from Queens does "Italian American" differently than her sister who resides in suburban San Diego, few of us think of our own selves, and of how we relate to those around us, as place responsive. Neither within the academy nor beyond it have we yet been able to explain how Queens might call out a different semblance than in San Diego of "Italian American." Our inability to fully grapple with these topics is one reason why the people with whom I spoke were so often surprised by their own transformations. Sam, for instance, did not anticipate that on moving to Portland she would begin to think of herself as "stone butch," nor how this would alter very intimate parts of her life, such as whom she chooses as a partner, her membership in social groups, and even how she organizes her intimate life, such as by embracing polyamory.

How Places Make Us

I did not intend to write a book about how cities shape us. At the outset, I sought to explore lesbian migration to small cities and the role those lesbians played, both intentionally and not, in gentrification. Instead, the more people with whom I spoke and interacted, the more I became fascinated by why identity cultures are place specific.[11] This eventually reoriented the project to focus more directly on perennial questions many of us ask ourselves: how do we know who we are? Why do we change?

In 2007, I began interviewing individuals who identified as LBQ in Ithaca. Over the next six years, I interviewed a little more than 170 LBQ individuals and observed their lives in four cities: Ithaca, San Luis Obispo, Portland, and Greenfield.[12] I selected the study cities because they fit the profile of the type of place to which lesbian couple migration was most orientated at the 2000 census (the available census when I began conducting research—although more recent Bureau of the Census, American Community Survey, and Treasury Department data affirm patterns evident in 2000).[13] These are small cities with many natural amenities, such as lakes, mountains, and hiking trails, and institutions of higher education.[14] Consider that the three US counties with the highest proportions of lesbian couple households are Hampshire County in western Massachusetts, which is home to Smith College; Tompkins County, New York (Ithaca is county seat); and Franklin County in Massachusetts (Greenfield is county seat).[15] These semirural counties, with moderately sized county seats, are not the metropolises with which we associate "gayborhoods." Nor are they the suburban tracts to which we might imagine today's married lesbian couples with children finding a niche.[16] This intrigued me.

Beyond their popularity with lesbian households, the cities share additional traits. They are all small, politically progressive cities; each has at least one institution of higher education; and each serves as county seat. They all have predominantly white populations, relatively high median incomes, and vibrant local foods movements, and each is two to four hours from a major city. In Ithaca, residents hike gorges and kayak on Cayuga Lake, while in San Luis Obispo residents hike the Seven Sister Peaks and walk the beach in outlying coastal towns. Portland and Greenfield are each home to burgeoning food scenes, with Greenfield emphasizing farm-to-table fare and Portland attracting Boston and New York tourists with high-end and cutting-edge restaurants. Finally, each contains a growing proportion of same-sex female couples (Bureau of the Census 2000, 2010). In this sense, the sites constitute "like cases," deepening the puzzle of why each city possesses a distinctive identity culture.[17]

Yet the cities are not identical. They have different population sizes, ranging from 17,456 (Greenfield) to 66,194 (San Luis Obispo). The cost of living is different in each city, as is the economic base, the character of local educational institutions (from Greenfield's community college to Ithaca's Cornell University), region, proportion of lesbian households, duration of lesbians' institutionalized presence (from quite longstanding in Ithaca to relatively new in San Luis Obispo) and of lesbian-friendly reputation, the ratio of lesbian to gay male households, municipal and state policy regarding gay marriage, and precise distance from a major city (Gates and Ost 2004 and Cooke and Rapino 2007).

The homogeneity of the full sample of informants (across sites) also contributes to our puzzle. Beyond the fact that most are white, highly educated and have the privilege to relocate, most of the individuals I studied—nearly all of whom identify as female—also hold professional positions, do not have children, and are politically progressive. Why, then, do such similar individuals identify differently in different cities?

The chapters that follow draw on five data sources: extensive field observations; interviews; a survey of informants regarding age, income, networks, and housing; analysis of online, print, television, and radio material in each city; and of census 2000 and 2010, FBI Hate Crime, and American Community Survey data.[18]

I collected field notes in settings LBQ residents frequent, such as bars, concerts, and potlucks, and at the annual Dyke March and Pride Parade; in total, I spent a summer or the equivalent in each city, with multiple extended visits for further observation and follow-up interviews. I also observed city-wide events: block club meetings, farmers markets, festivals, and religious services. While the former reveal the character of LBQ networks and scenes, the latter reveal how LBQ residents relate to their broader city.

Before and shortly after arriving in each city I spread word about my research by contacting local nonprofits, businesses, and university and activist groups. I also posted notice on Internet forums and sought out people to interview by relying on informal networks, ultimately formally interviewing just over one hundred seventy individuals who identify as LBQ; among these are a handful of those who identify as gender-queer or transgender individuals. Because very few in my sample explicitly identified as "male" at the time of interview, I analyzed these interviews separately from the rest. However, I typically refer to informants as "individuals" to mark the fact that a handful does not identify as "male" or "female" and to reflect the perspectives of the few transgender male individuals I spoke with. In the pages to come, we will encounter people who consider themselves "gender-queer," people who consider themselves "butch dykes," and, yes, some who refer to themselves as plain old "lesbians." The specificity, and the variety, of these terms are a key to my story. As a result, I have tried to honor their own choices for how they refer to themselves by referring to them in general terms as "LBQ."[19]

Recorder in hand, I engaged residents in conversation about the places they had lived and why they had moved from each place to the next, as well as their daily habits and the ways they participated (or didn't) in their city. Sitting in living rooms, kitchens, and in a range of public venues, from Ithaca's Gimme Coffee to San Luis Obispo's Linnaea's Café, I made certain that these conversations also traversed beyond this particular focus, as meaningful discussions nearly always do, into the larger and knottier topics central to who we are: what our networks consist of, both family and friends, where we went to school and what we do for work, how we define who we are, and how we fulfill our aspirations. I encouraged those I met with to tell me about the neighborhoods in which they grew up, their first loves, and favorite local places—from beaches to bars. I very rarely introduced identity terms, letting each informant introduce her or his own language, and in every interview I posed the same basic questions and conversation starters. Because my initial interest in the topic centered on LBQ individuals' residential choices and gentrification, I prioritized interviews with LBQ individuals who had moved to the sites within the last decade. However, in each city about ten percent of the sample includes some who have lived in the cities for a decade or more.

In each city, I worked to construct a sample that reflects the local LBQ population's heterogeneity in terms of race, class, age, and relationship and family status, with the important exception that my sample includes a disproportionately high number of publicly engaged individuals.[20] Because I had only minimal success relying on local institutions to recruit participants, my interview and observational samples span a variety of organizational nexuses. Likewise, stops and starts in the research process—partially a result of reentering the sites to conduct follow-up research after my initial fieldwork and also a result of initial access troubles—helped to ensure that the sample spanned multiple friendship and demographic groups.[21] The heterogeneity of the sample is also partially a result of the limited scope of the study population. Even in US cities with disproportionately high numbers of lesbian couples, the population of LBQ individuals remains relatively small. As a result, in each city I spoke or interacted with a sizable proportion and broad cross-section of local LBQ individuals.[22]

The more people I spoke with, the more I kept hearing about how the way they related to others and thought about themselves changed with their moves. One woman described how she sees new arrivals to Greenfield change: "I see other women who have moved here. [In Greenfield whether you are] gay or straight, it doesn't matter. They come up here and are feeling like they can just be themselves, [like] it doesn't matter who my partner is, it doesn't matter who I am. It doesn't matter that I'm a lesbian."

Initially, it didn't make sense to me that these individuals were describing themselves so differently from one another in each of the four cities, especially since the people I spoke with and the cities themselves otherwise seemed so similar to one another. Why do LBQ residents of Portland celebrate "particularized" identities while LBQ residents of Greenfield increasingly eschew identity labels? Academic literatures on identity did not provide a ready explanation for why similar individuals in similar cities would have such different ways of approaching sexual identity and difference. And popular ways of understanding how we become who we are provided few tools for the individuals I interviewed to explain their own transformations.

I began to find my way out of this puzzle—that is, to recognize that places shape identity—by recognizing the inadequacy of what most sociologists and likely most readers would consider reasonable explanations for the differences I had uncovered. For example, before I started talking with people in Ithaca I assumed that LBQ demographics produced identity differences.[23] Scholars document how differences in age, class, or race produce different ways of approaching "lesbian," "gay," and other social identities.[24] However, there are three reasons why this explanation fails to account for my findings.

First, while the demographic profiles of informants in each site are not identical, on the whole they are quite similar (e.g., most are white, possess at least a BA, and have the privilege to relocate). We tend to want diversity in a sample pool, to ensure that it represents the population at large, but in this case, a homogenous group is more useful because it allows us to isolate how and why distinct identities emerge in each city. In this case, the fact that the individuals I interviewed share so many traits—from class, to educational background, to occupations—reveals that identity differences do not emerge from demographic differences by city. For instance, identities do not vary by city because lesbians in one place are old and lesbians in another place are young or because lesbians in one city are rich and in another city are working class.

Second, within each city there are differences among LBQ residents, particularly in age, income, and education. Yet, this heterogeneity does not produce marked differences in identity, suggesting that something other than a narrow set of shared identity traits guide sexual identity cultures. Indeed, even in Greenfield—the only site with dual identity cultures—identity culture variation does not neatly correspond with generation or other demographic features; recent migrants of a variety of ages, from twenty-somethings to retirees, eschew an identity-politics orientation.

Moreover, cities such as San Luis Obispo and Greenfield where informants are, on average, slightly older than those in the others cities, have dissimilar identity cultures. This challenges the common assumption that
generation determines lesbian identities; for example, that baby boomers
identify as "lesbian feminist," whereas recent college graduates identify as
"queer."[25] For these reasons, I came to recognize that informant demographics do not account for differences in sexual identity across the cities.[26]

Some suggest that gay and lesbian individuals with the privilege to choose
where they live will seek residence in places that affirm or complement their
existing identity orientations.[27] By this logic, a gay man who regards sexual
identity as ancillary is more likely to seek residence in the suburbs than in a
"gayborhood."[28] Extending this logic, we might presume that cities' identity
cultures are self-sustaining; that LBQ individuals, following friends and word
of mouth, seek a city that affirms an existing approach to identity.

However, this book suggests that the role of chain migration and self-
selection in sustaining place-specific identities is at best modest. Instead,
professional opportunities, partners' schooling or careers, and family responsibilities drive most migrants' relocation. One described economic motivations for her move: "When I first moved . . . I was in Northampton and
the economy was really bad and the only job I could get was in Greenfield."
Another said that family called her to Maine: "I have some family in the
area. I was living in Minneapolis and yeah, I just, I was mid-twenties and
I decided that I didn't want to set down roots so far away." And a young
woman explained that she moved to Portland when her boss at a Boston
Whole Foods offered her a position in Maine. None of the LBQ individuals I
encountered specified relocating in search of a specific culture. In fact, most
report that they simply assumed that all "lesbian-friendly" cities cultivate
similar ways of approaching LBQ identities.[29]

Moreover, across the sites many had lived in the same places, such as
Jamaica Plain (Boston) and Park Slope (Brooklyn).[30] These common origin
points suggest that identity is not neatly transportable; if it were, we would
expect those relocating from Brooklyn, Northampton, or San Francisco to
arrive with and maintain San Francisco or Northampton versions of LBQ
identity. Instead, LBQ migrants move from many of the same places only to
adopt distinctive orientations that complement their new cities.

The fact that few anticipate identity culture in advance of moving further
disproves the notion that identity cultures exist because LBQ migrants seek
them out. Indeed, many express surprise about their new city's culture. For
instance, Portland initially disappointed Sarah, a feminine social worker

and local activist. She had not anticipated how distinct Portland's LBQ identity culture would be from that of the small, lesbian-friendly Midwestern city where she attended college. Specifically, as the partner of a trans man, in Portland she felt pressure to rearticulate her identity:

> I guess the thing that I didn't think about was that I was part of a pretty separatist lesbian community in [the Midwest]. . . . We never called ourselves separatist, but we definitely were and we participated in things like Michigan Womyn's Musical Festival. . . . And we were just, you know, a lot of us were Women's Studies students or just really like lesbian feminists and so I guess I didn't really think about what it would be like to move into a community where the majority in my community would be trans guys and their partners who used to identify as lesbians. So that was overwhelming. I was lonely. I also got a lot of, just a lot of flak for keeping my lesbian identity. I guess I was supposed to get rid of that and I didn't get that memo.

After moving she did not stop thinking of herself as lesbian, but she did come to identify as lesbian and femme, an adaptation to the predominant practice in Portland of hyphenating identities.[31] Her account underlines the degree to which Sarah, despite visiting the city a few times before moving, underestimated how Portland would call out a new orientation to identity.

Not all such surprises are disappointing—some are appreciated. For instance, Linda anticipated that LBQ individuals in Greenfield would express hesitancy about being "out" and "proud." Instead, "Surprisingly I've met a lot [who are out and proud]. . . . It feels like we have a big population of gay people." Likewise, Arlie was shocked to discover that Greenfield is "just an awesome little lesbian bubble."

These accounts of disappointment and welcome surprise underline the fact that chain migration or self-selection cannot account for place-specific identity cultures.[32] Instead, migrants move from some of the same places— for example, Park Slope—to distinct locales and find that their identities change; some experience growing pains as their identity shifts in their new city, while others report feeling that have finally come "home."

These—demographics and migration driven by advance knowledge of a city's identity culture—are just two examples of a plethora of plausible explanations for city-specific sexual identity cultures that I found to be ultimately insufficient.[33] By winnowing down possible explanations and carefully considering hints about the origins of their identity shifts in informants' words and interactions, my attention turned to the role of the cities themselves. That is, I came to recognize that the cities themselves drive identity culture, despite my initial expectation that something else must produce identity differences.[34] Indeed, some LBQ migrants describe how their identities evolve with moves. In the pages to come we will see again and again variations of the same essential revelation: that the identities of many of these individuals change with their moves, and that their sense of self and orientation to neighbors responds to city conditions.

But if places make us, how do they do so? Because the cities are so similar I swiftly recognized that I could not attribute differences in identity culture to basic categorical features of the cities, such as urban versus rural versus suburban, or southern versus northern, east or west coast.[35] Nor could I attribute identity differences to finer categorical differences across the cities, such as whether one is a "college town" or "county seat."[36] Ultimately, I came to recognize that what calls someone to reject identification as "lesbian" in Ithaca and embrace it in San Luis Obispo relates to more subtle—but ultimately quite consequential—differences between the cities.

Despite their many shared characteristics each city feels slightly different; one would not mistake downtown Portland, with its brick streets and tourists, for slow-paced downtown Greenfield, where a twenty-something man once exclaimed as I finished a busy day of fieldwork, "I've seen you on Main Street four different times today!" Relatedly and crucially, each city provides a different kind of life for its LBQ residents. Sexual identity cultures take shape in relation to dimensions of city ecology that influence what it feels like to be a sexual minority in a place; dimensions of place that, for instance, produce the feeling that sexual difference, in the words of one woman, "doesn't matter" in Greenfield, while it is quite consequential in San Luis Obispo. Specifically, LBQ identities respond to abundance and acceptance, or the proportion of other LBQ households and affirming institutions, and feelings of safety and belonging; to place narratives and frames or the stories cities tell about themselves; and, finally, to the demographic and cultural characteristics of existing LBQ populations in the city, such as the intellectual and professional character of Ithaca's LBQ residents. Together, this combination of features influence how LBQ migrants relate to heterosexual neighbors, other LBQ individuals, and, ultimately, themselves. These three dimensions of city ecology serve as touchstones as LBQ residents establish a sense of self and of group that are responsive to city conditions.[37]

Each dimension plays a distinct role in shaping LBQ lives and identities. Abundance and acceptance, specifically the proportion of lesbian households in a city, the ratio of lesbian to gay male couples, and measures of safety and acceptance (such as the number of affirming religious institutions), play a pivotal role by orienting LBQ individuals toward or away from identity politics. LBQ migrants de-emphasize identity politics—or the notion of sexual identity and difference as an inimitable and stable facet of the self that connects one to others who also identify as lesbian—in places in which they feel especially safe and accepted, and in which they encounter an abundance of other LBQ individuals. In cities that propagate feelings of insecurity and scarcity, and in which LBQ residents experience conflict with heterosexuals, identity politics flourishes.

Place narratives—or the stories residents tell about their city to themselves—offer models for who and how to be in a place.[38] In Greenfield, for instance, the town's slogan "Everyone's Hometown" embodies a broad and influential narrative that presents Greenfield as a wholesome place where one's specific attributes ought not prohibit membership. In turn, Greenfield's recent LBQ migrants present themselves as family- and community-focused individuals who celebrate Greenfield as a place where membership at the YMCA and food co-op affirm their sense of self.

On moving, migrants not only encounter early evidence of numbers and safety and place narratives but also observe indicators of the "socioscape"—the demographic and cultural profile of the city's population. These newcomers are particularly attentive to the traits of other LBQ residents. In turn, features of the local LBQ population influence how newcomers think about themselves. For instance, the highly educated and creative profile of Portland's LBQ residents shape how they "do" identity politics. Most embrace creative, flexible, and intellectualized approaches to identity politics and celebrate the notion that to be LBQ in Portland is to debate and perform identity around dinner tables, on stage, and at marches. Newcomers recognize these characteristics and come to emphasize their own creative, intellectual approaches to identity.

Place narratives and socioscape sometimes influence how LBQ individuals interpret indicators of abundance and acceptance.[39] For instance, in Ithaca a narrative about how the city is "Ten Square Miles Surrounded by Reality" encourages LBQ residents to overemphasize feelings of acceptance. They substantially underestimate the local hate crime rate and avoid acknowledging instances of harassment or threat that conflict with their notion of Ithaca as a bubble of safety and acceptance.

While abundance and acceptance, narratives, and socioscape all interact in complex and sometimes unpredictable ways, these three dimensions of local ecology are nonetheless quite consequential for LBQ residents across the four cities. They explain how demographically similar individuals come to have distinct orientations to a common subject; they explain why at the same moment in four progressive US cities LBQ residents articulate contrasting perspectives on matters of great debate, such as whether sexuality ought to define us, whether a life built around other sexual minorities is desirable, and whether there are linkages between our gender and sexual identities.

As I have begun to outline, in this book the city is not a backdrop to the lives of those it houses. Instead, the city is an active force. Any city is a collection of buildings and streets, a bundle (often vast and inchoate) of institutions. Needless to say, the city is not alive. Buildings don't think; institutions don't breath. And yet from a different perspective, our cities—especially those cities that we love—feel abundantly alive. They are powerful. They rise and fall; they grow and shrink; they are a palpable presence in the daily lives of more than half the world's population.

In the stories to come we will feel how, from afar, many prospective migrants envision the inert city, only to find on arrival the pulsing city and see in the process how cities shape them in ways they never thought imaginable. In a sense, these migrants come to take on some of the shape of the city; they stretch to fit its profile.

At the same time, the city responds to their presence; their being alters the city however so slightly. In this sense, the city is truly an actor; it is active and responsive.[40] It has an evolving character that adjusts in relation to its many features, including the profiles of those who live there, but it also gives character to those who build a home in the shadow of its buildings and who walk its streets. We make places, but they also make us.

New Approaches to Sexual Identity and Place

The arguments in this book build on and advance strategies for identifying and explaining why our identities and, more generally, our cultural orientations, are not identical. By uncovering how cities shape identities, I challenge popular explanations for identity heterogeneity: that identity is a product of the individual, demographic group, or epoch; in other words, that it is the self, the group, or the time period that makes us. These factors—our individual attributes and sensibilities, the group we belong to, and the period we live in—are no doubt influential, but this book reveals that they do not cancel out the impact of the place we live. Even if we watch the same television shows, read the same books, and listen to the same music, local context shapes much of the content of our daily lives and marks how we think about ourselves as individuals and as members of social categories or what I refer to, borrowing from Brubaker and Cooper (2000), as our self- and group understandings.[41]

This book is not the first to document identity variation. Gender and sexuality scholars increasingly attend to how social position influences identity, challenging approaches that treat sexuality as innate or universal.[42] They emphasize how, for instance, male and female sexual minorities identify differently and how identities vary by class and race.[43] Catherine Connell (2014) demonstrates how institutional differences matter for approaches to coming out and Emily Kazyak (2012) reveals differences in gender performance across urban and rural contexts. In so doing, they build on queer theorists' attention to how gender and sexual identities are contingent rather than essential; one might have a primary attraction to a person of the same sex, but context—the decade in which one comes out or the institution in which one is embedded—at least partially determines how attraction shapes one's identity.[44]

Despite this increasing recognition of identity as contingent, identity scholars, in Dawne Moon's (2012) words, generally stop short of demonstrating how identities "may be constituted differently, even among people in ostensibly the same social position" (1337).[45] Sociologist Wayne Brekhus (2003) calls us to recognize how *place* helps to constitute identity, writing, "Who one is depends, in part on where one is and when one is" (17).[46] He calls for recognition of "sites and times" as "identity settings for how to feel, how to act, and even for who to 'be'" (ibid).[47]

The notion that place is influential may not surprise the reader. After all, sociologists and others increasingly consider what place does or accomplishes. Neighborhood-effects scholars, for instance, examine how specific place conditions shape community outcomes, such as residents' health and education levels.[48] While they typically do not look at identity or other cultural outcomes, others do.[49] Those who study regionalism demonstrate how residents adopt regional identities; for instance, some think of themselves as "Midwestern" or "Southern."[50] Still others demonstrate how residence in a specific category of place—a suburb, a city, a rural town—lends residents identity; residents become "urbanites" or a "small town person."[51] However, this research does not consider how *specific cities* shape identity or, beyond this, the precise dimensions of city ecology that influence identity.[52]

Why is this? Neighborhood-effects scholarship aside, we are in the habit of thinking of places as belonging to broad categories, and to thinking that it is categorical differences, such as whether a place is urban or rural, northern or southern, that are consequential.[53] Relatedly, we often pursue broad trends and generalities, rather than conducting what Eve Sedgwick (2003) terms "reparative reading" of texts (or, in our case, of places or people); that is, we tend to shy away from localized theories that leave room for contingency and surprise. On top of this, we rarely conduct comparative studies, and when we do we tend to study across different categories of place or person; this encourages us to conclude that it is category that drives any differences we uncover.[54] In contrast, building on the study of four small cities, this book reveals the processes by which places make us, and even more intriguingly, the ways that similar places make us different.

In this sense, this book builds on growing attention to how sexual identities are contingent, as well as on our increasing curiosity about what places, especially cities, *do*. We will find a novel argument about the origins of identity heterogeneity; one that highlights the impact of city ecology on one's sense of self and group—even overriding certain within-group differences, such as those that relate to generation or class. We need not simply accept that group cultures are idiosyncratic and vary randomly; nor do we need to rely on neat categorical explanations for variation in identity that we do uncover. Rather, the chapters that follow reveal that we can identify the precise ecological conditions that call out particular approaches to self, group, and neighbor.

Local Communities

The stories that follow offer a novel argument about the origins of identity heterogeneity; a story that highlights the impact of cities on how we see ourselves and those around us.[55] In the process, the book also demonstrates how interactions and relationships respond to city ecology, which, in turn, underlines the role of interactions and relationships in shaping identities. Local ecology influences how LBQ individuals relate to heterosexual neighbors and other LBQ residents; in turn, these local ways of relating to one another play a crucial role in directing how one thinks about one's self.[56] For instance, in the cities in which neighbors and coworkers treat a woman as "different" because she has a same-sex partner she is more likely to think of her sexuality as life- and self-defining and to emphasize traditional identity politics.[57]

In the four cities, the ways in which LBQ migrants interact and connect with LBQ and heterosexual residents, like identity, falls loosely on a spectrum, from the very intimate and bounded community of lesbian-identified women in San Luis Obispo, to ambient community in Ithaca—in which ties are predicated on shared place, beliefs, politics and practices, more so than on identifying as a lesbian. Portland does not fall neatly on either end of the spectrum, although it falls closer to San Luis Obispo than Ithaca, as LBQ residents enjoy microidentity communities predicated on very specific facets of the self, such as femme identity or punk-queer identification, as well as an LBQ umbrella community. Finally, in Greenfield some longtimers belong to a lesbian feminist community, closely mirroring that found in San Luis Obispo, while most newcomers—and even some longstanding residents—experience ambient community like that found in Ithaca. In this sense, Greenfield's newcomers fall with Ithaca's LBQ residents on one end of the spectrum, while most of Greenfield's long-term residents tend to fall on the other with San Luis Obispo.

As the chapters will detail, the distinct ways in which LBQ individuals define and experience "community" underlines the diversity of forms that contemporary ties take.[58] That diversity urges us away from a pessimistic view of community dissolution—the idea that, for instance, we all now bowl alone—that rests on one-size-fits-all expectations.[59] A variety of social arrangements provide LBQ individuals with support and conviviality, some of which come closer to the scenes many of us imagine when envisioning "community," such as the gay or lesbian bar where "everyone knows your name" or formal membership in the PTA.[60]

In this sense, the heterogeneity of ties across four cities is a rejoinder to popular thinking about and scholarship on "community"; there has been much fretting over the last several decades about how our ties with one another are weakening, and much blame about the causes of that weakening—everything from suburbanization to more women in the workplace or to technological changes.[61] This book reveals that "community," like identity, is more varied and adaptable than we often assume. As the social world changes, ties do, too—they do not vanish.[62] And how we understand and frame our ties—and even whether we think of them as constituting "community"—has much to do with how we understand ourselves, as individuals and as members of broader groups. Moreover, local ecology calls out different ways of interacting with neighbors, with most LBQ migrants establishing networks of support in a form that complements the city that they are in and corresponds with their local approach to identity. In Ithaca, for instance, LBQ residents mourn the passing of ties predicated primarily on shared sexual identity *and* celebrate ties they forge with those who have similar beliefs and engage in similar activities, like fellow peace activists or runners. In turn, these local communities—the novel human interactions and ties we forge with one another in the places where we live—influence how we think about who we are and the groups of which we are a part.

This book's contributions to our thinking on community and identity rest, in part, on the fact that it takes up an understudied population in an understudied type of place: LBQ individuals residing in small cities. The bulk of scholarship on place and sexualities attends to the lives of white gay men residing in major cities, such as Chicago, New York, and San Francisco. While there are important exceptions, we know far too little about the lives and geographies of LBQ individuals, and even less about the small cities where lesbian-couple migration is most oriented.[63] This book, with others before it, begins to fill that gap, and in doing so speaks to the much broader questions many of us ask ourselves about place, identity, and community in a changing world.

What Follows

In the pages to come I take the reader to each city, in the order in which I encountered them, beginning with Ithaca, followed by San Luis Obispo and Portland, and ending with Greenfield. Once there, we meet the LBQ individuals who reside in each, learn how they came to live there, their expectations before moving, their experiences in the new place, and how those experiences impact ties with neighbors (heterosexual and otherwise). Ultimately, the book reveals how their moves shape how they approach their sexual identity and difference by immersing them in a new ecological and interactional context.

In each chapter, via informants' words and actions, a rough image begins to form of how cities influence ways of relating to heterosexual and LBQ neighbors and approaches to self- and group identity. However, precisely how abundance and acceptance, place narratives and socioscape shape identity cultures comes into full focus at the end of our exploration. For the people I spoke with, just like with all of us, the specific ways that place makes identity remains murky and hard to articulate. Thus, our story ends with an extended comparison across all four cities; it is that broader perspective—built from these individuals but reaching beyond and between them—which brings the sources of variation into sharper relief.

Our exploration to come is only possible because of the many people who shared their stories and invited me into their lives. Let's turn now to the four cities and the identity cultures they nurture, letting the cities and the words and actions of their LBQ migrants paint a picture of the novel worlds that our new residents encountered, help to further cultivate and have, in turn, been created by.

ONE

Ithaca:
Integration and Post-Identity Politics

In 2006 I moved to Ithaca, New York, to teach at Cornell University. Before moving, I knew what many Northeasterners might know of Ithaca: that it was famous for its steep ravines and gorges; that it was home to Cayuga Lake, Cornell University, and Ithaca College; that visitors flocked to the Moosewood, a natural foods restaurant and cooperative; and that it was remote—tucked into the Finger Lakes Region of upstate New York, more than three and a half hours from New York City.

On arrival it seemed nearly every car sported one of two bumper stickers: "Ithaca is Gorges" or "Ten Square Miles Surrounded by Reality." My first night I ate, naturally, at the Moosewood, and found the place dominated by three groups, so distinct that they almost felt like caricatures of themselves: students, academics, and "hippies," both aging and youthful alike. In the days after I shopped at Wegman's Grocery, the co-op, and the Farmers Market, discovered big-box stores on either end of town, and learned a network of running and hiking trails that wind through the gorges surrounding downtown. I learned that Cayuga Heights, which sits above Cornell, houses senior academics and other affluent folks in gracious homes, while cottages, camps, and terraced houses surround Cayuga Lake. In neighboring villages such as Trumansburg and Lansing, professionals live alongside farmers and working class families. A walk through neighborhoods near downtown revealed concentrations of poor, working class, and African American residents, and even months later, the drive out of the city still surprised with its pockets of enduring rural poverty.

Not as obvious, but just as important, was another discovery: the unmistakable presence of a large population of lesbian, bisexual, and/or queer (LBQ) individuals in and around Ithaca. I watched women holding hands with abandon. Playgrounds often contain two-mom families alongside heterosexual couples. Women with short hair wearing Carhartts and hiking boots work behind co-op and coffee shop counters. These recognizably LBQ individuals appeared nearly everywhere: on the bus to Cornell, on hiking trails, at the co-op, Wegman's, and Staples, behind coffee shop counters, in restaurants, and at the library.[1] Both the abundance and ubiquity of LBQ residents in nearly every space I entered was undeniable. These were not just pockets of young queers, nor merely the remnants of legends I had heard of lesbians who moved to Ithaca in the 1970s to live on rural communes or to mingle with other politically progressive residents.[2] Nor were they just university students, eager to experiment beyond the watch of mom and dad. Rather, these were LBQ individuals of a variety of ages and from all walks of life. And they were everywhere.

Data affirm my armchair observations about the breadth of the LBQ population. By the best measure—2000 and 2010 census data on same-sex couples, and US Treasury Department data on married female same-sex couples—Ithaca has an unusually high and growing proportion of lesbian couples.[3] Indeed, in 2000 and 2010 Tompkins County, of which Ithaca is seat, had the third highest proportion of same-sex female couples of all US counties, and the proportion of lesbian couples increased between 2000 and 2010.[4] The year I first lived in Ithaca, *The Advocate*—a leading gay, lesbian, bisexual, transgender, and queer (GLBTQ) periodical—named Ithaca one of the top ten "best places to live" in the United States.[5]

However, what neither the data nor feel-good stories like the *Advocate's* could tell me is *why* Ithaca possesses a disproportionately high number of lesbian couples. These sources communicate even less about what it *feels like* to be LBQ in Ithaca. A year later, as I left Ithaca for a position in Chicago, I decided that these questions were at the foundation of the project that led to this book. Not long after I returned to Ithaca to begin identifying answers.

Ten Square Miles Surrounded by Reality: The "Lesbian Friendly" City and LBQ Migration

There are three standard arguments explaining how lesbians choose where to live. Some suggest that lesbians' choices are financially driven; that due to economic constraints lesbians, whose households tend to be less affluent than those that include gay or straight men, live where they can afford to do so.[6] Others point to the role of ideology, particular when considering the establishment of lesbian-feminist-separatist communities in places like Berkeley.[7] A more recent argument purports that, especially for young women, sexual and gender identity are no longer paramount and that the notion of sexual identity enclaves is outdated.[8] "Post-mo" or "post-gay" LBQ individuals can live anywhere and do live everywhere.[9]

LBQ Ithacans explain their moves in terms that largely depart from these accounts. First, while Ithaca's cost of living is relatively low, there is much competition for jobs. Many report that they make professional or financial sacrifices to move to Ithaca—in large part because they have heard, from friends and books and magazines—that Ithaca is notably politically progressive and, relatedly, "lesbian-friendly."[10] For instance, over lunch at a downtown Indian restaurant Chris, a gender-queer educator whose partner heads a social service agency, said, "I think that is one of the hugest issues to face everyone of any background in this town. Finding work that pays a living wage and finding work period. There are tons of people who are unemployed and underemployed." Chris added, "I was sort of shocked at the cost of living here compared to other places where I've lived—everything from energy prices to lettuce."

This perspective is abundant; many recount periods of unemployment and underemployment. Ithaca is home to LBQ bartenders, baristas, waitresses, carpenters, and nannies, no matter their advanced degrees. The *Ithaca Times* featured a story on highly educated individuals occupying working-class jobs in Ithaca, and many of those I interviewed could afford to reside in places with a higher cost of living.[11] Affordability, in other words, drives few if any moves.

Second, none of the people I spoke with articulated a separatist ideology—that is, they expressed no desire to live apart from men or around only other lesbians. Indeed, most volunteered distaste for what they regard as an obsolete separatism.[12] Young women were not the only to offer criticisms of 1970s-style separatism. Jan, a butch fifty-something woman with short, dark hair who wore loose jeans and a button down shirt, criticized her youthful separatism, saying, "I identified as separatist for all of six months. It didn't last long. My male friends had an issue with it and told me to get a grip. You know because I liked them, too . . . So it didn't last long." Lilith, whose gray hair reaches halfway down her back and who often wears long, flowing skirts, came out in the 1960s and has long resisted separatism; in her twenties she joined a gender-integrated queer commune.[13] None of my informants moved to Ithaca to join separatist communities.

Third, despite their rejection of separatism, none are indifferent to the hospitability of a city for sexual minorities; most of my Ithaca informants told me that they felt comfortable moving to Ithaca because it has a large LBQ population, or because they had heard or read that it is "lesbian-friendly."[14]

However, virtually none suggested that they moved simply because Ithaca is lesbian-friendly and has a large LBQ population. Instead, on their account a large LBQ population and a lesbian-friendly reputation was necessary but insufficient information to permit a move; most followed work, education or a partner to Ithaca.[15] In this sense, it is crucial to note that, as this chapter elaborates, in retrospect many find this information about the scale of the LBQ population and Ithaca's lesbian-friendliness to be at once accurate and misleading; while technically accurate, it does not facilitate the formation of lesbian identity politics and lesbian-only networks that they anticipated finding in a progressive city like Ithaca.

An attorney recalled a typical notion of the city, from a moment she had years prior to her move: "I was driving . . . [years ago] and there was a sign [for] Ithaca and I was with a girlfriend . . . and we both said, 'Oh gosh, we have heard about Ithaca.' . . . It was like a little image of you go in, you check in, [and they say] 'lesbian 49 million has arrived.'" A much younger woman recounted a similar impression: "I heard there was a good woman's community. . . . I'd never been a part of a big, strong gay community. I'd never walked into a bar filled with lesbians."

Many others knew that Ithaca was "lesbian-friendly" and happily anticipated that they could be "out" about their sexual identity; this is another indication that they do not move without regard for sexual identity. Chris recalls: "I remember saying, 'Oh, there are a couple cities like West Hollywood, California, and Ithaca, New York, where they even have non-discrim laws.' [Ithaca] was well known, even [twenty years ago], as sort of a place where people could come, live and be a part of a community and a social fabric. They would be valued; they would be respected." Jan said: "If [my queerness is] not acceptable, I'm not there." Likewise, the attorney, Rebecca, said she always discloses her sexuality in job interviews: "I didn't care because if they didn't want me as I am then they shouldn't hire me. I always talk about my partner. . . . Everywhere I have been, everybody knows I am a lesbian. . . . I pretty much tell them right away because I am proud of it." Another said, "I don't want to have to educate or defend or explain myself. So I just assume you know, this is me and this is you and if you like it, fine. If you don't, leave me alone." Yet another said, "I am out in my resumes." LBQ mothers assign extra import to being "out." Andrea, a thirty-something, feminine professional said: "We're out in my kid's school. . . . That was a criteria for finding a place where it was okay for me to be out and [for my son] to be out."[16]

Thus, LBQ residents here present a portrait of moves motivated by a host of reasons, from work to family to love. However, Ithaca's large LBQ population, and the common perception that LBQ residents feel safe and accepted, affirmed the choice of nearly everyone I spoke with to relocate here, and, crucially, set expectations for the life they would build in Ithaca. Their sense of Ithaca's recent history—as a city renowned for its progressive politics and educational atmosphere—guided their moves, and their sense that Ithaca would be a place in which, as LBQ individuals, they could comfortably pursue a career, build a family, or simply live in a beautiful and semi-remote place.

What They Find in Ithaca

After arriving LBQ residents find that Ithaca meets their core expectations: it is a "lesbian-friendly" place and has many LBQ residents. I asked all the LBQ individuals I interviewed about their perception of the size or proportion of the local population that identifies as LBQ. One woman said, "Fifteen percent? Twenty percent? I mean maybe on a good day, maybe thirty percent." But all my informants greatly surpassed census counts, and several insisted that the census underestimates Ithaca's LBQ population. In other words, the breadth and visibility of Ithaca's LBQ population do not disappoint.

Indeed, across the board LBQ residents celebrate their city's LBQ population and consistently report greater safety and acceptance than in other places they have lived, including more well-known gay destinations like San Francisco. On the Ithaca Commons, which is lined with bookstores, bars, gift shops, cafés, and the occasional empty storefront, women walk arm-in-arm. Residents do not try to hide their sexuality, whether they work as baristas or behind a spa or co-op counter, or as university or college professors. In 2008, the Women's Amateur Softball Association, which is popular with LBQ residents, maintained eight teams—an impressive number for a town of less than thirty thousand. As Maura, a thirty-four-year-old social worker, said, "Here everywhere you go you see lesbians. Like I'm going to get a massage today by a lesbian. My chiropractor's a lesbian. Everywhere you go, they're just there." Before stepping into her silver convertible, a middle-aged attorney who has lived in large US cities told me that she concurs, saying that, despite Ithaca's small size, "you go out and see a zillion lesbians . . . you have never seen before." A twenty-five-year-old musician, who wears her hair short and tends to wear men's shirts and skinny jeans, suggested that the LBQ population is not only large but powerful: "It's great. . . . The police are obviously here to protect us, which I have never found to be the case anywhere else." Indeed, several people proudly told me that a prominent elected official identifies as lesbian.

However, two surprises await LBQ migrants to Ithaca. First, many report disappointment with what they refer to as "community"; a disappointment few anticipate before moving.[17] For instance, one said, "I don't really feel a part of *any* community," and another describes her "sense of community" as "Zero. *Absolute* zero." However, this disappointment does not emerge from a dearth of meaningful connections to others; LBQ residents—even those who complain about the absence of community—detail a wealth of support from their neighbors, heterosexual and LBQ alike. They told me excitedly of friendships forged with fellow gardeners and knitters, the support and company of a meditation group and parents' association, and the daily pleasure that comes with even casual interactions with their polyglot neighbors.

This paradox—disappointment with the absence of "community" amidst the discovery of rich local ties—emerges from specific dimensions of Ithaca's city ecology that inform what it feels like to be LBQ in the city.[18] Specifically, that paradox is possible *because of* the breadth of the LBQ population and its successful integration into Ithaca's social, cultural, and political spheres, and the safety and acceptance that LBQ individuals feel in these "Ten Square Miles Surrounded by Reality." Part of the reason why Ithacan LBQs say they don't feel a strong sense of "community" is because they are so accepted, and because there are so many of them in the town. In Ithaca, rather than constituting an isolated or even persecuted group who would bond with each other more fervently and thus feel a more palpable sense of community, they are part of the mainstream.[19] Most report that their inclusion is largely something to celebrate—but they are equally mindful of, and, justifiably or not, wistful about how inclusion has altered the character of their ties and, relatedly, their identities.

The manner of relating with neighbors—both heterosexual and LBQ—that these dimensions of city ecology cultivate helps to encourage a second surprise, one that we'll see throughout the book: a transformation of ways of thinking, talking, and feeling about the self and one's membership in a broader social category or group. LBQ migrants to Ithaca come to adopt a "post-identity politics" orientation. That is, they come to eschew lesbian identity politics, which regards sexual identity as a defining and inviolate facet of individual and collective self-understanding. Traditional identity politics emerge from the notion that a group of individuals has a common set of interests, concerns, and shared experience and perspective because they share a trait.[20] LBQ Ithacans are dubious about the notion that sexuality continues to produce shared experience, concerns, and interests—that shared sexuality is their "glue"—and challenge the implication that to advance and defend their group they must emphasize their commonalities and advocate on behalf of a shared set of interests.[21] On living in Ithaca, they come to embrace the idea that they live in a time and place that enables them to emphasize facets of the self that they "choose", such as one's profession, or being a parent, or a backyard gardener—facets beyond or other than sexuality.[22]

This chapter traces how LBQ Ithacans perceive city ecology as producing "costs" and "benefits" for social relations. Informants tell me, again and again, that their ability, in Ithaca, to forge ties with heterosexual neighbors and to eschew bonds predicated on shared sexuality threaten a sense of true "community," by which they mean an inclusive, place-based network of individuals who share a social identity and experience social marginalization. Here, they specifically evoke lesbian-only networks that they associate with other places or times; their images closely mirror textbook descriptions of "social movement community," which sociologists Verta Taylor and Nancy Whittier define as a "network of individuals and groups loosely linked through an institutional base, multiple goals and activities, and a collective identity that affirms members' common interests in opposition to dominant groups" (1994, 172). Although they rarely explicitly associate it with social movements, older women typically suggest that they were a part of this kind of a network in previous decades and/or more recently in other cities. Younger residents suggest that such networks used to exist, or that they've observed them in other, less LBQ-hospitable locales. They do not present these networks as perfect, but they do uniformly present them as *missed*. Yet, they also propose that Ithaca's large population of LBQ residents, feelings of safety and acceptance, and place narratives about Ithaca as a lefty-bubble promote a strong sense of what one woman refers to as *ambient community*: a sense of belonging and connection that arises from informal, voluntary ties with a diverse mix of people with whom one shares place, beliefs, politics, and practices, and secondary identity traits, such as age or profession.[23] Thus, while Ithacans mourn "community," they experience neither a loss of place-based ties nor newfound freedom therefrom—outcomes we might predict as a historically marginalized group experiences increasing integration.

Instead, they report a shift in the origins of or basis for place-based ties, not in the number or strength of their ties or the degree to which they feel connected and supported. Their local ties are not narrowly and explicitly predicated on "hard" status-based identity attributes, such as shared sexual identity, but, instead, on "softer" identity attributes, such as shared beliefs, practices, politics, and place of residence.[24] Their sense of loss reveals that they assess community, in part, by the traits of those with whom they forge ties or the reasons for forging them (necessity versus choice), rather than by the number or strength of their ties. Of course, they may overstate the lack of agency that LBQ individuals experience in other contexts, as well as their own freedom and flexibility to cull together ties in Ithaca. Most importantly, they romanticize alternate nodes of connection forged under circumstances that require sexual minorities to band together for safety and security. But their sense of ambient community and their certainty about the novelty thereof is nonetheless real and, in the Ithaca context, nearly universally articulated.

The transformation of Ithacans' ties challenges the prevailing expectation of many scholars, as well as a common notion of community (one that many LBQ Ithacans share as well): that place-based ties best flourish among marginalized residents.[25] Instead, in Ithaca we see that when the conditions in which we live change, the ties we form (or the impetus for forming them) change, too—they do not simply disappear. Specifically, they alter *how* LBQ individuals construct ties in a new place without producing either their "loss" or "liberation."[26] We will also see that dimensions of city ecology— the proportion of LBQ residents, feelings of safety and acceptance—do not just alter ties, but also, at the same time, change how residents think about who they are and how they relate to those around them.

Baking Contests and Affirming Religious Institutions: Integration in Ithaca

For LBQ residents, Ithaca encourages heterogeneous social circles, predicated on shared place, beliefs, politics, and practices—indeed, predicated on pretty much anything besides sexual identity. That was true even for those LBQ residents who told me about how they moved to Ithaca anticipating endless opportunities for interaction with other LBQ individuals.[27] After all, in a city with a "zillion lesbians" why wouldn't one find limitless lesbian networks? Sarah is a nurse and high school prom queen who lives with her partner and daughter in a restored Victorian; their open-concept living and dining area is overcome with children's art, toys, and books. She boasts, with a laughing surprise, at the gap between her expectations and Ithaca's reality; her block, she told me, "has an annual pie baking contest and they invite us. We are a part of that kind of stuff." The street, with its venerable trees and wide front porches, practically calls for such events. She delights in pie contests and her daughter's play dates with the children of heterosexual neighbors, but she can't get over her surprise at how different these occasions are than the lesbian dances and dinner parties she had envisioned.

At Ithaca's lakeside Farmers Market, LBQ mothers and heterosexual parents picnic with their children or chase toddlers down the long rows of vendors selling vegetables, fruits, and crafts. Their children dance together at one end of the market, where a string band plays folk songs. At Gimme

Coffee, housed on the first floor of an old wood-frame house on a residential block, young LBQ women share tables with straight men and make social plans with heterosexual couples. On any given day, the children of LBQ and straight residents play together, infants grow up together, and passive newborns become willful toddlers in the same playgroups sharing blankets on the lawn at Dewitt Park, shaded by impressive stone buildings that first housed Ithaca College.[28] During the sermon at Ithaca's First Baptist Church on Father's Day, an African American pastor substituted "parent" and "caregiver" for "father." The substitution seemed to surprise only this ethnographer, as children bounded forward for the children's sermon and story, and parishioners looked on with appreciation and, at most, mild bemusement.[29]

Over and again informants remarked on how their place on the inside, alongside other professors, artists, and social workers, was worlds away from exclusions—some subtle and some much less so—they experienced in other cities. Indeed, some emphasized fear they experienced in other places. A middle-aged white woman who had long lived in Brooklyn recounted violence she experienced in other cities:

> Two times I was at construction sites in Texas and no cell phone service, no one around, just got the living daylights just like kicked out of me. . . . And the one in Albany the police report, I mean these guys are like kicking me and beating me up and they're calling me "Dyke! Dyke! Dyke!" . . . but in the police report the reports never said anything about that they were yelling dyke and I was like, "Well why doesn't it?" and they're like, "Oh we didn't want to embarrass your family."

Thankfully, such accounts of overt violence were rare, but informants nonetheless describe feeling more safe and at home in Ithaca than in other places they have lived. For instance, one woman could not put her finger on why she felt less safe in coastal California than in Ithaca: "It is an indescribable feeling that you get. . . . I just feel like so fortunate like I'm in this little bubble of wonderful people." Similarly, a young woman spoke of feeling "really unsafe" in her Los Angeles neighborhood, and another recalled being shouted at in an area of Pittsburgh "where there are a lot of straight bars."

One longtime resident, a mother who favors jeans and T-shirts and can sometimes be found out at bars and restaurants with friends, said that twenty years ago even Ithaca used to be less accepting; she is grateful for the sense of welcome she experiences in Ithaca today. She recalled: "I mean there were a couple of times, like I said, at the beginning before the local laws came in that it was a little touch and go. I remember one time. . . . I was out mowing the lawn. We lived at a corner and this truck came down the hill and stopped at the stop and then yelled out 'lesbian' or something like that. I remember this little shiver of fear that was so odd, going through me." LBQ Ithacans celebrate a life relatively free of shivers of fear and other reminders that some regard them as "other." Having experienced exclusions and worse in other places, few take for granted their inclusion in Ithaca's baking contests, parenting groups, and workplace social networks.

LBQ residents emphasize that their inclusion is predicated on acceptance, not merely tolerance. Seated in her book-lined office, Jenny recounted a moment that marked how local politicians have come to embrace the presence of LBQ residents:

> We added [protective status for] gender identity and expression . . . and I went to the County Board when they . . . passed it, and you know it was pretty much a love fest. It was very cute. . . . We had, you know, the guy . . . who always gets up and talks about the fact that we're all disordered and . . . everyone goes right back to what they're doing. They don't argue with it. . . . They go, "Okay, you've got five, four, okay, bye." But you know the chair of the County Legislature got up holding, you know, *Stone Butch Blues* and said, "You know, I wasn't good on this issue and I didn't understand it and I didn't know what you were talking about and I thought, 'These people are just weird,'" and then of course it was like . . . "I read this book and I understood." And I was like, "Yeah, *this* is Ithaca. It's so cute."

Such signals of acceptance allow LBQ residents like Jenny to move with ease through Ithaca's various social worlds—from the political to the cultural and social—without nearly as much dissonance as they've experienced in other places. Ten years in, Jenny so takes this for granted that the county legislature's display of acceptance strikes her as "cute" rather than revelatory.

LBQ residents suggest that Ithaca's accepting atmosphere reduces their need to socialize with other LBQ individuals; as we will see, it also simultaneously reduces their need to think of themselves as a part of a sexual minority. Indeed, even those who moved to Ithaca with excited anticipation about the scale of the LBQ population find that it no longer seems important. One said that the LBQ population "doesn't need to be a lot. I think ten-percent or so is fine. *As long as it is a tolerant climate* . . . We don't need to have a lot of lesbians around us as long as it is a safe and accepting place." Another specified that the fact that "we don't need a lot of lesbians around" depends on how heterosexual residents interact with LBQ individuals: "You know, [I interact with] a good mix [of straight and gay people], but that's only because, in this town, it's such a positive mix because all of the straight people I know are just so open." In other places, she found that she actively sought out other LBQ individuals, and thought of herself as "lesbian."

Paradoxically, they detail how this sense of not needing to be around other lesbians in fact is a result of the fact that there *are* so many LBQ individuals in Ithaca; they argue that the density of the LBQ population partially produces their inclusion in Ithaca's broader social, political, and cultural milieu. My interviewees implied again and again that the breadth and visibility of LBQ residents normalizes their presence *and* provides a mechanism of social control that contributes to an ethos of acceptance. As Kelli reports, "If you were homophobic, you're not allowed to express that here." Tanya described her rural neighborhood outside of downtown Ithaca: "There [are] a lot of Cornell staff and faculty side by side with a lot of farmers and people who grew up here and are more conservative. And we all make it work. We talk to each other. We share plants. Our neighbors are eighty years old. . . . We were nervous to tell them we were going to adopt. We were matched with a birth mom and . . . they were so sweet. They brought over diapers and stuff and they were just so sweet to us. We all make it work there." Separately, her partner suggested that this acceptance was predicated on the fact that they are not the only LBQ residents of their neighborhood. Indeed, each reported that more than half the houses on their street, nestled between farm fields, contain LBQ individuals. In this sense, regardless of whether their precise count is accurate, they feel a fascinating paradox: the high number of LBQ residents helps to enable integration into Ithaca's broader social life. Surrounded by lesbians, this couple finds that they have more or less stopped socializing with them and, increasingly, have stopped thinking of themselves through the lens of sexual identity and difference.

Despite an awareness of how the breadth of the LBQ population enables integration, there was a clear limit. None of the people I spoke with want to be surrounded only by other LBQ individuals. I asked each person a hypothetical question: "In your ideal neighborhood or town what proportion of the population would share your sexual identity?" One said, "It would be nice if it was at least twenty-percent, I guess. . . . [More] would be overwhelming." Another said, "I would say probably like a quarter. . . . I think about 'oh it should be half and half' but in some ways I like being not part of the mainstream. . . . So I would say a quarter would be ideal."[30]

These individuals are mindful that they *could* choose to live in places with either a lower or higher proportion of LBQ residents than Ithaca possesses. For instance, Rebecca, who says "twenty-five percent is okay," vacations in Key West because "it is totally gay down there. It is just gay." However, she specified that she does *not* wish to live there, saying, "It is fun being in that fantasy for a couple weeks but it is fun to come back." Indeed, many report that they once lived in "lesbian neighborhoods" in places like Seattle and San Francisco. Though the promise of an all-encompassing lesbian world sounded heavenly, these women said that they and many of their neighbors experienced both physical and social isolation; one of the draws of Ithaca was that they wished to live outside the "ghetto."[31]

However, while they wish to be included in conversations and in pie-making contests with straight neighbors, they do not wish to disappear or blend. Meaningful integration does not require disguising, hiding, or even downplaying one's sexuality. Ithaca provides a context in which LBQ residents feel that they can be "out" about their sexual identity and difference, and indeed they emphasize the import of being frank and open about their sexuality. LBQ Ithacans generally presume that all other LBQ residents are "out" about their sexual identity. This presumption was revealed one evening in a lesbian-owned bar just outside downtown. An out-of-town friend affectionately refers to the small venue as the "pie bar," in honor of the homemade fruit pies sold alongside wine, beer, and old-fashioned cocktails.[32] There are also seasonal drinks made with herbs and fruit picked in the owners' garden, like the basil-raspberry martini my friend was drinking that night. Most if not all the bartenders are LBQ individuals under the age of forty-five, but the bar regularly draws a mixed crowd—from Cornell and Ithaca College faculty to a handful of just legal students of all persuasions. On any given night, one might encounter, for instance, tables of forty-something lesbians, a heterosexual, fifty-something house painter seated at the bar with a few LBQ members of his staff, and gay male faculty sharing a patio table with a few straight, female professors and a bisexual author who teaches at the college. After their game, softball players from several different teams, many of whom are LBQ, find a place on the porch and beside the bar, and begin raucous conversation that occasionally spills out onto the sidewalk and the quiet street. The bartenders know many of their customers' names, particularly those of the weekly meet-up groups that gather—the knitting group on Tuesdays, progressives on Thursdays—on the couches beside the bar's piano.

Twice per week the bar hosts live music, and this particular evening the musician, an LBQ singer-songwriter, drew a typically mixed crowd. Early in her set she encouraged the audience to applaud a couple, Jane and Ashley, each of whom had just graduated from Ithaca College. Everyone cheered, until the singer-songwriter noticed Jane's mother; blushing, the musician said, "Oops! Your mom is here tonight, too. I hope she knew you were a couple!" The crowd silently absorbed this note of caution until, a moment later, quiet gave way to nervous laughter; like the singer-songwriter, the crowd realized a moment too late the error of presuming that all are out about their sexual identity beyond the "ten square miles" of happy bubble that is Ithaca. Despite this awkwardness, this is the type of exchange LBQ Ithacans celebrate and on which they feel their ability to integrate rests: instances in which they forget that some remain closeted or moments when they presume that all, like them, are out. Thus, despite their appreciation of ties to a variety of residents, informants nonetheless express desire to be around other LBQ individuals and to be "out" about their sexuality.[33] This commitment to being out, partnered with commitment to integration, is a core feature of the local identity culture.

In this sense, many celebrate Ithaca as a place where they can lead a "normal" life without hiding their sexuality; where a woman attends her street's pie contest with her wife and child.[34] Moreover, some come to regard a social life predicated on common secondary attributes, such as the kind of work one does or how old one is, and practices, such as hiking or brewing beer—rather than shared sexual identity—as a defining personal trait. That is, LBQ Ithacans emphasize their ties to heterosexuals in their conversations with me to convey not only the significance they attribute to integration, but also to tell me about the kinds of people they think of themselves as being: nonheterosexuals who are "post-identity politics." As one said, "It's interesting because there's a lot of lesbians in this town. And it's really great and really exciting and . . . some of them hang out mostly with other lesbians but a lot of them hang out with all different kinds of people. And that's always been sort of my way is to hang out with all different kinds of people." In fact, this is not only her "way" but also the way of nearly all LBQ Ithacans I encountered, and perhaps "the way" of anyone with the freedom and flexibility to forge ties outside a context of oppression. It is to this way of thinking about the self and LBQ-group that I now turn.

Becoming Post-Identity Politics in Ithaca

Two seemingly contradictory proclivities—discomfort with strict adherence to narrow identity categories and the belief that others should accept them (embodied by nearly always being "out")—reflect a commitment to integration apparent among nearly all I interviewed. This commitment, which extends from the practice of engaging in integrated networks described above, constitutes a core, orienting feature of the identity culture I came to recognize among LBQ Ithacans. That is, integration fuels and compliments a vision of identity that emphasizes frankness and openness about one's sexual difference, but that simultaneously regards sexuality as only one facet of the self—not as the defining or organizing trait or as a source of inimitable common ground. LBQ Ithacans think of and present themselves as, for instance, therapists, professors, mothers, runners, and environmentalists who "happen" to also not be straight.

In their conversations with me, LBQ residents emphasized their ties to heterosexual neighbors to articulate a dimension of city ecology (the sense of abundance and acceptance that enables integration) that shapes self-understanding and to underline their post-identity-politics orientation; that is, to present themselves as multifaceted. Lucy, who is forty-eight, explained why a network composed of LBQ residents would not satisfy, "I've always hung out with people that live on the outskirts of the norm, doing theatre, doing music, you know, folks that are night owls. . . . [In Ithaca] the majority of them are straight." She elaborated: "You know, I'm LGBT but I'm also Asian. I'm creative. I play music. I write. I do script writing. I do storyboarding. . . . I mean, it's all part of everything."[35] For Lucy, in the Ithaca context sexuality is one part of the "everything" that constitutes her sense of self, and it was important to her that I know this.

Likewise, a middle-aged single feminist said, "I have a core group of friends who are also gay but I also have friends who are straight, you know, and what brings [us] together has to do with our politics and how we look at the world." She emphasized her participation in groups unpopular with other lesbians: "I have connections at Cornell and also with the congregation that I'm a part of. . . . And I don't do softball. . . . For me, sometimes you can take sisterhood and shove it."

Most acknowledge that they have not "always" sought taste- and activity-based ties nor have they always thought of themselves as post-identity politics. Lilith, a white woman in her sixties, primarily socializes with heterosexual members of an Ithaca cooperative that she was a part of in her youth. She lives in a rural hamlet and does not have any LBQ immediate neighbors. These ties and this location complement her sense of herself as a woman romantically involved with other women but whose sexual identity and difference do not begin to wholly define her. However, this is not how she understood herself in New York City. Indeed, Lilith suggests that in Ithaca she has established political and practical rather than identity-based ties and a sense of self that complements those ties: "In New York City where a lot of my friends are lesbians and most, I would say, they socialize, mostly, with other lesbians. . . . I think maybe because [Ithaca] is a smaller town . . . it's easy for people to sort of overlap and know each other in different ways."

Alice, an Asian American native of Indiana who was pursuing a graduate degree at Cornell, offers a parallel account of identity transformation. However, she emphasizes her increasing comfort with being out and open about her sexuality in Ithaca. To her surprise, this openness leads her to think less about her sexual identity than she did in her home state. When I spoke with her, she had lived in Ithaca for a year. Over a beer in her small downtown apartment, Alice described a year brimming with change: beginning graduate school, sharing a home with her girlfriend for the first time, and, most momentously, a shift in how she thinks about her sexual identity.

Before her move, Alice suspected that she was moving to a context in which having a female partner would have different meaning and significance than it did in rural Indiana. However, she underestimated the degree to which this would impact how she thinks and feels about her sexual identity. Of Ithaca she said, "People are nicer to gay people." Laughing, she added: "Welcome to the East Coast intellectual community."

Before moving, she debated whether she should be out about her sexuality in Ithaca. She recalled, "My mom was very concerned about me coming [with my girlfriend] and she was like, 'Do you really want to establish yourself with that identity, like do you want people to think of you that way?' . . . And so I was trying to kind of keep it on the down low because I just didn't know." She recalled, "I just didn't know what it would be like and. . . . [being out] wasn't something we did for a variety of reasons in [Indiana]." On arrival she was embarrassed that she had given so much thought to being out, and, more generally, to her sexual identity. In Ithaca, she realized, being in a same-sex relationship was not a big deal. "I was so embarrassed because people were so open about it. I was being outed left and right because nobody, it didn't occur to anybody that it was like private. Across like a crowded room like at the happy hour they have for the students they were like, 'Where's your girlfriend? We were hoping to meet her.' People were so like open about it . . . and it was sort of like a new identity I'd never had before."

Like others, Alice says her identity changed because of the kind of acceptance on display at the happy hour, and because much of Ithaca is, in her words, "very super lesbian." The breadth of the lesbian population provides the sense that "there's sort of this safety in numbers." She added, "It's like welcome to Lesbianville. . . . That's a really big culture shock." As a result of this sense of acceptance and of "safety in numbers," other facets of the self have become more central to Alice's self-understanding. She said: "I feel so much more at home here and that they are people who share my interests. . . . Like everybody here likes organic food." She elaborated, "People [don't] care that we are gay here and like it never occurred to us that there would be this whole other set of things that would make life so much better. . . . Like just the focus on being outdoors."

Echoing Alice, Nancy, a woman who has lived in Ithaca since the 1980s, suggested that shortly after her arrival she recognized that the city was different than other places she had lived, primarily in the rural South. She recalled, "It was not the usual way. It was different." It took some time for her to fully absorb this difference: "I think within that first year. I don't think it was immediate because I just wasn't thinking about it or expecting it, but definitely when I walked into [my first job] and people were, like, you know, 'Welcome lesbian.'" Nancy also recounts how Ithaca has changed in the twenty-plus years she has lived in town—and that as the city has changed she has changed, too. Ithaca is no longer a place, she implies, where co-workers say "welcome lesbian"; after all, to do so would be to draw attention to a facet of self that is supposed to be unremarkable. She described the "old days" when she was a "real lesbian": "They broke up and we broke up and then we had, you know, how lesbians do. Back when I used to do that. Back when I was a *real* lesbian." Here, she suggests that "real" lesbians are a part of lesbian-only networks (characterized by the serial monogamy and insularity she hints at by saying, "how lesbians do"). In a changing Ithaca context, in which lesbian-only networks are decreasingly relevant, she finds that she thinks of herself as lesbian less and less, identifying more and more as parent and social worker.

On first glance, Nancy's account, together with Lillith's and Alice's, nearly affirm the notion, forwarded by some other authors, that sexual identity has become secondary or ancillary for LBQ individuals.[36] Indeed, many Ithacans, particularly those in their twenties, eschew what they regard as an outdated view of sexual identity as static, as well as identity labels. A petite woman in her mid-twenties who was preparing to marry her female-to-male transgender partner does not claim a particular identity. She said, shyly, "I've noticed that it's mostly a seasonal thing where it's like I never like women and men both at the same time—it's like different seasons. I like different people." Likewise, a forty-something woman said she is cautious about labeling her sexual identity because, "I don't want to say I'll never get any new information about myself again." A recent college graduate, who remains in town to participate in athletics, said: "I don't actually officially identify. In all practical terms I'm gay; I'm a lesbian but I don't actually identify." Here, she recognizes her sexual difference, but implies that she does not want others to think of her through that lens—and does not primarily think of herself in that way. Another elaborated: "I don't like labels, so it's really hard for me. I'm really very Aquarian, so I kind of go through not wanting to be labeled and I'm different all the time and always changing." This was also true of some older residents. Sitting in Gimme Coffee on State Street, Jan said that she "identifies" in "two ways. One is I do identify as a lesbian but the other is I prefer to be more queer identified because I make a distinction that queer is more inclusive and has a political nature to it that I appreciate."

However, the same individuals who purport that they do "not identify" or identify in a way that emphasizes the fluidity of identity (e.g., as "queer") nonetheless emphasize the import of being "out" and of living near a robust population of LBQ individuals. In this sense, they do not regard sexual identity as ancillary. Instead, they wish to "do LBQ" in a different way than women in other times and places—and, in many instances, in a different way than they have done it themselves in other times and places.[37]

Collectively, their stories of how their identities have changed since moving to Ithaca or, in the case of longer-term residents, as Ithaca has changed, paint a picture of identities that are highly responsive to dimensions of city ecology. Specifically, LBQ Ithacans report again and again that an enduring sense of acceptance in the city, the high number of LBQ households, and Ithacans' celebration of their city as a progressive bastion (in Alice's words, "East Coast Intellectual"), enable their integration into sexually heterogeneous social circles and their closely related post-identity-politics orientation. While they do not say this explicitly, it likely also does not hurt that Ithaca's LBQ population—those who, for LBQ migrants, compose a core feature of the local "socioscape"—tend to be highly educated and intellectual and therefore better primed than most to debate, in academic terms, the merits of traditional identity politics. The rest of the chapter considers the paradoxical position many in Ithaca find themselves to be in, as they navigate the benefits and burdens of integration and acceptance and, fundamentally, of thinking of themselves as post-identity politics. Even in a context that enables the establishment of rich and varied ties, some yearn for what they and I refer to as "lesbian community"—that is, ties built on a foundation of shared lesbian identity and a common sense of difference.

Consequences of Integration

Ithaca's critical mass of LBQ residents, residents' commitment to LBQ inclusion, and abundant narratives about Ithaca's embracing atmosphere enable LBQ and straight individuals to forge ties with each other, predicated on living in the same place and sharing similar beliefs, politics, and practices. However, LBQ migrants do not experience this freedom as an unambiguous good. Instead, they offer vivid accounts of the "costs" and "benefits" of integration and concomitant shifts in identity.

"Being Separate Was Wonderful": Perceived Costs of Integration

The fact that local ties primarily rest on shared place, beliefs, politics, and practices, rather than shared sexual identity, contributes to one of the most common themes I found: a disappointment with "community." Of the more than forty residents with whom I spoke, about half vehemently articulated this disappointment, and most others shared a less pronounced version of this feeling. This disappointment was particularly paramount for middle-aged partnered women who moved within the last decade, many of whom reported having experienced alternate forms of community in different times and places.[38]

Many readily volunteered their dissatisfaction with community—sometimes before I asked about it. One said, "It was really hard to meet people when I moved here." Another said, "There are times I feel really lonely." Kelli, a single social worker whom I often encountered with her friends at the Farmers Market or a craft group at the LBQ-owned bar, said, "I don't really feel a part of *any* community right now, to be honest."

Kelli's emphasis is revealing: most people instinctively used "community" to refer to lesbian networks. While some mentioned other social circles—for example, "the music community"—the bulk of references to "community" implied LBQ networks. For instance, before I posed any specific questions about community, Tanya referred to the "gay community" and "the community I came out in" and Jackie, a twenty-five year old artist originally from a northeastern suburb, mentioned the "gay community."

Indeed, most interpreted one of my first such questions—"How satisfied are you with your sense of community?"—as pertaining solely to their ties to other LBQ individuals. Given that this followed a general line of inquiry about friendship and networks—many of which were forged with local heterosexuals—this presumption underlines the fact that they regard "community" as explicitly identity based; that is, as ties forged with other LBQ individuals simply because they are also LBQ.[39] For instance, Rebecca responded, "Zero. Zero. *Absolute zero.* Gay Pride came and went. I don't think Ithaca did anything for it." Indeed, several women suggested that in place of a Pride celebration some rallied for marriage equality. Joking, Rebecca added, "Maybe there really aren't very many lesbians in Ithaca. Maybe it's a myth, like Bigfoot. And we all move here because we think it is true and it's not." Likewise, Jenny said:

I don't think Ithaca is a hostile place to be queer. You know I really don't, but I don't think there's a whole lot of queer community. . . . If you go to a place like San Francisco, I mean you still have—there's the rich white gay guys but they have stronger senses of community. . . . This is a real lesbian baby boom place. So there are a lot of folks that are more interested in nuclear family and play-date kind of set-ups than they are in any of the more sort of traditional forms of queer community and we only have two half-gay bars . . . and one of them is way, way, way out of town.

Notably, Jenny did not respond by complaining about the number of her local ties or about her sense of support. Instead, her disappointment arises from the absence of a "traditional" gay community she associates with San Francisco, Pride Parades, and bars.[40] This disaggregation of "community" and "ties" allows those like Jenny to mourn lesbian bars and women's bookstores, while also acknowledging and celebrating the flourishing connections that they have forged with disparate individuals.

Julie, a forty-something white woman whose partner is a college professor, had lived in Ithaca for just two years when she spoke with me. Sitting at her home in the countryside just outside Ithaca she distinguished between "lesbian community" and "lesbian presence," thus offering a clear sketch of what LBQ Ithacans like Jenny mean when they say that Ithaca does not have a lesbian or gay community. Julie told me, "There's not a lesbian community that I've been able to tap into. There's, you know, *lesbian presence.*" In her experience, the absence of lesbian community is particular to Ithaca; in another college town she found "lesbian community." She recalled, "There are a lot of lesbians in Santa Cruz and there was a community there." By describing why Ithaca cannot sustain a lesbian community, Julie specified better than most what she considers to be the constitutive characteristics of lesbian community: the inclusion of all who are LBQ, an anchoring institution, and ties forged out of necessity.

First, by highlighting the absence of a formal LBQ center in Ithaca she suggested that lesbian community is marked by a formal meeting place that is open to all who identify as LBQ: "There are a lot [of LBQ women] here. There's just not a central place to find them." Second, she suggested that "lesbian community" is found in places in which such a center is forged out of necessity. In Ithaca, she said, "We kind of want it, and we kind of miss it—*but we don't need it.*" She underlined this by saying that she and her partner socialize with other LBQ residents, but that these events stop short of constituting community, because they are informal, infrequent, and predicated on pleasure rather than necessity: "We have game nights where we, you know, we invite [LBQ] friends over to play board games and card games and just laugh. And I like having a lesbian night. So we'll have . . . a lesbian game night where we can hoot and holler and it's just us. So I try to make little community opportunities but I don't get a sense that it's needed." She links the absence of lesbian community to increasing acceptance of LBQs across the United States, but especially to the specific local context, which she finds to be remarkably embracing: "Maybe that's a sign of our times. We don't have a literal physical center. . . . And you know, we're out and we're welcome on the bus. Even if there's some people who are like not thrilled with it, they're outnumbered." In this sense, Julie implies that the reasons for forging ties—that is, for pleasure rather than necessity—play a role in whether she regards them as constituting "community."

Informants' implicit distinction between the local ties that they value and what they think of as "lesbian community" (or between their lives as they experience them, day by day, and their lives as they imagine they could or should be) is also apparent in responses to a related inquiry: "Tell me about the communities of which you are a part." Amber, who is a young and newly coupled mother, answered with a lengthy description of (disappointing) evenings at an LBQ-owned bar, using these recollections to explain her disappointment with lesbian community. Yet a moment later when I asked with whom she socializes, she did not sound disappointed at all, saying, "Most of our friends are straight and it's mostly coworkers. . . . [I] hang out with other parents sometimes and we go to a lot of potlucks. That's what's great about this town, too, is all the potlucks. . . . We go to vegan family potluck every month. . . . We also go to raw food potlucks. . . . We've been going to the CSA [Community Supported Agriculture] potlucks." Like many, Amber distinguishes between the reality of her diverse ties and activities and her perception of an ideal "community," depicting the latter as necessarily homogeneous and discrete; a community one might find in a lesbian bar or bookstore.

Ithacans provide several accounts of what they miss about lesbian community. Many argue that Ithaca has a large but dispersed LBQ population, suggesting that they miss "cohesiveness." One, relying on nostalgia for what she thinks of as older forms of lesbian connection, said, "[In the past] it definitely seemed like [there was] more cohesiveness. . . . There was a stronger sense of community. . . . Now we're kind of all over. We're spread out. It's a fairly substantial LGBT community, but we are all over the place." While she may be looking at "lesbian community" through rose-colored glasses, she is not alone in her sentiment. Another concurs: "I know there are a lot of people who are gay here, but . . . it'd be great to have more gay friends here. . . . I wish we did have more of a community here."

Second, others wish for lesbian organizations that would aid the formation of ties based on shared sexuality. Toni, a gender-queer retail employee said, "I don't really consider myself to be a part of a community, and that's what's kind of sad to me about Ithaca. When I lived [in a less queer-friendly town] there was a community gay group. There isn't really one here." Toni's sense of isolation from other LBQ residents surprised me, as I could not think of a time when I had entered Toni's workplace when I had not encountered at least a handful (and usually more) of LBQ individuals staffing the store, shopping, or dining: a young, LBQ woman stocking the dairy aisle, a middle-aged woman selecting produce, and a woman in her sixties behind a cash register. Over and again, informants like Toni report that they are disappointed by the absence of homogenous LBQ networks anchored by institutions or markers of common identity, such as a Pride Festival or lesbian-feminist bookstore.

Like Andrea, many articulate the dilemma this produces through complaints about the absence of an LGBT community center, which they blame on the fact that "Ithaca is so gay." Sarah, the nurse, said that a student of hers "was starting to struggle with her sexuality. . . . It was really disturbing for her and I didn't have a place to send her. It was just kind of like—*if you are [queer], you [just] are.* Ithaca is the kind of place if you are, you are."[41] Her partner agrees, saying, "I think it would be nice if there was some kind of community center. . . . There is not a space here. . . . All of Ithaca is queer, but . . ." Likewise, despite working at a business staffed by many out, LBQ residents, Amber said, "It's sad because Ithaca is so gay that there really aren't any formal [gay places] that I know of. . . . It's kind of sad because we don't meet a lot of gay people."[42]

Those who had long lived in Ithaca fondly recalled with me a longstanding women's bookstore that sat on a tree-lined street just outside the city center. While its closure reflects the widespread pressure chains have placed on independents, several used it to illustrate their increasing integration by referring to the fact that in lieu of that store two chains now contain lesbian or gay sections, and one hosts a queer book club. For instance, Chris recalled that before (s)he first visited Ithaca a friend "would write me letters about this mythical Ithaca place and how there were . . . nine different softball teams. . . . I would be like, 'You're full of crap. This place does not exist.' She was like, 'There is a woman's bookstore.' That's another huge change . . . but again, that change mirrors what's happened all over the country too. . . . Is it good or bad that you can find gay and lesbian books in Barnes & Noble?" Likewise, many note that an LBQ-owned bar resists identifying as a gay bar and attracts a heterogeneous crowd. Thus, they mourn symbolic anchors for lesbian culture and social support.

By their own account, the disappearance of such institutions results from living in a place where, in Sarah's words, it is "a nonissue to be lesbian" (and therefore also a place where one doesn't have to identify as "lesbian"). She said, "I think that it is also a place where it is a nonissue to be lesbian so that there is no community because *you don't need to be together*. And I think that is to our detriment. . . . There is no Pride Festival, you know. You kind of don't need it" (emphasis mine). She added, "It's the plus and the minus of . . . living in a place that is so accepting that it is not a big deal [to be lesbian]." Likewise, Kelli, who was moving to the West Coast, said she looked forward to living in a place with *fewer* lesbians:

> Ithaca is ten square miles surrounded by reality. I'm going to be in for a shock because I'm going to be back in reality. . . . If you're in most towns you see a lesbian and you do a little eye contact thing. Like familiarity, like "How's it going?" Here you don't do that because *there's just too many of them*. You don't need that.

Another echoes this, reporting that she does not feel the need to join an informal LGBTQ social group—one of only a handful that I heard of—because "there is a critical mass here."[43] Here, she eschews the need not only for formal lesbian institutions but also for the informal, such as a coffee group for middle-aged women (indeed, the founder of the group said that she struggled to get others to attend).

Third, some miss how a sense of shared "outsiderness," in their view, cultivates lesbian networks and institutions: "[In the past] it wasn't as mainstream; you were still more of an outsider. You know, *there's something about oppression that brings people a little closer together* that may not ordinarily hang out together. And so as we become more assimilated *it gets dispersed* and therefore *different things take over*" (emphasis mine). This means that different "things" organize ties, such as politics, beliefs, and practices, but also that "different things take over" how one thinks about oneself. Tanya referred to what is lost on leaving the "ghetto":

> I had an interesting conversation about meeting people [with an acquaintance]. . . . We were both saying how hard it is to meet lesbians here. And she said, "Well, you know, we both come into communities expecting a center,

a core [of] lesbian-based activities and times have changed. We're not ghet-toized anymore and so it's harder to meet lesbians because there's no central place. You just have to stumble upon each other in the course of doing some-thing else."

Chris referred to this as "the unintended . . . effect of having a lot of things be really integrated."[44] Chris regards the absence of an LGBT community center as indicative of the extent to which LBQ residents are integrated into Ithaca's broad social fabric:

I have lived in a lot of communities where there's sort of the LGBT Center or stuff having to do with orientation and identity sort of over here some-where. . . . Here it's really become rather embedded, which is great—except I think it's pretty hard for newcomers to find what they're looking for. There's no central referral place . . . "How do I find a cool dentist? How do I find a realtor? Why isn't there a community center? Can you do therapy for me?"

In the process of telling me what they miss about the organizations that sometimes anchor "lesbian community," they offer arguments about why Ithaca does not have them. While they propose that their absence relates to broad social changes, they also suggest that it emerges from city context. Again and again LBQ Ithacans report that they experienced greater exclu-sion in other places where they recently lived, and that in those places they found lesbian community marked by institutions. But in Ithaca, by contrast, specific dimensions of city ecology enable integration: namely, a markedly heightened sense of safety and acceptance, broad narratives of Ithaca as a progressive bubble, and the high proportion of LBQ residents—many of whom, like most of those who are in positions of authority in Ithaca, are white and highly educated. Seated on a porch on a quiet stretch of Cayuga Street, Andrea noted that in other cities, she relied on gay community cen-ters for community.[45] She misses "gay community," but also said that she moved to live where such a center is irrelevant:

We belonged to an LGBT parenting group in [Los Angeles] and there were over a thousand families—families—not people, families! And you know we had our own playgroup for children in my daughter's age bracket and we had a [monthly] newsletter . . . and we had like three big parties a year. . . . And it was so very strange when I moved here and there was no LGBT Center and there was no physical place where my daughter could go. . . . There was nothing, nothing visible. So that actually I wondered for a little bit if I did the right thing kind of to pull her and take her out of a community she was comfortable in.

Not only has Andrea lost a community that she and her daughter were "comfortable in," she has also lost a sense of self as a person who joins LGBT parenting groups and visits the LGBT Center.

She later acknowledged that she struggled to reconcile integration in Ithaca with the formal modes of connection with LBQ individuals she knew in Los Angeles, saying:

> [My daughter's] teacher is a lesbian. . . . But . . . we've gone to a number of parades already since we've lived here and my daughter's wondering where the rainbow flags are and where the men dressed as women are. . . . Gay Pride was very important to our family in [Los Angeles] and there was a children's corner or a garden and so those things are very different. And I miss those things for myself and for her. . . . So *[in Ithaca] it isn't so separate, which is what I think I always hoped for.* That's part of why I wanted to be here but at the same time it almost felt like we just disappeared. . . . [I had] this sense of pride and I really wanted my daughter to have a lot of that because the world's an ugly place and I want her to feel secure and not always in a minority. . . . *I think that what we traded in was being separate, [which] was wonderful.* (emphasis mine)

As Andrea aptly states, in Ithaca LBQ residents find the safety and acceptance that drew them to Ithaca, but they also experience an unanticipated loss of identity-based networks—in Andrea's words, a sense of being separate that is simultaneously "ugly" and "wonderful."[46] Of course, it is only from the position of relative inclusion and acceptance—in Ithaca—that Andrea can reflect back on feelings of being "separate" in other times and places as having been "wonderful."

The 2011 Ithaca Festival Parade embodied the dilemma Andrea sketches: the inclusion of Ithaca's LBQ population and the absence of LBQ-only spaces and groups. Before the parade, which was held on a bright and breezy early June evening, dozens of residents participated in a one-mile run along the parade route. Participants included many families with elementary-aged children, as well as a few women with Down Syndrome who earned hearty cheers of appreciation and encouragement from the crowd.

For well over an hour after the race, a seemingly endless line of colorful and entertaining floats progressed along Cayuga Street. LBQ individuals appeared with many groups, such as a synagogue, a nonprofit that serves the homeless, and an after school program. Yet, *none* of the floats or organizations that participated in the parade were explicitly composed of, or even geared themselves toward, LGBT residents. This absence was particularly striking given the number and heterogeneity of interests represented: a group advocating the end of drone attacks in Afghanistan, former Peace Corps volunteers, motor scooter commuters, individuals who engage in specific water sports, a Volvo ballet complete with men in ballet costumes on the Volvos' roofs, and the co-op, which marked its forty-year anniversary by distributing carrots to the crowd and displaying banners such as, "Party Like its 1971." Countless childcare centers and afterschool programs participated in the parade. One childcare center carried a banner that read, "Where your child is the Center!" and members of a family reading partnership held alphabet letters above their heads. A large contingent of La Leche League members in bathrobes, some carrying babies, walked en masse, while a community drumming group performed from the back of a pickup, and a bookstore float sported children dressed as book characters—including a young boy in a tutu. Among the tiny handful of groups celebrating or marking a formal identity were the Latino Civic Association of Tompkins County and Ithaca Scottish Games and Celtic Festival—a departure from Cornell's College of Veterinary Medicine, Ithaca Carshare, Taoist Tai Chi Society, AIDS Ride, an antifracking group, a birthing support group ("Supports Your Birth Your Way"), and Roller Derby groups that dominated the parade. Thus, the parade affirms Andrea's observation about the low profile of sexual identity–based organizations, as well as the extent to which, despite this, Ithaca presents opportunities for LBQ inclusion, alongside the abundant opportunities for alternate modes of identification—primarily around beliefs, practices, politics, and shared enjoyment of Ithaca. After all, many LBQ residents walked with the Roller Derby group, and others with the co-op, daycares, and other organizations. LBQ residents had an unmistakable presence in the parade but were somewhat separate from one another, clustering instead with those with whom they share other commonalities, such as politics (e.g., environmentalism), beliefs (e.g., a common faith), or practices (e.g., kayaking or dancing).

Despite complaints about the absence of a community center and LBQ residents' dispersion evident in the parade and in their accounts, the LBQ residents I spoke with readily acknowledged that Ithaca is, in fact, home to some organizations and groups that provide opportunities for LBQ interaction, including the following: "gay AA," lesbian parenting groups, an LGBT book club, an LGBT elders group, gay-straight alliances at the area's high schools, university GLBTQ offices, a transgender support group, and gay bowling and softball teams. Several of my interviewees had been involved in establishing such groups: a playgroup for the children of LBQ mothers, a coffee group for LBQ women over fifty (and another for those under fifty), and a rugby team.

However, despite awareness of and some participation in such groups, many yearn for "lesbian community" that would span beliefs, politics, and practices. Yet even most of those who call for a formal embodiment of this community via an LBQ center admit uncertainty about whether they would use it because in Ithaca they do not depend on it, neither for ties, nor for safety, nor for a sense of belonging. Instead, many imply that a center would be of greater symbolic than practical value; it would symbolize the community they expected to find in Ithaca: one predicated on sexual identity and a sense of shared fate. Thus, there is reason to doubt that such a center would effectively alter—that is, improve—their sense of community. Despite their professed yearning for such a center, given their integration within the city and their post-identity-politics orientation, it is unclear whether they need or truly desire the support it would provide.

To be clear, despite their sense of loss of community none of those I interviewed or observed presented a portrait of a life of isolation or loneliness. This is because while integration and acceptance may spell the loss of "lesbian community," they do not destroy ties or support structures. In a town with many LBQ residents and high levels of acceptance of sexual difference, "different things"—in the words of one of the above women—"take over." Specifically, shared place, beliefs, politics, and practices, rather than sexual identity, are the foundation for ties that LBQ residents form with heterosexual and LBQ neighbors alike. For some like Lucy, this produces ambivalence about the state of "community" in Ithaca and simultaneous satisfaction with one's social life. She told me:

> Community [is] definitely out there. . . . If you lived here it wouldn't be uncommon for me to see your softball game or to see you at like a Take Back the Night Rally or you know serving up slop at Loaves and Fishes [a church soup kitchen] . . . and that's I think how the LGBT community in this town . . . live life. I think that's what I like about it. . . . Their life is part of who they are and they are part of life. They're interested in . . . helping out at Loaves and Fishes or interested in writing theatre. They're interested in attending free musical events. They're interested in supporting whomever. They're going to the Common Council meeting. You see people all over the place and that's part of their life. All of these things affect their life and so they happen to be LGBT identified but they also happen to really care about "What are we doing to our kids in school? What are we doing with the dog park, folks?"

Notably, Lucy mourns the loss of lesbian community. However, she simultaneously appreciates the freedom to form ties predicated on beliefs, politics, and practices rather than on sexual identity. And Lucy doesn't just exercise this freedom in her social life; she regularly rents a room in her house to Cornell graduate students, typically to heterosexual women.

Such interactions, across different groups but based on common appreciation for music, was apparent at a May 2008 night at a bar in Collegetown—a hilly portion of the city a few blocks from Cornell University that is home to many student rentals and businesses catering to undergraduates. On this evening the bar hosted three very different music acts: a lesbian singer-songwriter and guitarist from Chicago, with long brown hair; a queer female singer-songwriter and keyboardist from Ithaca, wearing a loose T-shirt and jeans and having closely cropped hair, who sings about, among other topics, an Ithaca street; and a folk country band, headed by a heterosexual couple, that labels its music "folk country for country folk." The band's repertoire ranged from a song about appreciation for women's butts to a cover of the song "Both Hands" by the musician Ani DiFranco, whose fan base, at the height of her fame in the 1990s and early 2000s, included many young LBQ individuals. Aside from the musicians, the audience included a handful of LBQ women in their twenties, two tables of middle-aged straight couples, and a large party of straight couples in their early twenties who became quite drunk as the evening progressed. While the scene was not idyllic—from disruptively tipsy twenty-somethings to a fifty-something woman who fell dramatically down a set of steps during one of the performances—the marked heterogeneity of both performers and audience exemplified a core feature of life in Ithaca, a feature celebrated by most LBQ residents whom I had interviewed.

Indeed, most told me that ties that emerge from shared beliefs, politics, and practices meet many of their social, emotional, and practical needs. Yet, they also complain about how this, combined with the high concentration of LBQ residents, facilitates the formation of small and sometimes insular networks—some LBQ only and others that include heterosexuals. This fragmentation exacerbates their disappointment with community, because it contrasts sharply with their vision of "lesbian community," which they depict as inclusive of all who share a lesbian identity and therefore spanning smaller social circles.[47]

We tend to think of integration as a coming together, a coherence. But it has the seemingly paradoxical effect of (at least for some people) also creating the opposite reaction, and fragmenting or pushing apart certain pieces of a community. For LBQ residents, we might imagine that integration is an answer to isolation and loneliness borne of exclusion. However, LBQ Ithacans report that integration does not produce a seamless collective; bracketing off still happens, but it is driven by facets of the self that are largely unrelated to sexual identity, like whether one has kids or plays softball. And while integration provides relief from the internal conflict and insularity that can characterize "lesbian community," it also affords the distance therefrom to recognize cleavages—or fragmentation—within and beyond the LBQ population.

Many recognize that they play a role in this fragmentation via membership in these smaller social networks, which some informants implicitly criticized by calling them "cliques." One said, "I have a lot of different sets of friends." Lucy described the multiple networks she is a part of, listing, "The academic . . . Let's see, music, theater, writing . . . I'm mixed into many different [networks]." Likewise, Mary, a forty-something entrepreneur and mother, said, "I'm just so connected in so many different [groups]." She elaborated: "I go to Rotary. I'm nineteen years sober, so I'm in Alcoholics Anonymous. I'm involved with Ithaca College athletics. I still dabble a little bit in doing real estate and in the business world most everybody knows who I am. . . . It varies." Notably, the bulk of social circles that these women identified are belief or activity based, and, despite listing a plethora of memberships and ties, many of these very women complained about the absence of "community." This suggests that while some believe *ties* may span sexual identity groups and arise out of shared politics, beliefs, and practices, constituting small "c" communities, they nonetheless regard "real" community as identity based (i.e., as lesbian community) and as spanning or obfuscating the opportunity for the formation of smaller networks.[48] For the reader who enjoys memberships in a women's book club, a mother's group, and a young professionals organization, the distinction between small "c" and "real" community that my informants make may seem overstated. However, LBQ Ithacans bring a powerful image of lesbian or "real" community to the table. This is, of course, a romantic image, as it glosses over the exclusivity and conflict that can characterize networks predicated on necessity and shared identity.[49] Yet this does not diminish its power in the minds of Ithacans encountering a new basis for connection. Indeed, some LBQ residents who report having been a part of lesbian community in the past or in other places are simultaneously aware of the limitations thereof (e.g., one recalled with frustration a moment when lesbian feminists in Rochester accused her of not understanding the patriarchy) *and* nostalgic for a sense of belonging and connection forged under conditions they consider deplorable. Thus, we ought not read attachment to lesbian community as either entirely naive or uncomplicated. We also should not assume that by articulating nostalgia for lesbian community they mean that they would trade what they have found in Ithaca for it; after all, beyond all else, to be a part of a lesbian community predicated on a shared lesbian identity politics would require LBQ Ithacans to revise how they have come to think of themselves—as post-identity-politics integrationists—in the context of their city.

Criticisms of fragmentation extends even to ties among LBQ residents, which some find disappointing because they are predicated on shared beliefs, politics, and practices, rather than on shared sexual identity. New residents complain that it is difficult to enter preexisting friendship networks formed around these nodes and describe Ithaca's LBQ population as highly compartmentalized. For instance, sitting on the porch of a rental shared with several other young, LBQ women, Jen, a twenty-two-year-old, described the Tuesday scene at an LBQ-owned bar, when bartenders screened episodes of a lesbian soap opera: "It's difficult to get into the groups. . . . It took me a really long time to meet girls. . . . I used to come for *The L Word* every Tuesday night with my two roommates and we would just like be by ourselves, because we were in our own group of three and everyone else had their own group of three and it's impossible to go talk to people like that." At one such screening a patron gestured to different portions of the room, "Look, there's the [natural foods] co-op lesbians, there's the knitting lesbians, there's the coffee shop lesbians, and there's the Cornell lesbians . . ." Rebecca, an avid tennis player, articulated a similar sentiment:

Ithaca also has a lot of cliques. . . . There's like the mama lesbians, then there's the professor lesbians. . . . There are people that are belly up to the bar—blue collar workers. And then there is people who are kind of more, I would think that are a little bit less polished. There is a little crowd of them. There is a little crowd of drinkers. There is a crowd of golfers. But there really isn't a little crowd of lesbian tennis players. What is up with my sisters? Where are you people?

These narrow LBQ social circles, forged around shared practices, contrast with their imagined lesbian community in which, for purposes of support, ties would necessarily span small groups and there would be ample opportunity to meet those whom Rebecca refers to as belonging to different "crowds."

These women aptly describe countless scenes I observed in Ithaca. At the *L Word* bar nights Jen describes, LBQ individuals in their distinct small groups spent much time looking at and discussing one another, but cross-group interaction was limited.[50] According to those who have lived in Ithaca for several decades, this fragmentation is partially a product of the (longstanding) breadth of Ithaca's LBQ population. A woman who moved from New York City in the 1970s to live in a gender-integrated gay commune recalled deliberating over *which* lesbian collective she should align with, and Mary recollected a party designed to draw together fragmented LBQ networks. Sitting in the remodeled kitchen of her colonial, she explained:

> We had a woman in town who . . . was wild and she wanted to put together a women's New Year's Eve Party. So she got nine women in different communities and I was the woman representing the business community. And we all got together and met and put on this New Year's Eve Party and that's how I met [my partner]. . . . It was fun. We did this back in probably '94. . . . We did it for three years. . . . [My partner] was from . . . the pot-smoking hippies.

Thus, the sheer size of Ithaca's LBQ population and LBQ residents' integration do not entirely diminish ties among LBQ residents, but they do encourage the formation of narrower networks predicated on more than shared sexual identity.[51] Ultimately, for reasons Julie outlines, they do not experience this as constitutive of "real" or lesbian community, and even these ties contribute to the sense that they have lost a kind of connection they once associated with cities with "a zillion lesbians."

Perceived Benefits: A Sense of Ambient Community

As may already be clear, despite disappointment with the absence of what they consider "lesbian community," LBQ residents take great pleasure in alternate local ties. Specifically, many suggest that integration produces a welcome sense of belonging and connection forged around shared place, beliefs, politics, and practices. For instance, when I asked Edith, "What are the communities that you'd say you're a part of in Ithaca?" she could not name any. I soon came to recognize that this was because she assumed I wanted her to talk about *lesbian* community. As she went deeper into an account of her actual, lived ties in Ithaca she expressed a sense of tremendous good fortune at the social life she's built in Ithaca, "It's a very generous community. It's a very charitable community. It's a very human service community."[52] If not lesbian community, what is this alternate community that is "generous" and "charitable"?

Tanya, who, like many others, expresses sorrow about the paucity of lesbian community, nonetheless also describes the welcome discovery of an alternate set of rich, supportive ties. Better than most, she described the precise character of the ties and of the welcome sense of community they generate for her:

> I have a nice *ambient sense of community* here that I didn't have in [Boston] or San Francisco and by that I mean I don't have to know everybody here to still feel like most people are sort of part of my community. Most people are liberal. Most people are not going to beat me up on sight. Most people here are actually really nice compared to other places. If I am on a bus . . . and I realize I don't have my wallet, I can ask people I ride the bus with, 'Can I borrow the money?' And the bus driver will say, 'I recognize you. It's okay.' This would *never* happen in the cities I have lived in. If I am on the street and something were to happen, you just flag somebody down. People offer to help here. It is nice to be in a place where people will like me.

Admittedly, these ties and the sense of connection they generate do not fully meet Tanya's vision of lesbian community, which she anticipated forging in Ithaca. Yet, she acknowledges that her sense of ambient community—what I propose we think of as her feeling of belonging, safety, and ease of casual communion with her polyglot neighbors and coworkers—satisfies her basic social needs.[53] On moving, straight neighbors welcomed her with plants and purchased diapers when she adopted a child, and on a more daily basis she finds herself chatting with people of all walks of life on the bus. Like Edith, she finds that she is enmeshed in "charitable" and "generous" networks, and a regular participant in impromptu friendly interactions with a variety of residents. These connections, largely predicated on shared politics, beliefs, and practices, are perceived as abundant and even "in the air" for most LBQ residents of Ithaca.

Lucy recounts how she came to recognize the alternate sense of connection and support ambient community provides after initially seeking lesbian community in Ithaca: "As far as socializing with gay people, I think when I first moved here I'd always try to go to [a gay bar] and seek a community. I just don't think it works. . . . I've done a better job finding neighbors or people or just being like, 'Oh they also do this or this or this.' Then there's more compatibility." Another, Mary, mentioned that heterosexual Alcoholics Anonymous members ushered her into sobriety and remain an essential source of support. Indeed, a diverse array of individuals regularly poured in and out of AA meetings held in a community building on a quiet residential street; this was not the "gay AA" Mary might have joined, and yet it provided a vital lifeline. Others referenced friendships forged through Compost

Education, conflict mediation groups, book clubs, work, children's schools, craft guilds, and the Farmers Market. For instance, Kelli said that community gardening "was a big socializing thing too. . . . It was a great place to hang out and chat with people." When I asked, "What kinds of people would be there?" she replied, "Just people into gardening, which is pretty diverse, too." As these words suggest, while Tanya was especially articulate on the subject, nearly all express appreciation for their "sense of ambient community"; that is, they highly value the variety of ties they've forged with a range of Ithaca residents.[54]

This sense of ambient community emerges from informal ties and a sense of belonging, but it is not rooted in a specific institution or space (e.g., the Unitarian Society), nor does it preclude intimate ties.[55] Indeed, while it grows from inclusion in community gardens, craft guilds, and religious institutions, it also depends on more intimate friendships that enable and extend from interactions in the public realm.[56]

As is evident in discussion of membership in arts groups, inclusion in block parties and potlucks, and participation in local politics, many reference how specific dimensions of city ecology produce a sense of "ambient community."[57] Many highlight the import of feeling accepted and included. Tanya expresses this by saying that "people will like me here." Likewise, Chris takes comfort in Ithaca's nondiscrimination policy. Others emphasize the sense of ownership of one's place of residence that feelings of acceptance generate.[58] A small business owner, Trisha, said that proprietors and residents of all kinds "opened their arms to me." She celebrates her sense that she is welcome throughout Ithaca: "I'm in love with Ithaca. . . . [I'm] pretty good friends with some of the people [in my neighborhood] and it feels good. You can walk anywhere you want." Lucy celebrates freedom to forge ties beyond local gay bars—an institution long regarded as essential for LGBTQI social support.[59] Others tout their (sexually) diverse friendship networks and everyday interactions with a range of residents: Mary takes comfort in the plurality of residents who support her sobriety, and Kelli enjoys informal interactions with community gardeners, most of whom happen to be straight. Standing in her restaurant kitchen, Trisha told me that she celebrates movement between groups, such as neighbors, Swing dancers, proprietors, and an ethnic association, saying: "I have bits and pieces of all over. . . . It's not just one set of community." A gender queer parent said: "We hang out with families, and most of them are straight. I don't think that we even hang out with any other families who are gay. . . . Obviously, they're cool heterosexuals or I wouldn't hang out with them." Several of these attributes contrast with those that produce an identity-based "enclave" community—in other words, the kind of place-based lesbian community many anticipated finding in Ithaca.[60]

The sense that one belongs, in a range of local settings, facilitates informal ties that require minimal obligation.[61] For instance, one said, "I'm kind of like anti-groups. I don't mind going to these potlucks because they're laid back and you can come and go as you want." This informality and the absence of obligation contrast with the kinds of ties LBQ residents attribute to ideal typical "lesbian community." Indeed, they contrast with the kinds of mechanisms most of us imagine generating community; scholars have long argued that formal institutions (e.g., church, family, government) or primordial ties (e.g., ethnic, familial) root local relations.[62] Few examine alternate mechanisms for a sense of place-based community or consider how mechanisms change as social identities evolve (or how the ways we interact with one another call out new social identities).[63]

How is it that LBQ Ithacans experience a strong sense of "ambient community" even as they mourn "lesbian community"? They suggest that the same conditions that cause fragmentation of identity-based ties—the breadth of Ithaca's LBQ population, acceptance, and narratives that highlight Ithaca's embrace of difference—produce ambient community. In other words, the same factors that they believe diminish "lesbian community" enable their sense of ambient community. As Sarah mentioned, this is "the plus and the minus of living in a place that is . . . so accepting."

Ambient community also emerges as the Ithaca context calls out new ways of framing or thinking about social ties. The discovery, once in Ithaca, that there are roadblocks to forming "lesbian community" encourages recognition of ambient community. In turn, the alternate set of relations that facilitate ambient community signal the loss of ties primarily rooted in shared sexual identity and marginalization, in turn producing nostalgia for an alternate form of connection. For this reason, it is not a coincidence that Ithacans' richest descriptions of the ties that foster a sense of ambient community are embedded in their complaints about the loss of lesbian community. For them, the loss (whether real or imagined) of one basis of connection and discovery of another are inextricably bound.

On the Limits of Ambient Community

Members of groups who experience marginalization may be more attentive than others to the extent to which local networks are welcoming and thus mindful of the sense of ambient community such networks can generate.[64] As an illustration, a thirty-five-year-old biracial lesbian suggested that the delight she takes in Ithaca rests, in large part, on membership in a running club primarily composed of white, heterosexual men. She described with fondness weekend runs along wooded trails, which culminate in beer-infused celebrations. Arguably, the joy this brings her is predicated on the safety and belonging she experiences in the woods with her corunners; feelings she might not experience in another place or time.[65] Some of her corunners are likely less aware than she of the significance of the belonging she experiences on those trails.[66] Those who, as a result of a variety of privileges, do not regularly experience anxiety about their membership may be less aware of the sense of ambient community such runs produce.

Yet, I do not wish to argue that my informants are necessarily alone in their sense of ambient community. After all, we know that dimensions of city ecology produce ambient community, and all residents experience this ecology, even if their ramifications vary from one group to the next. I suspect that the straight professor and carpenter who cross paths at Cayuga Street's Gimme Coffee, and many of the farmers and musicians who work the Farmers Market, experience a similar sense of casual belonging and connection. Indeed, there were moments during my time in Ithaca when broad belonging was tangible, such as when a siren on Cayuga Street interrupted the serious work and quiet conversations of the dozen or so of us seated in Gimme Coffee—from young, LBQ baristas to straight, tattooed artists, Cornell graduate students, Ithaca College faculty, and a heterosexual, middle-aged musician. Nearly everyone in the intimate seating area instinctively looked up, following the siren as it progressed toward downtown. Breaking the silence, a straight, white graduate student said, "Someone must have forgotten to recycle"; laughter broke out across the room, as we shared in this joke on our town and in so doing experienced brief recognition of a common set of meanings we share. This is to suggest that, while minority groups may be particularly aware of it, it is unlikely that LBQ Ithacans are the only residents to possess a sense of ambient community.

Yet, do *all* in Ithaca have equal claims to ambient community? My informants report that this is not the case. Indeed, many are mindful of how their own inclusion in Ithaca's ambient community rests on their economic, racial, and cultural privilege (even as their marginalization heightens their awareness of the existence of ambient community). As part of a broader related narrative, in formal interviews seven explicitly discussed exclusions predicated on racism and many more talked about classism as endemic.

As is true of all communities, the networks that produce feelings of ambient community are not wholly inclusive. For instance, Ithaca's much-celebrated ten square miles exclude, both spatially and symbolically, rural poverty surrounding the city.[67] Moreover, informants report that the bubble extends only tenuously to a portion of Ithaca south of downtown that is economically underresourced and in which a high proportion of African American residents reside. These seven women implied that many Ithacans take the idea of the exceptional "ten square miles" too much to heart, too readily drawing boundaries around the surrounding, less affluent communities. One said:

> I would like it if [Ithaca] was more diverse. I know that people are working on racism and their own ideas about race in Ithaca but I think that most people, almost everybody, probably still have a long way to go in that area. There's still a lot of like personally intentional segregation that goes on which I would like to see go away. . . . It still strikes me as strange that, you know, all the black people live on the south side and everybody else lives somewhere else. . . . That's something that I really would like to change about Ithaca.

Another echoes this:

> There's this Ithaca that most of the people I know never see. You know? This is a really poor area. I mean obviously Ithaca's not as poor as the surrounding areas but, you know, there's serious poverty here. . . . It's just a whole population that is totally invisible to most of the people around Cornell connected with Ithaca proper.

Here they register awareness that not all experience the ambient community that they so appreciate; this at once highlights their inclusion or "insiderness"—as well as the biases that preclude certain others from attaining full membership.

The experiences of LBQ residents of color reveal the things that most beneficiaries of ambient community take for granted. Ithaca's largely white and middle- and upper-middle-class LBQ population assumes that they belong to this community, if they so chose; but as women of color told me, that assumption does not apply as neatly to them—their membership must be earned, they often feel, and largely depends on their class and cultural capital. Indeed, LBQ residents of color who experience ambient community told me about rare but unsettling moments in which they recognize that their belonging is more tenuous than that of white women; in these moments the sense of belonging and acceptance on which ambient community depends was, for them, shaken. One said that if she could change anything about Ithaca she'd change "the racism." She went on:

> There was a woman that actually said to me, "Do you think he [a neighbor] is Native American?" And I thought, you don't know I'm Native American. It was like, okay. . . . I prefer neighborhoods that have people of color and also gay people. We don't [live in a neighborhood like that]. We live in a white neighborhood right now and I ride on a white bus to work. There is actually more people of color [on the bus] now that there is a low-income housing project near the hospital and there are a few Cornell staff on the bus with me who are also of color who ride occasionally. So it is not all white anymore and that's nice. And [Phil] who used to be my boss is black. But he's not my boss anymore. And the faculty here tends to be all white.

At the time of her interview, such interactions had not alienated her from a sense of ambient community; indeed she vocally celebrated her inclusion therein. However, she was less confident about the durability of her sense of belonging and ownership than any of the white women I interviewed.

In response to similar microexclusions, a Latina resident spoke of seeking cultural (dance and music) groups to connect her to other people of color; she considered this labor necessary to make living in Ithaca—a place she prioritized for its beauty, "lesbian-friendly" character, and commitment to natural living—tolerable. Her efforts to connect with other people of color not only underline the tenuousness of a sense of ambient community for some women of color but also suggest that post-identity politics does not prevail for all. City ecology encourages a post-identity-politics orientation for LBQ residents, but LBQ individuals of color suggest that in Ithaca they are not "post-identity politics" when it comes to race and ethnicity. One Ithacan—say, a Latina LBQ individual—may find that in Ithaca she adopts a post-identity-politics orientation to sexuality, but that she cannot do the same when it comes to her racial identity. Of course, this ought not surprise. Just because a city is hospitable to LBQ residents does not mean that it is equally hospitable to other minority groups; nor does it mean that ecological conditions—such as the breadth of a minority group's population, which helps to create a sense of "safety in numbers" on which ambient community relies—are equivalent for all.

Thus, LBQ Ithacans—even those who are white and upper-middle class and especially those who are not—are aware that Ithaca's ambient community is bounded; even "diverse" and "inclusive" networks are not endlessly embracing.[68] Of course, lines of inclusion are often fuzzy; they at once decry the exclusion of poor and working-class residents from most of their net-works and note, for instance, how conservative, working-class neighbors—the farmers who bring diapers—help to amplify this sense of ambient com-munity. It is precisely the fuzziness of the lines dividing the included and the excluded that makes their community "ambient" and not predicated on strict membership qualifications such as a single identity trait or residence in a precise neighborhood.

Why do white and middle- and upper-middle-class individuals under-line others' exclusion, even as they celebrate Ithaca for being casually inclu-sive and welcoming of difference? I propose that their talk of underlying exclusions highlights their sense of good luck at being a part of ambient community, and simultaneous recognition of the tenuousness of inclusion therein. Above all, by speaking of exclusions they implicitly remind them-selves of their place on the inside—a novelty of history and geography that they greatly value and that some, perhaps rightly, fear they may come to take for granted, especially since more than half of interviewees raised con-cerns about racial segregation. When and where else, their accounts ask us to consider, would LBQ individuals—at least those with the resources to live in Ithaca proper, most of whom are white—be so assuredly on the inside?

In fact, when LBQ residents were fully honest—and when this ethnog-rapher watched closely—it became apparent that even in Ithaca the accep-tance of LBQ residents on which ambient community rests is not universal. As a result, maintaining a sense of LBQ inclusion requires effort on the part of straight allies, as well as LBQ residents themselves. The (largely invisible) labor this necessitates ranges from the pastor who omits mention of fathers at a Father's Day service to politicians who recognize same-sex marriage and neighbors who sublimate their homophobia. LBQ residents too work to promote and maintain a sense of ambient community.[69] For instance, when I asked whether they had experienced any sexual identity-related violence or harassment in Ithaca nearly all replied that they had not. However, after a pause many grudgingly acknowledged instances, ranging from taunting to threats of violence and being driven off the road. Yet even those who even-tually acknowledged such events universally dismissed them as harmless anachronisms. In this sense, they work (perhaps at a cost to themselves) to highlight indicators of belonging—rather than exclusions—that facilitate a sense of ambient community.[70] One can imagine that this work must feel all the more essential when one recognizes the exclusion of proximate "others" or, in the case of LBQ residents of color, instances of direct exclusion or re-minders of how full, unguarded membership rests on, among other things, a set of racial, ethnic, and economic traits.

Conclusion

Ithaca suggests that many—from straight residents and, to a lesser degree, white middle- and upper-middle-class LBQ residents—take the local ties that produce a sense of ambient community for granted, treating them, like traffic noise or a mélange of voices and music, as background to more explicitly identity-based ties, such as "lesbian community," as well as to the intentional ties that compose "liberated" communities (Wellman 1973).[71] Just as it is precisely the (largely) unplanned compilation of voices and noises that composes much of the audio content of the places we live, so too the conditions that produce a sense of ambient community, however unintentional or disharmonious, loom large over our lives. In fact, this "noise" looms large even for those—such as sexual minorities—long imagined to possess a special claim to "real" or automatic community, and, for them, that noise serves as both problem and promise.

Ithaca also demonstrates that place-based ties flourish outside the ghetto and enclave.[72] It also reminds that ties vary not just in relation to economic and technological change. Social and cultural changes, such as shifting local attitudes about sexuality, influence ties and residents' experience thereof. Finally, Ithaca complicates the premise that narrow social identities foster community.[73] In Ithaca the inverse is at least partially true: alternate nodes of identification and connection, resting on nonessential facets of the self, such as shared beliefs, politics, and practices, enable ambient community.

Ithaca also reveals that the beliefs and sentiments that each resident brings to their interactions shape their assessment of community. The people I spoke with revealed a pervasive nostalgia for "lesbian community"; simultaneously, these individuals expressed an equally strong commitment to integration and a desire for freedom from forms of obligation associated with narrower sexual identities, which meant that they also appreciated Ithaca's ambient community. Indeed, their commitment to a kind of personhood that de-emphasizes sexual identity and difference in favor of other features of the self encourages appreciation for ambient community. For this reason, to assess "community" we cannot simply count ties or institutions; we must also learn how people experience and conceptualize the ties they create. Community has much to do with the concrete circumstances under which we encounter one another, but it also emerges from and has the power to shape how we think about what our ties should be like and even who we are.

Finally, the experiences of these individuals in Ithaca helps to confirm what I suspect we already intuitively know: that that there is no single, uniform "lesbian community" to be found in a place like Ithaca. This reminds us that sexual politics and sexual communities are not always mutually constitutive (D'Emilio 1983); the ties that LBQ individuals create, and the degree to which they forge ties with other sexual minorities, varies by place.[74] Specifically, the ways that LBQ residents interact with each other, and with their heterosexual neighbors, are forged by the city itself, and, in turn, orient how LBQ residents think of themselves and other sexual minorities. Indeed, we have heard accounts of how LBQ migrants change on moving to Ithaca, embracing integrationism and a closely related post-identity-politics orientation.

The following chapters, though, give pause to any notion of the universality of this shift for LBQ residents and others, as well as about the precise relation between such shifts and orientations to and practices of community. Despite the sense articulated by many Ithacans that they are caught in a moment of broad and universal transformation, Ithaca is one way, but far from the only way.

TWO

San Luis Obispo:
Lesbian Identity Politics and Community

San Luis Obispo—or, as it is sometimes called, "San Luis" or "SLO"—is a city of around forty-five thousand, located on California's Central Coast. It is about a dozen miles from the Pacific, a little under two hundred miles from Los Angeles, and a little over two hundred from San Francisco. Surrounded by coastal tourist villages and mountain ranching communities, the city is home to California Polytechnical Institute (CALPOLY), as well as to vineyards and wineries such as, to name just a few, Edna Valley, Baileyana, and Claiborne and Churchill. Tourists, many escaping the heat of the Central Valley, stroll San Luis' biweekly Farmers Market, shop at boutiques and galleries, hike the Seven Sisters, and dine at seafood restaurants in the group of small coastal towns that cluster around SLO, such as Morro Bay, Avila, Pismo, and Cayucos. In 2011, Oprah Winfrey, following the author Dan Buettner, christened San Luis the "happiest place" in the United States; the city readily embraces this label.[1] Temperatures are moderate, with an average daytime high of 76° F, and the mountainous coastal landscape is striking; hiking trails and restaurant patios, some abutting the creek that runs past the restored Mission San Luis Obispo de Tolosa—founded in 1772 by a Spanish priest in an area populated by the Chumash—and through the bustling downtown, are nearly always busy. Like almost any passenger arriving at San Luis Obispo's tiny airport, I was never underwhelmed by the surrounding hills—golden in the summer, green in the winter—that greeted me.

After Ithaca, I began research in California, staying in a variety of small homes near downtown across several extended field visits. During some stays the weather was hot and sunny; during others winter rain and cooler temperatures dominated. But always the impressive Seven Sisters Peaks, dramatic Pacific coastline, and eucalyptus-scented air served as a crucial point of contrast to Ithaca. Despite differences in climate and landscape,

I assumed that my time in San Luis Obispo would affirm the lessons I had learned in Ithaca: that contemporary lesbian, bisexual, and/or queer (LBQ) Americans, at least those with the privilege to move to college towns like Ithaca and San Luis Obispo, who tend to be white and middle or upper-middle class, increasingly reject lesbian identity politics; that is, they reject the notion that sexual identity is their glue. They don't assume that they'll have more in common with someone just because they're gay, or that being nonheterosexual will define their life.[2] But I was very wrong. San Luis Obispo's LBQ residents consistently challenged my assumption that LBQ individuals are moving beyond identity politics, that Ithaca's norm was a universal trend. Identities in San Luis Obispo and Ithaca are not merely variants of one another, but distinct species. Whereas Ithacans downplay sexual identity and emphasize sexuality's fluidity and social construction, San Luis Obispo residents embrace identity politics. Nearly everyone I spoke with regarded sexuality as life defining and static; most took for granted that sexual identity produced shared experience and therefore common ground with other "lesbians." Just as important, nearly all were adamant that this common ground spanned other areas of difference, such as those that relate to age, race, and class.[3]

If a post-identity-politics orientation emerges from and reinforces "ambient community"—a general sense of belonging forged with heterogeneous neighbors who share place, beliefs, and practices—in Ithaca, San Luis Obispo's insistence on identity politics both emerges from and reinforces lesbian-only networks. Not long after I arrived, lesbian-identified residents of San Luis Obispo and surrounding coastal and ranch towns began to invite me to attend their events, and I found myself attending a monthly Lesbian Chips 'n' Chat event at the Gay and Lesbian Alliance Center, a potluck group for "mature" (read: mostly those over fifty-five years) women, a Sunday Night Social group that meets at a Mexican restaurant, weekly games at a coastal pool hall, and both formal and impromptu dance parties at downtown bars.[4] While only one had a clever name, all these events were, by definition, only for lesbians. On a very active listserv—Central Coast Lesbian—lesbian-identified residents frequently invite one another to participate in any number of additional events, from beach bonfires to game nights and backyard barbeques. Moreover, such events—both formal and informal—habitually include a mix of women: young and old, white and Latino and Asian, attorneys and doctors, domestic workers and manual laborers. These game nights, "Chips 'n' Chat" evenings, and afternoon hikes are at the center of the lives of many LBQ San Luis women. In short, the social lives of these women are a far cry from the ties Ithacans cultivated—with a polyglot assemblage of neighbors and coworkers via yoga, vegan potlucks, and the PTA. Indeed, San Luis lesbians' ties epitomize what Ithacans (and many of the rest of us) think of as "lesbian community": out of a sense of common ground and shared fate, LBQ residents of San Luis Obispo nourish social circles that are demographically heterogeneous but primarily lesbian, which also are reinforced by formal organizations.[5] In other words, if Ithaca upends traditional expectations about the LBQ individual who seeks residence in a progressive city with a large lesbian population, San Luis Obispo does the opposite.

How can two college towns offer such vast differences in identity and ties? If feelings of acceptance, an abundance of LBQ residents, and talk of the city as a beacon of acceptance produce Ithaca's post-identity politics and ambient community, subtle differences in city ecology propel identity politics and lesbian community in San Luis Obispo. As with so much about urban life, this enormous difference is caused both by the physical and demographic shape of the city itself and, as important, our feelings about and experience of that city. Lesbians in SLO tend to feel that their population is small and geographically dispersed; the result is a sense of scarcity. Similarly, these residents feel their city is only partially hospitable to LBQ residents, in part because of their encounters with pockets of moderate and conservative social politics in greater San Luis Obispo. And finally, these residents try eagerly to embrace their own version of the popular local narrative about San Luis as bucolic retreat—the "happiest place in America." All these experiences and feelings encourage cultivation of a common lesbian identity, and unite disparate lesbians in a network marked by inclusivity, heterogeneity, and frequent contact.[6] Of course, as we will also see, inclusivity is not always fun or easy; conflict and divisiveness sometimes surface among those who share a social life in San Luis Obispo.

SanLezObispo: Lesbian Identity Politics in SLO

Almost universally, SLO informants identify, without reservation or qualification, as simply "lesbian" or "gay." This way of describing the self extends from public settings, such as parties, dance clubs, pool halls, supper clubs, and game nights, to the more intimate realm of my one-on-one interviews and small-group conversations with residents; while it might start as a collective, local way of talking about sexual identity and difference, it alters how LBQ residents think, quite privately, about their sexual and social selves.[7] This way of describing the self continued to surprise me, not only because it departs from trends in Ithaca but also because many SLO informants had, at one time, been married to or had romantic relationships with men; in another context they might describe themselves as "bisexual" or "queer;" indeed, a few spoke explicitly of how they identified differently in other times and places. However, with few exceptions—a twenty-something mother and a forty-year-old woman who identify as bisexual, three women in their early twenties who occasionally use the term "queer," and a thirty-something professional who identifies as "butch"—nearly all of more than three dozen informants and many others I observed in San Luis Obispo and surrounding ranch and coastal towns use "lesbian" and "gay" to describe themselves, as well as others. Instead of variety and complexity, these women share a guiding belief: that the desire for another woman is innate and life defining, and that those who share that desire share common ground. That is, LBQ San Luis Obispo residents favor "lesbian" not because their life experiences are identical or because they have, universally, only had sexual and romantic attachments to other women, but because in their view any heterogeneity of experience, between one woman and another, or even between your identity at twenty and your identity at sixty, pales in comparison to the significance of not being "straight."

A sixty-something grandmother, seated opposite me at a Denny's near a San Luis shopping center, spoke without hesitation of her lesbianism, leaning forward in her seat, work boots crossed at the ankles. She made no effort to disguise her long-term marriage to her children's father, but she also did not hedge when I asked about her sexual identity, replying promptly and definitively, "lesbian." Over and again, when I asked, "How do you identify in terms of your sexual identity?" women promptly answered: "I'm lesbian" (retired civil servant); "As a lesbian" (forty-year-old loan officer); "I identify as a lesbian" (twenty-two-year-old gas station attendant); and "Lesbian" (fifty-something educator). Setting and personal background have minimal influence on the terms these women use to describe themselves; a pair of women in their eighties who share a home in a trailer park for retirees identify as "lesbian," as does a stay-at-home mother in a high-end coastal residential development, a community college student at a lesbian-owned coffee shop, and, seated across from me outside a strip mall, a store manager who regularly visits gay bars in Los Angeles and San Francisco. The homogeneity of identity talk in San Luis Obispo upturned my expectations again and again. It departed so starkly from that which I encountered in Ithaca. But it also surprised because of increasingly dominant accounts of how LBQ identities are generation specific, as well as the increasingly prevalent notion that many today reject identity politics or are "post-mo" or "post-gay."[8]

Indeed, the sense in SLO of sexual identity as immutable is so powerful that it was the only city in which residents almost never shared accounts of how their identities changed on moving. This is a small detail, but a crucial one. Indeed, the rarity of such accounts epitomized their way of thinking about sexual identity, in which their past, present, and future are all rendered as "lesbian"—even if their actual sexual and romantic history included men.[9] It also mirrors a larger narrative about San Luis Obispo as a place: it is a city where one comes to "be" (happy). In San Luis Obispo, one discovers who one "is" and then you simply *are*. On the one hand, this might seem like a Californian or West Coast approach to sexuality and to life more generally; it conjures an image of, for instance, the laidback California surfer. Indeed, it is possible that regional and coastal differences play a role in generating distinctive identity cultures in San Luis Obispo and Ithaca, and especially in informing the place narratives that constitute a dimension of city ecology.[10] However, coastal and regional explanations only take us so far—because they cannot explain differences in identity cultures in the three non-Californian study cities, all of which are in the Northeast and two of which are in New England.

San Luis lesbians do not just frame their own lives in either/or (read: gay/straight) terms. They speak of others' identities similarly. For instance, a middle-aged woman described an informal group that plays kickball, saying, "I guess they're not all gay, but . . . it was still nice to get out," and, later, referred to the "gay community" (a sharp contrast to the words of those in Ithaca who insist that "there is no gay community" there). A young woman with short, sculpted hair referenced the "lesbian community" and an internet group "for lesbians," and, most tellingly, described a woman some of her female friends had dated as "straight. . . . Well she has a boyfriend but she goes gay for us sometimes." This underlines the degree to which San Luis women frame sexual identity in black and white, as a defining, essential, and transparent facet of the self.[11]

The names of local organizations and events furthered this clarified vision of sexuality: the SanLezObispo (a social networking website), the Gay and Lesbian Alliance (GALA), LezMingle, Central Coast Lesbian Listserv, and Lesbian Chips 'n' Chat. Such titles defy a contemporary trend that I assumed was universal: the commitment to recognizing both the heterogeneity, and the ambiguity of LBQ identities, and the increasingly long acronyms—for example, LGBTQI (lesbian, gay, bisexual, transgender, queer, and intersex) organizations—that result.[12] Most substantially, all this reveals the proclivity to interpret, label, and categorize facets of local life—from organizations to acquaintances to ties—based solely on a singular notion of identity and to approach "gay" and "straight" as occupying distinct, if not opposing, camps.

Seated in the kitchen of her North County doublewide trailer, her dogs at our feet, Catherine, a woman in her seventies, told me her coming-out story:

> I had come out when I was about fourteen. . . . I wanted to play with boys, like sports and things like that and cars and whatever you do when you're a kid, but I never was interested in having sex with them. I kissed a couple of boys when I was young but it didn't do anything for me. . . . The first lover I had, she was two years older than I am . . . and so she sought me out and we used to play games. You know, chase and I'll get you. . . . And I tried to tell my mother at one time. I remember the scene really well. She was washing her face at night, washing the makeup off her face and I was trying to tell her that this woman was chasing me around and I was kind of confused but she didn't . . . I didn't get the reaction [from my mother] that I thought I'd get. . . . She was just kind of like, "Well, ok. What do you think she wants? Well, you know? She wants a kiss." So anyway, I think Kinsey's book was out about then. . . . So I went to the library and read it. [And I thought]: "Oh, that's what I am." And it explained it and I thought, yeah, that's it. . . . And then I met this woman, another woman in high school who kissed me. . . . [She got a job at the factory in town] and then there were quite a few lesbians working for that company. . . . And I must have known ten or twelve of them. . . . [My girl-friend] met these two women who had lived together for years and years . . . and one day she was on the elevator with them . . . and she asked them if they were lesbians. They said, "Well, yeah. Come over."

Here she emphasizes her early self-knowledge, forthrightness about her identity, and longstanding membership in lesbian circles. Throughout, she made certain to provide explanations for any behavior or feelings that might be interpreted as a departure from her conception of what it means to be lesbian. For instance, she confessed that she once cheated on a female lover with a man, but presented it as an understandable derivation from her true, core identity: "I don't know why. I guess one of the reasons why is because I was like twenty-one or twenty and everybody I knew was getting married and the peer pressure was really something." Likewise, early sexual experiences with adolescent boys were discounted as merely experimental. Moreover, her narrative of self-realization culminates with her discovery, via her girlfriend, of a confederacy of lesbian-identified women.

Another, an arts educator in her forties, one of the rare San Luis informants to identify as bisexual, presented her sexual identity as nonetheless fixed: "Well, it seems I'm bisexual, *truly so*." At another point in our interview—on a sunny patio outside a small restaurant near San Luis's train depot—she went out of her way to present her sexuality as stable over time: "I've been going back and forth from men to women for years and years and years." With similar certainty, a middle-aged mother distanced herself from the possibility of a bisexual identity despite her earlier marriages to men. Without a moment's hesitation, she told me that she identifies as lesbian: "Lesbian, yeah. It just took me a hell of a long time to come around to it, the realization—staying up way too many nights late at night watching *The L Word*."

Some told me that this orientation to identity, as fixed and life defining, was not universal, only nearly so. Karen, a young, bisexual mother, noted differences between the identities of some CALPOLY students and those of the bulk of San Luis's LBQ residents, most of whom she described as identifying as lesbian. She commented, "I see more women identifying as bisexual, curious, or open to whatever. There is a term I found on the Internet, sapiosexual: intensely attracted to intelligence in either sex." This suggests at least some variation in how those in San Luis Obispo identify (although, despite Karen's assertion, the bulk of CALPOLY students I encountered during observations described themselves in the same terms as much older women). Yet it simultaneously indicates, in contrast to Ithaca, that in San Luis Obispo departures from lesbian identity—when they occur—are novel enough to note to a researcher, and, as exemplified by Karen's definition of "sapiosexual," inspire research and reflection.

This dominant either/or framework for sexual identity also influenced how these women interpreted me and spoke about my identity. Most presumed that, like the other women around them, I must not only be coupled with a woman (as I am) but also share their precise self-understanding. Indeed, women in San Luis Obispo frequently asked me, "Are you a lesbian?" or "Are you gay?" Informants in the other cities were typically far more circumspect—waiting for me to hint about the gender of my partner, or to indicate the term I use to describe my identity (whenever possible I simply echoed the term my informant used—e.g., in San Luis I was "lesbian"). But San Luis women extend their "lesbian" (which some occasionally use interchangeably with "gay") identity to others with ease. At a party I caught up with a woman, an elementary school teacher whom I hadn't seen for more than a year. Sitting in chairs at the edge of the dance floor, we spoke over the music. She told me about her new girlfriend and job, and asked how I had been. I was at the close of my final field visit, and, feeling more forthcoming than usual, I mentioned my new job and told her about the birth of my daughter. She paused for a moment before saying, "I have a memory that you are gay. Is that true?" Here, she left no opening for me to define myself in different terms and revealed her assumption that there is unambiguous "truth" about one's sexuality.

Accompanying this either/or method of identification is the belief that sexuality is innate and inviolate, rather than something that changes as one ages or as the world evolves, or even—heaven forbid!—that sexuality is merely a performance or role that can be put on or traded out; it is, as the teacher's question to me reveals, a "truth" that can be definitively answered.[13] This belief was readily and collectively articulated at a monthly potluck group for "mature" women. Attended primarily by women aged fifty years or more, the meetings were held in a bank's staff room in Los Osos. Over the course of a meeting that I attended in January 2009, nearly a dozen women entered the staff room and found a place under the glare of the room's fluorescent lights. Everyone sat in orange chairs around a long, brown table. Most dressed casually in jeans, with short gray or graying hair. Two pairs of women wore sweater vests over button-down shirts in homage to the cool evening and Los Osos's perennial fog. Aside from an African American woman and two couples, the attendees were white and single. After much chitchat—about tourism, the economy, Obama's fiscal policies, and outdoor activities—a woman, Emily, asked whether I had read a recent New Yorker article about a roaming band of 1970s lesbian separatists, the Van Dykes (Levy 2009). Over plates of lentil salad, chicken, guacamole, and cake, her question launched a broader conversation about separatism and the nature of sexual identity.

After a moment of casual back and forth about separatism, Emily said, "I'm not a separatist and I never was back then. It is about sex. It is physical for me; about desire. If I could have been with men I would have. And I tried. I thought it was a matter of practice. I practiced and practiced. It is not. Some of these separatists weren't really lesbians. [For them] it was about politics, not sex." Nearly all the women indicated their assent, nodding or muttering, and shortly the conversation turned to a New York Times article about gender, sex, and sexuality (Carey 2005). Emily's partner, Sarah, repeatedly stated that the article indicated that women have greater sexual response than men to visual stimuli. Using this as her evidence, Sarah told us that she has come to believe that the popular stereotype is wrong, and that actually women are more sexual than men. As the conversation progressed, a lone voice—that of Ariana, an artist who had recently moved to the area—proposed that differences in male and female sexual response reflect the fact that young men are socialized to suppress feelings of arousal generated by other men. The group briefly fell into debate about the merits of Ariana's argument. Their words indicated that all were familiar with the concept of socialization; indeed, many had likely debated its merits in undergraduate classrooms. Despite (or perhaps because of) this familiarity, after five minutes of extended conversation, the group came to near consensus that socialization *cannot* influence physical measures of arousal. Having neatly presented lesbianism as originating in desire, and desire as purely physiological, they moved to other topics. As they chatted about a birthday party, politics, dogs, and grandchildren, I tried to get my mind around how casual their belief was in sexuality's immutability. Indeed, the room seemed to take for granted that immutability just as much as Ithacans assumed that everyone and everything was fluid. For these San Luis women, the notion of sexual fluidity was worthy of brief conversation, but nothing more. By the end of the debate, if it can be called that, even the newcomer, Ariana, had fallen into line; I did not encounter another instance in which anyone proposed that identities are social or that sexuality might be political. At this potluck, as at so many other gatherings, the dominant frame for approaching sexual identity was briefly examined and ultimately reinforced.

While the potluck conversation is revealing, the intellectual character of the conversation is not particularly representative. As Emily's words imply, many San Luis Obispo lesbians read texts like the *New York Times* and the *New Yorker*; they are, for the most part, women with college and, in some cases, advanced degrees. And yet, as we have begun to see, they do not typically emphasize learned or heady debates. They do not, contra those in Portland and even in Ithaca and Greenfield, spend much of their time together discussing the nature of identity or sexuality. You are who you are, they imply. Part of this emerges from their lesbian identity politics; from their certainty about the unambiguous quality of sexuality. However, it also relates to a broader way of life in San Luis Obispo, which, despite being home to a major state university, is a place in which residents emphasize fitness and leisure; wine, hiking, and walks on the beach. Why spend your time debating identity when you could be dancing at a bonfire on the beach or navigating a back trail at Montana de Oro State Park? To be sure, residents communicate the dominance of lesbian identity politics to newcomers, just not typically via debate about recent academic studies and lesbian history. This ethos contributes to their broader disinterest in self-reflection related to how their sexual identities have changed over time, contributing to the distinction between the abundant narratives of self-transformation I encountered in Ithaca (and, later, in Greenfield and Portland) and the paucity thereof in San Luis Obispo.

Ariana is not alone in learning, after establishing a home in San Luis Obispo, about the dominance of lesbian identities; no one reported having knowledge of the prevalence of lesbian identities before moving. Instead, most report that they were initially attracted to San Luis Obispo for reasons only indirectly related to sexual identity. Some report that knowledge of the area's progressive reputation provided a sense of security, but that they considered relocating for professional, family, or other lifestyle reasons, such as desire to retire to the coast or to assist an aging parent. For instance, one informant, a Latina domestic worker, reported moving to San Luis to live near her partner, with whom she had rekindled a romance when they were each visiting their Central Valley hometown. She didn't imagine that San Luis would be as lesbian friendly as Seattle, where she had been living, but she thought it would be hospitable enough.

Others actively sought a more hospitable place than they had found in the Central Valley—the noncoastal agricultural heart of the state, which tends to be much more politically conservative than other areas—or other parts of California, but argued that if acceptance of lesbian identity had been a primary motivation, they might have opted to live in San Francisco or Los Angeles. Like women in the three other sites, many instead emphasize how the area's natural beauty and proximity to a major city attracted them, from Morro Rock, which rises above the harbor in the nearby town of Morro Bay, to the trail up Bishop's Peak in San Luis Obispo. One woman said, "I've always wanted to live on the West Coast, but I wasn't sure where. . . . My partner at the time came out here. . . . She described [San Luis Obispo] to me over the phone, and I said, 'Yup! That's it!' . . . She said it was like Avalon." Another echoed this: "I lived in a really congested city, and . . . I had just had it. I didn't like the traffic. . . . I had met a girl that lived down here. . . . Then I came down to visit one weekend. As I came over . . . and entered Los Osos, I just fell in love with it; so then I moved. . . . As I came over the hill, it just felt like home. I like being on the coast, and the air. . . . And it gets dark at night. I like that."

Others suggest that economic motivations influenced their choices. Anna recalled:

> We just kind of randomly came down. It was just kind of on a fluke actually. We saw it on the map. . . . We were totally priced out of Santa Cruz and we wanted to live coastally but there was just no way in 2000 that we could possibly afford that, and so we came down here. I just saw the name on the map. I'd never been here before. We had no connections. We knew no one, no job possibilities. We just came down here and I saw how beautiful it was and Morro Rock. It was like, yup. This is it.

As Anna's words suggest, despite its high cost of living, many regard San Luis Obispo County as affordable when contrasted with other parts of coastal California, particularly progressive coastal cities such as Santa Barbara, Santa Cruz, Los Angeles, and San Francisco. However, those who offered affordability explanations for their moves were in the minority. Many more emphasized family connections, work opportunities, appreciation for the landscape, or a desire to escape the Central Valley.

As their words suggest, unlike the expectations of migrants to Ithaca, few move to San Luis Obispo hoping to find a lesbian haven. This makes lesbian identity politics in San Luis Obispo all the more remarkable, for few of us associate lesbian identity politics with cities that are *less* hospitable and *less* densely populated by lesbians than the Ithacas and Northamptons of the world.[14] As we will see, it is precisely the fact that the local context does not feel entirely hospitable or abundantly populated by LBQ residents that calls out lesbian identity politics in San Luis Obispo.

Indeed, despite their certitude about their sexual identities, San Luis Obispo's LBQ residents are less resolutely "out" than their Ithaca counterparts. Most of the women I spoke with had come out as "lesbian" or "gay" to family and friends—some later in life and despite their families' conservative religious and political views—but they were far from universally out to neighbors and coworkers, and carefully assessed the costs and benefits of "outing" oneself. For instance, Judy, who works as an elementary school classroom aide, explained how she came to conclude that she should *not* be out at work in San Luis Obispo County—a possibility she briefly explored by wearing a rainbow ring to work. On a couch in her seaside rental, a cat crawling across our laps, she recounted:

> One of the kids in [the class] has two moms. I thought oh, cool, but then they have two [other] aides and a teacher in that classroom . . . and they were actually making fun of this kid, talking about two moms. . . . I'm hoping the kid didn't pick up on it, but I don't know. . . . I'm up in front. I see everything. . . . And the other thing was the young man said, "Oh, I just love rainbows," you know, and the teacher says, "Now so and so, you know, not everybody loves those rainbows."

After this comment, my informant ceased wearing her rainbow ring to work. Like her, others hesitate to announce their sexual identity. However, some of these people also rely on symbols—whether rings or photographs—with the hope that they might invite candor with heterosexual neighbors or coworkers. Over coffee at Linnaea's, a venerable downtown San Luis Obispo coffee shop especially popular with hippies and nature aficionados, Lauren, a short woman with long, dark hair who worked as a loan officer, said, "I don't feel the need to really tell people, you know. On my desk at work I have pictures of, you know, me and my girlfriend. . . . You know, I don't hide it, but . . . I don't introduce myself by saying, 'Hi, my name's [Lauren]. I'm a lesbian.'" Some are not even comfortable relying on subtle symbols of their identity. For instance, one explained that she refrains from putting pride stickers on her car, for fear that it will out not only her but also by association the lesbian business owners whose establishments she supports. She told me that her lesbian friends who own local businesses fear being "outed."

These strategies—from using subtle indicators of identification to intentionally masking such indicators—indicate the degree to which lesbian residents proceed with caution when it comes to being out. At least some of these women were aware of how being out in San Luis compared to other places. A white woman in her thirties who works as an educator described how in San Francisco she was "out all the time. In San Francisco if you have a problem with diverse sexuality, then you're a freak and you need to go." In San Luis Obispo, however, she is much more cautious: "Here where it's a Democratic town but it is a more Republican—a more conservative—county, there is no official gay bar or anything like that. We have to hold dances, things like that." Here, she suggests, there are welcoming spaces and opportunities, but not the expansive welcoming feel of San Francisco—where you could be "out all the time."

As this suggests, caution about being out emerges, in part, from a general sense of mild and somewhat unpredictable conservatism and, less frequently, from specific experiences that generate fear or anxiety. Lesbian residents report occasional harassment in their neighborhoods, especially in the smaller towns outside of San Luis, as well as in San Luis's downtown. One described an incident at San Luis Obispo's biweekly Farmers Market, a place that on the surface—abounding with organic vegetables, local bands, and booths run by community organizations—seems to embody the ultimate progressive, college-town scene. She said: "We were right next to the GALA [Gay and Lesbian Alliance] booth. Some guy was asking us questions in a more aggressive manner, and he wasn't satisfied with our answers. As he turned away he made a comment." Another recounted her dismay on encountering homophobia at CALPOLY—best embodied by a sign that a student house displayed, but relating to broader patterns she noted on campus—which she had expected to be the epicenter of acceptance in the region.

I am not political like that and it usually does not bother me that much, but . . . Did you hear about the incident at CALPOLY? One of the Ag[ricultural] houses put up a sign. Did you hear about it in the news? The Confederate flag. They put up a sign that said: "No fags, no niggers, no hippies."

Another woman told me that because of moments of overt conflict or intolerance like these, "There is a very underground closeted element to a lot of people."

Several described San Luis Obispo County as particularly fractious in the months prior to the 2008 vote on Proposition 8, which sought to ban gay marriage. One woman recalled the explosion of what she interpreted as symbols of intolerance during the lead up to Proposition 8: "'Yes on 8' written on cars . . . cars that had the no [gay marriage] stickers on them or some other demonstration of supporting [Proposition 8]." Another couple described how Proposition 8 changed how they experienced the Farmers Market and, more generally, San Luis Obispo: "We were among the protesters that basically flooded the Farmers Market. We do a weekly Farmers Market here on Thursday nights; it's big; it's a big family good time, hang out with friends." Her partner interrupted: "Except when you are dealing with politics." Marcy continued:

So we were out with our signs saying we would really like the right to be married and not be a second-class citizen. And just to see everybody with the Yes on Prop 8 signs. Those are kids. They are kids. . . . Stickers, booths, signs, T-shirts. They made balloons and tied [them] to kids' wrists and little tiny toddlers and stuff. Very sad. . . . It was almost like gang wars. Like all their signs were yellow and all of our signs were blue so you could tell allies and stuff like that. It was hard to see; to take over like that. It is usually so positive and now when I look around I don't know; you know what I mean? Just the stigma stays with me.

Her partner added, trying to put things delicately, "There is a lot of *not-allies* in this area and Prop 8 brought all of that kind of to a head." While no one explicitly mentioned it to me, San Luis Obispo County was the only coastal county between Los Angeles and San Francisco with a majority of voters who supported the gay marriage ban, and the referendum's outcome became a stinging reminder of how San Luis Obispo is less unabashedly politically progressive than other parts of coastal California between the state's two largest cities; San Luis Obispo has, for instance, a higher proportion of registered Republicans and a lower proportion of registered Democrats than

Santa Barbara County.[15] As Marcy suggests, the homophobia that resistance to same-sex marriage embodies "stayed with" LBQ residents well after the vote.

Yet, when Marcy stopped to think about it, she thought that perhaps the intolerance that emerged during the Proposition 8 battle should not have surprised. She said, "I grew up here. So I knew that there's [conservatism] depending on what part of the county you live in. South and North County are both agricultural and kind of hickish, you know? And this [because of the college] is the most liberal area." Thus, San Luis Obispo County is approached as a hospitable place, but also as a place that requires a certain strategic positioning. One has to determine when and where one can be out and therefore where one ought to work, socialize, and live.

Indeed, on occasion women receive explicit instruction to proceed with caution in San Luis Obispo. For instance, one couple recounted how a realtor led them away from certain towns and neighborhoods, while another realtor encouraged women to seek out accepting institutions within their new town. One woman reported, "We asked [our realtor] how would we be accepted here. She says, 'I don't think that would be much of a problem. . . . I've got one gay friend, I'll ask her.'" After speaking with her friend, the realtor reported that there was a monthly lesbian gathering in the back of a lesbian-owned bookstore. This, in turn, led them to participate in a separate monthly lesbian supper club. Thus, while they were not warned of hate crimes or otherwise made fearful, they were encouraged to seek out explicitly lesbian spaces. Moreover, the fact that the realtor's response wasn't immediate—that she needed more information before answering their question—implicitly communicated uncertainty and a general lack of knowledge—despite her "one gay friend"; this suggests separation between straight and lesbian residents. At the same time, these newcomers interpreted San Luis Obispo as a welcoming enough place that they felt comfortable asking their heterosexual realtor for information about what it would be like for them to live there as lesbians. This is the complex terrain— between acceptance and exclusion—that many describe navigating.

Given the degree to which San Luis's lesbians experience sexual identity as a core feature of self, this sense of caution and discomfort is a source of pain and frustration. One woman spoke of having to keep her sexuality under wraps around those with whom she spends her days: "I know some gay nurses in North County but they are not particularly out about it. I've never been able to be out as a nurse in this community with any degree of comfort. . . . I worked at a nursing home I dearly loved. It is arguably the best in the county, but it's run by Christian churches and I thought that if the administrator ever found out I was gay, I'd be out on my ear in a minute. In a New York minute, I'd be out the door. It's not safe. That's it." Another said, "I do not have any identifying stickers on my car of any kind. . . . I [do] not want to have something unpleasant happen to my car like getting it keyed or who knows what."

San Luis women report that they negotiate professional and neighborhood ties with heterosexuals by being "out" in some contexts and "closeted" in others. Many suggested that they "do not advertise" their sexual identity, relying instead on an informal policy of "If You Ask, I'll Tell." One woman, a private tutor, described her concern about her relationship with a new girlfriend:

> I'm letting people come to their own conclusions when they see us together although I'm not afraid to hold her hand anywhere. I'm not afraid to kiss her anywhere. I will do it. The only thing that I feel that I have to be careful about being out is around . . . I have a lot of homeschooled students who are Mormon and they are fundamentalist Christians and very, very, very, you live by the word of God or you will go to hell. . . . And they love me as a teacher, but if they found out that I was in a relationship with a woman I'm not sure if they would continue with me. They would find some reason, they would just say, "You know our daughter's just too busy right now. We're going to stop." I don't think they would be you know like, "You're going to hell." But I don't want to lose that, so I'm very careful publicly. Facebook? No way.

A retiree retains much of the caution she practiced with regard to outing herself during her working years: "Some [coworkers] knew, some didn't. If it came up I would indicate something, but if it didn't, I didn't bring it up. . . . [Now that I'm retired] if it comes up, I'm very open about saying who I am. If it doesn't, I don't raise it." From her words and those of others in San Luis, a portrait emerges of a California distinct from the popular image of San Francisco, and even Los Angeles, as places where sexual identity is either a nonissue or is boldly displayed.[16] However, informants also distinguish San Luis Obispo County from the far more conservative Central Valley, like Bakersfield, Fresno, and Stockton. In its politics and inclusivity of LBQ individuals, San Luis, they imply, falls between either ends of the California spectrum.

In response, perhaps, to their fear of being "out" at the wrong time or place, some lesbian residents stigmatize others for being readily identifiable as lesbian. As an example, Joan, who came out after her children were grown, recalled the anxiety she felt on coming face to face with a volunteer at the Gay and Lesbian Center: "She was absolutely my typical nightmare of what

a lesbian in my head was, which was the dyke with the tank top and tattoo
and short hair and shorts. . . . And I'm going, naw." For Joan, this woman,
with her tattoo, tank top and short hair, was uncomfortably legible as
"lesbian"—and therefore constituted her worst "nightmare" of what a lesbian could be. Later, she hesitated to attend a Lesbian Chips 'n' Chat event
after observing "biker" women walk into the event ahead of her. Again, for
Joan, their visibility and legibility produced deep discomfort. Indeed, as
her anecdote suggests, bikers and tattooed women with a "butch" aesthetic
are minorities in the San Luis scene; many, although not all, of San Luis'
LBQ women dress in a nondescript manner. A typical weekend or evening
outfit, particularly for women who are forty or above (who constitute much
of the membership of San Luis lesbian social organizations), consists of
comfortable jeans, sneakers or boots, and sweaters. Most wear their hair
at shoulder length or shorter, and most faces are relatively free of makeup,
with some wearing the occasional mascara or lipstick, but few appearing
fully made up. This aesthetic might be out of place at a downtown San Luis
Obispo boutique or gallery populated by CALPOLY students, tourists, and
affluent retirees from San Francisco, Los Angeles, and the Central Valley,
but is much less exceptional at the pool hall, bars, Mexican restaurant, and
beaches where LBQ residents frequently congregate. One woman recounted
how her aesthetic has changed since she moved to San Luis Obispo—here
she feels she has found her "truth": "I've gone through chopping my hair off
and wearing men's clothing and never wearing makeup. . . . Mostly in Santa
Cruz. . . . What I found was I wasn't being true to myself."

In this sense, many San Luis LBQ women share a casual aesthetic that,
intentionally or not, permits them to "pass" as heterosexual in some contexts—an ability many value. Yet, despite the discomfort with lesbian stereotypes and caution about being out that some articulate, San Luis Obispo's
LBQ residents nonetheless embrace lesbian identities. That is, their discomfort with the highly legible lesbian—who, in their minds, sacrifices the ability to blend—and caution about being out do not produce reticence about
lesbian *identity*; their uncertainty is limited to the question of when and
where to be forthright about their sexuality.

There is one key exception to this pattern of caution about being out. As
we have glimpsed, many actively resisted California's Proposition 8, which
sought to overturn a judicial decision that had briefly permitted the state's
same-sex couples to legally wed. In so doing, many became much more
"out" in San Luis Obispo than they had ever been. Some informants appeared at a candlelight vigil in downtown San Luis one evening in March
2008, held across from the Post Office against a backdrop of pale pink

terracotta buildings housing retail chains, such as Pottery Barn, and upscale boutiques. At a minister's behest, a group of couples affirmed their marriages and relationships; one woman in her early twenties stood beside her girlfriend, wrapped in a rainbow Pride flag. With Donna, a frequent presence at Chips 'n' Chat and other events, I moved through the pockets of men, women, and dogs that composed the crowd, helping to light tea candles in mason jars. This was a rare instance in which I observed gay men and lesbians coming together. Despite the fact that male same-sex households outnumber female same-sex households in San Luis Obispo, the two populations almost never comingled during my time in the field (as was also true in the other three study cities). Instead, lesbians habitually socialized with other lesbians. In this sense, the fight for same-sex marriage provided an unusual opportunity for unity across gender lines.

In the months before and after the vigil, LBQ residents spoke of marriage rights to the newspaper and television reporters, advocated for marriage before crowds like the one near the post office, gathered signatures, and breathlessly awaited news of the vote's outcome and subsequent court decisions. Why were they willing to take this risk? Over the course of my time in San Luis Obispo, women formed and ended relationships, some were legally wed when it was legally permissible to do so, and others exchanged rings privately or before friends and family. Throughout, none expressed hesitation to me or in my presence about the fight for marriage equality (about which some residents of the other study cities were critical—preferring, for instance, that gay, lesbian, bisexual, transgender, queer, and/or intersex (GLBTQI) social movement organizations emphasize transgender-inclusion and nondiscrimination policies) or about the institution of marriage itself. In fact, after very directly asking, one woman learned that my partner and I had not legally married despite ties to Massachusetts (a state in which we could do so), and her partner, a very active anti–Proposition 8 activist, redacted her offer to participate in an interview. In this way, more so than residents of the other cities I studied (even more so than residents of Portland, which faced its own statewide referendum on gay marriage while I conducted research), San Luis lesbians articulate values and engage in practices that mirror a dominant, contemporary agenda of national GLBTQI groups: the fight for marriage equality. This likely reflects the ambiguities of their city: a place where they do not feel comfortable being always out, but a place in which, when push comes to shove (as they felt it did when faced with Proposition 8), they feel the latitude to fight for their cause.[17]

As their caution about being out might suggest, while they wish for safety and security related to their lesbianism, that is for heterosexual neighbors, co-workers and family members to, at the very least, tolerate their sexual difference, they do not explicitly celebrate the formation of ties with those who do not share their identity. Indeed, most informants' social lives are organized around ties to other lesbians, both close friends, and a broader circle encountered via formal and informal social groups for lesbians, many of which advertise events via the local listserv. In turn, this membership in lesbian-only circles reinforces lesbian identity.

Indeed, the vast majority answered my question about their "ideal neighborhood or town" by stating a desire—however fanciful—for a place where lesbians constitute a very sizeable minority, if not a majority. A banker answered by saying, "It would be nice if they all [shared] my sexual identity!" Others were more realistic, but were unswerving in their desire for a higher number than they find in San Luis: "Oh, I'd like to see more. Realistically it is never going to be a majority or even a half." Another echoed this, joking, "They wouldn't have to share [my identity]. They would just have to glorify it. . . . I think I'd like about half; a third would be okay." Still another specified a place on which she'd model her ideal city with regard to the proportion of lesbian households: "I would want it be like Boulder" (here she evokes a narrative common across the sites that presents the ideal LBQ residential locale as a small city, typically a college town, in a semirural part of the United States—and, indeed, recent census and Treasury Department data suggest that same-sex female couples do tend to concentrate in this type of city more than in any other).[18] One resisted my attempt to induce her to provide a number. Instead, she described the atmosphere she desires— one that, as Ithaca begins to suggest, likely flourishes in places with a particularly high proportion of LBQ residents:

> I guess enough [lesbians] that it feels normal. It would probably be like San Francisco; like a city where people don't assume. I was watching [a movie] recently. It was on TV. You know the one with Liam Neeson. [He] is the father, and he has the son that wants to try and get the American girl. The son is totally crushed out on this girl. Well, before they find out that it's the girl . . . the father says to the kid, "Is it a crush?" You know something's bugging the kid. "Is it a crush? Is it someone you like at school?" The father says, "Some girl? Some boy?" This is a mainstream film, and it had that "whatever it takes for that." That's what [my ideal city] has to be.

By celebrating the father's "whatever it takes for that" attitude she communicates desire for a city in which heterosexuals are nonplussed by sexual difference. As this and the words of other women suggest, SLO lesbians desire acceptance, but at least in San Luis—which most believe falls short of Boulder or San Francisco in terms of the magnitude of the lesbian population and heterosexuals' embrace of them—they prioritize ties with other lesbian identified women.

"Lesbian Community"

San Luis Obispo's LBQ residents primarily forge ties with one another. Their connections to heterosexuals are primarily limited to family members, such as siblings, elderly parents, or adult children, who reside in the area. For most women, the fact that their social life is composed primarily of other lesbians goes without saying. Women who have recently come out or are new to San Luis Obispo are the exception to this rule, still marveling at their newfound lesbian network. For instance, one described the novelty and relief provided by a lesbian-dominated social life in San Luis Obispo County:

> [My social life] was all straight for a good seven years because I didn't know anybody. . . . I would say it completely changed as soon as I came out [in San Luis]. When I started meeting a lot of other women I felt so comfortable finally being in the company of somebody that I could relax with, and I could talk to on a very real and intimate basis that I was not ever afforded the opportunity to do before.

The more time I spent with these women, the more I realized that their networks shared three common ingredients: inclusivity, frequent interaction (read: very busy social calendars!), and heterogeneity of participants. These defining attributes can be seen throughout the lesbian community in SLO and are what birthed the deep feelings of informality and intimacy that so many of those I spoke with described.

For the most part, LBQ social circles in San Luis are remarkably inclusive. Time and again I was the beneficiary of this inclusivity. Almost immediately after unpacking my bags in San Luis Obispo I was invited to gatherings organized and attended by a diverse array of LBQ women; these included gay bingo, Lesbian Chips 'n' Chat, a game of pool, a dance party, a bonfire, a Proposition 8 protest rally, a potluck for older women, a going-away party, and game night. More often than not, during my interviews the woman would offer to hike, or dance, or drink with me, or would introduce me to their families, or would make sure that I was planning to attend an upcoming dance or party. Without fail, in one way or another, nearly every woman opened her home and social life to a researcher they had just met.

One evening at a bar, the bartender momentarily forgot to serve me a beer that I had ordered, and the woman I was meeting insisted on calling this to the bartender's attention. Later, a friend of hers informed me that I needed a slice of orange for my beer, and yet another clamored to request it. These efforts to welcome me to the area stood out on the heels of fieldwork in Ithaca, where LBQ residents were slow to participate.[19] In fact, at the close of my San Luis Obispo field visits I struggled to keep pace with the social calendars of women who were much older and had far less flexible work schedules than my own. It seemed that SLO offered no end of opportunities for lesbians to socialize with other lesbians.

My experience was not atypical; this was not a special benefit bestowed on a researcher. When new LBQ women move to town or come out they are, more often than not, readily embraced, even earning leadership roles shortly after arriving. For instance, shortly after coming out, a working-class single mother became the organizer of LezMingle, a monthly lesbian social gathering; without quite meaning too, Amy became a public face of the San Luis lesbian population. Over sandwiches in a packed deli on the edge of downtown San Luis, Amy, a slight woman with long curly hair, expressed not the slightest surprise about how quickly she had acquired her leadership role. Likewise, just months after moving to San Luis Obispo County a stay-at-home mother established picnics and play dates for LBQ families, hosted women's beach bonfires, and planned a scavenger hunt in her large rental in a gated, upscale seaside development. This sense of inclusion and unity, which shares a close relation with the adoption of a uniform, collective sexual identity, provides a protective barrier in an area that many LBQ women regard as only somewhat hospitable.[20]

In addition, the "refreshing" of the social pool provided by the ready inclusion of newcomers, who, during my time in the field seemed to arrive in a steady trickle, helps assuage informants' anxiety that the lesbian population is too small to fully satisfy friendship and dating needs. New arrivals do not go unnoticed, and having them join social events—and even come to lead them—generates genuine excitement and enthusiasm among longer-term residents. This was true of single and coupled newcomers alike.

For instance, when a couple that was new to the area introduced themselves via the listserv, several women responded with warm words of welcome, as well as with invitations. One wrote, "If you two are up for [it] there is a happening party Saturday in Los Osos! It's my 40th b-day party. . . . Are you up for some Karaoke and fun? Great company and laughs? Come on out and enjoy the wonderful women we have here on the coast. Hope to see you there!" Here, she expressed zero reticence about inviting strangers to celebrate a momentous occasion with her; this comfort, I came to recognize, is generated, in part, by confidence in the notion that because they are lesbian they are fundamentally alike. Likewise, when a newcomer attended the Supper Club, nearly three dozen women crowded into the comfortable living room of a cul-de-sac ranch and, over coffee and cake, took more than an hour to introduce themselves to her, detailing occupations, place of residence, and relationship status, and providing light-hearted summaries of how they had spent the holidays.

On several occasions, women preparing to move to San Luis Obispo County posted notice of their move on the lesbian listserv. Posts sometimes included requests for help with housing and even with carrying boxes. In every instance residents responded promptly and with enthusiasm, loaning trucks, unpacking boxes, and providing recommendations. Here is a typical request:

> Hi everyone. This is [Alice] (. . . moving from [Washington]) . . . still on schedule to arrive late Saturday, [August] 20 or early the 21st, and hopeful of taking advantage of the offered muscular support (will post details later) . . . BUT I'll be making a visit later this week to find a place to rent and get acquainted . . . I thought I'd wander the Thursday eve Farmers Market and perhaps attend the Friday eve Chips "n" Chat. Feel free to contact me during my visit . . . Thanks . . . I'm VERY excited to meet everyone.

While I never encountered a social occasion that literally included "everyone," listserv members swiftly offered to join her at the Farmers Market and encouraged her to come to Chips 'n' Chat. Although I was in Chicago during the week of her visit, I would not be surprised if, across the two events, she met twenty or more lesbian residents.

These traditions, and the shared identity politics underlining them, enabled lesbian-identified women in San Luis to readily embrace a researcher. Indeed, at the aforementioned supper club, women greeted me warmly, and the event's organizer asked me to give a five-minute summary of my research over dessert. Sometimes enthusiasm for newcomers even produced confusion, such as when a woman wrote to ask me to meet for coffee. I presumed that she wished to be interviewed, but, instead, she told me that she merely wished to socialize (despite being fully aware of my research). However, my ease of access to dinner parties, potlucks, gallery openings, and dances was an extension of a general tradition of inclusion—a tradition that enables (and is enabled by) a uniform notion of who the lesbians are and of what "lesbian" means.[21]

The sense that other—read: straight—San Luis social circles are unavailable to most lesbians also facilitates the inclusive character of LBQ ties. One woman, who grew up in the San Luis Obispo area, spoke of how a low-level sense of intolerance prohibited a broad sense of "community," built on connection to the place itself. As a result, the lesbian community is all the more important. In response to a question about this "sense of community," she told me, "I think as far as the gay community, yes [I have one]. As far as the rest of the community goes I am fearful of what is going on in everybody else's head. . . . I don't have a sense of community as far as San Luis Obispo goes. . . . I'm not proud of this community as far as the way they treat anyone that is different." Another explained why she consciously decided to turn to lesbians for conviviality and support:

> I got tired of playing the pronoun game. I got tired of just being careful. . . .
> For a while I probably was out there in the straight community as well as the
> gay community . . . and all of a sudden I went out to dinner with three other
> lesbians and I thought, you know what this is really nice. I could just relax
> and not watch myself, monitor what I say because even though I—if I want
> to be truly friends with a hetero—[that] is what I call them—if I truly want to
> be friends with them they need to know who I am 'cause I need to be able to
> relax, but even so . . . it's like [local heterosexuals] didn't really want to hear
> about it.

This sense of exclusion from heterosexual ties is not universal, but many articulate it. This drawbridge effect—the sense that others have cut off at least direct access to mainstream San Luis Obispo—further strengthens ties among lesbians, as well as the celebration of a common, lesbian identity. Why create divisions among your fellow lesbians when you believe you are already always apart?

The degree to which so many are included—to which everyone knows your name—is partially evidenced by the fact that my informants regularly complained about the scarcity of dating options in the San Luis Obispo area. Several informants suggested that this results from the limited population of LBQ residents—despite the fact that San Luis Obispo has a higher than average, and growing, proportion of lesbian couples, and that one San Luis suburb, the coastal town of Los Osos, possesses a particularly high proportion of lesbian couples.[22]

Thus, San Luis Obispo discourages the thriving sense of "ambient community"—a general sense of belonging forged with heterogeneous neighbors who share place, beliefs, politics, and practices—that Ithaca fosters, instead assigning great import to ties with other lesbians and encouraging a spirit of inclusivity among exclusion, or an "outside togetherness." Specifically, lesbians do not articulate a broad sense of belonging and membership in San Luis Obispo as a whole, nor in sexually heterogeneous networks. Neither do they articulate the sense that their membership in lesbian circles is entirely voluntary; with other social options partially foreclosed, lesbians are the individuals who, for the most part, they depend on for both the burdensome and light aspects of life. These conditions fuel the sensibility that "everyone is welcome" that is so central to social life in San Luis Obispo.

What does "inclusivity" look like? The presumption that shared sexual difference provides common ground, in conjunction with a reduced sense of safety and of exclusion from a larger heterosexual social world, draws a diverse array of residents—from affluent business owners to domestic workers—into a common social scene. Indeed, San Luis Obispo social networks are quite diverse—particularly in terms of age and class. The moderate size of San Luis's LBQ population—a figure that increased between 2000 and 2010, but that is nonetheless lower than our other cities—works together with shared identity politics to unite a diverse set of lesbian-identified women.[23]

As an example of the group's heterogeneity, a 2011 going-away party for Sarah, a recent community college graduate and well-known organizer of lesbian social events, included retirees, professionals in their fifties and sixties, community college students, a professor, and food service employees. The party, housed in a rented room in a small industrial park on a long stretch of former agricultural land near Trader Joe's and San Luis's small airport, featured music, dancing, an array of food, and a speech honoring Sarah's friendship and leadership role in organizing and sustaining social opportunities for lesbians. Students in their late teens and early twenties danced on one end of the floor, not far from the professor and her date. A successful business owner led a flash dance, and Sarah's grandmother sat near the buffet with lesbians in their sixties and seventies. An elementary school teacher and an arts therapist greeted me and, half-shouting over the music, told me of how they had met and started dating.

While drawing a larger crowd than many other events, the heterogeneity of the going-away party crowd was not atypical for San Luis Obispo. I regularly encountered such diversity: an attorney, banker, and working-class women seated side by side on a Wednesday evening at a dimly lit beachside pool hall in Pismo, a popular tourist destination, and a doctor, ranchers, construction workers, nurses, and educators conversing over Mexican food before caravanning to a retired woman's ranch-style home for dessert, coffee, and more conversation in a mountain town fifteen minutes from downtown San Luis

Obispo. Lesbian Chips 'n' Chat events, held at the small offices of GALA (which has since relocated) in a San Luis strip mall, drew a diverse crowd, regardless of topic: from game nights to a scavenger hunt, to a talk I gave about lesbian geographies. At my talk, a petite Latina lesbian in her early twenties sat shyly on a couch in the back of the room beside retirees, grandmothers, and a fifty-something auto mechanic, while women in their thirties and forties—including graduate students, a nurse, teachers, and a small business owner—were seated closer to the center of the room.

At such events, difference seems quite nearly sublimated, replaced by shared sexual identity. After my talk, the bulk of women caravanned to a downtown bar for dancing, where the crowd was at least as diverse as those at my talk. Friendship and flirtations cut across age, occupation, class, and, to a lesser degree, race.

I walked into the bar with Sarah, the forty-something community college student, as well as with a small business owner, Jen, and a teacher, Leah—each of whom is in her late thirties or early forties; Sarah and Leah are white, while Jen is Latina. As we approached the door the women paused so that I could introduce myself to an auto mechanic who is in her fifties, who was finishing a cigarette before entering the large, dimly lit bar. As we entered, I noted, just to the left of the door, two women, Maria and Susan, at the pool table. Maria is Latina and a mother, and came out within the last decade. On this evening she wore an oversized sweatshirt. Susan, who is Caucasian and athletic, wore her long brown hair pulled back into a ponytail beneath a baseball cap.

Seated at one end of the bar were two straight men. They steadily ignored the growing crowd of lesbians in the club, which usually draws a heterosexual crowd. Early in the evening Ariana volunteered to run to her car for a Joan Armatrading CD that she hoped would encourage more women to dance. "Honey," Sarah said, "No one dances to Joan Armatrading." This moment, which I momentarily suspected might become one of overt generational or cultural conflict, softened when Sarah and Ariana agreed that a compilation of songs from the seventies would be just fine. Indeed, generational differences seemed to be of little significance to the women gathered at the bar. Early in the evening, a woman in her twenties was the sole person on the dance floor. She wore a skirt that reached her ankles, which twirled as she moved to the music, and her long hair was pulled back from her face with barrettes. Later, she danced alongside a woman with a buzz cut, also in her early to mid-twenties. As the evening progressed, Lucinda, a middle-aged, white physical therapist arrived in a cowboy hat, boots, and fitted jeans, and paused at the bar to talk with younger women, including a twenty-two-year-old gas station attendant who also walked in late, wearing a shirt and tie. Later, Robin and the twenty-two-year-old flirted and danced despite an age gap of more than two decades. As they moved together on the dance floor, their bodies nearly touching, one woman whispered to me, "I'm trying to wrap my brain around that," but others simply looked on with expressions of interest, curiosity, and bemusement.

For much of the evening I managed to overlook a pole in the middle of the dance floor—an accomplishment given that it was literally luminescent, with sparkles that move from floor to ceiling. The pole only came to my attention when I noticed Robin scrubbing it with rags, which she requested from the bar. As we watched Robin work, Lucinda told me that the last time they were at the club a number of women performed pole dances. Bobbi, joining the conversation, said of the woman with long hair and barrettes, "But the best one, the one who stole the show was little schoolmarm one over there. It was like a movie where the schoolteacher lets her hair down and goes crazy. She was amazing on that pole. We were going wild." I take a moment to absorb this information: this is the selfsame "schoolmarm" who had just told me that she was uncomfortable participating in an interview because she is hesitant about being "out." I ask, perhaps naively, why Robin is cleaning the pole. As if to underline exactly what it is that brings this menagerie of women together, Bobbi, having overheard my question, retorts, "We're all women. We know what gets on there!" I blush, while the women around us laugh and wait, excitedly, for Robin to dance. In this moment, all eyes on Robin and the pole, I became fully cognizant of the degree to which, as we have seen, a common understanding of a core feature of their identities—their lesbianism—ties these women to one another (here, actors presume that we—lesbians—are all "in the know"). Belief in the significance of their common gender and desire for women unites them. Other differences—in age, politics, occupation, and class—seemed to fall away in anticipation of Robin's dance.

San Luis Obispo lesbians sometimes pause to acknowledge the economic and generational heterogeneity of their networks; some even promote it. For instance, one mentioned diversity in an email sent over the lesbian listserv intended to reassure a newcomer about the virtues of lesbian ties in San Luis. The newcomer reported in an introductory email that friends in the Bay Area warned her that San Luis Obispo "has no community." Not only is there community, a writer responded, but *diverse* community:

> Much Aloha to You [name redacted]! I know you will find SLO to be very "community" orientated! The inviting diversity, in both the people and beautiful land and seascapes of the Central Coast, will give you daily affirmations

of WHY you chose [sic] to STAY! (I myself have been here 35 years. . . .)
WELCOME!

Another wrote to the listserv to celebrate generational diversity: "We do
have a great community; women of all ages supporting each other." Intentionally or not, LBQ residents nurture this diversity—a defining feature of
their network—by maintaining organizations and regular events, such as
Chips 'n' Chat, Pride dances, and GALA events, that enable them to come
together across differences in age, finances, and even interests (whether one
likes board games, pool, hiking, or dancing). They nurture it, too, by talking
about it—signaling, in person and via the listserv, their diversity and therefore the principle that all are welcome.

Over the course of several extended research trips to San Luis Obispo,
most of which were two to four weeks in duration, I found that rarely a
week passed without the opportunity to attend at least one formal event
and often at least one additional social gathering announced via the Central
Coast Lesbian Listserv. This frequent contact underlines the degree to which
lesbian residents depend on one another for support and conviviality. It
also is a core mechanism via which they make strides toward inclusivity
and heterogeneity; the sheer volume of opportunities for connection helps
ensure a place in the fold for many lesbian residents.

I was consistently amazed by the sociability of SLO lesbians. Bobbi
suggested that this social fecundity did not always exist. She spoke of the
closure of San Luis's gay bars, and how, following this, LBQ residents frequently complained that there was not enough to do in the area. Tiring of
these complaints, Bobbi took action. With a friend, she founded the listserv, which women use to organize events. When we spoke in 2009, she
estimated that there were approximately one hundred fifty official listserv
members. Indeed, she suggested that women in the San Luis area now encounter an opposite problem: sometimes their events are overattended. For
the most part, she said, they have stopped organizing events at restaurants,
because "it is too overwhelming for the restaurants. Thirty to forty women
often show up." Instead, they caravan to San Simeon, about an hour north
of San Luis Obispo, to observe elephant seals, host living room game nights,
and organize dinners or potlucks. Residents also use the listserv to distribute
notice of annual events, such as those surrounding San Luis's Pride celebration and a women's camping weekend.

In a typical week, especially in the warmer months, the listserv advertises
a dizzying array of activities and events. On a *single day* women used the
listserv to promote the following: the annual Women's Campout, a Breast

Cancer Walk, Hearst Castle tour, and dinner at a lesbian-friendly restaurant. Likewise, over a week and a half women encouraged others to attend an Indigo Girls concert, a dance night at a downtown bar, build-a-burrito night at Lesbian Chips 'n' Chat, a softball game, a pavilion dance, Rainbow Bingo, Saturday Club, a Pride BBQ, a Blame Sally concert, a game night, a dinner club for women over fifty, a beach day for kids of same-sex parents, and a Pride dance in a south county town.

The diversity and frequency of events helps to ensure the heterogeneity of lesbian networks. For instance, you do not have to drink alcohol, dance (indeed, women explicitly encouraged nondancers to attend one dance), or play sports to attend one of the above events. Women without Internet access—whether permanent or temporary—told me about receiving telephone calls from friends, notifying them of events that they might attend. Thus, women of a variety of ages and classes, and with a variety of tastes and abilities, are able to find a place in the social scene. Moreover, the frequency of events enables consistent contact, and a near-constant accessibility of lesbian networks for purposes of practical and emotional support. Likewise, repeated contact encourages the development of both friendly and intimate ties, as well as romantic connections. One woman sent a note of gratitude to listserv members, thanking them for attending an event, stating that she very much appreciated the opportunity to see "some of my best friends . . . love you all!" This statement, while particularly effusive, was not uncommon; with frequency of contact this type of community affirmation cements ties and bestows contact with meaning and significance.

Some imply that the abundance of social occasions is a valuable antidote to the comparatively small size of San Luis Obispo's lesbian population; they feel that San Luis' lesbian population is limited, at least in relation to the perceived size of the population in places such as San Francisco and Los Angeles, and even of smaller cities, such as Boulder, Colorado. By visiting with one another often, residents suggest, they keep loneliness at bay. Some take concrete steps to combat this sense of loneliness. For instance, after my first field visit, an informant wrote to tell me of the creation of a website (now defunct), SanLezObispo. She and others hoped it would connect lesbian residents by providing another resource for learning of activities and opportunities for social engagement. They also hoped that it would attract additional women to the area by making visible the vibrancy of existing networks. In so doing, they hoped to bolster the San Luis lesbian population and thus to expand dating and friendship pools.

Others take smaller, more personal steps. A loan officer told me, "To me [the local LBQ female population] doesn't seem that big. . . . It seems small."

And yet, she acknowledged that she and her former partner, from whom she had recently separated, did not often socialize, and that she was beginning to discover, despite the relatively small size of the lesbian population, a plethora of social opportunities. One such opportunity had helped her to begin dating again:

> [My friend] is much more active and outgoing than I am. She was really involved with the Proposition Eight, you know, fighting Proposition Eight and marriage equality and all that stuff, so she actually knew a lot more people than I did because I'm not that political so I wasn't really into all that stuff, but she had heard about [kickball] and she mentioned it one time to me. . . . And I didn't have anything to do and I was like I need to get out or I'm never going to meet anybody and so I finally got up the courage to go one day and it was a lot of fun. . . . We went to the bonfire a couple weeks ago and that was cool. . . . A lot of people showed up for that. Maybe like 40 or I think actually last night somebody said there might have been 52. . . . But you know people were coming and going so I don't know how they kept track, but it was a lot of fun. They, you know, somebody brought out a boom box and it was just down on the beach, brought some firewood and we danced and talked and ate and drank and mingled. So yeah, that was a lot of fun.

In a context in which the lesbian population does not seem "that big," and in which lesbian residents proceed with caution about announcing their sexual identity to heterosexual neighbors and coworkers, and in which identity politics dominate, women take great comfort and pleasure in the number and frequency of their social occasions. Indeed, as the loan officer's words suggest, such occasions can be life-altering, ushering her from one relationship to another and into a lesbian-world of games, bonfires, and dance nights. Paradoxically, the small size of the lesbian population produces an unexpected breadth of opportunities for contact. One woman recalled that while living in San Francisco, a city with an abundance of LBQ residents, she remembers thinking: "You know what? I don't have any gay friends, and I don't have a partner now. And I live in *San Francisco.*" Unexpectedly, she found the comradeship she had expected to find in the Bay Area in San Luis Obispo, a smaller city with a less established reputation as a lesbian haven and a smaller lesbian population. This, I propose, is not a coincidence: feelings of scarcity, coupled with concern about acceptance and safety, encourage frequent contact among lesbians. And, of course, this frequent contact encourages or reinforces lesbian identity politics, which, in turn, furthers the importance of frequent contact. This circularity is, of course, different in character from that found in Ithaca—where a sense of "ambient community" and post-identity politics reinforce one another—but, as in all the study cities, the circularity of ties and identity are nonetheless evident.

The formality of the venues in which some interactions take place, and especially of the avenues by which news of opportunities for social engagement are transmitted, help to reinforce the defining characteristics of ties among lesbians: frequency of contact, heterogeneity of members, and inclusivity. That is, residents do not have to rely on informal friendship networks to learn of social opportunities, but instead can turn to sources that are—at least ostensibly—open to all and advertised to many: primarily the GALA and the lesbian listserv. That is, these formal mechanisms for organizing social ties anchor and facilitate lesbian social interaction. With a note to the listserv or an email or phone call to the GALA office, one can find a place on the roster of two key mechanisms for distribution of news of opportunities for social engagement. As a result, many occasions span smaller friendship clusters. News of a dance, for instance, does not just get distributed among women who hike San Luis Mountain together after work—although the idea may begin there. Nor are plans for a Wednesday evening hike limited to those who appear at a Saturday bonfire. Like other dimensions of their community, the existence of these mechanisms, lesbians' reliance on them, and the emphasis they place on them are products of their sense of population scarcity and limited sense of abundance and acceptance and the closely related identity-politics orientation.

The first of the devices on which San Luis women rely to nurture and maintain ties is GALA, which provides an organizational umbrella under which several social groups for lesbians operate and/or are advertised: for example, LezMingle, the social group for "older" women, and the Saturday Club. GALA houses some meetings of the above groups, although with the exception of LezMingle, most groups adopt an independent approach, meeting off-site and primarily relying on GALA to distribute news of their activities via its website and newsletter. Over and again, women mentioned the organizing glue GALA provides. One said: "We'd go and do a hike here and there. I got to meet other people who organized the hike—who [advertised] it through the GALA group." Women who have established new activities, such as a supper club, typically notify GALA of their plans.

Many suggest that GALA is a particularly critical resource for those who have just moved to the area. One, who lived in the area before coming out, turned to GALA as she explored her sexual identity: "I looked up in the phone book like either under gay or lesbian and the GALA Center was listed under there. . . . So I checked that out a little bit and would go to like the Chips 'n' Chat, you know, years and years ago and so that's kind of how I was getting my feet wet as far as in the community around here and so I would attend dances." Another woman echoed this: "It was the GALA group, the local GALA group that I contacted—one of the very first places that I contacted."

In addition to serving as a bridge for newcomers to establish ties to LBQ women, GALA organizes two regular opportunities for which many women express appreciation: an annual Pride Celebration, and a booth at the weekly Farmers Market in downtown SLO. Women take pleasure in each. One described Pride: "It's a really nice Pride actually. . . . It's like a week long. They have different movies that they show at the Fremont Theater. . . . Then they have like drag shows that are pretty fun and neat." Several articulate appreciation for the sense of comfort and pleasure derived from the presence of a GALA booth at the Farmers Market. In the midst of an impressive stretch of vendors selling fruit, vegetables, nuts, and prepared food, I often encountered informants behind the booth, and lesbians regularly pause on their way to eat, dance, or purchase produce to talk with those staffing it. The booth provided an especially valuable anchor during the months leading to the vote on Proposition 8, when the market became a public battleground over gay marriage.

Despite enthusiasm for Pride and the Farmers Market booth, several complained that GALA is male dominated and more concerned with gay men than with lesbians. As a result, these women appreciate GALA but are more likely to be involved with offshoots of GALA or activities advertised by GALA, rather than those that take place at the GALA Center itself (which moved from its strip mall location to a historic home in downtown San Luis Obispo). This underlines the degree to which "community," for them, references lesbian networks, rather than a broader network of LGBTQI individuals. One said, "The GALA out here is very guy. . . . It would be nice to get something like that—like a Her Land started or something that is a women's resource center. So, yeah, that would be nice. That would be awesome." Here, she signals desire for a lesbian-only organization. Another echoed this, saying, "The guys dominate the GALA Center. The women don't want to go there. I don't understand that, but I'm not willing to be the woman to go there so that's just not my style." Likewise, another woman explained that GALA's membership isn't as age integrated as she would like. As their words suggest, most primarily regard GALA, with the exception of Pride and the Farmers Market booth, as a crucial communication device, rather than as constituting a community in and of itself. This is notable given that, in theory, such an organization *could* unite disparate LGBTQI individuals and encourage the formation of pansexual-identity ties. The absence of such a hyphenated network—with the exception of a network of anti–Proposition 8 activists—in San Luis emphasizes the degree to which LBQ women there are first and foremost lesbian identified and oriented.

The second organizational facilitator is the aforementioned Central Coast Lesbian Listserv, which provides a crucial point of entry for new residents and notifies a diverse array of lesbians of social opportunities. Over and again women indicate that the listserv provides a crucial resource both for newcomers and longstanding residents, informing them of activities and providing its own sense of connection. On hearing of my research, some even emailed me in advance of an interview to instruct me to pay attention to the listserv. For instance, one woman said, "There's an email group. . . . They have a lot of events going on." The listserv functions to spread news not only of GALA events but also of more informal events and impromptu plans, from birthday parties to game nights and bonfires. It also enables women to assist one another in times of need—such as when they are looking for housing, seeking to rent or sell a property, or searching for work.

The warm inclusivity of lesbians results, in part, from the fact that GALA and the listserv aid the habitual inclusion of outsiders and that they discourage identification with other facets of the self, such as with one's generation, profession, or race or ethnicity. With only a few exceptions, such as the potluck group for "mature" women, the subgroups and activities facilitated by or through such umbrella groups are organized around activity, not around other identities. This helps to minimize the splintering of women into distinct social groups and therefore works to counter some of their concern about the scarcity of the lesbian population, allowing them to serve as a united front in a less than totally hospitable environment.

However, we must consider why these umbrella organizations exist and serve such a crucial role in San Luis Obispo. As Bobbi's words above indicate, one explanation informants provide rests on the closure of a longstanding gay bar.[24] After its closure, lesbians had to find alternate methods to reach one another. According to Bobbi, this closure directly inspired the establishment of the listserv. However, this cannot fully explain the existence of umbrella groups, since three of the four cities this book features have experienced the closure of a gay or lesbian bar.

Rather, what makes San Luis distinct is not the absence of a bar or even the existence of GALA or the Central Coast Lesbian Listserv. Instead, a common lesbian identity and mild feelings of alienation (from heterosexuals) and of scarcity (of other lesbians) enable reliance on groups that include and appeal to a broad swathe of women. In other words, these (more or less) all-inclusive umbrella groups and LBQ residents' identity politics are mutually reinforcing. Without a common sense of identity or the drive to connect with those who share it, there might be little interest in or effort devoted to maintaining such organizations, and without such organizations, women would be less likely to maintain heterogeneous, inclusive networks marked by frequent contact. This underlines how dimensions of city ecology inform the existence, role, and features of local institutions for identity groups.[25]

Trouble in the Happiest Place in America?

After about a year of flying in and out of San Luis Obispo to conduct fieldwork, I began to think that the city was the perfect retort to the growing assumption—in Ithaca and elsewhere—that the "lesbian community" is in decline, if not already a relic. Here, community college students and grandmothers share dance floors, a doctor hosts a going-away party for a part-time food service employee two decades her junior, and the adult children of Central Valley farm laborers hike and play pool with women from upper-middle-class Los Angeles and San Francisco families. Moreover, such generosity of community does not require special entry or years of waiting before you are let into the club; as we have seen, newcomers are greeted with open arms. Nor are interactions limited to formal occasions or infrequent events, such as an annual Pride Parade. Marcia, caravanning with me from a potluck to a restaurant where I was to interview her, suggested that we take a detour to deliver a meal to a retired, Los Osos lesbian couple preparing for an extended trip; Adele spoke, in the air-conditioned comfort of the mobile home she shares with three small dogs, of the poker game she planned to host that evening for lesbians, some highly educated and some still in school, ranging in age from forty to sixty-five. If this is not the idyllic community for which Ithaca residents are nostalgic, what is?

After several of these remarkable encounters I repressed the urge to call my informants in Ithaca and tell them they had it all wrong. But perhaps I was being naive. Slowly but surely, this image of San Luis Obispo—as a shining counterexample to cynicism about lesbian community—was complicated by revelation of the distinct friendship groups to which the broader San Luis Obispo lesbian population belongs. This became particularly unmistakable at a dance party at a downtown San Luis Obispo club. For several months in 2009, a promoter hosted the event, marketed to gay and lesbian residents, on a bimonthly basis. On the party's opening night, I entered the upscale bar, which is decorated with white walls, a white bar, and sleek contemporary tables and stools. The bar extends onto a patio abutting the historic Mission San Luis Obispo de Tolosa and recently restored San Luis Creek. On entering, I found many of the LBQ residents I had encountered thus far in various settings, from potlucks to a Pismo Beach pool hall. However, I swiftly realized that women, who, at previous events, interacted across areas of difference, such as age and class, fell into distinct groups occupying different spaces within the bar; something about the party—perhaps its novelty or its noise, which prohibited conversation among large groups of individuals, or the atypical presence of gay men—revealed alliances and divisions. Despite participating in many activities and the dozens of interviews I had already conducted, I had been almost completely unaware that such fractures in the landscape existed.

As I moved through the space I encountered a handful of white women in their fifties and sixties whom I had met at several events advertised via GALA. They sat together on a couch at a distance from the dance floor. Nearby, a Latina couple, both in their fifties and employed as domestic workers, talked with a younger Latina friend. Later, the couple took to the dance floor for much of the evening, seemingly falling into their own, private world. This move may have been romantically driven, but in a later interview with one—in which she articulated a sense of being at a slight remove from San Luis lesbian networks as a result of class and race exclusions—suggests that romance might not have been the only motivation for their insularity.

At a series of cocktail tables stood clusters of women I had not yet met. One group was made exclusively of women in their thirties, most of whom were white and wore their hair in short styles popular with LBQ residents of San Francisco. At another table I found women with longer, blonde hair, seated at barstools talking and sipping expensive cocktails and wines.

On the opposite side of the dance floor stood a few professionals in their thirties and forties. I had met them several times, such as at an informal dance party and Lesbian Chips 'n' Chat. Robin and Bea, both white and professional, dressed similarly, in shorts and a button down shirt. Andrea wore a skirt and sandals. When I spoke with them they told me that they shared a ride to the event, and I learned that the three work for the same company. Throughout the evening they stood and danced together.

As the night progressed, a few women escorted me around the bar with the aim of introducing me to residents I had not yet interviewed. Midway through, Sarah, who, since I first arrived in San Luis Obispo, had been especially certain to make certain I was included in parties and outings, introduced me to a group of women in their early twenties. Seated on the patio, I learned that several are friends with the young, lesbian DJ—a tattooed woman wearing a vintage dress who lives in a small downtown apartment with her partner and dog (when I later interviewed them, I sat on a couch in their tiny combined living/bedroom, a foot or two from the bed where they sat, our knees nearly touching). A few young women on the patio were androgynous in appearance, but several others looked much like many other CALPOLY students on a Saturday night. They wore tight dresses, makeup, and long hair. One told me that she identifies as straight, although another, overhearing, loudly announced in a tipsy voice that she had just made out with her in a corner of the patio.

Around eleven p.m., hired dancers took to small stages above the dance floor: a woman wearing a short skirt and a bikini top and two men attired in leather briefs. Near the dancers stood a tall and broad white woman, Laurie, who is in her early fifties and has coifed, spiky hair. She dressed in white, wore angular glasses, and a small cluster of women of a similar age and style surrounded her. Sarah introduced me to Laurie, whispering: "She's the mayor of the lesbians." This surprised me, as to date I had not encountered Laurie or any of her friends at Chips 'n' Chat or the pool hall or dances and, frankly, had thought of *Sarah* as something akin to the "mayor of the lesbians" (although I had not thought to put it in those terms). While I pondered the likelihood of the San Luis area containing two "mayors," Laurie promised to participate in an interview and for the rest of the night encouraged me to join her friends on the dance floor.

Throughout the event I became privy to small pieces of gossip. I learned that two women were avoiding one another because of a recent break up, as well as about unrequited attractions, jealousies, romantic competitions, and infidelities. Individually, none of this surprised; I had long heard of breakups and new romances and hookups. However, put together in a single scene, in my notes from the evening, I expressed surprise about the distinction between how residents interacted at the dance party and how I had seen them interact to date—including in other casual settings, such as on the dance floor at another downtown bar. At this party, LBQ networks appeared decidedly less cohesive and culturally homogeneous.[26] In this new setting, women seemed to feel free to stick with their own "kind" or otherwise interacted primarily with close friends. In other words, at least at this event, "lesbian community" was not simply a melting pot of women united solely by shared sexual identity as women in Ithaca nostalgically imagine it to be; instead it appeared to be a compilation of more and less loosely connected friendship circles composed of residents who share certain traits, such as occupation, class, age, tastes, race, or hometown. Here, then, the existence of a common identity politics and of "lesbian community" does not prohibit the simultaneous existence of smaller friendship groups.[27] This ought not to surprise, as all communities are composed of smaller subunits. And yet, it did surprise me—perhaps in large part because I had heard so much talk from lesbian informants in San Luis Obispo about the inclusivity of their community.

Inspired by the evening, I looked back over my earlier field notes and found that they contain hints of divisions evident at the dance; such divisions simply had not been as obvious as they were that night. For instance, on the March evening when I joined more than a dozen women at a dimly lit bar on the edge of downtown San Luis Obispo, as I approached the bar I briefly fell into conversation with Julie, an auto mechanic who was smoking on a sidewalk beside the door. Her short grey hair is cut bluntly. She has bright blue eyes and a few missing teeth. She began to tell me a bit about her life—her grown children and her house in the country—when Sarah pulled me by the arm into the bar saying, within earshot of Julie, "I hate how [smoke] smells. How can anyone stand to smoke and smell like that?" I cringed at the thought that Julie had overheard the comments and realized, too late, that I had been used to assert or reassert a boundary—the basis for which I was not yet entirely aware and largely unprepared, but which I very much suspect was about class difference.[28] In retrospect, Sarah's gesture spoke volumes: it is okay to be working class and a part of San Luis' lesbian umbrella community, but women like Julie who are poor—who, for instance, might not have access to dental care—are at best on its margins.

In addition to such moments of overt exclusion, there are also, as in any network, gossip and rumors and struggles over reputation. On the same evening, one woman told me, in front of Ellen, that Ellen has dated "half the women in here." Ellen, looking uncomfortable, remained silent. "Everyone wants Ellen," the woman continued. "She's the popular one. She's standoffish and it drives women crazy." Like Ellen, I could not help but wince at the open antagonism these words communicated. And, of course, women shared stories of thwarted romance, such as flirtatious emails that were followed by in-person rejections. One woman told me that she had to physically resist the sexual overtures of another woman, and another resident was viciously attacked on Craigslist after placing an anonymous ad on its women-seeking-women page (perhaps for this reason, despite otherwise high reliance on social media, residents infrequently rely on the San Luis Craigslist site). Once, at the Pismo pool hall, two women who had recently begun dating kissed and caressed one another, despite the presence of a woman from whom one of the women had just separated after a decade together. For those of us who were not members of the new couple, the evening was, at best, awkward.

In interviews, a few women offered criticisms of local social dynamics. For instance, Camila, a Latina domestic worker—one-half of the aforementioned couple who took to the dance floor—contrasted social dynamics in SLO with other places she had lived, bemoaning the absence of a strong network of lesbians of color in the San Luis context, as well as the degree to which personality conflicts shape social interactions. She said, "[In Seattle] a lot of the women got together. There were a lot more women of color that would get together that would do outings, plays, theatre, conferences, and you know, more camaraderie. Because here we try to make a connection and we have made some connections, but it is like, 'Oh we don't invite so and so because of this and that,' you know. And my thought is, you know, is [that it should be] principles before personalities." In contrast to her former home, in the San Luis Obispo context, Camila felt pressure to let lesbian identity supplant other facets of her self-understanding, for her, most painfully, her racial and class identifications. She implies that this is a product of the fact that San Luis has a smaller population of lesbians of color, but I argue that it also emerges from the general emphasis residents—of a variety of ages, classes, races, and ethnicities—place on being lesbian as the defining facet of the self. This is a protective impulse, meant to enclose all (or at least most) local lesbians in a protective circle, but we see that it comes at the expense for some—such as a Latina domestic worker—of opportunities to organize and educate and connect on behalf of other concerns; concerns that may, in fact, overlap with one's interests as a lesbian—as her description of a community of lesbians of color in her former city implies. And, as a working-class racial minority in a white and middle-class–dominated network of lesbians, raising these concerns seemed to be entirely out of the question. In this sense, absent of that kind of open and honest exchange, this is not a fully or truly inclusive community.

Beyond this, in a context where LBQ identity is only rarely politicized (such as when women felt that Proposition 8 called them to defend their group), it is hard for principles, beyond the belief that sexuality is innate and life defining, to guide ties and interactions (recall that several women insist that they are "not political"). This leaves much room, as Camila instructs, for personalities to come into play. To be more overtly political would be to risk attracting unwanted attention to their group in a context in which, much of the time, they seek to live below the radar. It would also conflict with the broad and powerful local narrative of San Luis Obispo as a place one comes for quiet and beauty: to "be" rather than to transform or agitate.

Of course, the claim that one can ardently identify as lesbian without being political rests on a narrow view of "politics"—one that is deeply responsive to local conditions—that better serves some (middle-class white women) than others (a Latina domestic worker).

It is not an accident that it took obviously cliquish behavior at a dance to make the existence of factions and conflict apparent to me. Rather, as we have begun to see, many work to present their networks as unified and harmonious (e.g., sending notes to the listserv underlining the diversity and inclusivity of their community and their insistence, in interviews with me, on painting a portrait of an inclusive network). Like much else related to their ties, this presentation of community relates to their understanding of lesbian identity; they present both LBQ identities and ties as uncomplicated, conflict free, and steady, since this is how they wish—and perhaps even feel that they need—them to be. To acknowledge any instability within the community could introduce the possibility of identity instability; if Latina lesbians have their own microcommunity, might they also have their own microidentity? In this sense, San Luis residents' understanding of female same-sex desire—as a uniform experience—encourages their efforts to affirm notions of a seamless community and thus an unsplintered identity politics. Plus, they feel that they need one another for support and camaraderie, and to talk of conflict within the group is to risk the sense of security that derives from lesbian community.

Finally, their disavowal of conflict and division—embodied less by what they say and more by what they don't say, such as their relative silence about breakups and fading friendships—relates to how they perceive and talk about San Luis Obispo itself: as a bucolic escape from other parts of California, whether more urban or conservative. San Luis Obispo, they state repeatedly, is a place one comes to be content and happy. They refer to it as "Camelot," "Avalon," and "Middle Earth." To emphasize division and conflict within lesbian networks would cast doubt not only on the notion of unified, uncomplicated lesbian identity but also on what it means to live in the "happiest place in America."[29]

While conflict and divisions within San Luis's lesbian umbrella community were unmistakable at the dance party and, on second glance, in my notes and interview transcripts, my record of the evening of the dance nonetheless indicates the degree to which I struggled and ultimately failed to imagine such a menagerie of women coming together at a similar event in Ithaca (or, for that matter, in Greenfield). After the dance, writing into the early morning hours in my San Luis rental—a bungalow outside downtown—I reflected on the fact that while they may not have danced together or even talked, the evening was shared by retirees and college students, domestic workers and professionals, and women with a "straight" aesthetic and those with an "edgier" aesthetic who likely feel at home in the nightclubs of San Francisco or Los Angeles. I found myself thinking of an extended conversation I had at the event with a young gay man—an undergraduate on break from an elite Midwestern university. On a leather couch next to the dance floor, he told me that the breadth and diversity of the crowd was revelatory. This was not his parents' San Luis Obispo—and yet here were women, and some men, of his parents' age and older, sharing a dance floor with his peers. Where else, I wondered, might he encounter this diversity of individuals? Certainly, as he readily admitted, he would not find such a crowd at his university, nor was he likely to do so at off-campus bars in his progressive college town.

After all, a common lesbian identity gets nearly everyone in the door in San Luis Obispo. Despite this shared identity, distinctions and conflicts exist, but, because of their shared identity and reliance on inclusive, umbrella organizations, almost everyone knows almost everyone—even if they do not share close friendships.

This sense of familiarity is so great that some bemoan the absence of unexplored romantic opportunities. Seated at a bar, Lucinda expressed disappointment about the paucity of eligible women, comparing San Luis Obispo to Los Angeles: "It was better there, but not as much better as one might imagine." Another echoes this: "When [my partner] and I split up, I just didn't know a lot of lesbian women and I like having a partner and I want to meet more women and find somebody—a partner, you know. I like that. I think . . . I just like the company. I'm a care provider. I like . . . taking care of somebody or . . . having somebody around; a best friend. I do better with somebody than on my own. I get a little lonely. I've met a few women that I really like that will be friends, [but] you know I haven't met anybody that I would want for a partner."

This sense of scarcity, together with the presumption of shared identity, fuels the ready inclusion of newcomers into the scene, both for friendship and dating. As an example, after arriving in San Luis, Jean, who had moved from the Central Valley with her son, moved from one Central Coast romantic partner to another—dating both women who were regulars in the social groups I observed and at least one woman whom I rarely observed at such events. Just two years after Jean's relocation women indicated that they had her "ticket"; that is, Jean had dated enough women who knew one another that prospective romantic partners had grown wary of her intentions. In other words, friendship groups and even cliques exist in San Luis, but ties—romantic and otherwise—cut across them. In this sense, ties among

San Luis's LBQ population are intimate, heterogeneous, and marked by frequent contact, but they are also sometimes sites of conflict, gossip, and division.[30] Even more commonly, as the Maria anecdote suggests, the very intimacy and heterogeneity that a woman in Ithaca might long for produces, at least for some in San Luis Obispo, feelings of insularity and even loneliness.

Conclusion

Being LBQ in San Luis Obispo clearly means something vastly different than it does in Ithaca. The enormous contrast between the residents in these two cities reminds that there is no neat chronological progression out of the closet or away from gay and lesbian identities. Contrary to some popular assumptions, gay life in America has not moved away from identity politics; though the narrative is tempting, we have not stepped, in unison, from Stonewall to marriage registries and baby showers. There is, in short, no narrow and uniform set of guidelines about "how to be gay" (Halperin 2012).[31] At least in San Luis Obispo, even amid a string of legal and cultural victories, and with unprecedented mainstream acceptance of alternate lifestyles, identity politics—predicated on notions of a common "lesbian" identity—is alive and well.

The durability of identity politics should not, perhaps, come as a total surprise. Both recent scholarship and media accounts continue to highlight the prevalence of LGBTQI communities even in places that seem to be inhospitable, from the Bible Belt to rural America, not to mention the Middle East and Africa and other more conservative parts of the world.[32] And the more we look, the more we see how certain demographic groups, like some working-class Latino and African American men in Chicago and some gays and lesbians in the Bible Belt, depart from dominant scripts, such as norms about "coming out."[33] Yet, San Luis Obispo's departure poses a greater puzzle. After all, this is a progressive college town on the coast of California with a mostly middle- and upper-middle-class and highly educated LBQ population—exactly the kind of place where we would expect people to be out and proud and moving away from identity politics. In short, the existence of lesbian identity politics in a university town in twenty-first-century coastal California calls us away from strictly temporal and demographic explanations for the formation of LBQ identities, as well as away from a spatial map that only recognizes variation across blue and red states, rural and urban locales, and coastal and inland cities.[34]

How do we account for this culture that embraces lesbian identity and ties so eagerly? The gulf I found between my experiences in Ithaca and in

SLO helped to shape my understanding of identity: that scripts about "how to be gay" (Halperin 2011) are derived from or at least assembled in novel ways in their contexts. Specifically, the cities we live in both shape but also reconfigure broader narratives, making them locally comprehensible.[35] In San Luis Obispo, the sense of shared fate or common ground that drives lesbian identity politics emerges from measured feelings of exclusion and fear, the moderate scale and spatial dispersion of the LBQ population, and a narrative about the place that prioritizes the peaceful "good life" in a beautiful setting, further minimizing division and debate among lesbian residents.

We also find that being a lesbian in San Luis Obispo earns you a near-instant membership in a network of others who identify similarly.[36] The "lesbian community"—a network of women from different walks of life predicated on shared sexual identity for which some Ithacans are nostalgic—is alive and well in San Luis. Like the identities of individuals, the existence of this broader "lesbian community" emerges from dimensions of city ecology that inform what it feels like to be LBQ in San Luis Obispo.[37] In particular, feelings of scarcity and exclusion cultivate an inclusive community of LBQ residents who turn to one another for support, fun, resources, and a sense of belonging.[38]

Recognition of how place shapes identity and ways of interacting with heterosexual and other residents calls us to even more carefully assess the costs and benefits of San Luis Obispo's "lesbian community." After all, their community arises from a feeling of distance from and caution about the heterosexual majority, as well as from related (albeit mild) concern about the paucity of other LBQ residents and therefore of prospective friends and partners.[39] At least in San Luis Obispo, these conditions encourage a turn inward, toward one another, for support, conviviality, and romance. LBQ residents believe they can build a safe and affirming home here, but to do so they rely almost exclusively on one another.

In this sense, the conditions that foster their lesbian-only social circles are, of course, worthy of pause. At what cost do LBQ residents search for camaraderie and come to presume that this is best, if not only, found among other lesbians? When some, like those in Ithaca, romanticize "lesbian community," do we also, implicitly, celebrate unfortunate conditions—the feelings of partial acceptance and scarcity that lesbians in San Luis Obispo articulate? We need not only ask this question in relation to LBQ residents. The constellation of factors that produce identity-based ties among San Luis Obispo's lesbians may produce similar ties for other groups. This calls for caution about nostalgia for such ties, such as our frequent collective mourning for the lost-ethnic-enclave or the fading working-class village. This caution, though, should be counterbalanced with awareness, garnered from Ithaca, of what is lost and gained in a safer and more "integrated" world. Identity-based community may arise from conditions that few would wish to replicate, but in other contexts, like Ithaca, many nonetheless long for it.

San Luis Obispo also instructs that approaches to identity and community are mutually reinforcing. Despite subtle internal cleavages and occasional conflict, San Luis Obispo lesbians present their community as a relatively seamless and harmonious collection of heterogeneous individuals. It is not a coincidence that this bears striking similarities to how they present sexual identity: as a coherent and unswerving set of desires and attachments. In San Luis, the belief that female same-sex desire is singular, life defining, and innate encourages a confederacy of lesbian-identified women, despite differences that might separate women less certain of the common ground that joins them. In turn, the existence of this network reinforces notions of shared sexual identity among lesbians by presenting them as part of a (relatively) comprehensive whole.

Finally, by capturing how the identity-driven lives and ties of San Luis lesbians unfold beyond the lesbian bars and bookstores in which we might imagine "lesbian community" to take place, the chapter challenges not only the when and who of identity-driven lives, identifying them among an array of contemporary women in San Luis Obispo, but also the *where*.[40] Not only do these women live identity-driven lives in a place that we would not anticipate—a progressive coastal college town—they also nurture identity-driven ties in more or less unmarked spaces: in the staff room behind a bank branch, on the dance floor at a straight bar on the edge of town, and in a beachside pool hall popular with teenagers and tourists. This challenges notions of a neat binary between identity-driven spaces (the archetypal gay bar in a gay ghetto) and "post-gay" space in which lesbian-only gatherings become unnecessary and rare.[41] In San Luis, identity-driven congregation remains frequent and vital, without, for the most part, depending on demarcated locales.[42] That seeming contradiction calls for us to reassess the role of marked, exclusive places in fostering group identities, from the lesbian or gay bar to the ethnic neighborhood.[43] What alternate mechanisms nurture and maintain group understanding and connection? Among these, we have seen, are the Internet and reliance on an umbrella organization, as well as the practice of coming together at restaurants, bars, parks, and beaches. Just as we have found in contemporary San Luis Obispo an identity politics many of us associate with an earlier era or a different type of place, we might find identity politics and related congregation flourishing in parts of our cityscapes where we might not ordinarily look. Thus, for a full portrait of contemporary LBQ life we must look not only at the bar and community center but also at the room behind the bank and the group of women on a mountain trail.

THREE

Portland:
Hybrid and Hyphenated Identity Politics

I began fieldwork in Portland, Maine, in May 2009. I rented an apartment in an antique Cape Cod house at the crest of Munjoy Hill in Portland's East End. My living room and kitchen doubled as the art gallery of the woman who owned the house; her vivid paintings of landscapes and animals lined the walls. Almost directly across the street sat evidence of the neighborhood's advancing gentrification: a coffee shop, complete with youthful baristas in hipster attire, and a market selling local produce, fresh bread, and gourmet sandwiches, as well as a small curated selection of wine and beer. A few blocks away there were three restaurants, ranging from low- to moderately high-end that drew a combination of loyal local customers and tourists, a realty office, an Italian deli and convenience store (almost exclusively serving white working-class residents and immigrant families who lived on Munjoy Hill pregentrification), and a Laundromat. On my arrival, many lesbian, bisexual, and/or queer (LBQ) residents were boycotting the Laundromat because of the owners' opposition to same-sex marriage, signaled via a placard in a front window proclaiming "yes on 1"—a 2009 ballot initiative to reject a new law permitting same-sex couples to wed in Maine. At the end of the street sits the Eastern Promenade, a large grassy park on the slope of a vast, green hill overlooking the Atlantic and a series of small islands. A recent college graduate and artist described the "Eastern Prom" as "just this huge grassy hill where you can look at the whole entire ocean. Everybody who lives up here who goes there when it's nice always says, 'We live here!' Like we just look at each other beaming. We're like, 'Yeah, we live here. We live here.'" Indeed, in July and August—the only truly warm months in Maine—the promenade seemed to be a second living room for many locals. Each time I walked down my block I seemed to encounter someone whom

I knew—often, among them, some who were LBQ—splayed on the green grass, with books, picnics, and dogs.

Despite the vibrant ocean blues and sumptuous green grass of the Eastern Promenade, much of Portland loomed large, austere, and, in places, somewhat dilapidated; this was especially the case in May and June when cool, damp weather set a dramatic backdrop. I lived in the few sweaters I had packed, and the baseboard heat in my rental rarely clicked off. It was in the chilly spring rain that I began to navigate Portland's streets, some paved with cobblestones or bricks, as I rushed to interviews in the gentrifying East End, the upscale West End, Deering Oaks Park where the weekly Farmers Market takes place, the streets surrounding the University of Southern Maine with their gracious single family homes and duplexes, and to more suburban South Portland, with its strip malls and single family homes.[1]

Emails, sent well before I arrived, to organizers of Portland's Dyke March, as well as to administrators of an lesbian, gay, bisexual, transgender, and queer or questioning (LGBTQ) organization at the university, yielded no response, so I spent my first afternoons at the North Star: a coffee shop and performance space on Congress Street midway up Munjoy Hill, which closed a year after I returned to Chicago. Women, wearing T-shirts and cargo pants, whom I later learned identified as LBQ, worked behind the North Star's counter, and several days per week a small cluster of young female-to-male transgender individuals and their gender-queer friends talked politics and art over coffee. Butch-femme couples often appeared, especially when the café featured performances, such as slam poetry, or New England singer-songwriters. In the North Star, these LBQ women and trans and gender-queer individuals shared space with young hipsters, heterosexual middle-aged professionals, hippies with small children, and artsy teenagers. I came to recognize that the North Star embodies a key facet of life for Portland's LBQ residents: the existence of warm and welcoming sexually heterogeneous spaces within a broader city that residents find to be inconsistently hospitable to sexual minorities, and in which they find pockets of LBQ density and other spaces that are much more heterosexually dominated.

While perhaps the most reliable venue for locating LBQ individuals, the North Star was not the only place I encountered those who are LBQ. They passed me on their way to work in the Old Port (Portland's most touristy section, with its coffee and candy shops, galleries, clothing stores, seafood takeout, and expensive restaurants), in galleries proximate to downtown's Salt Institute for Documentary Studies and the Maine College of Art, on a running path along the Back Cove, at Whole Foods, and at Planet Fitness. However, outside of the North Star and a few other similar venues I only occasionally encountered LBQ residents with heterosexuals. Instead, I more often found them with other LBQ residents, making their presence in Portland all the more unmistakable—even if it is also geographically uneven.

After a slow start, I secured two interviews. The second led to an invitation to a party on Munjoy Hill, off of Cumberland Avenue. On the block where the party was held, young people, immigrants, and working-class Portland residents rented inexpensive apartments and even less expensive rooms within these apartments; these blocks stand in stark contrast to the restored Capes and Victorians that populate the crest of Munjoy Hill. At the party, one Portlander described the neighborhood in these terms: "[It] used to be perceived as the scary, immigrant neighborhood, but then artists began moving in and it is fairly gentrified now—but some people still think it is dangerous. Some of my female friends don't like to walk alone at night here." This last statement did not surprise, as I could not miss flyers, affixed to lampposts, publicizing the recent, severe beating and subsequent hospitalization of a queer individual walking Munjoy Hill at night.

Sitting around a backyard fire pit, which a young man kept dousing with gasoline—sending flames high into the cool, dark air—I met, to name a handful, a (female) librarian, (male) members of a punk band, an adjunct film professor (male), a woman from another Maine city who, with her female partner, makes dildos for a living, and a (male) sommelier. This heterogeneity of the gathering seemed to surprise no one. One person, a man who identified himself to me as queer, spoke with jealousy of the LBQ "scene" in Portland: "There's nothing like that for men here. It is just gay men. Not *queer*." Also at the party were a few twenty-something LBQ women who had recently moved to Portland and who were making ends meet via a revolving combination of waitressing, modeling, retail work, and sex work—all while contemplating whether to go to graduate school, performing at local galleries, and creating visual art.

These twenty-somethings served as my first ambassadors in Portland, posting notice of my research on Facebook, sending emails to acquaintances, and rallying local organizations to connect me with still others. Soon, I was walking several miles each day from interviews at people's apartments or places of work, to evenings of observation at a bar, or a performance, or a gallery opening, or a rally. A portrait of LBQ life in Portland came into view, concentrated on Munjoy Hill, but extending across the metro area.

Across Portland, and across the city's many walks of life, I encountered an approach to sexual identity quite distinct from that in Ithaca and San Luis Obispo. LBQ residents of Portland embrace identity politics; like those in San Luis Obispo they regard sexual identity as innate and life defining, as well as generative of a common set of interests and concerns. However, most of the people I met simultaneously conceive of the particularities of one's sexual identity as idiosyncratic and adaptable, and embrace a hyphenated sense of self, especially hyphenated gender and sexual identities.[2] In this sense, they reject the lesbian identity politics so prolific in San Luis Obispo in favor of a *queer* identity politics; here, beyond recognition of the salience of shared sexual difference, embrace of flexibility and hybridity itself reinforces a sense of inimitable common ground.

Complementing their identity politics, as well as their vision of the self as multifaceted, Portland residents participate in three tiers of community. These include communities predicated on microidentities, such as with other "gender queer" or "butch" individuals; an LBQ umbrella community spanning smaller microidentity communities; and "affinity communities" or communities composed of sexually heterogeneous individuals who share a common belief or hobby, which constitute friendly islands within the broader and not always friendly city.

This approach to community and residents' sexual identity culture emerge from a city ecology in which residents experience moderate hospitability and a constrained sense of safety, and, relatedly, concentrate in specific areas of greater Portland, creating a greater sense of belonging in some places than in others. They also arise from a sense that the LBQ population is neither abundant nor too limited; there are enough LBQ residents to permit clustering around narrower sexual identities, but not enough to generate the widespread integration and post-identity politics that flourish in Ithaca. Finally, a place narrative that celebrates Portland's urbanity and creativity, as well as a related narrative about the LBQ population as notably artistic and intellectual, encourages an identity culture that embraces intellectual debate and performativity. Residents' accounts of how their identities changed on moving underline how Portland calls out this self-consciously creative approach to identity politics.

More than Just One Way

A few days after the backyard party offers to participate in my research flooded my inbox and voicemail. One woman, who is in her mid-thirties with brightly colored hair and a career in fashion, told me in an email introduction that she identifies as a "queer kinky poly high femme dyke." Another immediately told me: "I guess I would identify as bi. . . . I'm in an open marriage with a man and dating both within and without my gender."

Another wrote, by way of introduction, "[I'm] ftm [female-to-male] trannyboy pre-op, loud, proud, and (slightly) out of control."

As these words begin to suggest, the people I encountered in Portland resist notions of identity as static or singular. They celebrate their own and others' unique amalgamation—and performance—of both sexual and gender identities. Around half of five dozen informants explicitly described their identity in hyphenated or hybrid terms, often uniting sexual and gender descriptors: for example, lesbian/queer, queer/dyke, queer-butch, queer-polytrans-boy, and masculine-dyke.[3] Here, they emphasize gender identity— along with sexual identity—to a degree totally unmatched in the other cities. Most prominently, they urgently embrace the notion that, in the words of Dyke March organizers, each of us can—and maybe should—"identify in more than just one way."

There are a variety of ways in which LBQ individuals in Portland "identify in more than just one way." Most obviously, they do so by articulating explicitly hyphenated or hybrid identities, like "queer kinky poly high femme dyke." Others capture what they regard as the fundamental multiplicity of sexual identity by embracing the term "queer"; again and again they suggest that queer communicates the possibility that one might "identify in more than just one way" over the course of his or her lifetime, or even in a given decade, year, or moment.[4] Finally, even the minority who primarily emphasize a single identity (e.g., lesbian or dyke) readily recognize, embrace, and even admire others' hybrid, hyphenated, and evolving identities.

In addition to approaching identity (one's own or others') as hybrid or hyphenated, there are other notable features of the Portland identity culture. Most fundamentally, LBQ residents simultaneously acknowledge that, while one's precise identity may shift, one's sexual difference or, in the words of many informants, one's "queerness," will itself remain unswerving and life defining. In addition, crosscutting specific microidentities, such as femmes, butches, queers, dykes, and lesbians, is the embrace of what residents describe as "intellectual engagement" with identity. They frequently join in collective work and play to explicate the meaning and significance of sexual difference. They especially engage questions about how gender and sexuality are related. And many Portlanders rely on habitual talk of who they are *not*—specifically, most reject the notion that they are "lesbian"—to communicate and reinforce the import they place on constantly refreshing how they approach identity. Finally, nearly all are "out" to friends, family, and coworkers, and in the public sphere.

Perhaps because they embrace the idea that specific self-understandings may evolve, LBQ Portlanders largely approach their identity malleability as unremarkable. Yet, some articulate how their identities took new shape in Portland, and many describe the sexual identity cultures they encountered in other cities as quite different from Portland's. One woman, who previously lived in Boston, told me:

> In Portland there's major femme identity, major butch identity. . . . Femme identity, butch identity they're very strong and that was new to me . . . coming from Boston where there, it seemed to me, [is] more of this gender fluid, gender queer, androgynous community. And that's what I was used to. And when I moved [here] . . . it was easier to transition into what I was comfortable with because it was mirrored in my culture. . . . [In Boston] it wasn't and it was almost like, you were almost jeopardized for identifying.

She did not anticipate growing in this way in Portland, but was pleasantly surprised by the opportunity for self-adjustment awaiting her there. In Portland, she finds that her new way of thinking about herself, as queer and femme, is, in her own words, mirrored by many other residents.

Echoing this, another middle-aged woman said that in other cities she did not think of herself as "butch":

> I never really thought about [butch identity], politically or anything. . . . I was out, and it didn't really matter. . . . When I moved to Maine, of all places, after living in San Francisco for eight years, I came much more into who I am, into being more butch, being more comfortable in my skin, figuring how I wanna identify, what's comfortable. In San Francisco, I was still trying to figure that out, and I never really thought about it. And that's the funny thing about it. It's, like, I'm in San Francisco, and I'm not doing that, but I move to Maine, and . . . I guess it must be the people that I'm around.

Now that she is "around" new people in Portland, her way of thinking about herself has changed; that is, her sense of who she is and of what feels closer to her "truth" evolved on moving to Portland. Crucially, she notes that this growth was unexpected; Maine was the last place she imagined exploring an identity frontier. The pages that follow detail how, as we have seen again and again, identities, and the ties that reflect and nurture them, respond to city ecology. However, they contain only a limited number of explicit accounts of how residents' identities changed after moving to Portland. This is because residents present personal transformation as unsurprising; sexual difference may be constant from one decade to the next, but they treat identity transformation as expected and unremarkable.

The Hybrid Self

If sexual difference provides fundamental common ground for LBQ residents of Portland, their common celebration of "personalized" approaches to sexual identity provides another layer of connection. As an example, celebration of hyphenated or hybrid identities and dedication to being "out" about them were apparent in the Butch Project, which markets itself as embracing multiple butch identities. Their website listed dozens: "trans butch," "drag queen butch," "survivor butch," "preggers butch," and "tea-drinking fairy butch." Members meet to go bowling or attend a performance, sometimes bringing friends or girlfriends along. Likewise, the performers at the 2010 Portland Femme Show reveled in their specificity and their multiplicity, identifying as a "High Maintenance Femme" or a "Fat Femme" and beyond.[5]

A year or so after I left Portland, a group of LBQ residents, including a designer, photographer, and stylist, created a Tumblr page called JackTar. JackTar frequently featured, among others, androgynous, butch, gender queer, and trans individuals dressed in preppy men's wear in Portland and other Maine settings; an androgynous woman poses in a button-down plaid shirt and jeans against a gray seascape.

When I asked, "How do you identify?" residents rarely offered a single descriptor. A recent liberal arts college graduate identifies as a "queer dyke" and describes an ex-partner as a "powerful dyke" and "gender queer." A middle-aged professor identifies as "queer-femme." A newly minted attorney identifies as a "stone butch dyke." This conception of self as amalgamation of sexuality, gender, and lifestyle attributes is not limited to one particular type of Portlander; those of a variety of ages, occupations, and places of origin describe their identities similarly. Informants report that in Portland they can be their "true" selves, especially if that truth is hyphenated and gendered. As we have already seen, several suggest that they came to this truth in Portland after living in other places; one becomes queer-femme after identifying as lesbian in a Midwestern college town, or stone butch after thinking of herself as simply lesbian in other Northeastern cities.[6]

Public recognition of hybrid and hyphenated identities was evident in the theme of the 2011 Dyke March: "Celebrating our Dyke Identities." On the June evening of the march, which, like Dyke Marches across the United States and beyond is intended to serve as an LBQ alternative to what is often the male-dominated Pride Parade, at a premarch rally in Longfellow Square—dominated by a statue of Henry Wadsworth Longfellow and bordered by tourist shops and restaurants—an organizer declared into a microphone that the organizing committee wished to celebrate the "multiple experiences [of dykes], especially of those who identify in more than just one way."[7] Organizers introduced themselves via specific dyke identities. With most in their thirties, professional, and femme identified, the committee drew laughter and cheers by describing themselves as, for example, "a Jewish dyke—who likes bacon," "gender queer," "gay for pay," "a queer, femme skater," and "a vegan with vegetarian tendencies." To be "out" in Portland is not merely to stand and identify as LBQ; for many, it is also to name other dimensions of the self.

Even those who do not introduce themselves in hyphenated or hybrid terms apply this formula to others. One woman said that while she thinks of her gender identity as "fluid," many in Portland "read" her as a "butch dyke." Despite some apprehension about this, she spoke with great respect for a couple that identifies as butch-femme and polyamorous. Another, who identifies as "queer," described her friends in one breath as "queer-friendly/poly/punk." Thus, while hyphenated identities, such as butch-dyke are not universally adopted, most everyone acknowledges and often celebrates them.

Roughly half of informants, as mentioned, include "queer" in their self-description—either as a stand-alone identifier, or with other identity descriptors, such as queer-dyke or queer-femme. As used in Portland, "queer" signals a conceptualization of identity as predicated on multiplicity—specifically on an assemblage of features of the gendered and sexual self.[8] It also rests on the notion that one's sexual *difference* may remain constant while specific features of one's self-understanding or behavior or practices, such as the gender identity of the person with whom one partners, may shift. Ty explained:

> I think that my sense of my gender has changed, has fluctuated a lot. . . . I felt . . . more masculine or feminine or something that is not categorizable at different points in my life and I also have been attracted to lots of different gender identities. So I feel like it's really, its really mutable and so "queer" to me encapsulates that openness in a way that bisexual seems like—just bi is just so sort of like black and white and doesn't allow for anything transgender. . . . So I like queer better.

Even in this definition of queer Ty implies hyphenation or hybridity, examining or referencing queerness as resting on both the gender of those to whom Ty is sexually attracted and on Ty's own shifting gender identity.

Another prefers identifying as "queer" as it leaves her the flexibility to identify as "butch" when she wishes to without permanently placing her in a "box":

> Queer is a more, I feel like it's a more encompassing word [because] . . . it's not necessarily . . . only possible for me to be attracted to just women. . . . I think it opens it up more instead of boxing me in. Like when people were calling me butch, I felt really boxed in. . . . Fairly recently I went through this thing where I feel like . . . I *am* butch. . . . I thought about it and I was like, I guess if I am in any box whatsoever, I'm a butch. But I still don't feel the most comfortable with that. . . . It feels too narrow, you know? . . . I can say that I dress butch. . . . I mean I wear ties and suits and things like that, you know, when I dress up.

She prefers to think of herself as a queer person who dresses butch and some-times calls herself butch, rather than as someone who is always, and rigidly, butch. Here, she reacts to the frequent engagement with gender identity in Portland.

Still others describe themselves as queer (as part of a broader hyphen-ated identity) to mark the fact that their partners' identities may be fluid or that they might partner with individuals who identify in any number of ways. One woman alternates between femme dyke and queer:

> Queer is also to me like political and sexual and also I think keeps open the possibility of being involved [with different people] and I think I also live in a gender community in a sense that a lot of people I've known in differ-ent kinds of ways have not occupied traditional gender categories so I think part of being queer is about not just showing this idea of being a woman-identified-woman who has sex with other people identified as women, neces-sarily. So my own gender seems incredibly stable to me, but I think people I've been involved with tend to, especially of late, no longer identify as female in one way or another.

Another, in simpler terms, echoes the idea that some adopt queer to best reflect their partners' identities: "It means that I haven't shut any doors. My partners have been pretty much split between trans men and women since I came out."

Thus, by emphasizing hybridity—either via identification as queer or re-liance on hyphens—Portland's LBQ population displays pride about micro-sexual and gender identities, and the pleasure they derive from emphasizing each person's unique amalgamation of attributes (e.g., stone butch, poly-femme, and queer-Mainer) and sharing these with the world. Here, common ground emerges at once from shared distinction (and exclusion) from those who do not think of themselves as LBQ, as well as a sense of connection with those who regard the self as a product of multiple and often shifting facets of identity.

The Gendered Self

As is already clear, gender identities—from gender-queer to butch and femme—have a prominent place in self-understandings and self-descriptions, and informants welcome the opportunity to use interviews with me as an extension of conversations they frequently had with friends and neighbors. The centrality of gender identities is readily evident in public life; in my short time in Portland I attended performances by gender-queer slam poets, a whole variety of burlesque shows, and several by troupes of drag kings, and then there is the more banal but no less consequential tendency at marches for the organizers to publicly pronounce their particular gender identities. Such awareness of gender was just as abundant in the privacy of living rooms and kitchens. The residents I spoke with routinely talked about gender performance and gender fluidity as nonchalantly as if we were talking about the weather. One told me: "Gender performance is really important to me." Another said, "My gender presentation is so fluid." These were not eager college kids trying out the vocabulary they had just learned in their Intro to Gender Studies class. Rather, such descriptions were just the norm; Portland is peopled, I heard again and again, by LBQ residents who are self-reflexive about gender. One said, "I think I also live in a gender community in the sense that a lot of people . . . have not occupied traditional gender categories."

This attention to gender identity extends well beyond those who emphasize gender as a primary facet of self-understanding, such as those who explicitly identify as gender-queer. Many who primarily identify as queer or lesbian or bisexual also describe themselves as femme or butch or gender fluid. Indeed, more than one out of ten informants identify as butch or femme (usually as part of a hyphenated identity), and about half explicitly mentioned gender. Thus, informants described themselves to me as "queer and butch," "lesbian/bisexual/femme-presenting," "trans boy," "femme dyke," and "soft butch." One young woman even suggested that *not* identifying as femme is an essential component of her identity. An immigrant and a person of color, she said that she favors makeup, dresses, and painted nails. Yet, consciously flouting the dominant trend in Portland, she specified: "I identify as lesbian and as *not* femme."

As her words imply, residents especially emphasize gender-queer and butch and femme identities; this woman was an outlier in insisting upon "lesbian" as a descriptor. Informants were eager to share the meanings they assign to these terms. They also characterized conversations with me as an extension of a local discourse. One woman explained why she is butch:

> I like things that are traditionally considered masculine things I guess. I like to build, I like to be really physical, I like to hash things around, you know. I like to work out but . . . I'm not going to go jump around in the aerobics room. . . . I like to do the weights and stuff like that. Also, my dress is not reflective of a femme in that I don't feel comfortable in skirts; I've always felt more comfortable in pants and in suits and ties. I like more masculine scents than I do feminine scents, I like more like bergamots and limes and cedars. Yeah, so I consider myself more butch.

Borrowing from a similar logic, another woman told me: "I totally identify as butch, because I would rather wear a tux than a dress. So there you go. . . . I think that's the basic baseline of butch/femme." Another instructs that femme and feminine are not synonymous: "And femme for me means that I am—while I'm feminine there are certain characteristics that I identify with that are more 'femme' than 'feminine.'" Here, she specifies and values awareness of the enduring history and culture of femme identity.[9]

Despite their popularity, gendered forms of identity are not monolithic (e.g., the woman who identifies as not femme). Moreover, while these terms were quite firmly entrenched in the local identity culture during my time in Maine, some people mentioned that while attention to identity hybridity is longstanding, the specific focus on gender identity—especially butch and femme identities—is relatively new. A butch-identified woman told me that since she moved to Portland less than a decade ago, "other people have become . . . have identified as femme," and she has learned a lot about butch and femme. Another echoes this:

> That led to some sexual identity conversation, but since then . . . I feel like the majority of conversations that I have with people are more about gender identities. There's a lot of butch/femme conversation. . . . In the beginning or maybe the middle of my relationship with [my best friend] there was a lot of trans identity conversations.

In telling me that attention to butch and femme identities is recent and possibly even temporary, informants emphasize that it is not the precise content of identities that stands out in Portland. Instead, it is the emphasis they place on hybridity and intellectualization, and their certainty that sexual difference is the defining facet of the self.

The Non-Lesbian Self

For many informants, underlying the embrace of identity as hyphenated, or hybrid, and gendered is a rejection of the notion of a lesbian identity. Many offered explicit explanations for their distaste for the term and what it stood for. One said, "There's something about the term lesbian that's always kind of bugged me." Jen, a forty-something woman with short dark hair who favors jeans and T-shirts, lives in South Portland on a leafy street of small houses a few blocks from the water. She offered a detailed explanation for why she does *not* identify as lesbian, referencing a sketch from a recent performance we had both seen. She said,

> I identify as queer. . . . You're recording this, right? Or [I identify] as a dyke. I don't like the term lesbian. I just don't like it. . . . I don't like the way it sounds. I don't like the way it looks when it's written. I have a certain idea in my head. I generalize. It's really bad. Like, I generalize lesbians a certain way. Well, you were at the show, you saw "Lavender Rainbow." . . . I think of, like, these women that are just kinda . . . not necessarily New Agey, but, you know, they're . . . they wear lavender, and they're really, like . . . you know, it's all about the Goddess, and I just . . . I can't do it. I can't do it. And I feel, like, being . . . identifying as a dyke or as queer . . . it helps. I think it's a little rougher. It sounds a little rougher, and I don't look like your typical lesbian. . . . I'm more masculine looking and a little . . . I don't like when people call me lesbian.

The skit she referenced, "Lavender Rainbow," was performed by the drag king troupe, Kings of the Hill, as part of their "Stimulus Package" revue. Set to a medley of songs, including pieces by the Indigo Girls and Melissa Etheridge, the skit featured two women seated on stools, wearing, between them, Birkenstocks and Crocs, a bandana, and loose, casual clothes. For the duration, the women did nothing but strum on a cat scratch pad and a guitar. A litany of cat photographs surrounded them. The skit, which included references to "17 life partners" and Subarus, drew raucous laughter from the crowd.

It is tempting to conclude that the sketch and broader criticisms of "lesbian" identity such as those Jen offers are the result of generational conflict

or division.[10] However, some of the performers were in their forties—
roughly the same age of the two characters onstage—and the age of the
audience itself varied widely (although there were only a modest number
of women over fifty). More than underlining generational differences, the
sketch pokes fun at lesbian identity as stable and homogeneous. In Portland, the sketch instructs, you are supposed to mix it up—by being "masculine" as Jen above suggests, flouting serial monogamy (perhaps by embracing polyamory), or by exchanging lesbian-feminist androgyny—embodied
by the performers' Birkenstocks, ill-fitting vests, and flowing button-down
shirts—for high heels or men's dress shoes. Moreover, it is not, as one might
also be quick to surmise, to reject identity politics, but, instead, to embrace
a different version thereof; that is, one that embraces gender hybridity and
sexual flexibility as foundational.

Many went to great lengths to dismiss the notion that they might identify
as lesbian. Sitting in the front yard of her Munjoy Hill apartment, a thirty-
something graduate of a women's college said: "I will go with dyke or queer.
I really hate the word lesbian. . . . For me it implies like this Birkenstock-
wearing kind of gender-ambiguous but female-type person. And for me I
identify as butch." For her, butch is a subcategory of dyke or queer—much
as femme is for those Portlanders who identify as femme-dyke or femme-
queer. Another thirty-something professional, Jay, offered a similar argument for rejecting the lesbian label: "Lesbian doesn't quite make sense. . . . It
is just a term that doesn't quite make sense for me." Seated opposite Jay in
a light-filled office downtown I asked, "Why is that?" Jay replied, "Because
I don't identify as 'woman' or 'female' necessarily. . . . I would say butch
is my gender identity." A femme-identified woman concurs: "I like girls
but . . . my appearance is really important to me. My gender performance
[as femme] is really important." For these informants, "lesbian" is too narrow a box, a label that degenders sexual identity and inhibits hyphenation
and therefore a full representation of self-understanding.

Such dismissal is not universal, however, in Portland. More than one in
ten informants identified themselves as lesbian in interviews. However, even
some who identify as lesbian embrace the idea of "mixing it up." One said:
"I'm a butch lesbian. . . . But I'm a soft butch. I'm not a hard butch. And I'm
not a stone butch." An educator specified that she identifies as lesbian at
work—in her view a more acceptable and recognizable identity descriptor—
but as a dyke or femme in other realms. A medical professional initially told
me she identifies as lesbian, but then qualified her answer: "I'm a lesbian,
but, you know . . . well, I mean, technically, I'm probably bisexual. I haven't
been with men in probably 10 years, 15 years. . . . I was femme presenting,

and so no one . . . no one questioned that I might not be heterosexual."
Here, she felt compelled to share a portrait of her gender identity or performance—as femme—even though she never explicitly presented it as a crucial facet of her identity. In this sense, like several others, while she answered
"how do you identify" with the term "lesbian," she sought to demonstrate
that lesbian for her is, in the words of another Portlander, "personalized."
That is, she makes an effort to imply that not all lesbians are the cat-loving,
androgynous, serial monogamists in "Lavender Lesbian." After all, for many
Portlanders, who strive to be cutting edge and creative, lesbian is simply too
mainstream and traditional to feel right—indeed, in Portland, it is worthy
of parody by Kings of the Hill.

The Intellectual Self

Many people seemed determined to demonstrate to me, not to mention
themselves and one another, that these dimensions of self-understanding
were not casual or stumbled upon. Thinking about, discussing, and otherwise engaging with identity are projects many in Portland wholeheartedly
engage. Along these lines, several informants read books such as *Butch is a
Noun* and *Gender Trouble* for pleasure, and two carried such a book to meet
me for an interview. On the first occasion, I sat in Arabica Coffee on Free
Street, in the Old Port, the sunlight streaming through large windows and
reflecting off of its red brick interior wall. I found myself glancing at my informant's copy of *Gender Trouble*—an elephant on the table between us. I
wanted to know why she was reading the book, but also why she carried it
with her on this day, to an interview with me. Was this an intellectual feint?
Was she trying to impress me? Eventually, I came to recognize that this intellectualized approach to identity is not reserved for *Gender Trouble* or interviews with academics.

Residents do not just read and study alone. Many told me about their
involvement in "group education"; engagement with and research on identity is here a collective project. As Jo, a thirty-something organic farmer (and
graduate of a highly selective East Coast liberal arts college) suggests, identity is a frequent topic of conversation and engagement: the term "dyke" "is
something that my friends and I have been talking about recently. We realize
we don't really have a word for [our sexual identity] anymore." Instead of
rejecting labels altogether, as many in Ithaca do, they discuss a variety of
approaches to articulating how they think about their sexual selves. Beyond
reflections on the evolving meaning of dyke, the more general concept of

identity is a frequent conversational topic at the weekly dinners she and her LBQ friends host.

What is the broader content of these and similar conversations—over dinner, beer, and walks on coastal trails? Bea suggests that identity is a constant topic: "The conversations I think tend to be more on the academic side of like what does it mean to identify as butch and femme." She indicated that conversations about identity sometimes are as complex as those she has engaged in at the seminar table: "I do identify as butch and I have never ever been able to answer [what 'butch' means] in a way that did not make me sound like a stuttering idiot." She clarified that her discomfort was not with the academic tone of conversation, but with the possibility that she might inadvertently define someone else's identity for them: "Usually if someone starts a conversation . . . on like butch/femme identities, I can have that more academic conversation, but . . . what I shy away from is [from] making it specific to *my* idea of what butch is and then it takes away from someone else's ability to define." At least for her, the academic tone of discourse has the benefit of keeping identity discussion from becoming overtly contentious. The question is not how "I" or "you" or "we" ought to identify, but how identity works and what identity is for each of us.

Part of what lends an academic tone to these conversations is Portland-er's frequent engagement with academic texts (like *Gender Trouble*), but also with gay, lesbian, bisexual, transgender, and queer (GLBTQ) histories. As an example, in advance of the 2009 Pride Parade, a photography exhibit documenting 1990s AIDS activism in Portland appeared in a downtown gallery; an impressive crowd appeared at the opening discussion and reception. LBQ individuals of a variety of ages and walks of life examined black and white photographs of ACT-UP protests and sit-ins, and listened attentively as a panel of academics and activists spoke. Later, many lined up to purchase a booklet of photographs from the exhibit. And engagement with these histories extends beyond formal events. A twenty-something marriage-equality organizer said: "If people were going to talk to me about the history of the butch/femme dynamic, I wanted to be able to say, 'That's my history.' . . . There's the understanding that I have a history."

References even to the particulars of queer theory pop up in ordinary interactions. For instance, a social worker in her thirties told me:

It's interesting to have those really very personal identity conversations with somebody else for whom, you know, queer theory is something that they know and talk about and study. . . . It's sort of like that interesting shift between, you know, like, queer theory and, you know, personal lesbian identity politics.

The conversations this woman referred to led her to decide (at least for now) that, regardless of the identity of the individuals she dates, she identifies as lesbian and femme. Likewise, a thirty-something professional who attended school and began her career in Boston, described how she came to identify as queer-femme via what she called her "self-education" over the last several years she had lived in Portland. She said: "My femme identity is something that as a feminist . . . it took a really long time to come to and sort of more of a *self-education* that I had to do on how I identified *within the community* because I think if you were to take pictures of me, you will look at somebody who looks gender-queer through most of my incarnations." Here, she outlines how self-education, and specifically her growing awareness of the prominence of femme identity in Portland, enabled her to publicly articulate a queer-femme identity that stands in contrast to her earlier "incarnations" in other cities. Another, a middle-aged South Portlander, echoes this, explaining how "political" conversations encouraged her to identify as butch on moving to Portland. Now, she "educates" others—not only by conversing about identity but also by being a performer in Kings of the Hill.

As her troupe exemplifies, such intellectual engagement is not merely serious; engaging with identity in Portland is often public, playful, and collaborative. This is not a surprise in a city that is home to many theaters and galleries. At a Youth Pride event in a central Portland park, a twenty-something gender-queer slam poet stood against the backdrop of a brick building and described himself as a "girly-man." Raising their voices to compete with street noise from Portland's bustling downtown, the female-dominated audience of several dozen cheered. Likewise, at public events such as Pride Parade and Dyke March—each held in the same week—two Portland women with short punk haircuts sold T-shirts behind a booth with the slogan "Individualized Visibility for Your Identity."

At a performance, Kings of the Hill, which is mostly made up of LBQ professionals in their thirties and forties, played with, among other things, New England identity, lesbian stereotypes, and the Catholic Church. In one of their most New England–loving sketches, a man collects sap for maple syrup from a maple tree (to the sound of Def Leppard's "Pour Some Sugar on Me"), and then a few minutes later he ends up simulating oral sex with the spout that releases sap. In 2011, a second drag troupe, 5G, played with Maine identity at the annual Dyke March, lip syncing to "I Wanna Be Your Maine Man"—in lumberjack and lobsterman attire. If attending and participating in such performance is part of "group education" in the Portland context, it is a pleasurable educational experience. To describe reception of these troupes as enthusiastic is an understatement; during their multinight runs Kings of the Hill readily draw crowds to the 286-seat Portland Stage theater, and both troupes habitually bring audiences to their feet.

A burlesque troupe, The Dirty Dishes Burlesque Revue, was a regular performer at Dyke March, Pride Parade, and other public events. On Facebook, the troupe describes itself as "a sex-positive, queer-positive, and feminist burlesque group—playing with all the contradictions and ponderings of what it means to be feminist." Here they explicitly embrace the notion of identity as complex or contradictory and assume that pondering the meaning of feminism will appeal. And, indeed, it does. Crowds cheered at Portland Pride as the revue's members performed a collective strip tease to "Hungry Eyes," slowing removing their skirts and dresses until they danced in bikini bottoms, tassels covering their nipples. Members suggest that such performances, along with members' stage names (e.g., Rosie Rimjob and Ophelia Hiney), are meant to titillate and challenge, while simultaneously embracing and promoting difference. One told the *Portland Press Herald*:

> Burlesque explores and plays with sexuality. . . . When we say we want to provide a "safe space," we aim to create an environment that allows people to be themselves, both on the stage and in the audience, a space that is safe for queer or taboo or alternative representations of sexuality. Burlesque has the ability to literally create a space that does not generally exist in the world, for anybody who does not fit the traditional image of what is sexy. (Olcott 2011)

They also underline the individuality of identity: "Feminism has influenced how we understand ourselves as sexual beings and how we think about performance, presentation of our bodies and representations of sex, gender, and sexuality. Our burlesque is informed by our own particular experiences with feminism, and we understand that our experiences are not the same as [others']" (ibid). During the months I was in Portland, the troupe was composed of—at least as far as I could determine—both straight and LBQ women. However, this combination did not stop them from performing at several Dyke and Pride events, and from generally becoming enmeshed in the broader LBQ culture.

In short, LBQ residents actively celebrate their intellectualism; indeed many describe this, together with an emphasis on hybridity, as a defining feature of the Portland LBQ scene. One, a young, white femme-dyke who advocates for marriage equality, described the LBQ community as full of "a lot of brilliant, brilliant women. . . . Luckily, in this community we have very brilliant women who are so smart." She believes that Portlanders bring intellectualism to bear on identities, sometimes provoking conflict that she finds to be educational and therefore productive:

> I would play devil's advocate on someone's gender identity, not to be disrespectful but just really to get out of someone like really what they were trying to convey. . . . Sometimes when you get a whole bunch of women together, I'm not going to lie, there's some cattiness. But in this community I mean above all there are some incredibly intelligent and just inspiring women.

She described moments in which she challenged how others articulate their identities, asking them to name and defend how and why they frame their identities in a specific manner. Her description captures a vital mechanism that reinforces Portland's particular identity culture: intellectualized conversation and debate. These debates seem remarkably friendly and respectful. Most report that these debates center on the issue of identity itself, rather than a person's particular choices, thus rendering identity partially abstract and depersonalizing differences of opinion. Partially as a result, identity-based conflict is relatively rare. Whether intentional or not, such abstraction is a valuable tactic for a relatively small and bounded population.

What is the source of this intellectualized engagement with identity? This seminar-style engagement is surely a product of the biographies of Portland's LBQ residents. Many attended elite, private Northeastern schools with lefty reputations, such as Sarah Lawrence, Hampshire, the Seven Sisters Colleges (i.e., Barnard, Bryn Mawr, Mount Holyoke, Radcliffe, Smith, Vassar, and Wellesley), Bates, Bowdoin, and Colby, as well as other elite New England schools.[11] Several explicitly reference college classrooms and lesbian, gay, bisexual, transgender, queer, and intersex (LGBTQI) centers as crucial resources in the development of their approach to identity, and some carry with them to Portland the debates about identity taking place on those campuses.

However, biographies do not tell the full story, for many LBQ residents of Ithaca (and, as we shall see, of Greenfield) have attended the same or similar schools, and, in fact, a higher proportion of informants in those sites have advanced degrees. Indeed, graduates of Hampshire and the nearby elite women's colleges cluster in Greenfield, as much if not more than in Portland, yet Greenfield residents rarely adopt the hybrid and intellectualized approach to sexual identity so popular in Portland. What else is it about Portland? A few residents speculated that conversation is a vital antidote to the isolation of Maine's cold winters. Much more crucially, the fecundity of opportunities for artistic expression in Portland, from galleries to theatre troupes, extends an ethos about the pleasure of creative introspection and in so doing aids the proliferation of public conversations about identity. While only a few speculate on their source, nearly all suggest that conversations about identity are a crucial basis for connection and conviviality. Intellectual exchange on identity has become part of how many residents understand themselves—as individuals and as a body. On arrival, newcomers find an indisputably intellectualized and performative atmosphere, one that ineluctably shapes Portland residents—inducing them to mirror the contours of the small city they call home.

The Out Self

All this talk about identity, however, only spills from the privacy of the home to Portland's stages and streets because people are committed to being out. A graduate of an elite private college and drag performer said: "I'm . . . very out, definitely. . . . Since I'm a drag performer I'm sort of almost a queer public figure who people can identify." Her absolute commitment to being out is typical. Another said: "I always wanted to be out. Once I realized I was a lesbian, I wanted to be out and the army didn't fit to do that, you know?" In Portland, she finds, she can be quite out. Yet another said: "I'm all the way out. I'm out at work, I'm out at home." A young transgender man who, with a handful of other transgender men I met in the field, frequently socializes with LBQ residents, said: "[I'm] very out. Extremely out. I don't know if I can get more out unless I come up with a new label." As an aside, the inclusion of at least a handful of transgender men in Portland's LBQ umbrella community, and, by default, in my interview sample, reflects how commitment to being out and especially to identity heterogeneity, allows transgender men a place on the inside of LBQ circles that is unmatched in any of the other cities.

This commitment to being out is notable, given that residents report an inconsistent sense of abundance and acceptance in the Portland area; in some neighborhoods they feel embraced, but in others they feel much less so. That awareness of possible danger and discomfort, rather than causing residents to hide their identities, seems to drive their determination to perform who they are, and their certitude that shared sexual difference produces common ground. If Ithacans describe an uninterrupted sense of welcome, and if San Luis Obispo residents report that even spaces that "should" welcome them sometimes do not, Portlanders indicate that a few treasured spaces constitute bubbles of abundance and acceptance, while others are ambiguous or unwelcoming and sparsely populated by LBQ residents.

Informants readily recounted threats of violence and, much more commonly, harassment. Two told me of a neighbor who threatened them with a baseball bat when they kissed on a sidewalk near their home, charging toward them and cursing, calling them "fucking dykes." Others suggested that verbal harassment was commonplace, sometimes ignorable and sometimes scary. Sitting in her small backyard, a petite, butch woman recounted the "normal crap" she experienced:

> Not physical violence or like threats or anything like that . . . Like yelling and just like . . . there's like some stores I like to go to in the Old Port and it's like always a mistake. It's just like—it just feels like there's a lot of people down there and I don't know, people have said not very charming things. . . . If I'm like, you know, holding hands with my girlfriend and somebody says . . . "I'll show you what a real man can do" or like something directed at the person I'm with, which happens a lot. . . . Or "you're not a man" or whatever.

A single mother with long hair recounted the "welcome" she received on moving to her subsidized apartment complex: "My first night here . . . somebody wrote on my car in mustard, they wrote 'gays die.' . . . Yeah, it was scary. . . . They probably saw me and my butch friends moving me in. . . . So that was a little bit scary but I decided that I wanted to live here and not be wondering if my neighbors—if any of my neighbors had written it."

Residents report a patchwork quilt sense of abundance and acceptance, one that relates closely to gentrification. That is, they feel safest in neighborhoods that house many creative professionals. One woman recalled that, before Munjoy Hill began to gentrify, "I *never* wanted to live on the East End [where Munjoy Hill is]. . . . My impression was always that, you know, apartments in the West End were nicer, and maybe they were a little bit more money, but they were safer neighborhoods." Another suggests that today's East End is now safer (and yet more "wild") than other parts of Portland: "There's like a couple hours of walking I can do all over the East End with my dog totally off leash and, like, never bump into another person. That's really nice. And this . . . this end of town feels . . . I guess just, like, a little bit safer, too, than other parts of town." Here, they propose that the East End, and Munjoy Hill in particular, is becoming more and more like the West End— and perhaps even outpacing it in terms of providing a sense of abundance and acceptance for LBQ residents. Others suggest that this transformation of the East End, particularly of Munjoy Hill, was not happenstance. Priced out of the earlier-to-gentrify and more gay-male–dominated West End, LBQ residents regard themselves as key pioneers in the "settling" of Munjoy Hill; indeed, it is a swiftly upscaling neighborhood.[12] Some celebrate this role, whereas others sought to express their concerns about how they were transforming and perhaps harming Munjoy Hill's "character."[13]

Despite this narrative of progress, residents are cautious about how welcome they really are in places like Munjoy Hill. Many recounted a beating of an LBGTQ individual on the Hill that occurred shortly before I arrived in town. And, indeed, walking down the hill along Congress and entering downtown my partner and I experienced a taste of the verbal harassment that residents suggest is common, when a car of young men yelled: "Lady Dykestras!" (The fact that the harassment centered on rather creatively naming our identity was not lost on me, in the midst of a sea of individuals notably dedicated to naming and playing with identity).

While LBQ residents do not feel entirely welcome or always safe in Portland, they nevertheless celebrate their identity publically, such as during the Dyke March, drag revues, and burlesque shows. In addition, nearly all are committed to being out about their "individualized" identities on a daily basis. For a sizable minority, this includes acknowledging one's gender identity, most frequently as butch or femme. This forthrightness serves to mark their discursive and political space in an inconsistently welcoming environment. It also enables articulation of sexual difference as life defining and as producing a common set of interests and concerns, while still acknowledging that one's precise identity may evolve.

Individualized Communities for Individualized Identities

Tier One: Microidentity Communities

LBQ informants eagerly claim membership in Portland's microcommunities, predicated on their particular gender and sexual identities. Whether hybrid, hyphenated, or both, a very small, and very specific, community existed for nearly everyone in Portland. And these microcommunities, which are not merely predicated on friendships, but, instead, on shared identities, were constantly apparent. At a Dyke March After Party, held at One Longfellow Square, several butch/femme and polyamorous couples sat together in the balcony, while young, queer-identified women danced together. A small cadre of lesbians in their fifties arranged themselves in a row facing the stage. Likewise, at a North Star performance by a queer folk musician, gender-queer and transgender slam poets sat at one cluster of tables, while femme-dykes sat at another.

Residents readily provided vivid sketches of their microcommunities. One said, "There's the kink community." Another referred to "my, like, queer punk community." A butch woman claimed membership in a femme/butch community. Some were even more specific. Describing her core community, a woman in her early thirties depicts women united both by life stage *and* by a specific LBQ identity: "Most of them tend to only date women. And I would say, I mean, like, if we all, had to pick a word, we would probably just say, like, 'lesbian' or 'gay' or, you know, something in that realm. . . . And, like, they're all, like, partnering up and, like, looking into having babies." Here, identifying as "just" lesbian helps to earn one membership in a microcommunity; a notable departure from the near-universal lesbian identification and community in San Luis Obispo. Moreover, she suggests that weekly traditions sustain this microcommunity: "Every Monday night we have a little family dinner here at my house." Em, a gallery worker in her early twenties, provides a similar description of her microcommunity, constituted by people who are around her age and who are part of a "community of queer sex workers."

Members of this fledgling community invited me to a queer-feminist pornography viewing on a July evening at Em's house off of Munjoy Hill's Cumberland Avenue. We sat on couches and chairs in her cool, dark living room, the room falling uncomfortably quiet as they screened a film featuring a series of women having sex with one another. Afterward, over beer in the kitchen, women spoke about a queer-feminist-anarchist collective one had encountered on the West Coast. Not everyone at the screening was a sex worker (in fact, only a minority called themselves this), nor did most have more than a casual interest in pornography. Yet, having some in the room with knowledge of feminist pornography and others who identify as queer sex workers provided a way to talk about the feeling of edginess and commitment to political and sexual exploration that the women in attendance felt that they shared.

Some people, like Em, belong to microcommunities predicated on an identity with which they do not explicitly identify. A professional woman in her twenties who identifies as femme-dyke or lesbian (depending on context) described membership in several microcommunities, beginning with "the trans community." She said, "I have a lot of friends that are in the trans community." When I asked, "What is the trans community like here?" she said, "Um, candidly, it's the Tranny Shack. It's a joke that we all have. . . . [It] is this house . . . and they all ended up living together in this

Tranny Shack—well okay, in this apartment but like the amount of trannies that have lived in that apartment in the past five years is insane." For her, the "shack" and those who live in it serve as a vital source of conviviality and support—a notable departure from the other three cities I studied, in which, during the period of study, transgender individuals tended not to be included in the orbit of LBQ circles. Likewise, she describes herself as a peripheral member of the butch community. Just as the "Tranny Shack" helps define the boundaries of the trans community, from her perspective an organization helps root the butch community: "The Butch Project is fantastic and I'm definitely an ally for them. . . . It's just a group for butches really to get together and have shared space with one another. . . . So it is community so that they know that they're not alone." Despite these allegiances, she is most centrally a member of the femme community. She associates the femme community with an organization, too—despite the fact that the organization is now defunct: "The femme community, what small femme group there is, it started off with the New Femme Regime, but that kind of failed." Thus, she does not regard organizations as necessary to sustain community—after all, the femme community has sustained itself despite the failure of the New Femme Regime—but they provide a reference point, as well as some highly visible opportunities to socialize.

Even life outside of Portland aids these microcommunity bonds. An educator in her forties whom I met at a Foursquare game described how she forged community via the Michigan Womyn's Music Festival. She described how she met the first member of what is now her core social circle: "I had met her when I was working at a work shift [at Michigan] and she said where she was from, and I was, like, 'I'm from Portland.' . . . And so that was exciting. And then we just kept running into her and her partner [in Portland]. . . . And so there was just this Michigan connection. . . . And they're sort of like the barbeque central." She describes a social life initiated by Michigan and maintained by barbeques and drag shows. What she doesn't say, but what is apparent from afar, is that what unites her friends is age (early middle), occupational status (mostly professional), and an explicit identification as "feminist" that encourages drag revues and regular attendance at Michigan. Another who is part of the same microcommunity sought to articulate why Michigan brings them together: "It was really nice to. . . . be around other people who knew about Michigan and, you know, had that sort of funky vibe."

Of course, community is not all drag revues and lighthearted barbeques. A trans man in his twenties described the support of transgender men and gender-queer punks:

I love the sense of community. That's like my favorite part. One night I had just written a piece because they have a Take Back the Night here. . . . So I went up on stage and I was like shaking or whatever. . . . And like I got all the way through it but it was really, really difficult and like my friends were outside listening to it because you can't smoke inside and like they were howling through the window and like the people here would like clap or like hoot or whatever when they liked a part. And when I got off stage I just kind of like broke down and almost started crying or whatever and everyone was there and they just hugged me and it was really sweet.

Helen, a medical professional in her forties who identifies as bisexual similarly described her microcommunity—middle-aged lesbian- and bisexual-identified women—as her "gay family." Alongside her birth family, she turns to these women for support: "Friends that are totally there you know . . . they are family, you know. . . . I'll go to my family for Christmas and I'll go to the gay family to you know exchange presents at the end of the day."

Crucially, these are not random friendship groups or networks that are only implicitly organized around shared identity. LBQ individuals readily announce the emergence of ties from and sustenance by those who share specific microidentities. These identities, in turn, are likely reinforced by the existence of crucial support networks—of, in Helen's words, "families"—predicated on those identities. A yearly visit to Michigan Womyn's Festival reinforces the common ground that a collection of middle-aged feminists on a Foursquare court shares, as do Butch Project outings and queer-feminist pornography screenings. Communities of those who share one's identity serve as a mirror through which one sees one's self (Cooley 1902); the woman who says that she enjoys the "funky vibe" of other Michigan goers in Portland implies that she also likes her own "funky vibe." Of course, this looking-glass function reinforces not only individual identities but also collective identity.[14]

Of course, microcommunities do not just provide support; they are also sites of conflict. I spoke with Jo, a butch-identified, thirty-something woman who had recently ended a relationship with a femme woman. She said, "You know there is like a butch group." I asked, "Are you a part of it?" She responded simply, "No." When I asked her to elaborate she said, "My partner left me for my best friend [another member of the Butch Project]. We were sort of in what was under the guise of a polyamorous relationship." I asked whether she was ever part of the project, and she said, "Yeah . . . I went to some of the events." Thus, while she didn't put it precisely in these terms, she seemed to have opted out of, or felt that others had pushed her from, the butch microcommunity.

Her story was not atypical, although her sense of intragroup dating as disrupting community was more acute than that of anyone else with whom I spoke. Individuals repeatedly emphasized Portland's small size and how in that context intragroup dating is unavoidable.[15] Yet, most spoke of intragroup dating in a nonchalant manner, and some suggested that it facilitates ties to others within one's microcommunity. One insisted that dating within your microcommunity actually strengthened connections: "My girlfriend is my best friend's girlfriend's best friend. So that's all nice and connected, as it should be." Another echoes this: "[I] met them, like, through my girlfriend [Jenna] who is not my girlfriend anymore. We broke up last fall. Or, you know, [maybe I met them] through her sister. And then they would date people, and I would meet their partners and then, like, break up with someone. . . . I think a lot [of community] is through, like, who's dated who and it just kind of builds on itself." Not only have these women dated one another, she suggests, they also share other attributes that bring them together: "They all do really good work. Like, domestic violence or, like, violence work in general or work in the school systems. They all do some sort of, like very, very people-oriented work."

In this context, why are breakups not as devastating for ties as they might otherwise be? Why don't breakups, infidelity, and other sources of intragroup schism produce widespread dissatisfaction? Part of the answer rests, as some above suggested, in Portland's size; with a population of over 66,000 and as Maine's largest city, Portland is a place in which there are enough LBQ residents for microcommunities to form but not large enough to avoid dating those who have also dated one's friends or with whom one already regularly socializes. Again and again informants said that Portland's moderate size provides much incentive for avoiding intra-microgroup conflict. Some make light of the small size of the LBQ population and of the necessity of working to embrace what one describes as the incestuous quality of microcommunities: "It's such a small community . . . you know . . . I joke . . . like, 'Which one have you slept with?' . . . You know, this one slept with that one, who slept with this one, who dated that one, who dated this one, who slept with both of them, who was kinda sorta seeing her behind her back." Residents are also mindful that when conflicts arise it is nearly impossible to avoid those with whom one has fallen out, which gives everyone incentives to repair ties and minimize ongoing drama; in Portland, there is no avoiding friends or enemies.[16]

Tier Two: An LBQ Umbrella Community

These endless little dramas aren't as destructive as they might seem from the outside, because, while microcommunities are a crucial source of pleasure and support, they are not the only networks on which LBQ residents rely. Most also depend on a broad and inclusive LBQ umbrella community. For instance, Jo, whose girlfriend left her for her best friend, still had ties to LBQ residents outside the butch/femme community from which she was alienated.

Middle-aged, lesbian-identified Portlanders might have weekly "family dinner" and exchange holiday presents, but supportive networks do not stop there. Nearly all LBQ residents turn to a broad array of other LBQ residents for a broad array of reasons: for conviviality and support, and to explore ideas about identity, and to cultivate an LBQ presence in the city as a whole. This umbrella does not constitute what Elijah Anderson (2011) terms a "canopy," which envelops (nearly) all whom are beneath it in places where it flourishes, such as certain parks and markets. In contrast, the LBQ umbrella extends across a variety of scenes and embraces those who share a sense of sexual difference, specifically an LBQ identity.[17] In Portland, this unifying sense of sexual difference—of "otherness"—brings a diverse set of residents together again and again.

Both the many microcommunities—from punk to butch to femme—as well as an umbrella LBQ community, are evident at events such as Dyke March, slam poetry and songwriter performances, drag shows, and Dyke Nights hosted by a downtown gay bar. Residents tend to arrive or sit with others who share their microidentity, but interactions and ties cross these lines. This is not to suggest the existence of a single, conflict-free LBQ body; indeed, informants report occasional conflict and exclusions. However, such clashes are usually seen as par for the course and do not prohibit a sense of belonging in a larger body of LBQ individuals.

The words of one woman, Kate, illustrate this. She took pains to tell me that she feels alienated from the microcommunity of femme-identified women, several of whom are Dyke March organizers or have other leadership positions in Portland. She said, "There's a lot of the queer community that I don't really socialize with. . . . Like members of the Dyke March and that contingent of the queer community . . . like, none of my friends are the friends of those people." When I asked why she thinks this is the case, she suggested that the decision was not her own. Instead, for reasons about which she was uncertain, these women don't seem to include her in their inner circle.

Despite her unhappiness with what she describes as exclusion, Kate is content with her friendships. For her, exclusion from a microidentity community does not produce isolation because, by virtue of her sexuality, she has near-automatic membership in the LBQ umbrella community.

I have good solid friends, really good solid friends that are fun and not necessarily all queer, but queers and allies . . . and also through just being around Portland and . . . being someone who walks everywhere and usually has funny looking hair. People are like, "Oh, I saw you on the street." . . . So I end up knowing just a lot of people. Because there is a community here, like everyone gets together for Youth Pride . . . and everyone comes out for Youth Prom, like all the adults. . . . And the Dyke March is like everywhere and doing things.

Part of what Kate appreciates about this umbrella community is how it is inclusive of and appreciated by a broad range of LBQ individuals:

Everybody goes to events. . . . There are like dances at the North Star and there are picnics and game nights and like all sorts of stuff. Open mics. And people support each other. And if someone has a band, people go see that band. . . . A lot of that probably has to do with how small the town is so if there's only one thing to do, everyone's going to go do that one thing. But I mean it's still awesome. It's cool to have a *built-in community* that you can count on to support you kind of no matter what. . . . I know that if anything were . . . like anything horrible were to ever happen even if I'm not friends with everyone in the community I know that they would have my back. Like where else [would that be true]? Nowhere else. (emphasis mine)

Here she carefully distinguishes between being "friends with everyone" and "a built-in community"; to have a strong sense of membership in the broader LBQ community and to trust that it will provide support, you don't have to be friends with all lesbians, and you may even feel excluded from some circles. Rather, simply being LBQ enables membership in this "built-in community." Kate indicates that she has not found built-in community in other places and suggests, accurately, that Portland's relatively small proportion of LBQ households (vis-à-vis other "lesbian-friendly" locales) calls out umbrella community, as does the sense that, in this sometimes inhospitable city, one might need to "have" other LBQ residents' "backs." In this sense, cities make identities, and they make communities, too.

Kate's sense of belonging in an umbrella community also calls her to support others' efforts and concerns. In the face of the 2009 ballot initiative, she lobbied for marriage equality, despite her ideological resistance to marriage. She said: "I'm not really a supporter of marriage. . . . I identify as poly[amorous] and so the whole fight really isn't mine, but . . . you know, I wrote letters and I tweeted the entire hearing [on marriage equality] in Augusta. . . . Because even if it's not for me it's for a lot of my friends."[18] Kate's words imply that, when push comes to shove, she recognizes her membership in and allies with a body of individuals united by sexual difference—even if this means acting against another commitment, like her resistance to marriage. She feels that in Portland LBQ individuals constitute a body—a body that warrants protection—for which one ought to lobby. In this sense LBQ residents provide mutual protection, and a sense of mutual protection buoys their umbrella network. As Gerald Suttles (1974) writes, "It is in their 'foreign relations' that communities come into existence and have to settle on an identity and boundaries" (13). In Portland, these "foreign relations" are an ongoing (although typically not all-encompassing) part of life: how you define yourself as LBQ hinges in part on how you deal with a man with a bat, or with another man who harasses your girlfriend in an Old Port store with claims that he will show you what "a real man can do."[19]

Beyond support, membership in an umbrella community colors everyday interactions. A young, queer-identified college dropout and waitress told me: "Honestly, being in Portland is the first time that I felt part of a truly queer community." She described the pleasure she takes in "being in a city full of queers. . . . This is the first time that I've really embraced that." While she uses the language of "queer" when she told me about those who constitute this "community" it was clear that her community encompasses far more than those who specifically identify as "queer." Indeed, when I encountered her at a gallery showcasing her work, on sidewalks, and at the vegetarian restaurant where she worked I often found her conversing or laughing with other LBQ residents. Among these were her friends or intimates who share her microidentity, but they also included friends of friends and other acquaintances. Like Kate, she suggests that Portland's small size is partially responsible for producing this sense of queer community: "I think the fact that it's such a small city and you can really go, you can walk down Congress Street at any time of day, except for like two in the morning, and see ten of your friends. . . . And really everyone is very tight."

But who, exactly, is included in this "everyone"? Over and again, informants underlined its inclusivity. One said, "I'm part of the queer community, which is always and ever growing here. Basically everybody in the GLBT spectrum is part of it: trans people, gender queer, people that are asexual or agender; everyone basically." Here, she included "G" in her acronym, but actually excluded gay men from her more detailed list of members. This reflects dynamics I observed in Portland; while they were not overtly excluded or avoided, I rarely encountered gay men in social scenes peopled by LBQ and transgender individuals. A professional and single mother also emphasized inclusivity (forgetting entirely about gay men when she mentioned "queer"): "The queer community, it's incredibly diverse. It's like, you know, people who identify in all kinds of ways." An educator in her forties pointed out that the community is inclusive by age as well: "Queer community of people from, you know, pretty broad ages. You know, but I'm 46, and most of, you know, my friends are fifty-something down to twenty-something. . . . So that's the community in Portland." However, the heterogeneity that they highlight is nearly always sexual, economic, and age based; there was only minimal heterogeneity in the scenes I observed by race or ethnicity or education level. The mostly white residents I encountered in Portland—living, after all, in one of the three whitest states in the United States—seem mostly oblivious to racial and ethnic homogeneity, which helps to facilitate their own self-confidence in the diversity of their community.[20]

To a remarkable degree, microcommunities and umbrella communities seamlessly interface. A professional in her thirties described her own and others' micronetworks and a broader "lesbian community":

> There's like a smaller group of people who are my friends and peers that I spend time with. And then there's the lesbian community. . . . There are some groups even there. You know, there are like jock-y kind of women who play rugby or softball. And then there are like people who are really, as far as I can tell are mainly interested in hanging out at the bar and who do their socializing at the bar. And then, you know, there are like more activist kind of folks who like social justice work of various kinds, and I say that that's probably where I fit in there. . . . And then all of those are divided into like older and younger. . . . And then there's like the queer identified and trans community. And there's some overlaps and dating overlap.

Another echoes this: "The more people I meet the more I realize that like they already know people that I've already met and it's sort of hard to distinguish between communities." She draws a parallel between the structure of Portland's LBQ and music communities: "It's just like everybody seems to know everybody already. . . . It's just like with the music-playing crowd. They all know each other even though their styles of music are totally different." This statement not only underlines how LBQ individuals with distinct sexual identity "styles" are included under the umbrella, but also gestures to the possibility that city conditions that encourage microcommunity and umbrella community among LBQ residents impact other population groups, such as musicians. A woman who had recently moved from Boulder credits Portland's small size, as well as a sustaining institution—the North Star Café—with facilitating the fusion of multiple microcommunities under an umbrella: "Boulder's really cliquey, which I think Portland is too—but people still know everybody [here]. . . . I think everybody's kind of always sort of mixed together here. . . . I think the North Star builds a lot of community."

LBQ Portlanders sometimes explicitly harness local institutions to shore up their umbrella community. A Dyke March organizer, for example, emphasized the group's intentional efforts at inclusion:

> A handful of us identify as femme or as butch, but it's really spread across the spectrum. And one of the things about the Dyke March that we've been really, really intent on is that it's an inclusive environment. And so, you know, the Dyke March is for dykes *and the people who love them.* You know, we're committed to anyone with a current or past connection to the lesbian/dyke community. And so we all had people in our lives who were trans-identified who had been dyke-identified or lesbian-identified and . . . were no longer in same-sex relationships . . . so being inclusive of that life is really always really, really important for us. . . . Dyke March community incorporates a lot of folks with different identities, as well. . . . One of the sort of funny and quasi-practical ways that it works out is when we need volunteers to act as crossing guards, I go ask my trans guy friends first. . . . And for some of them, it's the best way [to participate].

Thus, residents work to make their umbrella community as welcoming and inclusive as possible—at least of those of whom they are aware. And they are often successful. At one Dyke March I watched as two bisexual women ran out of a Thai restaurant, where they had been dining with their husbands, and joyfully joined the march, embracing friends and laughing about the husbands they had (temporarily) left behind.

Yet, in Portland as seemingly everywhere else, inclusion has its exceptions. The two most obvious, as mentioned, are class and race. The vast majority of LBQ members of the umbrella community are white; a fact that certainly is not lost on a handful of women of color I interviewed who are often burdened with advocacy and education. The Portland LBQ umbrella community is also composed of a notably privileged collection of individuals. While there is substantial variation in income and occupation—from waitresses to doctors—most are college educated, with degrees from elite institutions, and many have advanced degrees. In my time in Portland I did not encounter any explicit exclusions predicated on class (recall, in San Luis Obispo, uncharitable gossip about a woman who worked as a mechanic and struggled financially), but in a state with poverty levels at around 14 percent it reasonable to assume that these individuals exist—even if they never get so far as to enter the orbit of those who tend to people the sidewalks, concerts, grassy parks, and café tables where so many Portland LBQ individuals congregate.[21] But there is one other noteworthy exception: gay men are fairly absent from LBQ networks and many of the events and spaces in which they flourish. LBQ residents suggest that gay men occupy a distinct sphere and, to a degree, distinct neighborhoods—with more men concentrating in the gentrified West End.[22] One woman said: "I think [the queer community] is really divided. It's divisive by nature. For some reason men and women can't share the same space and hang out and have it be the same feeling." Yet another agrees: "There's the gay male community which I actually don't know as much about." Another said: "There's a lot of division between gay men and lesbian women in Portland."

I rarely encountered gay men in the scenes I observed. There were few gay men at Dyke Marches, or at the concerts, parties, and games I attended. Bars, however, were an exception. Shortly before I began fieldwork, a lesbian bar had closed and this encouraged gay and LBQ individuals to share bar space, much as they shared space at the Pride celebration.[23] On Thursday night "Dyke Nights" at Styxx, a gay bar and dance club in the Old Port, a crowd of LBQ women took to the dance floor, played pool, and claimed spots at the bar. Gay men were present, too—but constituted a minority. At two West End gay bars, gay men were nearly always present (and in one always constituted the majority), but I observed very few interactions between men and women in these "shared" spaces. One woman complained, "Styxx is just . . . first of all it's very gay-men centered. There's Dyke Night on Thursday nights but that's about it."

Sometimes LBQ residents mistake the lack of interaction between GLBTQ men and women in spaces like Styxx for complete spatial and social separation. For instance, in advance of Pride in 2009, women provided advice about which events I should attend. Several advised me to skip a pre-Pride party on the water in the Old Port, because only gay men would be in attendance. When I arrived to observe the party anyway, I was surprised to find at least as many women present as men. However, for the most part the men and women once again occupied distinct spaces; there they literally shared space but seemed to avoid interaction.[24]

Conflict also sometimes colors interactions within this umbrella community. As mentioned, the New Femme Regime had already disbanded before I began fieldwork, but it nonetheless maintained a prominent place in conversations LBQ residents had with one another, as well as with me. The New Femme Regime, everyone seemed to agree, threatened the delicate balance between an LBQ community predicated on inclusivity and the simultaneous existence of microidentity communities, thus serving as a negative example of how best to navigate that balance.[25] Secondarily, they used criticism of the New Femme Regime to underline the import they place on emphasizing identity's individual and idiosyncratic nature—"individualized visibility for your identity"—and the central role that they believe this plays in ensuring the harmonious inclusion of disparately identified individuals within the city's LBQ umbrella community. That is, again and again residents instruct that the New Femme Regime ran into trouble not because it embodied a single microcommunity (e.g., the Butch Project, which is also predicated on a microcommunity, is nearly universally celebrated). Instead, it ran afoul because of the manner in which the New Femme Regime marked microcommunity: as exclusive and internally homogeneous.

Jane, a thirty-something, politically active butch woman spoke of the exclusion she felt.

> The Femme Regime, which was trying to I think just to kind of have this sort of celebration of this identity. This femme identity. And it was weird for me because I was always like hanging out with [one of the initiators] all the time but they would have these meetings and we weren't allowed. And I went to a party that they did have where everybody was allowed to come and they were talking about, you know [Anna] was talking to some people about it and this one butch lesbian was like, "What party?" and [Anna] was just like, "Oh, you're not invited, honey." You know? And I was just like, what is this? You know what I mean? Like are we dividing the community now, is that what we're doing? . . . During the Dyke March . . . they had these ribbons that they passed out to all the femmes that said Femme Regime on them and my wife took one but she didn't wear it. She like took one, she looked at me and she's like, "I don't know what to do with this." You know?

Jane's specific complaint was not, as it might have been in some cities, with celebration of femme identity, but instead with what she experienced as the exclusion of nonfemmes from certain events and assignment of femme identity (rather than letting residents articulate their own "personalized" identities). She said: "If we're going to have a conversation about femme identity, why not have it with everyone? We should all honor this and know what this is.'" Like others, Jane told me that the New Femme Regime "died really quickly," attributing that demise to its exclusionary practices.

Another butch-identified woman also reported that the New Femme Regime "didn't last long." However, she associates its failure with the narrow vision of "femme" identity the Regime organizers embodied, which prohibited some prospective members from identifying with the group. By presenting a narrow portrait of "femme," she suggests, they inadvertently excluded some prospective members, and violated a guiding norm of Portland's identity culture: that all identities are "individualized" or idiosyncratic. She said, "The people kind of leading [the New Femme Regime] are like feminine in similar ways. I mean [one organizer] is like high femme and like you know just like very intentional about her feminine gender . . . and then the other person was also very like overtly femininely expressed. So I think some people were like, you know, "So femme is like a really polarized thing," and "Do I belong?" . . . A lot of people felt like it was really cliché and they wouldn't have a part there, so they didn't last really long."

Thus, some residents worried that the New Femme Regime conflict threatened the equilibrium on which an umbrella LBQ community containing smaller, microidentity communities rests. However, rather than letting the conflict upend the umbrella community, these women harnessed the episode to remind themselves and others of their shared core principles: the notion that all Portland LBQ individuals constitute a single body and that the heterogeneity that body contains should be embraced and celebrated. Thus, rather than uprooting community, the conflict collectively reinforced defining characteristics of the local identity culture, as well as their corresponding membership in an inclusive umbrella community.

However, the rift created by the Regime required repair. Resident after resident spoke of the conflict and of the conversation it induced—conversation that, at least by reaffirming commitment to inclusivity and heterogeneity, seemed productive, albeit painful. The Regime's organizers readily spoke to me of their errors. Moreover, they and others suggested that this repair work was a labor of love and necessity. And repair they had, for with only a few exceptions LBQ residents embraced the organizers and their femme identities. Indeed, as we have already seen, several who do not identify as "femme" or "butch" spoke of their respect for those do so. Indeed, the crowd at the 2011 Dyke March was wildly enthusiastic about the femme identities that the organizers articulated ("femme-skater," "femme-professional," and so on).

The work that the LBQ umbrella community requires does not always stem from conflict, nor does it always feel like "work." One woman recounted the ad hoc basketball game she organized for years in the East End, which drew a heterogeneous assemblage of LBQ individuals and, for her, came to embody a facet of LBQ community:

> Seven years ago we decided we wanted to like have fun and exercise. So we started a basketball game on Sunday mornings. . . . I met a lot of people that way, actually. There were no rules. . . . It was like meant to be fun so if you didn't know how to dribble the ball you didn't have to. I mean you were encouraged to try, but we had another friend who would bring her daughter who was like eight at the time, maybe even seven. . . . She would come and she would get to play. And like people were fair and there wasn't competition. And so like if [the little girl] would get the ball, everybody would like kind of stand away and give her a shot at the basket to practice and she would shoot. . . . There was one time when we all played in dresses. And then one time they dressed up as pirates.

Such habits, like the Dyke March, poetry slams and concerts at the North Star, Dyke Night at Styxx, burlesque shows, queer art exhibits, and Kings of the Hill and burlesque shows, help to sustain the umbrella community. In turn, the pleasure residents take in one another's company helps to fuel these habits and rituals, which in turn reinforce the strength of the umbrella community as a whole.[26]

Thus, LBQ residents invest in their "groupness." Their success in this regard is notable given that they negotiate a simultaneous emphasis on individualized identities and microidentity communities. This success, they suggest, rests in part on milder versions of the same mechanisms that encourage lesbian community in San Luis Obispo: some trepidation about their safety and inclusion in the city and, closely related, mild feelings of social and spatial isolation, as well as the perception that the local LBQ population is necessarily small and thus that they must have one another's back. But there is one key difference between residents of San Luis Obispo and Portland that enables the latter's identity-heterogeneous LBQ umbrella community: a collective embrace of identity heterogeneity as a defining feature of what it means to be LBQ in Portland.

Tier Three: Affinity Communities

Tracy described how, in the decades since she left home for college, she has felt embedded in an LBQ community in several different parts of the country not unlike what LBQ residents in San Luis Obispo describe; places in which

LBQ individuals provided nearly all her support and engagement. In contrast, her experience in Portland is quite different. Here she is buoyed by her micro–queer-feminist community and by the larger LBQ umbrella community. And finally, for her and many other Portland residents, there is a third tier: what I propose we think of as "affinity communities"—demarcated networks predicated on secondary identity traits, such as shared place, beliefs, practices, and politics.[27] These affinity communities are numerous and varied, but all are not shaped by sexual identity, as they consist of both gay people and straight people.[28] As a result, inclusion in these groups permits her some spatial separation from the LBQ community. She spoke at length about why she values this distance:

> I don't live in the West End [the Portland neighborhood with the highest proportion of gay male couples] or anything. [My neighborhood is] more residential. It's more family. . . . I live in a duplex. A very Italian family lives in half of it and then my roommate and I, who I went to high school with, live upstairs. . . . I love it. I don't know if I would leave now. I know that for the [queer] community, more the East End and the West End are community centers. I don't have a particular draw to live in either of those places. . . . I lived in Park Slope. . . . I lived there for two years and it was 2000. It was right as the babies descended. . . . I don't have a need to live where my community lives but that's me personally. . . . I don't need to. I like knowing where they are. I like going and visiting. . . . I think that our [queer] communities tend to be small and then living in a place like Portland, for example, it is already a small city. And the type of work that I do overlaps really heavily with the [LBQ] community. It's nice to not always be seen or seeing. [I like] to be more in the general population where I live and not just have like queer identified in the area.

Here, in her appreciation for membership in a community that extends beyond the LBQ population, she sounds much like the women who enjoy the "ambient community" of Ithaca, that general sense of belonging in a variety of settings. However, there are two key distinctions between ambient and affinity communities. First and most centrally, in stark contrast to LBQ Ithacans, Tracy claims membership in an LBQ community. That is, even as she speaks of living apart from other LBQ individuals she names that umbrella community as essential, as "our community." Secondly, as I explore below, in contrast to Ithaca's broad-reaching ambient community, Tracy's affinity communities consist of pockets, or islands, within Portland's broader social milieu. In contrast to "ambient community," which provides LBQ Ithacans with a general sense of belonging in their city, affinity communities rest on narrower nodes of connection with similar others; they constitute islands of welcome in an otherwise inconsistently embracing city.

Indeed, most LBQ residents specify membership in particular segments of Portland's broader population, specifically with individuals with whom they share place, politics, beliefs, or practices, or other secondary identity traits. For instance, in the kitchen of her bungalow on Portland's western edge, dogs at our feet, Angela described what this concept of community by affinity means to her: "A group of people who maybe organize around a particular thing, not necessarily political but you know social activity or something like that." She pointed to her volunteer work and her partner's book group as examples of activities that helped them forge ties of affiliation in Portland.

Most LBQ Portlanders echo at least two facets of both Angela's and Tracy's narratives. First, like Tracy they express appreciation for their ability to step outside both their microcommunity and the umbrella community. However, whereas Ithacans describe "ambient community"—ties forged with a heterogeneous collection of individuals that are predicated on shared place, beliefs, practices, and politics—as pervasive and as a network in which LBQ individuals are assured membership (indeed, LBQ Ithacans note that those on the outside looking in tend not to be LBQ, but, instead, to be poor and working-class African Americans), in Portland most describe a sense of membership in *pockets* of Portland, among segments of the population who explicitly embrace their sexual identity and difference and with whom they share beliefs, politics, and practices; in contrast to Ithaca, in Portland there is no tacit sense of inclusion in straight-dominated circles. In this sense, while they are confident that they will find opportunities for belonging (predicated on commonalities), they understand that such social opportunities are not endlessly pervasive (are not, in other words, "ambient"). Instead, they constitute valuable islands of hospitability in a city that is otherwise only moderately inclusive.

Second, like Angela they regard ties forged around shared, beliefs, politics, practices, and other secondary identity traits as genuine and sustaining—even if they are not as intimate as ties with LBQ residents. Affinity communities can take shape around virtually any area of allegiance or common ground, but LBQ individuals speak most frequently of membership in several specific types: political communities; groups based around belief or activity; networks forged around cultural tastes (e.g., "punk") or life stage (e.g., parenting); or ties forged via shared place (spatial or institutional).

Many describe themselves as members of political communities. One said, "I'm . . . generally part of the queer community and . . . [the] activist/

political community." When I asked her to elaborate on her political ties she described separate islands that share a political kinship: "You've got Equality Maine, People's Alliance . . . Civil Liberties Union, League of Young Voters. The list can go on and on and on. There are organizers. There are lobbyists and all that. And then you have the artists. Dancers, visual artists, musicians. And they overlap [with the activists], but I see them as separate [communities]." Another describes membership in the "organizing community." Still another says: "So there's like . . . the radical community. . . . I used to really spend a lot of time with . . . this self-identified group of anarchists."

Les, a young activist, suggests that shared ideology and identities, such as "radical" and "freak," connect her friends in Portland. A recent graduate of the Gender Studies program at the University of Southern Maine, Les told me:

> Portland's a very queer town and in a lot of ways, not just the sexual orientation or gender identities. Politically there are a lot of really radical people here. Something a little bit more than just sexual orientation or gender identity. It's about politics and it's about the way that you choose to live. I think there are a lot of people in Portland who are straight but who are freaks somehow. Society would see them as not quite normal and that's what I love about this place: everybody is different somehow.

It is in her community of "freaks"—straight or queer—that she feels at home.

Others align less in terms of explicit political values or practices, and more in terms of cultural tastes. A middle-aged woman said, "I'd say I was like part of the poet community." A young woman who identifies both as "queer" and as "punk" appreciates how her LBQ umbrella community intersects with the music lovers and the punks:

> There are definitely queer people in most of the communities here. . . . I think there's definitely a lot of overlap. . . . There's . . . a music community. There's sort of like a punk community. I call them the 'dirty butt patch kids.' They're pretty easy to distinguish. There's them. There's definitely the roller derby community.

Others belong to affinity groups predicated on life stage and/or family ties. Several described the (biological) family they had in the area as constituting a "community." Recall the woman who suggests that her birth family constitutes one community and her "gay family" another: "I'll go to my family for Christmas and I'll go to the gay family to you know exchange presents at the end of the day." Another native Portlander, a single mother of an elementary school–aged child, echoes this: "My first community is probably just my family and close friends."

Others gesture less to family and more to ties predicated on the life stage created by their family status, but independent of their actual biological family. A young mother described how straight, married couples came to constitute much of her social network: "There's people who I know because of my son so I spend a lot of time with them because [of] play dates and all. . . . I was just saying to someone the other day [that] all of my friends are married straight people." Another offers a similar description of her experience parenting: "We knew a lot of families with young children, because we had a small child." These "families with young children" had heterosexual parents, and while immersed in the endless tasks of early parenting, she said, "I found that we were much more inclined to gravitate towards them than the lesbian community."

Still others, such as Marcy, a forty-something educator, emphasize activity-based communities: "I'm also . . . part of the figure-skating community." Before finding membership in a figure-skating community, she cherished ties she cultivated at a YMCA populated with a variety of Mainers. She explained why these activity-based ties are important:

> Maine is too small to decide that you would like to hang out with a bunch of middle-aged lesbians. I mean it's just not big enough. And it's too small even to say I just want to hang out with people that have X, Y, Z view of every military action. I mean . . . there's no way to have a sort of life that involves you know a lot of different people . . . so you know, I liked hanging out at the Y.

Here, she implies that, because of Portland's small population, LBQ micro- and umbrella communities cannot entirely fulfill her. On Marcy's account, LBQ individuals join affinity communities because they must. In contrast, Tracy (with whom I opened this section) suggests that one joins affinity communities because one *can*. Such affinity is a good that is not available to LBQ individuals in all times and places and therefore is an opportunity to seize. Crucially, both imply that elements of local ecology—such as, to name a few, the city's population size, especially that of its LBQ population, and the degree to which LBQ individuals concentrate in specific neighborhoods and feel accepted in straight networks—play a role in determining their ties. Both suggest that local conditions shape the accessibility of affinity communities for LBQ residents, and the degree to which those communities play a role in one's social life and support system. Yet affinity community also emerges from and reinforces a basic approach to sexual identity in Portland—the notion that it is personalized. One size does not fit all; thus, residents acknowledge how various facets of the self influence both our understanding of self and our ties to others.

Despite comfort with and appreciation for ties to heterosexual members of affinity communities, LBQ Portlanders do not blindly forge ties with heterosexuals. Instead, they look for indicators of acceptance of their sexual identity from prospective members of affinity communities. One shared the delight she feels when a prospective heterosexual friend or acquaintance passes muster:

> There was a guy I met. . . . He's a straight guy. I met him at The Snug [a Munjoy Hill bar] a few years ago. We were just drinking and having a good time and I started talking and he said he was a photographer and I was like, "Do you do any pro bono work?" He's like, "Every once in a while." I [was like], "Oh we could really use a photographer for Gay Prom for the kids." And he gave me his contact information. . . . He did that for two years.

Here, she hoped—but felt that she could not assume—that a straight man would accept her sexuality; she felt comfortable asking him about Gay Prom, but found his willingness to get involved to be exceptional and memorable. The uncertainty that underlines this interaction captures a key dimension of what it feels like to be LBQ in Portland and likely in much of the United States—although it stands in notable contrast to how those in Ithaca describe what it feels like to be LBQ in their city.

It is not a coincidence that Amanda befriended a straight man in The Snug on Munjoy Hill. The Snug is located next to the North Star, which, as we have seen, many LBQ individuals heralded as the spatial heart of the LBQ umbrella community. Owned by a woman with long dark hair and many tattoos, The Snug is an opportune locale for interaction between LBQ individuals and heterosexual individuals who might not only be open to forging ties with LBQ residents but also share some of their interests or beliefs. On occasions when I entered the bar with an informant, we were rarely the only LBQ individuals present, although the majority of patrons and staff appeared to present as heterosexual. Several indicated that they regard the bar as friendly territory. Indeed, the after party for a Portland-produced performance of Boston's Femme Show was held at The Snug; LBQ cast, crew, fans, and friends shared booths and tables in a corner of the bar, drawing minimal notice from the straight men who occupied most seats at the bar.

Beyond The Snug, many suggest that certain parts of the city are home to particularly dense clusters of affinity communities accessible to or welcoming of LBQ residents. Several reported that Munjoy Hill is a rich site for affinity communities: "I really appreciate the sense of community. It's a very close-knit place. . . . People really make an effort to create a friendly atmosphere. . . . They have this Munjoy Hill Gardens Day where you can take a tour and go to everybody's gardens. . . . Or we have a festival." Another describes most of her block as constituting a supportive affinity community:

> We have a next-door neighbor who's a very elderly gay man. . . . And then on the other side of us we have a young couple who are both teachers with a young son, who also have a dog. . . . We have dog play dates and I've actually babysat for his son since he was four months old. . . . And next to them, we have a group of guys who live in a house that, you know, is just mixed. It's just a mixed group of guys shacking up together. . . . And then next to them, we've got some nice women who live in a house. And next to them it starts to get a little sketchy.

Here she instructs that she offers aid—childcare and assistance to an elderly neighbor—to those with whom she shares a street. She, too is the beneficiary of support:

> We all take care of each other. One night, for example, we had a . . . new puppy. . . . He decided he wanted to go outside, and . . . he got his neck caught underneath the fence, and he was freaking out. . . . We rushed outside. The neighbors next door came outside, and guys from down the street next to them came over to see if they could help. That's the kind of community we have. That, you know, one dog makes a big peep, and boy, the whole family's there.

While she describes her neighbors as "family," she also notes that on one end of her street "it starts to get a little sketchy," suggesting that she does not feel equally connected to all. In this sense, her affinity community is spatially, socially, and economically delimited, with gay men, heterosexual teachers, and progressive twenty-something men constituting her affinity community. She did not specify why some residents are not a part of the community, but based on our broader conversation I had the sense that class and political differences separated one end of the block from the other. Of course, this exclusivity is a basic characteristic of affinity communities. Like any other instantiation of community, every affinity community, while sexually heterogeneous, rests on a mutually acknowledged common ground, thus defining itself—either implicitly or explicitly—against those who don't stand on that same common ground.

Residents imply that the density of—or likelihood of joining—affinity communities is a factor to weigh when looking for a place to live (just as they also consider the density of LBQ residents in a neighborhood). They also suggest that a certain space, like Munjoy Hill, by virtue of its physical (and social) separation from the rest of the city, "provides an additional basis for social differentiation and social cohesion" (Suttles 1974, 28), partially enabling LBQ residents to rub shoulders with heterosexuals with whom they share beliefs, politics, or practices.[29]

Another points to the role of institutions in helping to forge affinity communities in a space like Munjoy Hill. She presents the North Star Café on Munjoy Hill as a crucial resource:

> The North Star community. I'm looking at the owner right now and she's winking at me. It's fabulous. It's fabulous. . . . It's pretty multigenerational, sort of mirroring the East End. I feel like this is sort of one of the hubs of the East End. You know this is like where you come and get your coffee but also get your food and also can come hear music and hear stories get told and hear spoken word. So the spoken word community is definitely a little microcosm within the North Star community and it varies from night to night depending on what the entertainment is in terms of the demographics of people. . . . If I don't go I miss it.

Indeed, founders of the North Star explicitly hoped to cultivate a common space for multiple-affinity communities and, in this sense, to embody the community spirit they associate with Portland's East End, especially Munjoy Hill.[30]

Some report that affinity ties, partially cultivated in places like the North Star, moderate their dependence on other LBQ residents. A young artist said:

> When I came here I definitely did put a lot of emphasis on meeting queer people, like getting to know all the lesbians and dating. But now I don't think that I care about that as much. I just kind of want to meet cool people regardless of their sexuality and especially positive people. That's important here because there are some long, cold winters and you can get in a slump so easily so you need good productive people around you.

Yet, despite appreciating her ties to heterosexuals, she acknowledges that most of her ties are with LBQ residents. However, her affinity ties with heterosexuals build certitude that she connects with LBQ individuals not only because of their shared sexual difference but also because of common affinities: "I guess [my community is] probably like 80 percent, 90 percent still [LBQ]. But I guess the difference now is that I'm not necessarily socializing with them *because* they're queer. Because when I first came here there were definitely friends that I made who I had nothing in common with besides our sexuality." That is, largely as a result of the fact that she has affinity ties with heterosexuals, even if they compose only 10 or 20 percent of her ties, she experiences her preponderance of ties to LBQ individuals as driven somewhat less by necessity.

She especially appreciates the possibilities of affinity because finding like-minded artists was one of the things that drew her to Portland. She is not alone in this regard. While many move for professional or educational opportunities, or because of family ties in Maine, a desire to live around poets, leftists, or environmentalists also motivates some.[31] Others move because of a desire to be in Maine and to be in a city; within this predominantly rural state, Portland is the most urban option. With this comes anticipation of meeting other "urbanites." Thus, anticipation of one or another of the many manifestations out of which affinity communities emerge encouraged some to move.

Few report disappointment. A small business owner and musician hoped Portland would be home to many musicians: "I love the community. . . . The first thing that I did when I got into town was get hooked up with musicians." Likewise, the arts community drew others: "I came down to Portland one night for a show, and met all these amazing people who had just started a local art space called The Door Yard." Indeed, on any given weekend night, I could pass a handful of LBQ residents amongst the crowd in a number of (heterosexually dominated) galleries and music venues.

Of course, LBQ residents are not indifferent to indicators of Portland's LBQ friendliness, even if some profess that pre-move they were most concerned about other features of the city, such as the arts culture.[32] One described her decision to leave the South for Portland: "I didn't want to be in the South and I wanted to be out so I guess moving back to Maine, part of that was that. I thought that I could come here and be safe and be safe to be out." Yet, many place as much weight on anticipated affinity communities as on perceived lesbian-friendliness. For instance, a middle-aged woman considered moving to "San Francisco because I thought it was really gay friendly." However, despite its gay-friendly reputation, in San Francisco she could not find the affinity communities she hoped for: "It's more like gentrified and very like hyper-masculine, hetero-normative, white. . . . I'm all set with that." Instead, she moved to Portland where she trusted she would find not only out LBQ individuals, but also affinity communities of which she could be a part.

Prospective residents' confidence in finding affinity rests, in part, on Portland's public persona, or place reputation—everything from how Portland portrays itself to the world and how the media presents it.[33] The "Visit Portland" website, for instance, immediately announces the notion that one can find one's niche or niches in Portland. Under the heading "Authentic—By Nature" the site describes Portland in terms that emphasize nearly endless opportunities for cultural and social engagement, from nature to food, culture, art, and fashion. The site reads: "With its heady mix of artistic and outdoor adventures, our region is stylish and sophisticated, yet remains genuine and unpretentious, a place where grey flannel and plaid flannel coexist companionably."[34] The site and other media representations and self-promotions also emphasize this notion of companionable coexistence; one can find one's place—whether on a boat, at a restaurant table, behind a bar, in a gallery, or on the shoreline—in Portland.[35] Indeed, a local paper (Routhier 2012) notes that Portland frequently makes "best city" lists—numbering thirty-five in thirteen years—that offer a glimpse into the city's many affinity communities: from third-best city for kids (*Parenting*) to fifth-best for hipsters (*Travel & Leisure*), and a top vacation resort for people with dogs (DogFriendly.com).[36] As informants' words suggest, the city does not disappoint LBQ residents who move anticipating that Portland is a city in which one can find a niche—even if that niche does not stretch without interruption across the city limits.[37]

This is not to suggest that Portland is bucolic or all-embracing. We have heard accounts of violence directed at LBQ individuals and other expressions of homophobia, from slurs on the street, to threatened violence, and hateful graffiti. And LBQ networks in Portland are primarily constituted by white residents with a BA degree or higher (often from highly selective private institutions). This reflects broader racial and economic segregation in the city, and the concentration of immigrants of color in select residential pockets, and related barriers that prevent some from achieving access to the affinity communities my informants celebrate. However, despite instances of violence and harassment, LBQ respondents do not feel compelled to exclusively belong to LBQ networks, even if they also do not articulate a sense of being on the inside of the social world or of a boundless (for white and middle- and upper-middle-class LBQ individuals) affinity community. This directs them away from either end of a spectrum: away from both San Luis Obispo's "lesbian community" and Ithaca's "ambient community."

In Portland, as elsewhere, culture positions community. There are obvious parallels between the embrace of individualized, hyphenated identities in Portland and the individualized hyphenated communities that residents form. The widely embraced and heralded notion of identity as individual encourages residents to cobble together not only personalized identities but also personalized networks. For some, affinity communities play a very large role; for most others, its weight is moderate. Some constantly engage with the umbrella LBQ community, whereas others are more entrenched in their particular microcommunity. LBQ individuals in Portland embrace this variation in community assemblage, just as they celebrate and embrace identity differences; this is personalized community for personalized identities. Together, this underlines a lesson with which the reader is increasingly familiar: how identity and community closely influence one another. Identity, along with local ecology, influences the ties that each of us cultivate; and the shape and character of ties, which emerge from interactions, alternately calls out and reinforces ways of thinking about self and group.[38]

Many LBQ individuals in Portland are quite satisfied with having affinity communities play a secondary role in their public life, since they are relatively content with LBQ networks. No surprise then, that integration is not a celebrated goal (as it is in Ithaca and, increasingly, in Greenfield). This is evident in their response to a question about the proportion of residents who ought to share their identity. One said, "Probably like 80 percent, 90 percent," and another, "My specific sexual identity? Well, it couldn't be all queer dykes because that would just be too crazy. It's good to change it up. There would be endless drama, endless. But I think that 50 percent to 75 percent would be good. I like dykes." One went further: "All of them. We're talking utopia." Another explained that she lives in suburban South Portland because "there's just more lesbians." Here, while some say that they could not only live around lesbians, they nonetheless call for a very low proportion of heterosexual neighbors. For most, finding a place among sympathetic straight residents is a perk of living in Portland, but it is not a primary goal.

Despite the high value they place on connections with other LBQ residents, they repeatedly report that affinity ties play a vital social role. They also affirm their sense that Portland is in their own image; that is, it is a city in which LBQ residents are on neither the outside nor the inside (precisely the cultural position in which many locate themselves, as highly educated, creative, and transgressive individuals). After all, many LBQ residents express uncertainty or ambivalence about efforts, such as the fight for marriage equality, to stake a place in traditional institutions; they neither wish to be excluded nor lose their outsider perspective, which they recognize helps produce and sustain their rich ties to each other. Beyond marriage debates, this informs broader politics.[39] Some protest the consumerism of the annual Pride Parade. A queer/punk woman told me: "Last year in the Pride Parade, there was [an action by a queer visibility group of which she is a part] that's . . . coming in and saying, we are a movement of queers, we are not a market. We are not Budweiser, rainbow flags!" Yet, when push came to shove, LBQ residents labored to prevent their exclusion, such as when, in 2009, it began to seem that the amendment banning same-sex marriage might pass in Maine. At the Dyke March After Party the crowd responded with warm applause when a representative from Equality Maine acknowledged that it was a moment when fighting for insider status had, from her perspective, become necessary. A middle-aged woman with short blonde hair, she said: "Whether marriage is your issue or not is irrelevant at this point." Indeed, in the months that followed, many reported that they found themselves aligning with gay organizations, such as LAMBDA Legal and the Human Rights Campaign, that they believe promote the "normalcy" of GLBTQ lives—and a few mentioned, with both nostalgia and optimism, the gradual closure of local debate about marriage as more and more began to lobby on behalf of marriage.[40] This parallels their somewhat divided desires when it comes to community: to be outside and inside at the same time, and to enjoy both identity and affinity community.

Of course, we have already seen how this desire is locally grown; how it emerges from dimensions of city ecology—limited acceptance and safety, a moderate and spatially uneven sense of LBQ abundance, narratives of Portland (and its LBQ residents) as urban, creative, intellectual and cutting edge—that shape visions for one's self and community. Portland is a place of personalized identity politics and personalized communities. It is a place between the ends we have encountered in Ithaca and San Luis Obispo; a city in which one can carve out affinity communities with heterosexuals, but in which much pleasure and support is nonetheless derived from LBQ microcommunities and the umbrella community.

Conclusion

In retrospect, one of the first events I observed—the 2009 Dyke March—was both a distillation and a display of Portland's identity culture. Indeed, a core lesson Portland offers—one instructive across cities—is about how public display, from marches to drag revues, communicates and reaffirms distinctive features of local LBQ life. Portland residents' proclivity for playing with and discussing identity, itself borne of Portland's broader intellectual and artistic character, make public display particularly prolific and visible. However, recognition of this mechanism at work in Portland highlights the (subtler) role of display in the other cities, too. It is to this lesson that I turn first.[41]

The official theme of the 2009 Dyke March was "for dykes and the people who love them." Unofficially, the event celebrated microidentities, largely by engaging butch and femme identities. Stickers and placards—from "Love Your Femmes" to "Butch is Beautiful"—were affixed to backpacks and T-shirts, and waved by marchers. An after-march show included a litany of performances that engaged and/or played with femininity and masculinity. Performances included four belly dancers; a skit featuring a drag king whom a woman tied in a chair before writing a "W" on his forehead in lipstick; a performance by a woman in drag wearing a suit and dancing with a picture frame around her face—which she eventually smashed; a strip tease to a song containing the lyric "the queerest of the queer" by a performer in lingerie and fur; and a drag performance featuring women in boas and heels fighting over a drag king—whom one woman ultimately carried off the stage slung over her shoulder.

Performances ranged from those displaying and celebrating gender performance (e.g., the strip tease) to those actively disrupting binary-gender categories (a woman in drag with a "W" on her forehead, a frame smashed on the floor; a woman carrying a drag king over her shoulder). Here, for me, core features of Portland's identity culture came into focus.

But I was not the only one taking cues at the Dyke March. For residents, the event and others like it displayed and affirmed the local identity culture, and likely shaped self-understanding of numerous people in numerous ways. It would be difficult to walk away from Dyke March without the sense that Portland's LBQ residents celebrate the notion of identity as individualized, intellectualized, and mutable, and embrace the value of announcing sexuality with pride and forthrightness.[42]

Secondarily, the event reflected and affirmed local ties. Marked by shared humor and pleasure, the evening underlined membership in a common community, an umbrella with room for variation in age, income, and identity style. Here, "groupness" rests on the sense that sexual difference provides common ground and on the shared embrace of identity heterogeneity. A forty-something Equality Maine volunteer in jeans and a T-shirt had a place on the stage, as did a middle-aged androgynous comedienne, as did a young "dyke."

Why doesn't commitment to identity politics and engagement with the umbrella community—embodied by the fact that so many residents attend events like Dyke March—work against the individualization of identities and microcommunities? At the same time, how do Portlanders prevent emphasis on individualized identities from disrupting a difference-spanning identity politics and their umbrella community?

Several overlapping mechanisms permit this coexistence. First and foremost, as we have seen, feelings of moderate acceptance in their city, and the sense that their population group is of moderate size, encourages a sense of common ground and even of mutual dependence. In turn, this nurtures identity politics and an umbrella LBQ community. Over and again, LBQ individuals describe the comfort and pleasure they take in building a broad and inclusive (of different microidentities) LBQ network in which they take frequent, even daily, refuge. Imagine the woman who came into the LBQ-owned North Star Café after having passed a flyer reminding her of a recent attack on a queer resident. At the North Star, surrounded by polyglot LBQ individuals, she could come in from the cold. Here, common ground—and the warm feeling of belonging it sometimes generates—emerges at once from shared distinction (and exclusion) from those who do not think of themselves as LBQ, as well as a sense of connection with those who regard the self as a product of multiple and often shifting facets of identity.

Secondarily, place narratives and residents' artistic and intellectual biographies encourage an intellectualized and theatrical approach to identity, as well as the embrace of microidentities. Under this rubric, one is nearly always LBQ plus something else, or at least mindful that others are. Recognition of hybridity as a unifying local approach permits a common, umbrella identity politic—without necessitating the abandonment of microidentities for the sake of the umbrella; part of what earns one *entrée* here is an embrace of sexual heterogeneity.

Finally, intellectual engagement and playing with identity are part of the discursive work LBQ residents rely on to negotiate prospective tensions between umbrella and microidentities and ties. This parallels the stories Ithaca's LBQ individuals rely on to present their city as "LBQ friendly" (despite some counterevidence), as well as the talk of "inclusivity" and "heterogeneity" that San Luis Obispo lesbians rely on to maintain a reasonably cohesive "lesbian community." Over and again, Portland's LBQ individuals affirm their "groupness"—via Dyke March, Kings of the Hill shows, or a Saturday afternoon at the North Star. Although they sometimes falter in this task (the year when Dyke March organizers distributed "femme" stickers to some), they typically succeed in celebrating a collection of LBQ residents united, in large part, by commitment to individualized identities. Quite often, this celebration was quite literal: the Dyke March theme of "Celebrating our Dyke Identities," for example, or the "Individualized Visibility for your Identity" T-shirt vendor.[43] Through play and talk, they stake out space for "personalized" self-understanding and networks within the safe enclosure of umbrella community. If one believes, fundamentally, that there is no "right" or singular way to be LBQ then there is much room for identity heterogeneity and exploration; difference and experimentation do not threaten a sense of common ground if part of what constitutes that common ground is a belief that identity is flexible, evolving, and individual. And this sense of common ground nurtures and responds to the existence of the umbrella community; Portland's identity culture and community dynamics inform one another.

The fusion of hybridity and identity politics in Portland offers an additional broad lesson. First and foremost, it disputes presentations of post-identity or post-gay politics as ascendant, especially among young, highly educated individuals, and of a neat temporal shift between an era dominated by identity politics and one characterized by a retreat away from it and an embrace of queer politics.[44] In Portland, "queer" and "identity politics" are not opposed, but, rather, fused. From Portland, an image emerges of a flexible and adaptable identity politics: of a *queer* identity politics. Portland's LBQ residents are unambiguous in their sense that sexual identity provides inimitable common ground and shared interests and concerns, but they marry this with an embrace of flexibility and a hybridity that we more typically associate with those who reject identity politics. In Portland, nonnormativity is itself an identity category; one that, despite its embrace of instability, rests on recognition of the constancy of one's "otherness" or "outsiderness."

This may surprise some, as recent scholarship on sexual heterogeneity explores sexual differences across different types of places or the constitution of distinct sexual "scenes" and "fields" (Green 2008) within a city.[45] Instead, Portland at once reveals a remarkable range of microidentities within a single city, and less city-level heterogeneity than accounts of "sexual cultures" (Irvine 1994; Hennen 2008) and "fields" predict, since Portland possesses an overarching, unifying identity culture. This culture unites what might have, had my observations been less comprehensive, appeared to be distinct scenes or fields. For instance, had I only surveyed the cadre of women who attend Michigan and socialize on Munjoy Hill, or focused only on femme individuals, I might have missed the common cultural logic that unites disparate microidentity communities and their spaces.

This is not merely a methodological issue.[46] When we put Portland into conversation with the other cities it becomes apparent that cities set parameters for identity heterogeneity among residents; certain city conditions enable (or restrict) identity flexibility within a place—and thus the likelihood that a city will engender multiple microcommunities. This calls us to consider not just the scene or small group but also the common crosscutting elements undergirding them. Had I not looked across Portland—from Munjoy Hill to Deering Oaks and beyond—we would not have a full sense of the vivid and heady social world LBQ residents cultivate in Maine's largest city, or of how "queer" and "identity politics" can fuse. Of course, most of the time we do not look at a whole city to evaluate sexual identities and communities, since we associate them with demographic groups, specific institutions, or friendship circles. Recognition of citywide sexual identity culture calls us to adopt a more holistic way of viewing and engaging sexualities.

FOUR

Greenfield:
Lesbian Feminist Longtimers and
Post-Identity-Politics Newcomers

Two hours from Boston and fifteen minutes from the southern border of Vermont, the small city of Greenfield, Massachusetts, rests on the northern edge of the Pioneer Valley. The Valley, which traces the Connecticut River, is a bastion for progressive politics, especially environmentalism and antiwar activism. Its unofficial cultural and economic capitals are Amherst, home to Amherst College and the University of Massachusetts Amherst, and Northampton, location of the venerable women's college, Smith College, and seat of the county with the highest proportion of lesbian couple households in the entire country.[1]

Greenfield is just a thirty-five-minute drive from Amherst, and even closer to Northampton, and yet is distinct from the Valley's flagship cities. In contrast to Amherst and Northampton, Greenfield boasts a single, and more humble, institution of higher education: Greenfield Community College. The city, and especially its Main Street, has struggled to recover from the closure of tool and other factories, and the ongoing pressures of big-box stores. Yet, Greenfield is seat of Franklin County, which possesses the second highest proportion of lesbian-couple households in the United States, and over the last thirty years the picturesque hill towns surrounding the city have experienced unmistakable upscaling (Gates and Ost 2004).

When I began fieldwork in the summer of 2010 I could not miss the cluster of lesbian, bisexual, and/or queer (LBQ) recent Smith graduates lunching outside the Greenfields Market Co-op, LBQ women serving burritos, and multiple tables of LBQ residents in a new and bustling brick oven pizzeria on Bank Street. Nor could I miss indicators of broader change afoot in Greenfield by the time I finally left the field, in 2015: the development of a new Arts Block on Main Street, and the opening of a new bookshop and whiskey bar near the long-empty hulk of a shuttered bank.

This book has already sketched how LBQ residents respond to the ecology of the city in which they live; we have seen how a person's ties, and their orientations to sexual identity, take shape in response to what it feels like to be LBQ in that particular place. We have also seen how approaches to identity and ties extend across a city's LBQ population, uniting relatively disparate individuals as they negotiate a common place. In Greenfield, however, something different is found: there is more than one identity culture, and more than one approach to the ties that develop there. Longtime LBQ residents, as we'll see, articulate a lesbian feminist identity politics that shares many traits with the identity politics of LBQ San Luis Obispo residents. In contrast, newer arrivals (the bulk of those I encountered in the field) articulate post-identity politics and, mirroring those in Ithaca, celebrate "ambient community" or a general sense of belonging forged around shared place, beliefs, politics, and practices.

Lesbian feminist longtimers are as certain of their sexuality and of its significance as those in San Luis Obispo. Take, for instance, my morning of observation at Greenfields Market where LBQ women gathered for the "Big Gay Brunch," organized via the Lavender Lips Listserv.[2] Conversation among the women, most of whom were in their forties and fifties and dressed casually in jeans and sweaters, was light and friendly. However, it became more serious when one mentioned "lesbian bed death."[3] Martha spoke of how hormones influence desire and proposed that female and male sexuality are inherently distinct. She spoke candidly of her declining desire for sex with her partner, whom everyone at the table knew, although she took care to tell us that she finds her partner attractive and delights in her company. Martha argued that women's libidos are less powerful than men's and that bringing two women together inhibits their ability to maintain sexual passion. Add to this the propensity of lesbians to remain in relationships for a long time and hormonal changes associated with menopause, and, in her view, lesbian bed death is unavoidable. A narrative about sexuality (and gender) as biological and immutable underlined her explanation, and nearly everyone at the table offered agreement. A relatively recent migrant from Philadelphia briefly challenged this formulation, but the general tone was one of happy accord. In this and all other conversations, everyone seemed to delight in speaking openly about intimate features of their personal lives; everyone turned to shared sexual identity and an underlying current of feminism as bases for connection. As I listened, it seemed as though I had magically traveled to a potluck table in San Luis Obispo, at which women of a similar age, class, and racial background (mostly early to late middle age, white, and middle class) offered similar pronouncements about the biological roots of desire. In both cities, a newcomer was the only one to articulate any opposition to dominant arguments, and shared identity invited candor and intimacy.

Yet, in stark contrast, a short walk from Greenfields Market, an LBQ couple, each of whom is white and in her thirties, lives in a small apartment. When I visited them there, they labored in their tiny kitchen to make a meal for a farmer—a white heterosexual man—who was recovering from a work injury. The couple happily described networks that not only include but also extend beyond LBQ residents. As Lori tossed a carrot salad, and while chickens roasted in the oven and her partner pared apples for a crisp, she told me that she does not think of herself as having a sexual identity. She said, "You know, it's kind of funny, 'cause I don't, really. I don't really identify. I think that humans are humans, and the sexuality spectrum is really broad, and at different times we fall at different places, and I feel like most people are kind of in the middle somewhere." Of course, this approach to sexual identity is a far cry from that articulated at brunch. Not only was Lori's view of sexuality—as fluid and as only one facet of the self—quite distinct from that at the "Big Gay Brunch," so too were her networks. As these two scenes suggest, a few blocks apart two different visions of sexuality and the ties that these visions help to establish flourish.

Despite the coexistence of distinct identity cultures in the city, Greenfield's LBQ residents only partially depart from the broader pattern we've found of city-specific identities and communities. That is, Greenfield is not an identity free-for-all. Instead, there were two groups: lesbian feminist longtimers (both longtime residents of Greenfield and/or of the Pioneer Valley), who compose one migration cohort, and a growing cast of post-identity-politics newcomers, who compose a second migration cohort. While post-identity politics is becoming increasingly widespread, each nonetheless persists. LBQ individuals find a home in one of these two camps, with a few older women (generally aged fifty years and above) beginning to adopt a hybrid orientation and a mix of ties.

As I spent time in the homes of Greenfield's newest LBQ migrants—many of whom moved from other small New England cities, or Boston or New York—it became increasingly apparent that membership in each group is not neatly reducible to age, class, or other characteristics.[4] Instead, the period of migration is the greatest predictor of identity and ties; Greenfield nurtures identity generations, but these are what we might call "migration cohorts," not generation or age cohorts. Why does the period in which a migrant arrived in Greenfield matter for how she conceives of her identity and develops her ties? New residents increasingly encounter a city that casts itself as a desirable destination and an LBQ haven in its own right—a far cry from the (relatively speaking) inhospitable cousin to Northampton that earlier migrants met—and they articulate a corresponding post-identity politics and describe a growing sense of ambient community. An earlier migration generation met a different and less hospitable Greenfield, one that called out a lesbian-feminist identity politics.

As Greenfield has changed, the identities of its residents have also changed, away from lesbian feminism and toward post-identity politics. That shift serves as a vital reminder that city "character" is not as static as extant literature suggests; residents describe a dynamic city, and orient identity and ties in relation to changing city ecology.[5]

Both then and now, among longtimers and newcomers alike, Greenfield is shaped in relation to Northampton, like the moon's steadfast orbit of earth.[6] Northampton's presence marks, and therefore elevates, the effects of Greenfield's mutability. Northampton itself is, of course, evolving as all places do, but in the mythos of lesbian America, Northampton is a touchstone, and a stable one at that, against which Greenfield measures itself.[7] Thus, Greenfield's LBQ residents are more mindful of their own city's changes than are residents of the other study cities (despite changes in each); indeed, the notion of Greenfield as changing is one of the most powerful place narratives that they encounter and to which they contribute. This hyperawareness accelerates the transformation of Greenfield's identity culture.

From Greenfield, two new lessons about how places shape identities and ties emerge. First, cities do not exist in a vacuum; other places matter, too. Local actors interpolate and experience place characteristics relationally. This is likely always true; for example, the sense that Ithaca exists in a "bubble" has much to do with residents' assessments of surrounding cities and towns. But Greenfield's adjacency to Northampton—also known as "Lesbianville, USA," and perhaps the most renowned lesbian enclave in the United States—renders this relationship particularly visible. However, the degree to which another city serves as an identity referent ultimately depends on the characteristics of the city in which LBQ residents reside. This relates to the second major lesson: as cities change, LBQ identities and ties change, too. As Greenfield has attracted over the last ten or fifteen years a more affluent and highly educated population, and as it has become a locus for organic farming and local foods, the position of LBQ residents has evolved and, with this, LBQ newcomers' identities and ties have also changed.[8] Concomitantly, the degree of Northampton's influence has waned.

Below I will briefly sketch the Greenfield in which recent LBQ migrants build a home, before turning to portraits of its two identity cultures, one of which is waxing and the other waning, and of a related shift in the foundation that residents' ties are built on. I close by charting the centrality of change in the narratives that people told me and the consequences of this emphasis on transformation. Throughout, the chapter pursues two guiding questions. First, why are there multiple approaches to identity and community in Greenfield? Second, why are cultures and networks changing—from longstanding emphasis on lesbian feminist identities and networks, partially forged with Northampton residents, to an increasingly dominant post-identity politics and local, sexually integrated networks? The answers to both, we will see, rest in Greenfield itself—and in changing perceptions thereof.

Locating Greenfield

To understand Greenfield's identity culture and ties, we must understand the space it occupies in western New England and how the city has changed over the last decades—how it is a city on the move. Greenfield is, as informants readily report, a multifaceted city. It is both a struggling former-factory town and the county seat; it is home to the bustling Greenfields Market Cooperative Grocery, which was founded in the 1970s and recently expanded to a neighboring town, and to the regionally celebrated Greenfield Community College, as well as to the annual Green River Music and Balloon Festival, held on the college's expansive grounds; and it also can feel like a small town that can't catch an economic break.

Drive not three miles from Main Street and suddenly the land is nearly rural, abutting a string of former dairy-farming communities nestled on slopes above the valley that Greenfield occupies. In 2008, residents established the Greenfield Community Farm, located on municipal land on Greenfield's northern edge that served as the town's "poor farm" until the 1950s; the farm sits near tree farms and fields containing cows, sheep, and horses. Other portions of the city appear suburban: neighborhoods of old Victorians and colonials, bordered by more modest neighborhoods of Cape Cod, ranch, foursquare houses, and affordable housing developments. Many houses, in affluent and working-class neighborhoods alike, sport front porches and large yards. And many of these "suburban" neighborhoods are in walking distance of downtown. LBQ moms push strollers from gracious single-family homes to the Farmers Market, while LBQ community college students walk from apartments to Greenfield's new nightclub or to pick up burritos at Mesa Verde.

On summer afternoons, young LBQ women park on the side of a shady dirt road to swim in a remote, rocky section of the Green River that is popular with hippies and hipsters alike. Meanwhile, a two-mom family journeys to the Green River Swimming Pool, a dammed section of the same river a mile and a half from Main Street. Here, their children climb the jungle gym and share the beach with school friends from white, working-class longtime Greenfield families and the children of Greenfield's professional class (some of whom attend private or charter schools), as well as with Puerto Rican kids from Greenfield, Holyoke, and Springfield. A handful of LBQ women hike at the Wendell State Forest or picnic at Poet's Seat Tower, which provides a view of both downtown and the Berkshire foothills. Others shop at Wilson's Department Store downtown or drive to a local farm to pick berries. Some LBQ residents are avid cyclists who take weekend rides on county bikeways in northern and southern Franklin County. Nearly all LBQ residents travel regularly to Northampton, thirty minutes to the south on Interstate 91, to shop, dine, or visit friends.

By many accounts, Greenfield's school system has struggled over the last decades, as has its Main Street. Wilson's, one of the last remaining family-owned, independent department stores in the United States, still serves as its anchor, but the half-mile stretch along the center of downtown has witnessed high turnover and vacancy rates.[9] Yet, despite struggles borne of deindustrialization (a nonissue in San Luis Obispo and only a moderate one today in Ithaca and Portland), which came to a head in the 1980s, possibilities exploded in the few years before I began fieldwork in Greenfield and continuing for the five years I was in and out of the field. Located beside furniture, stationery, clothing, craft shops, and the occasional empty storefront, restaurants occupy more and more downtown space. Two Thai restaurants opened, as did an Indian restaurant, a brick oven pizzeria, a Mexican restaurant, a local foods restaurant and bar situated in an artfully restored Polish social club, a whiskey bar, a bar and restaurant owned by the founders of a local brewery, and a sandwich shop. The arts, too, is abundant in a volume that seems incongruous with the city's economic struggles. The "Arts Block" sits in a restored brick building and includes a café and performance space.[10] A former bank, stripped bare in the 1990s by a fraudulent international "investor" who promised to save the city, hosts theatre productions, and for a time a used bookstore with storefronts in more upscale Massachusetts cities, such as Amherst and Cambridge, operated adjacent to Greenfield Coffee—itself an offshoot of an Amherst-based chain.[11]

LBQ migrants have had an unmistakable, if quiet, role in this revitalization. As a marker of this, when I first began fieldwork in 2010, LBQ individuals were owners or partners in six downtown restaurants, constituting a notable and highly visible dimension of Greenfield's commercial change. However, they were not the initial pioneers, filling in spaces first opened in the 1970s and 1980s by college-educated men and women who migrated north from Northampton and Amherst and their colleges and universities, and west from Boston, primarily settling on the abundant acreage in surrounding hill towns and villages that had once served as dairy and other small, family farms. For these migrants, Greenfield, together with Brattleboro, Vermont (twenty minutes north of Greenfield on Interstate 91), provided a shopping and service center, as well as jobs in local industry, from factories to a hospital, local government, and social service agencies.[12] From the start, some of those moving to the Greenfield area as part of this broader resettling of the area by progressive newcomers were LBQ residents, many of them white feminists. Indeed, feminists (LBQ and otherwise) have long been associated with certain Greenfield nonprofits, such as a battered women's shelter and rape crisis center that have been around since the 1970s.[13] A 1997 article traces the high concentration of lesbians (long before the 2000 census marked the county as having the second highest proportion of lesbian couples in the United States).[14] However, many of the LBQ Greenfielders I spoke with emphasized that they believe that there was an increase in the local LBQ population beginning around 2000. And certainly around the same time LBQ-owned businesses began to constitute a very visible presence downtown.

To understand Greenfield one must consider a broader geography that includes hill towns or so-called bedroom communities (because most residents sleep in their rural home but commute to work and shop in neighboring towns like Greenfield) that attracted professionals to Franklin County in the 1970s and 1980s. One must also understand Northampton and Amherst, which serve as economic and cultural anchors in what some call the "Happy Valley."[15] Many LBQ migrants report that Greenfield's proximity to these anchors first drew them to the area. However, current LBQ residents are divided in how they approach this affluent portion of the southern Pioneer Valley, and especially Northampton. Some regard Greenfield as a northern outpost of Northampton, and others, primarily newer arrivals, present Greenfield as a valued alternative. On a practical level, Northampton serves as a perpetual resource, providing nightlife, social opportunities, and institutional support. But in a more subtle and perhaps more meaningful way, Northampton also serves as a yardstick for measuring identity and lifestyle. In the pages that follow, we will find that Northampton provides a touchstone that LBQ migrants—new and old—use to measure Greenfield's transformation. This produces acute awareness of Greenfield's changes, which, in turn, helps drive Greenfield's dynamic sense of identity and changing ties, specifically the movement toward post-identity politics and ambient community.[16]

Below the reader will find a greater space devoted to the experience of residents who reject identity politics. This is not happenstance. As I did in all the cities, I prioritized interviews with those who relocated within the last decade; nearly all these more recent residents celebrate post-identity politics and ambient community or a general sense of belonging forged with sexually heterogeneous neighbors with whom they share beliefs, politics, and practices. However, I nonetheless devote a disproportionate amount of space to the minority of residents who articulate a lesbian feminist orientation, because the identity culture heterogeneity that I found only in Greenfield offers broad-reaching lessons. I also attend to it because echoes of the lesbian feminist approach color life in Greenfield, even if its influence is waning.

Lesbian Feminist Longtimers

Most longtimers—those who relocated to Greenfield, and especially its surrounding hill towns, in the 1970s and 1980s—present themselves as "lesbian feminists." They see themselves through the lens of sexual identity; a common set of understandings about that identity undergirds ties, practices, and politics. Given that they live in the Pioneer Valley this should not surprise. After all, they regard themselves as populating an outpost of Northampton, which is renown among LBQ individuals for its lesbian-feminist identity-politics tradition. And some locate themselves among a lineage of lesbians and feminists who "returned to the land," and some have ties to "women's land," the shared acres on which women came to live in the 1970s, collectively and apart from a heterosexist society. You can picture these women: some fly a rainbow flag from their porch, others drive cars adorned with cat stickers and cluttered with gardening accoutrements, and still others have helped over the last decade to establish an archive of Pioneer Valley LBQ history.

Jo, a woman in her fifties who lives a ten-minute drive from downtown Greenfield, best embodies the lesbian feminist identity orientation of longtime LBQ residents; for that reason I highlight her words here. Jo's words, and my observation of her at events in Greenfield, such as on the Town Common during the Saturday Farmers Market or on the grass at a summertime Co-op Concert, also demonstrate how Greenfield's recent changes have shifted the ties of even longtime residents; a shift away from sexual identity–based networks and toward ties based on shared beliefs, practices, and politics. Jo described this change, quite aptly, as a move from "demographic" community to "geographic" community.[17] Yet, changes in Greenfield—that is, in LBQ residents' position in the city and in its broader cultural and economic dynamics—have not produced a wholesale change in Jo's ties; while her geographic community is expanding, her closest friends are lesbians like her, and she cultivates lesbian ties even as she also nurtures a geographic community with a heterogeneous group of locals who share her politics if not her sexual preferences.

Jo first moved to the Valley, specifically to Northampton, as a young woman almost thirty years ago. Sexual identity shaped her move. Referring to herself and the woman she was dating at the time, she said, "We wanted to live rurally where there was lesbian and women's community.... In 1979 this map was very small to me. It was Eugene, Oregon, and here." And, indeed, this is the life she built for herself: for nearly three decades, she has rooted herself in the lesbian feminist networks of this rural locale.

I interviewed Jo in her kitchen; we faced a bank of windows that frame rolling green hills. Her rural retreat seems worlds away from both Amherst and Northampton. But, crucially for Jo, that world—of Amherst and Northampton and their colleges and culture—is accessible, even if her house rests in hills closer to Greenfield.

Jo, who wears her hair short and favors loose button-down shirts and jeans, articulates her identity in black and white terms: "I'm a lesbian. . . . Through high school my sister was like dating and being all into boys and I was like, 'I don't think so.' . . . I was very much, you know, doing softball and riding horses. . . . I'm about to have my 35th anniversary of being a lesbian, and I intend to have my lesbian anniversary party—[a] sledding party." As her party planning indicates, a shared sexual identity provides a common foundation for her community, and she cultivates that community via women's softball, lesbian potlucks, and a women's history archive, and, as we'll see, by organizing an event—inspired by the Michigan Womyn's Festival—designed to "get the lesbians together."

The event, a performance of Carolyn Gage's "Lesbian Tent Revival," epitomized her desire to celebrate lesbian identity and to initiate ties predicated thereon. Held at Northampton's Unitarian Universalist Society, the night began with dinner, at which tables were organized around topics, including planning other events to "get the lesbians together." Then Gage walked in, adorned in a minister's robe, and took to the stage. After greeting the crowd she began singing "Age of the Clitoris" to the tune of "Age of Aquarius" and spoke of the import of valuing the "self-conscious lesbian." The crowd, which was composed almost entirely of women, mostly middle aged and older, cheered when Gage referred to the audience as a "miracle" for being constituted by "lesbian-identified women seeking lesbian company." Here, Gage and her audience celebrated themselves for *not* being "post-gay" or "post-mo"—for maintaining allegiance to identity politics. While they did not ordinarily spend evenings singing "Age of the Clitoris," the event nonetheless embodied the politics—and community—Greenfield's lesbian feminist longtimers forge with one another and with Northampton lesbians.[18]

And yet, despite Jo's firm identification as lesbian, woman, and feminist, she suggests that her ties increasingly extend beyond the type of community she sought to (quite intentionally) strengthen via the Lesbian Tent Revival. In Jo's words: "Until like 2001 or so . . . my community was more demographic than geographic and so I was really connected with lesbians in the community." Notably, her demographic ties spanned and extended beyond the Valley. While most of her lesbian connections were cultivated within western Massachusetts, her networks also extended well beyond the area. As one example, via Michigan Womyn's Music Festival she forged ties across the country. The "glue" connecting her to these individuals was, indisputably, shared sexual identity and the certainty that lesbian identity is life defining and provides a set of common experiences.

Within Massachusetts, her demographic ties concentrated in and around Northampton and Amherst. In the late 1980s, a job at an independent gift shop—a stalwart of Greenfield's downtown—strengthened her connection to Franklin County lesbians, but these ties, too, were predicated on being lesbians and being feminists. Jo happily described activities that undergirded these ties: "We would have these lesbian potlucks with twenty-five or thirty women in the '80s. Oh, the other big thing was softball . . . [and a women's outdoor organization]. Those were pretty much focused more around Amherst, Northampton. Not so much up here." She was also an active participant in Northampton's "Lesbian Home Show," which she described as "this annual event . . . that was a holiday sort of craft fair [and] potluck party [with] dancing . . . and it was the absolute see and be seen event." However, after getting to know each other on the softball field, more and more women came together to Greenfield-area potlucks. She and a former partner also joined a lesbian couples group, primarily composed of those who lived outside of Northampton. They selected a discussion topic for each meeting and shared a potluck meal. Jo recalled, "There have always been lesbians here [in Greenfield] and so I would know the lesbians here, but I really didn't get to know much else, the rest of the town or people in the town."

However, something has changed. She has begun to cultivate local ties; she has found networks within Greenfield and surrounding small towns that are open and welcoming. Jo suggests that the terrorist attacks on September 11, 2001, marked a turning point, when she began to think about building local connections that spanned identity groups. She said, "After September 11 there was all these people getting together in like church communities or whatever and I was feeling like I didn't have a place like that. And I wanted to connect and I got involved. That fall of 2001 was when I got involved in local food stuff, in the, like, local grown food thing." To her delight, she found that she was welcome in these sexually heterogeneous spaces. After years of assuming that she needed to inhabit a separate sphere composed of lesbians, this was a welcome surprise. Soon, she began participating in a weekly peace vigil in Greenfield, held on Saturday mornings at the Farmers Market on the Town Common, which sits alongside Main Street near the Greenfield Town Hall. Indeed, I would often see her standing on the Common with a small group of individuals, mostly middle-aged and older, holding signs calling for peace. The vigil in turn drew her into other Greenfield networks: "I used to shop at Stop and Shop in Hadley [near Northampton]. . . . I was in Greenfield every Saturday [for the vigil] and I started shopping at the Co-op. . . . So I got very sort of Greenfield focused and got to know people." Jo appears in my field notes at the Farmers Market and the Harvest Festival. Her byline also appears in the local paper, for which she writes a column. Moreover, she has become active in the rural town where she lives—advocating for the preservation of wildlife and participating in town events.

While this shift could be, as Jo describes it, an idiosyncratic by-product of 9/11, there are two reasons to be skeptical that this event alone transformed her networks. First, other LBQ residents who have lived in the Valley for a long period articulate a similar shift—that is, a movement from lesbian to sexually heterogeneous local ties. Jo's story, in other words, is not as novel as she supposes. Second, the timing of her shifting community coincides with a broader shift in Greenfield: the moment at which that new wave of LBQ individuals—those who, having adapted to present-day Greenfield, would be at home in Ithaca—started moving to Franklin County. Jo herself provides an account of how Greenfield had to change in order for her to access geographic networks. Thus, while 9/11 may have stirred Jo's interest in forging networks spanning sexual identity groups, a changing city made that new community possible.

What changed? As we stared out her dining room window one afternoon, Jo provided a narrative of how Greenfield has changed, and with that change, how she found a community quite different from the Lesbian Home Show and lesbian-couple potlucks. She describes herself now as "one hundred percent out," whereas in the past she was more cautious—especially when, years ago, she worked as an educator:

> 100 percent completely. . . . Through the '80s, I was not able to be out. It was before there was a nondiscrimination law in the state. The guy who had the job before I did . . . he had come out to the kids as a gay man a couple weeks before he left his job and the organization had a nondiscrimination policy that included sexual orientation at that point and after he came out to the kids the board met and took sexual orientation out of the nondiscrimination policy. . . . And so I knew that going into it. . . . So I could like sort of like shut myself down and then open myself back up. . . . And I got lesbian-bated. A bunch of the kids would call me "lezzy" or the boys . . . one group of boys . . . they called me "He-Man faggot."

This was not limited to work with children. Despite her love of contra dancing and Greenfield's national reputation as a contra-dance capital, she avoided dancing in Greenfield.[19] She notes that indicators of acceptance are now abundant and that the LBQ population has increased; together, these new conditions make her feel much more at home in the contra-dancing world and beyond. Jo described one time when she went contra dancing by herself:

> God, at one time in Greenfield—and Greenfield's better now—but there was a time where you couldn't dance, you know, you got shit. I mean I would dance in the men's line and dance with a woman partner. And then literally one time . . . there was this like an instantaneous moment where . . . I was in the men's line and so I went to swing this woman, you know, to the next thing, and she looked at me and went and literally walked away from the set. Ruined the whole set.

Today, she joins forces with heterosexual environmentalists and is otherwise deeply engaged in local food and farming initiatives—which are usually dominated by the same kinds of people who caused her to stop going to contra dances. She also described going to a wild-game supper at a technical high school in the area: "I was one of the very few women at this. And I'm sure the only lesbian. . . . So it was just like this other world. . . . So the food has given me this entrée into these other worlds."

Jo reports that freedom for LBQ residents to become more "visible" and the increasing avenues to join the wider community developed simultaneously. She said: "Lavender Lips [a now defunct online community for Greenfield lesbians] has made lesbian stuff more visible in Franklin County, too . . . and the whole 'we're here, we're queer, we eat brunch.' Those things . . . [and the] lesbian owned restaurants in downtown Greenfield." She also can no longer imagine heterosexual women ruining a contra dance to avoid having a woman as a partner; this reflects her broader sense of increasing safety and acceptance in the Greenfield area. These two things— increasing forthrightness about sexual identity and difference and desire to join sexually heterogeneous networks and institutions—took shape from a sense of increasing safety and acceptance in Greenfield; from the decreasing likelihood that children will call a tall woman who dresses in button-down shirts a "He-man faggot,"—and increasing confidence that the LBQ population is growing, both in terms of numbers and visibility. Thus, at precisely the moment when she might have located her demographic community in Greenfield and environs rather than in Northampton, Jo finds that she takes pleasure in geographic ties—some of which, to be sure, she forges with LBQ individuals.

To be certain, Jo's transformation has not been wholesale. She still very much identifies as "lesbian" and she has not forsaken her ties to others who identify in the same manner. Jo says, in stark contrast to most recent migrants, "I'm still part of the lesbian community, I'm still involved." Among other recent local events she mentioned her participation in a women's history collective and a women's singing group, as well as her local promotion of the Michigan Womyn's Music Festival. She added, "I mean my close friends are lesbians." Thus her ties—and even the ways she emphasizes her lesbian identity in "mixed" company (e.g., by openly advancing LBQ events in conversation with straight men)—remain distinct from those of most more recent migrants, few of whom consider themselves part of a "lesbian community."

The endurance of Jo's lesbian networks and lesbian feminist identity, even against the backdrop of increasing acceptance and a growing LBQ population, can be explained in two ways. First, Northampton remains a center of lesbian life, thus anchoring longtimers'—those who belong to the first migration cohort—lesbian feminist identities. For Jo, Northampton remains a bastion of lesbian identity and networks, and she describes the city as a perpetual destination for everything from film viewing to softball and academic panels. Surely many new arrivals to Northampton would disagree with this characterization of their city as a bastion of identity politics. But regardless, the disagreement itself is evidence of a larger truth: Northampton serves a symbolic function as much as a practical function and embodies an ideal of a lesbian community. For many, it represents the earlier Valley Jo first encountered on moving to Massachusetts—a place she sought for its lesbian feminist communities and for being the greatest bastion of lesbian-feminist identity politics in the United States (at least for white, middle-class women). Second, as Jo indicates by referring to a local lesbian networking site and the "Big Gay Brunch" (both of which have since fizzled), she no longer has to travel to Northampton to tap into these networks. By maintaining ties to other longtimers who, like Jo, long approached Franklin County as a rural outpost of Northampton, and who turn to Northampton as a social resource, Jo can renew her lesbian identity and ties closer to home. In other words, she is not immune to Greenfield—in fact, she is quite mindful of how Greenfield's changes have altered her social life—but by keeping one foot in Northampton, and part of another in Greenfield's network of longtime lesbian feminist residents, and still another in her memories of the Greenfield of yesteryear, her transformation is more subtle than it might otherwise be.[20]

The combination of an intimate circle of lesbians, as well as her broader food and activist-based networks in Greenfield, leave Jo quite satisfied. She told me: "I have an outrageously fabulous community. . . . It feels like geographically and demographically it's like been this blend from that original sort of demographic to now it's really feels like both." Her satisfaction with her networks was apparent when I watched her dance in the Energy Park as folk musicians played to a mixed crowd (nearly all white and mostly middle class and mostly heterosexual but with a notable sprinkling of LBQ individuals on picnic blankets and chasing children at the adjacent playground). Her satisfaction was equally apparent when she spoke quietly with other peace activists (again nearly all white, middle class, and heterosexual) at the Town Common.[21]

While I have given Jo's story a great deal of attention here, I do so because she embodies the broader story of much of her migration cohort. Jo is far from alone in her experience. Her words capture a broader trend among those who have lived in greater Greenfield since the 1970s and 1980s, and one that even extends to some LBQ individuals who have recently moved to Greenfield after residing in the Pioneer Valley for a decade or more, typically in or near Northampton. Like Jo, they have networks throughout the Valley that partially (and to varying degrees) insulate them from the immediate effects of Greenfield's transformations.

Take, for instance, Eleanor. She is a recent migrant to Greenfield, but moved to Northampton in the 1990s after hearing Barbara Walters refer to the city as "Lesbianville, USA." Eleanor identifies as lesbian and regards her sexuality as innate. Indeed, by way of introduction she told me how happy she is that members of her family share her general approach to sexual and gender identity. She said, "When I told my mom [I was having a mastectomy] she said, 'Oh honey, you are going to save your life and be the boy you were meant to be.' . . . And I got to hook up with this really great plastic surgeon who made me a nice boy's chest, which I wanted my whole life."

Eleanor's closest friend is lesbian, but, also paralleling Jo's experience, she takes delight in entering heterogeneous networks in Greenfield. Describing her "sense of community" in Greenfield, she said, "I feel like there's a really nice mix of everyone and everyone's very tolerant of each other." When I asked her to specify the places in which she feels most comfortable she listed a number of local businesses, several of which are LBQ owned. And when I asked her to describe the "communities of which you're a part," without hesitation she said, "I'm a member of the Co-op . . . and I also have been a member of the community kitchen. . . . I'm in a cancer writing group . . . and a yoga class at the Y and I do another writing class." Eleanor also described feelings of connection that come close to the sense of "ambient community" that women in Ithaca articulate and that many newer residents of Greenfield also experience. She said that she frequents the same coffee shop every morning and that the baristas there—three straight men—"are almost my best friends. . . . I have coffee with one of them almost every morning." In the same breath, she described dining out frequently in Greenfield and the sense of conviviality this generates. In this way, while Greenfield is not the uninterrupted bubble of inclusion that she depicts Northampton as being, for Eleanor there are enough safe spaces in Greenfield to experience belonging and broad sense of geographic membership that extends well beyond her intimate ties to other LBQ individuals.

Why does Eleanor, like Jo, maintain a lesbian identity, but, to use Jo's framework, increasingly turn to geographic rather than demographic networks? Like Jo, Eleanor describes Greenfield as in transition—as still somewhat homophobic (compared to Northampton). Like others, she describes occasional street harassment and some uncertainty about how neighbors will think of her once they learn that she identifies as lesbian. Yet for her, it is changing in ways that, directly and indirectly, inform what it feels like to be LBQ there. She said, "There's some pretty ignorant people in this town that reminds me of down south and what feels like homophobia. . . . They're a little more biased than they are in let's say Northampton or a lot of towns." Yet, Eleanor nonetheless expresses optimism about Greenfield's future and finds that the city offers welcome surprises: "I have to say I've been surprised that a lot of men are liberal here." She also expresses surprise at "how much it's grown in the past I'd say maybe three years. It feels good to me in a way. . . . The buildings seem to be getting refurbished and used.

It seems like there used to be a lot of empty buildings here. . . . Like it's going to raise the level of, I don't know, our community value or something."
Eleanor's experience of Greenfield as betwixt and between leaves her, like
Jo, with ties that are gravitating away from the demographic to the geographic, but that leaves her lesbian-feminist identity politics as yet relatively
unchanged. Perhaps, though, to borrow her language, the level of the "community value" will increase enough that her identity will eventually change,
too—becoming more like that of the new migration cohort.

Thus, longstanding LBQ residents (like Jo) and some middle-aged and
older women who are new to Greenfield but who have lived in the Pioneer Valley for a decade or more (like Eleanor) rely on identity politics as
a lodestar. Their approach shares attributes with San Luis Obispo's identity
culture. However, a Greenfield identity politics places much greater emphasis on feminism, even entangling "lesbian" and "feminist" in the manner
associated with classical 1970s lesbian-feminist identity politics; much like
Northampton (at least as they describe it), they are at once lesbian and feminist identified (in subtle contrast to the lesbian identity politics of San Luis
Obispo).[22] This ought not surprise in the Valley, which has an enduring reputation as a bastion of lesbian *and* feminist identity politics.

However, even these longstanding residents are not totally inured from
local change. Rather, while their identities remain (thus far) relatively steady,
their networks are in flux. As Jo so aptly puts it, as local conditions change,
opportunity for engagement along geographic rather than demographic lines
expands. Of course, the two are not mutually exclusive, and geographic ties
are not devoid of demographic connections. That is, they are not truly forging ties with *all* local residents based solely on shared geography. Rather, even
as their identity orientation remains fairly constant, they feel free—and even
driven—to take advantage of opportunities to engage around shared politics, tastes, commitment to voluntarism, or self-expression.

Post-Identity-Politics Newcomers

The more recent migrants I spoke with use a much wider variety of terms
to describe themselves and also emphasize their integration into the nooks
and crannies of Greenfield and downplay sexual identity, while maintaining
a commitment to being out and proud about their sexuality; these are the
core features of their post-identity politics. They also present themselves in
opposition to "Northampton lesbians" whose lives they regard as organized
around sexuality and affluence. Mirroring LBQ Ithacans, Greenfield's post-
identity-politics newcomers juggle twin desires: a wish to be known for facets

of the self that extend beyond sexual identity and a commitment to being out and open about their sexuality. As in Ithaca, they also aim to forge ties predicated on areas of connection that extend beyond shared sexual identity, such as shared place, beliefs, practices, and politics. Most describe a cautious sense of belonging in Greenfield, predicated on such areas of common ground. As in Ithaca, this provides a sense of "ambient community," or a generalized sense of belonging, albeit one that is slightly less expansive and less secure than that which Ithacans articulate.

Evidence of LBQ newcomers' membership in a variety of spheres of local life was particularly evident at community events that draw other middle- and upper-middle-class residents, many of whom espouse progressive political attitudes, such as weekly Co-op Concerts at the Energy Park along the railroad tracks in downtown Greenfield, the annual Harvest Supper, and the yearly Green River Music and Balloon Festival on the grounds of the community college. However, it was also evident in everyday exchanges between LBQ and heterosexual residents over restaurant counters, on sidewalks, and in stores. Here, they engage in the minutiae of everyday life—buying groceries, pumping gas, securing a car repair estimate—that is easy to overlook but, as informants report, a key component of their sense of belonging.

Below, I introduce the core commonality that binds these newcomers: their insistent presentation as multifaceted and "beyond labels"—as being post-identity politics. As an extension of this, they speak of how Greenfield and Northampton are distinct; a discourse that underlines their distance from what they regard as a more traditional identity politics. Next, I detail their commitment to being forthright about their sexuality. Finally, we'll explore the particulars of their "geographic" ties—that is, local ties based on shared beliefs, practices, and politics that provide a sense of "ambient community" or a broad sense of belonging. However, I also trace how and why LBQ individuals in Greenfield, in contrast to those in Ithaca, articulate little nostalgia for what Jo describes as "demographic" ties or lesbian community, as it has been traditionally defined by the pioneers of Northampton and elsewhere.

"Beyond" Labels

Some newcomers resist identity labels; indeed, their resistance to labels surpasses even that of the LBQ residents of Ithaca whom we have met. One, a woman with short hair who is in her forties, said, "I hate the fact when you do identify a certain way then you become a sex act . . . so I've just never really said one way or another and most people just assumed." She said that being identified by her partner's gender "makes about as much sense to me" as being grouped "because we both drive red cars." A social worker concurs: "I guess I'd identify as a lesbian but I forget that sometimes, which is nice. I like to think of myself just as a person, but if I had to identify that's what I would identify as." Another, a forty-something professor and parent, said: "I'm just [Sam]." A woman, in her fifties, who lives on rural acreage outside Greenfield, contrasted herself to some other LBQ women her age, specifically in Northampton: "They still identify very much as lesbian and I don't. You didn't ask me do I really identify as being a lesbian. . . . I don't." Here, she revealed her expectation that I would assume she identified as lesbian—and expressed her surprise (and abundant relief) that I had not. Even though many of the newcomers resist labels, the influence of the long-timers is still felt in the fact that "lesbian" serves as a touchstone via which they communicate their rejection of identity politics.

Seated on a sofa in the living room of her refurbished farmhouse near downtown, a retiree in her seventies instructed: "Maybe it's my age, but I'm not into it for an identity. I already have an identity. I'm not in that twenty-something-year-old-thing where I'm trying to figure out who I am and then I can say I'm gay. That's like *one* of the aspects of me and it's not the main one, frankly." While she suggests that her approach to identity may relate to her age, my findings suggest otherwise. LBQ newcomers of a variety of ages and backgrounds share her post-identity politics—from retirees like Ann to recent college graduates, and from doctors to bartenders and farm workers.

Some provided detailed explanations for how and why they identify by absenting themselves from categorization. Sam, who told me that they (Sam's preferred pronoun) identify as "just Sam," clarified, "So mostly I identify as a lesbian, you know, for political purposes. . . . I mean like in terms of being counted, you know, like on [the] census . . . you know, but I think of myself as somewhat transgender and you know butch and mostly just as Sam. Yeah, I don't feel like I fit really well and neatly in a box." Sam values Greenfield as a place where one can exist outside the "box."

Sounding more like those in Ithaca, another intimated that outside of our interview, she generally succeeds in avoiding affixing an identity label to herself. She said: "I usually don't really launch into labels or whatnot, but I would just identify as queer. . . . I think that I like queer just because it feels very inclusive of all the ways that people can identify, and, also, to a certain extent, a fluidity of identification." And recall that Lori, a professional in her early thirties, altogether refused to offer a label when I asked, "Tell me about how you identify?": "You know, it's kind of funny, 'cause I don't, really. I don't really identify. I think that humans are humans, and the sexuality spectrum is really broad, and at different times we fall at different places. And I feel like most people are kind of in the middle somewhere. It's kind of a funny thing."

Maggie, who is an educator and mother in her mid-thirties, recently moved from Northampton. She told me she identifies as "gay" but was very quick to qualify the term: "For a long time I didn't like being considered lesbian or gay. It felt too clubby. I've always hated the parades. . . . I mean this year I went to the Gay Pride Parade in Northampton for like a minute because I was trying to go shoe shopping with my straight friend. . . . I also start to feel like it's a club that I'm not [a] part of. . . . Like everybody's so happy to be gay and like it's this huge thing for them and it's never really been a huge thing for me, it's just been you know, kind of a matter of fact." When I asked her to reflect on why she does not feel that she belongs in the "gay club," she said it relates to her more general approach to identity—not just to sexuality. She said:

> I don't have any sort of identities that I like to join groups around. . . . I had this friend of mine who lives in Northampton and . . . for her it's a huge part of her life. Like she would never miss a Gay Pride and when I've gone to parties at her house it's all gay people and she's very in it. It's very interesting to me because like I'm just so different. . . . So I think that's why I didn't identify as [gay]. It just felt like dishonest. It's like yes, I have girlfriends but I can't really say that I'm a lesbian because I don't like parades.

Instead, she conceives of herself as a partner, mother, educator, and sister, and as someone who bikes and takes long walks. In addition, she resists not only membership in a "gay club" but also in other identity categories, such as with other adoptive parents.

Some are quite mindful of the dominance of post-identity politics in Greenfield. As we'll see, many of the people I spoke with conceive of themselves in opposition to "Northampton lesbians," whom they perceive to be lesbian identified and focused almost exclusively on nurturing ties with other lesbians. A mother in her thirties boasts that, to her, it feels like there are more LBQ women in Greenfield "than New York, but . . . it's just like, yeah. It's not primarily gay. . . . It's like a lesbian city council or a lesbian math teacher or a lesbian YMCA worker." Here she suggests that sexual difference is not ignored, but that it does not outshout other facets of identity, such as one's position (city councilor) or profession (math teacher).

Several specified that they did not always approach their identity in the manner they do in Greenfield, and that they have seen others transform on moving to the city. Here, they offer clear narratives of how the city shaped their identity. A middle-aged woman offered a general account about how where she has lived throughout her adulthood has shaped her identity: "I think it wasn't until I moved to Boston, honestly, and I started meeting a lot of lesbians and like then I really started to identify like that." Another said that, in Greenfield, "I have shifted." She elaborated, "I don't feel like I have to hide who I am here. I don't live in any sense of fear of that"—whereas in the past, "I had to be careful with my pronouns." Another observed others' identities change after moving to Greenfield: "I see other women who have moved here . . . feeling like they can just be themselves and it doesn't matter who my partner is, it doesn't matter who I am, it doesn't matter that I'm a lesbian, it doesn't matter that I identify with being bisexual or whatever else." Recently, on traveling, she was reminded of how distinct conditions for LBQ residents are in Greenfield than in some other places. In Greenfield, she said, "it's not like I walk into the bar up here and somebody says, 'Hey who you dating?' . . . Which is what I experienced in Australia. It's like, 'Where's your man?' I'm like, 'I don't really need a man.'" She also recalled how she identified differently in a different place and time. After college, she said, "we were still very much a lesbian couple with lesbian friends and stuff like that. And there was just this community and it felt really comfortable." In contrast, in Greenfield thinking of herself as lesbian is "not palatable. . . . Here, I just knew more and more . . . I can be gay. I can be straight and be bisexual. It doesn't really matter. I can just be me."

This way of thinking about one's identity—as "just me"—informs talk of others. When I asked a woman to describe her ties she said, "They're all different ages and I really have no idea of their orientation. I'd speculate mostly straight." Ann, a retiree, also said, "I don't even think about that [whether or not friends are straight]. I'd have to count; I mean, literally I would have to count." She spent a few minutes demonstrating her point by categorizing her friends one by one as "gay," "straight," and "bisexual." After a moment she shook her head and said, "I don't think that way, I really don't. So I would have to actually make lists and count. . . . It's not where we relate." For her part, before establishing a home in Greenfield, Arlie underestimated the degree to which the city constitutes what she calls a "lesbian bubble." By her account, she missed this because Greenfield's LBQ newcomers focus on "normal life"—that is, a less overtly LBQ-oriented life.[23] The result, she suggests, is that this approach actually complicates efforts to identify LBQ residents. She said: "It's just an awesome little lesbian bubble. It's just not in your face all the time, because a lot of them have families and live a different kind of lifestyle, where it's not, 'Hi, I'm a queer person, let's be queer together' kinda thing. They're just normal people who have their normal life." Another specified that Greenfield calls out this desire for "normalcy"— and the ability to achieve it: "I just want to be normal. I just want a normal life and as I have I think become more comfortable here and more confident here I realized that I [could be]."[24]

Echoing this, LBQ newcomers suggest over and again that Greenfield is a place LBQ individuals live well-rounded lives that not only acknowledge sexual identity and difference but also emphasize other dimensions of life and self, from work to family, and from food to community. This, as we will see below, reflects and supports a broader ethos about Greenfield as a place that is innovative or cutting edge in its return to the "basics": to a modern vision of a more traditional way of life or what one resident describes as *"Back to the Future* Town." This ethos is apparent not only in LBQ residents' words but also in, for instance, the city's website, which at once marks Greenfield as having a "quintessential American Main Street" and as a revitalizing place with an Urban Renewal Zone and Amtrak service to Burlington, New York, and DC.[25] Here, past and future—a quintessential Main Street and loft apartments in an urban renewal zone—intermingle. In addition, the Franklin County Chamber of Commerce boasts that "farmland vistas beckon, along with the taste of freshly-picked fruit or the creative cuisine of an expert chef. . . . Our chefs take pride in knowing their farming neighbors."[26] Borrowing from this broader logic, LBQ newcomers use talk of "normalcy" not to refer to what they regard as a narrower middle-class "normalcy" (which they associate with Northampton), but to gesture to a return to the basics or to life's roots. In Greenfield, lifestyle, broadly conceived, can outshine a sense of self and connection oriented around narrow identities.[27]

This embrace of the "normal" or wholesome also applies to that most "normal" of institutions: marriage. More often than not, LBQ newcomers agree with mainstream gay, lesbian, bisexual, transgender, and queer (GLBTQ) organizations in their push for marriage equality. Many are legally married to or intend to marry their partners. Several got married in a (relatively) traditional wedding ceremony. Many are raising children. That is, despite the fact that some describe themselves as "queer" or reject identity labels—seeming indicators of a nontraditional approach to sexual identity and difference—they embrace their more "traditional" unions and family units.[28] Dora explained why she and her (former) female partner chose to have a wedding and to consider themselves married (before same-sex marriage was legally recognized in Massachusetts). She said, "We wrote a little thing [for the ceremony] about what it meant to use the word marriage because we thought about whether or not we wanted to use that word. Because

I'd always thought marriage was very oppressive, very patriarchal and you know, like it's a way to subjugate women basically and why would you want to imitate that even if it was with two women? But we thought about what it means to make that kind of lifetime commitment and become a family and we realized that the word marriage really sort of brought all those implications without us having to create some new structure and so we decided to use that word." This approach to "normalcy" complements their framing of Greenfield as a place that is both somewhat traditional and also progressive or future oriented, in which LBQ families may find a quiet and unassuming life; a city in which they can love nontraditionally even as they live an otherwise traditional life.

Post-identity politics, not surprisingly, impacts the value LBQ newcomers place on living alongside others who share their sexual identity. Their answers to questions about their ideal city, specifically about the proportion of residents who would share their identity in a city, reflect their post-identity politics. Most of the people with whom I spoke in Greenfield care more about other areas of common ground, such as shared beliefs. A typical response from these newcomers eschews the import of the question: "[It is] less [important] that people share my sexual identity, more so that they are understanding." Another described her friends by saying, "I really have no idea of their orientation." Still another said, "Certainly a number of friends are [lesbian], but that's not why primarily we connect. . . . It's been really nice that we connect through activities. . . . It's not one of those, 'I'm gay you're gay we should be friends.' You're friends because you're friends." A twenty-something nurse said: "Oh gosh it doesn't matter. Probably the more people that are gay probably the more drama there's going to be so I don't care. To me it doesn't really matter so much I guess. Whatever."

A small business owner who maintains a rich circle of friends elaborated:

> I mean I guess the gay thing is not that important to me. . . . I mean the percentage would be more important to me if it was like people who, I don't know, like dogs. Like even like liking dogs would be more important to me. . . . I wonder like what is the defining characteristic of the people with whom I would like to share my community? I don't know, humble, humility. I'd like to live in a place that's like 100% humble.

Julie, a writer in her early thirties who is politically active, echoes this:

> I wouldn't want to be totally isolated in a queer bubble. I kind of already lived a life like that. In San Francisco. Not really on purpose, but it just happens. . . .

I was in it, and I was always pretty aware of it, but it's not reality. I like to have a mix of people around me. If anything, I would include more people from different countries or ethnic backgrounds into my population, more so than having more queer people in it.

Notably, each of these women had lived in a place that felt like a "bubble," such as San Francisco. And Julie suggests that she did not seek or even desire the bubble in San Francisco, but that "it just happens." In Greenfield, she and others like her find that something else "just happens"; they turn away from identity politics and toward connections that are only narrowly forged around shared sexual identity. But at least a few people I spoke with mentioned an important precondition: sexual identity can be ancillary in part because Greenfield is more and more accepting of sexual difference. One person said that being around others who are LBQ is "not important," and yet was very clear that "the acceptance of it is very important. Other people being the same, not important." When I paused for a moment, she clarified, "It might be important for the kids just to see other families. Maybe two or three percent [should be LBQ]."[29]

This insistence that one does not need to live around many other LBQ individuals is but one way in which Greenfield residents seek to distinguish themselves from residents of Northampton. Like residents of the other study cities, Greenfield's post-identity-politics newcomers communicate who they are, in part, by telling stories about who they are not. However, in Greenfield this mechanism is particularly pronounced, as they often accomplish this by emphasizing distinctions not between other people in Greenfield but by talking about how Greenfield is distinct from neighboring Northampton. They present Northampton as an anti-Greenfield—as a place in which LBQ residents emphasize identity politics and prioritize ties to other LBQ residents. In their imaginary, Northampton's LBQ residents would uniformly answer my question about their ideal city by stating a desire for a place entirely populated by lesbians.

One compared Greenfield lesbians to those in Northampton: "[In] Northampton there's been a lot of visible lesbians for a long time and [they are] out as lesbians. Greenfield lesbians were everywhere and they were in key roles and doing different things, but not as overtly. You know . . . [they were] sort of just doing their thing and lesbian wasn't the focus." Another echoes this. After telling me that she believes that there are equal numbers of LBQ residents in Greenfield and Northampton, she specified that identities are different in the two cities. She said, "I think it's a different type of queer." I asked, "How so?" and she said, "I think it's a toned-down type of queer [in

Greenfield]. . . . I think in Northampton they're kind of maybe fighting their own battles, whether either 'coming out' as themselves or 'coming out' as a family. So they're people . . . who are raising children and . . . dealing with you know 'coming out' in that way or helping their children deal with whatever in schools." However, she also specified that "I certainly know queer families in Greenfield"—suggesting that the difference she wishes to convey hinges on one's sense of sexual identity, not life stage or family structure.

A small-business owner proposes that differences between the cities in the way residents "do" queer reflects a general difference in their priorities:

> When you're in Northampton and you work in a restaurant everybody's like, "Well, what else do you do?" Like you must be a student or an artist or something and I wasn't and I liked how [in Greenfield] everyone was like, "What are you growing this year?" You know, like, "Do you have any extra seedlings?" Like everybody talks about their gardens and how they're brewing beer in the bathroom, and I really liked the fact that people were settled here in Greenfield and doing interesting things.

Another, a forty-something educator, echoes this, drawing parallels between class and sexual identity in Amherst and Northampton:

> With the lesbians that I knew in Amherst [and Northampton] . . . [they are] maybe slightly more sporty, more you know, caught up with—and this is not a judgment—but you know, wanting to drive a nicer car, wanting to you know, sort of be slightly more straightlaced middle class. And then the Greenfield folks . . . tend to try to be people . . . who have a sort of, loyalty to this community. . . . Or they really are looking for some sort of connection to the whole, you know, ecological or green side of things. Or the homeschool side of things, or the . . . more to the whole town culture.

Here, "straightlaced middle class" literally refers to how they express class position ("nicer cars"), but it also points to how they approach sexuality: in what she regards as a flashy or even ostentatious manner. In so doing, she posits a relation between one's city and one's sexual identity and suggests that ways of doing sexual identity are inextricable from the culture of the place you live.

Narratives about how the Northampton resident is distinct from the Greenfield resident underline the degree to which Greenfield's newcomers understand their city as distinct from what they regard as the prototypical lesbian enclave. In addition, the fact that they frequently volunteer references to Northampton when answering seemingly unrelated questions underlines the centrality of Northampton in their imaginations.[30] Clearly, the way they frame Northampton in comparison to Greenfield is quite distinct from that of lesbian feminist longtimers—but Northampton constitutes an equally powerful reference point for both groups; it is a goalpost against which Greenfield's LBQ residents measure themselves and their town. Indeed, it is when newcomers talk of Northampton that they reveal just how important their post-identity politics is to them.

Despite being "beyond labels," most regard being out as a responsibility or an inevitability. Here, they share with an earlier migration cohort commitment to being forthright about their sexuality, but they regard this forthrightness as separate from any need to label or explicitly identify one's sexuality. Having relocated from neighboring Northampton, a forty-something medical professional had anticipated a smaller LBQ population in Greenfield, as well as greater hesitancy among LBQ residents about being "out" and "proud." She said, "Surprisingly I've met a lot. . . . It feels like we have a big population of [openly] gay people. It almost feels like I meet as many gay people in this town as I do straight people." Thus, LBQ newcomers to Greenfield are at once open about their sexual identity and difference and downplay the import thereof.

A woman in her thirties, Logan, answered my question about how "out" she is by saying that she is totally out, despite occasional homophobia in Greenfield. However, she specifies that her ability to be out emerged with increasing acceptance:

> Completely, like 100%. Like the other day, somebody drops off *The Rainbow Times* at [her business], which is fine. . . . But these guys came in and they were like, "That's a magazine for gays!" And they were really freaked out about it. . . . There's still that element of the hill town like total backwoods Yankee like homophobia. . . . I remember walking down the street in Greenfield I don't know maybe 2001 or 2002 and having like a carful of boys like follow me like menacingly . . . like *Boys Don't Cry* style. And I don't think that happens anymore.

A more recent migrant, Ann, suggests that she is out in Greenfield not *despite* the local culture, but, instead, *because* of it. Ann said that she can be out about all facets of herself because, "Everybody else seems to be wanting the same thing. . . . You know this area is called Happy Valley not for no reason. There's a lot of ex-hippies who live here, people who are disfranchised one way or another either through economics or education or orientation or politics . . . and so we tend to clump together and form a body, you know. So there's a lot of leeway. . . . I really love that."

Most others concur, and yet even some who are fully out express reticence about this—because they want to ensure that their sexuality is not perceived as the most important part of their identity. For instance, two middle-aged white women dodged my question about how "out" they are: "I'm no more out about being a lesbian than anybody else is about being heterosexual. I just live my life." After a moment her partner clarified, "But we're fairly out here. I mean everybody at work knows," and her partner added, "[even] the pizza guy" knows. A younger woman, a writer in her early thirties, concurs. On "coming out" she said, "I didn't really have to do any of that. It was just kinda like, 'I'm a human.'" A nursing assistant in her fifties also said, "I guess it depends on your definition of what [being out] means. I think, for some people, it kinda means wearing their sexuality on the surface and on their sleeve, and, in that way, I don't feel like I do that. But I also don't hide who I am and the relationship that I'm in. . . . And so I'm not 'in,' I'm not 'out.' I don't care anymore. I'm just me." A much older woman, a retiree, suggested that being "out" in Greenfield means openly sharing facets of the self that include but also extend well beyond sexuality. She said that one of her favorite of Greenfield's attributes is "that I get to express the many parts of myself pretty easily, openly. They're welcomed."

In practice, such women are quite out. The nursing assistant clarified that for her the sense that coming out should be ancillary does not necessitate dishonesty. Instead, she shares facets of her life at work and in her neighborhood without resorting to labels or immediately announcing her sexuality. She described how this unfolds at work:

> I work [at a hospital] and when I first started out there it was like, you know I'm just going to be me. So they used to talk about their boyfriends and one day I turned around and I said, "Well, my wife . . ." And they're like, "Your what?" and I'm like, "Yeah, you know, I've been married to my wife." And they're like, "Oh, okay. Cool." And we chitchat back and forth and it just becomes about people. It's not about the sex. But I think again that's about living here.

Thus, while she does not announce her sexual identity, she is committed to being forthright about her wife; this is not a facet of herself or her life that she is willing to hide.

Thus, most newcomers wish for their sexuality to be known and acknowledged, but they do not wish to be known *by* that identity or status. In the words of the aforementioned writer, they wish for a world in which one is simply regarded as "human." Short of that, they want sexual difference to be one part of a broader portrait others paint of them, not the primary lens through which others see them. Of course, as some of their accounts suggest, this desire—to be "out" and to be regarded as multifaceted—emerges from the city ecology: from a contemporary Greenfield that, via growing acceptance, the expanding presence of LBQ households, and broad narratives of the city as a welcoming place—enables this self-presentation and understanding.[31]

Ambience without Nostalgia

Paralleling this dual commitment to being out and to being "beyond labels" is the appreciation that these newcomers feel for ties that emerge from shared beliefs, practices, and politics rather than shared sexual identity. That variety of connection is particularly interesting considering the *lack* of variety in other ways. Greenfield's newcomers tend to look similar to one another—they are mostly white and mostly middle class. And while they belong to sexually heterogeneous networks and related organizations, those networks are primarily constituted by others who share the person's socioeconomic status and race. White, LBQ residents who farm, for instance, tend to socialize with other white farmers—regardless of sexual identity; the mothers of young children socialize with the (mostly heterosexual) parents of their children's friends. That stratification by race and class, however, came up only occasionally in my conversations. Instead, friendships with straight men and women were mentioned by almost everyone.

Indeed, many of the newcomers I spoke with depict what I described in Ithaca as a sense of "ambient community": feelings of belonging and connection that arise from an assortment of ties. The ties that define ambient community, as we know, have three key qualities: they are fashioned around shared beliefs, practices, and politics, predicated on a sense of safety and acceptance, and forged with gays and straights alike. The structure of this community is nearly identical between Greenfield newcomers and Ithacans. However, there is one key difference: *none* of the LBQ newcomers in Greenfield articulate nostalgia for the identity-based (read: lesbian) ties that Ithacans rhapsodize about.

Most Greenfield newcomers report high levels of satisfaction with their ambient ties. For instance, a writer in her thirties happily described her membership in networks predicated on shared politics, beliefs, and practices. She began by describing political connections: "I was just recently elected to [a town board], so I've come to know a lot of people that are involved . . . in local politics." She also mentioned individuals she met as a bartender: "I have become friends with a few people that are sort of in the restaurant business. . . . There is definitely a restaurant community. . . . It's people that are about my age. . . . They tend to be creative types. . . . A lot of people are pretty into farming or respect farming and food and just agriculture in general and music." She added, "Oh, you know, I play soccer, duh. I play soccer in Greenfield once a week. It's a co-ed team."

Beyond mentioning that her soccer team is co-ed, her account was absent of any other mentions of identity characteristics. Before I closed the interview I asked her about the sexual identities of the individuals who compose her networks. She paused, seemingly trying to peg the identities of her friends. Eventually, she said: "Wow, let's see. Maybe 60 percent straight and 40 percent not so straight." She then turned to her partner and asked, "Do you think that's accurate?" It was clear, for her, that shared sexual identity is not the "glue" that binds her to others—although, on reflection, later in the interview she acknowledges that her networks include a disproportionately high (vis-à-vis Greenfield's population) number of LBQ individuals. Instead, shared work, politics, and activities provide the foundation for her local ties. Ann, a retiree, finds that the formation of such ties requires minimal effort: "My friends and my community keeps expanding. I mean it's just endless, you know, I keep meeting new people and then we're friends. I have met people through church, I have met people through, I don't know, the Y. I went to the Y for exercise, you know, I mean I went to . . . workshops at the community college and met people."

Ann elaborated, describing how in Greenfield she is able to nourish ties predicated on shared politics, specifically around concerns about the environment and sustainability:

> We started thinking about shared economics and before you knew it we had called together a group . . . which we've been doing now for four years. And we meet every month and it's been written up in the papers and it's been a model for other places. . . . We're a sustainability-focused group. . . . And that has completely felt to me like a home anchor. . . . And it's a mixed group, straight/gay, men/women, all ages. Well not as much younger ages as we'd like, but there is some.

Today she cultivates sexually heterogeneous ties predicated on politics; a possibility that never occurred to her in the Boston suburb where she spent her working years. This reveals how political views can serve as a basis for ambient community, as well as how newer migrants, regardless of age, experience a strong sense of ambient community. Ann's delight in how her ties are different in Greenfield than they were in Boston also underlines how places change our interactions and, ultimately, us.

The formation of these sexually heterogeneous networks is not limited to those, like Ann, with the time and flexibility to forge ties; nor are ties always restricted to those with whom residents share a plethora of traits. A couple with elementary-aged kids, Sam and Gabrielle, described a rich set of child-based and institutionally anchored ties. They suggest that their ties span not only sexual identity groups but also socioeconomic groups. Sam said:

> My friends are all my children's friends' [parents] now, which is fine . . . and they are people that I wouldn't necessarily know otherwise. You know, a lot more straight people. . . . What I like about Greenfield is the Co-op as an entity and also I go to Alcoholics Anonymous meeting every morning and that's a huge cross section and . . . I love that. I love knowing my town like in-depth.

Sam appreciates these connections to residents whom they otherwise might not know: "It's a transitional neighborhood [where AA meetings are held], you know what I mean? It's across the tracks . . . and they have been the most right there with me in terms of like [my wife's] illness and you know, they just . . . you know they're just really good people." Here, unlike most others, Sam describes ties that cross class lines. This additional heterogeneity seems to bolster her feelings of confidence in Greenfield's ambient community. Another echoes this, suggesting that forging connections with local residents sometimes takes effort because sexual identity is not the only difference they must bridge. She described the sense of belonging that these casual interactions generate as tremendously valuable: "I make a ton of chit-chat at [my business] and then like as I walk to the bank and I chitchat at the bank and . . . the copy store when I'm making menus, or grabbing a cup of coffee at the Co-op or . . . I have dinner at [a Main Street restaurant] like twice a week." Yet these valued interactions are not without effort: "When I'm at Foster's [a longstanding family-owned grocery] and I chat with the cashiers there and at the bank and . . . I'll strike up a conversation with somebody at the restaurant and we just will have completely different values and completely different backgrounds but . . . I always try to find something we have in common."

Sam feels that gender and sexual identity are a nonissue in AA meetings, and in the ties that extend beyond those meetings: "They're just picking up their lives so there's a great tolerance. . . . So I really belong to the subculture, you know." Moreover, Sam articulates an expansive sense of community membership that extends beyond child-based networks and AA. For instance, Sam said, "If I had more time, I'd be part of the co-op subculture, too." This perception—that connections can be numerous, that ties do not require a shared sexual identity, and that networks can be built on a vast range of interests—is palpable in today's Greenfield.

For Sam and Gabrielle, local institutions, such as the Green Fields Co-op and AA, help to produce a sense of ambient community, but informal networks play a crucial role, too. "We have great neighbors. . . . All of our neighbors are straight, I mean the neighbors that we are in close contact with and really enjoy. . . . But there's . . . I mean it doesn't matter to them in the least that we're lesbians, you know, that just isn't an issue at all." This sense of inclusion also extends to the YMCA, which many, especially (but not limited to) those with children, celebrate as a bastion of community. When I asked what she would most miss about Greenfield if she moved, Gabrielle said, "What would I miss? I'm going to say the Y, but it's not just the Y. It's that when you walk in there *everybody knows you.*" She added, "99 percent of my socializing is with straight people." Sam and Gabrielle regard this combined sense of both official (at the YMCA or the Co-op) and unofficial (via neighborhood interactions) inclusion and acceptance as quite meaningful.

Sitting on their wide front porch, dogs scampering at our feet, Gabrielle and Sam proposed that a sense of ambient community exists for two reasons: because Greenfield residents are accepting of LBQ residents and because the town is at an early stage of gentrification, with a heterogeneous coalition seeking revitalization. Sam elaborated:

> Well I definitely feel at ease here. I don't ever feel . . . like I don't question if I want to kiss you [to Gabrielle] on the sidewalk or hold hands or you know it's not a big deal. And I like that it's not overly shi-shi. I like that there's a sense of people working together to create a community as opposed to this, you know, sort of corporate influence or a cookie cutter community already in existence. So I think that's what I like about it most: that people feel a need to make community here because there's work to be done and so people really, you know, come together behind political candidates and come together around the Harvest Dinner and you know stand out on the Common . . . against war.

Indeed, they describe their town in storybook terms. As we've seen, Sam describes Greenfield as "the *Back to the Future* town. You know that Michael J. Fox movie *Back to the Future*? His town. That's Greenfield." Gabrielle added, "It's a *real* town. That's what I say. It has a center."

While Gabrielle, Sam, and Ann, like the young writer recently elected to a city board, are joiners—active in church, AA, the YMCA, their children's school, and the Co-op—such individuals are far from the only beneficiaries of ambient community. Dora, a medical professional who lives in a rambling Victorian with her partner, several children, and a housemate, intended to create "community" in Greenfield, only to find that it fell into her lap: "Before living here I didn't realize that community could happen without huge amounts of focused work. I didn't realize there were sort of like organic neighborhood communities like this." At this moment we paused our conversation so that Dora could answer the door (for the second time). When she returned, holding a glass bottle of milk, she said, "We take turns getting raw milk from the local dairy farm." Later she described neighborhood potlucks, regular parties in a neighbor's barn, and daily carpool to the alternative private school her children attend. Dora couldn't say enough about her good fortune, especially about how her sense of belonging in Greenfield is "in the air," requiring minimal output:

> It's the kind of community that I never thought existed anymore and we always had these fantasies that we would somehow create community from scratch. . . . We would buy land and have people all move together and declare their intention to be part of this community and we would all work really hard . . . and figure out how to live together. But as it turns out, we have all these neighbors. You know there is any number of people I could call up if someone needed a ride or you needed to borrow an ingredient or somebody needs to watch their kids. . . . I mean just a very supportive group of people. And we didn't have to do any work. All we had to do is just luck into it.

In subtle contrast, Maggie described a sense of ambient community—but one that was not primarily located in her immediate neighborhood and one that does not require the kind of mutual dependence—for milk or childcare or emotional support—that Dora described. Her children at summer camp, Maggie sat across from me in her cool, shadowed dining room, sipping water as we talked. She said, "I think the only community [I'm a part of]—I'm not a community joiner, I'm an anti-joiner—is the pool going community. [People] that go to the Greenfield pool a lot." She described summer days biking with her children to the pool—a dammed section of the Green River, complete with playground, picnic area, and lifeguards—followed by hours on the playground, in the river, and reading books on the beach. When I asked her to describe the pool-going community, she said: "Very loose, which is good. Like people see each other and say hi and that's it. And like parents sit back and kids play together. That kind of community." She added, "We do a lot with the YMCA so a lot of people we know there. The library community." She describes the feeling of community these interactions generate as literally without conscious effort, saying: "I don't have to think about it."

Here, by suggesting that she doesn't have to think about her ties, she evokes Herman Schmalenbach (1961, 334), who suggests that, unless they are disrupted, we are typically unaware of our community memberships.[32] For this reason, Schmalenbach argues, unless our ties are threatened we are more likely to recognize *others'* communities than our own. But, of course, Maggie thinks about her ties enough to articulate that she doesn't have to think about them. This may be because, as a member of a sexual minority group, membership in the kind of geographically based community that one "doesn't have to think about" is novel and valued—it is the "*Back to the Future* town" community that many GLBTQ individuals assume, even today, that they could only view from afar.

Confidence, of course, comes only with a sense of ownership—a sense of belonging so firmly rooted that a city feels like "ours" and not "theirs."[33] Despite the fact that she has lived in Greenfield for less than a year, Maggie reports, "I just feel like this town is *ours*. This town belongs to my kids. It belongs to me. Everywhere we go we're welcomed." That perception seems to require a palpable ethos of acceptance. Such tolerance of sexual difference is, not surprisingly, not universal—for instance, Maggie has one neighbor who will not allow her children to enter Maggie's home. Yet Maggie reports that for most people, "the word 'partner' doesn't raise eyebrows. . . . There's no sort of 'Where do these kids come from?' and looking back and forth." As a result, she describes relations as positive and friendly, and thus part of the "little things that make life good." These little moments make life good by bolstering her sense that she belongs and thus making that sense of ambient community possible.

Indeed, among this bounty of casual contact, Maggie actually resists forging ties that are overtly predicated on identity, such as being a lesbian or being an adoptive parent. Attaching ties to identity would force her to "think about" them or to approach ties with an intentionality she typically avoids; instead, she prefers to—and has the luxury of—associating community with something more effortless and "natural." She actively celebrates her ability to take part in, to borrow Jo's terms, geographic rather than demographic community; networks that do not require the active seeking that Jo described once relying on to cultivate demographic ties.

Maggie said, "I'm not sure [lesbians] are people we want to like commit to being friends with." When her partner met lesbian friends via a Northampton softball team this underlined her sense that such ties—originating in and predicated on shared sexual identity—are not for her: "I don't like that kind of thing. I went to a party here once and it was like 'oh, lesbians.'" Yet, much like Gabrielle and Sam and others, she readily acknowledges that her freedom to forge ties at the Green River Swimming Pool, the library, and the YMCA—rather than via softball—depends very much on her sense that "we don't look so special" on the streets of Greenfield: "That sort of comfort and naturalness . . . you know? It permeates everything."

To be clear, this desire to blend and for an effortless sense of community is not about eschewing community or intimacy. Indeed, on several occasions I observed Maggie with family and friends at a brick-oven pizzeria on Greenfield's Bank Row. Their table stood out for its warm interactions with other diners; I was not the only acquaintance that Maggie and her family greeted. During our interview, Maggie confessed, "I have decided that I want to search for a BFF, though. So watch out, Greenfield. I'm like fielding candidates. I might even allow a lesbian in for the ride." Her account suggests that her flippancy—she *might* let a lesbian along for the ride—is only possible because of local conditions, because of what she describes as the relative invisibility of sexual difference in Greenfield; a sense of invisibility that produces feelings of "comfort and naturalness" as she forges ties via her daily rounds.

As Maggie hints by joking that she might accept a BFF application from a lesbian, her sense of "ambient community"—of a generalized sense of belonging—does not necessitate the disavowal of ties to other LBQ individuals. Instead, her sense of "ambient community" derives from the basis for or foundation of her connections, whether to LBQ or heterosexual individuals; on the fact that she will not accept a best friend because she is lesbian, but might accept one if they share other commonalities. Echoing this, Karen, a middle-aged woman who lives on rural acreage outside of Greenfield, answered my question, "Have you been to lesbian potlucks here?" by saying, "Oh yeah, you know, they're just people. It doesn't matter." She elaborated:

> I also belonged to a group called Business Women's Alliance, which is a bunch of women that get together informally and we all sit down and we have food and their sexual orientation is not even [an issue]. . . . You know, this is what's normal: you get up, you go to work, go out and have a drink with your friends, you come home and you watch TV. That's like the normal connection. And these like lesbians they do the same thing. It's like they get up, they go to work, they watch TV. And they talk about it. And I'm like [their

sense of connection] is not about you being a lesbian it's about *this is what you do*. But they happen to like their partner and their partner happens to be female. And so sexuality doesn't—that's what I finally came to realize—the sexuality part doesn't really matter. And I think that that's part of the Franklin County thing. Like that's part of what makes here really awesome is just that the sexuality part doesn't matter.

In this sense, without eschewing ties to other LBQ residents, integrationist Greenfield newcomers readily embrace their ability to prioritize other bases of connection and to benefit from a generalized sense of belonging. And many, like Karen, recognize that this emerges from the place itself or, in her words, is a "Franklin County thing."

With all this overlap between Greenfield and Ithaca, how do we explain the absence in Greenfield of a wistfulness for "lesbian community" that dominates Ithacans' accounts? Put simply, Greenfield's LBQ individuals possess resources that Ithacans do not: multiple identity cultures *within* their city, one of which is organized around a common lesbian feminist identity, proximity to Northampton, an LBQ hub, and, emerging from and sustaining the two, an enduring lesbian feminist community (primarily composed of longtime residents) within Greenfield itself. At least in the imaginations of Greenfield migrants, networks predicated on shared sexual identity are, in theory, accessible to them—either via entering the established networks of Greenfield's earlier wave of LBQ migrants (who typically identify as lesbian feminist) or via accessing Northampton's LBQ networks. Indeed, some LBQ residents—even some who are relatively recent migrants to Greenfield—report ties to Northampton residents. It is harder to pine for lesbian community when it is right down the block from you—or at most, a short drive away in Northampton.

Are Northampton networks as Greenfield respondents imagine them to be: are they rooted in shared lesbian identity and inclusive of all or most "lesbians"? Without data on Northampton, we cannot be certain. On the one hand, as the next chapter documents, there are reasons to be cautious about this conclusion, since the more that LBQ migrants feel accepted and surrounded by others who are LBQ, the greater the likelihood that they will turn away from identity politics and toward integration. This would suggest that integration and post-identity politics would dominate in Northampton. Yet, the very high proportion of lesbian-couple households in Northampton, combined with its reputation as America's foremost lesbian enclave, may liberate Northampton from the broader pattern. Specifically, Northampton's elevated and enduring reputation as *the* lesbian college town in the United

States may result in enduring identity-based ties, despite city conditions (acceptance, a large LBQ population, and narratives of the city as exceptional) that would otherwise encourage post-identity politics and integration.[34]

Accurate or not, the *idea* (in Greenfield) that Northampton is a bastion of lesbian identity and community, together with the persistence of lesbian feminist identities and networks among Greenfield's longtimers, recuses Greenfield's post-identity-politics newcomers from nostalgia. Instead, they celebrate their membership in heterogeneous networks in a city that's "for everyone." Indeed, members of their migration cohort actively celebrate what their city is not, and, in turn, what they are not. Of course, having another migration cohort, composed of lesbian feminists, and Northampton—with its lesbian film festivals and poetry readings and singer/songwriters—at their fingertips plays a vital role in orienting them to Greenfield's—and their own—future, rather than to nostalgic visions of the past.

Narratives of a Changing City

How is it that Greenfield is home to two coexisting identity cultures? And why is there momentum toward post-identity politics and sexually heterogeneous networks? Throughout, we have encountered evidence of Northampton's practical and symbolic influence; Northampton provides material and symbolic resources that help to sustain longtimers' identities even in the context of a changing city, while simultaneously providing a point of contrast for post-identity-politics newcomers. Yet, if Northampton partially stabilizes longtimers' identities, how do we explain the rise of post-identity-politics? Why doesn't Northampton direct *all* ties and identities?

The following pages suggest that Northampton does not tell the whole story; in fact, Northampton is not the story; its role is supportive. Instead, Greenfield's changes, and perhaps especially residents' perceptions thereof, drive changes in identities and ties. Indeed, Greenfield's transformation, or at least local narratives thereof, directs how and even the degree to which different waves of migrants relate to Northampton.[35] Identities and ties take new form as LBQ residents—both new and old—increasingly regard Greenfield as an LBQ haven in its own right and, more generally, as a city on the move. They turn to indicators of LBQ acceptance (namely, declining homophobic incidents and welcoming organizations) and of a growing LBQ population as markers of change. However, they also emphasize commercial investments, and a more general sense, embedded in local boosterish narratives, that Greenfield residents are mobilizing to produce "revitalization" (such as via "urban renewal" and new commercial establishments).[36] Below,

I highlight residents' narratives of change. For Greenfield's LBQ individuals, talk of self and city are interwoven. Perhaps the best evidence of this is that, despite their differences, LBQ longtimers and newcomers present a common portrait of Greenfield as a *changing* city.[37] Of course, to date this narrative of change has been more consequential for a new migration cohort's identities than it has been for an earlier (1970s/1980s) migration cohort.

An articulate minority, best represented by Jo, explicitly suggest that Greenfield's changing landscape has produced change in LBQ residents; namely, movement away from lesbian community and toward ties forged around shared beliefs, practices, and politics. A twenty-something woman also noted a shift from a dominant lesbian-feminism to post-identity politics: "They would have the Big Gay Brunch on Sundays, which we went to a few times. But it was mostly the lesbians." Here, despite having a female partner and living just a few blocks from the restaurant that hosted the Big Gay Brunch, she did not consider herself to be on one of the "the lesbians." A few years later, the Big Gay Bunch has ceased, and this woman feels quite at home in Greenfield.

Many celebrate Greenfield's betwixt and between qualities: as up and coming, yet still gritty, down to earth, and antimaterialist.[38] A recent transplant described why she prefers Greenfield to the Boston suburbs: "Priorities are more on like relationships and like community and like being comfortable and having a good time and not as much on like appearances or you know aspirations and . . . status." Another echoes this, describing how on first arriving in town: "I liked Greenfield 'cause there was some grit to it, there was some tension and grit to it." Still another said: "It's like a lot more mellow. Every time I go to Northampton it reminds me of . . . growing up in the suburb of Boston." Another, celebrates Greenfield's "town-ness" and grit. Notably, by depicting Greenfield as "gritty" she communicates its humility and a sense of possibility closely linked to her perception of the city as changing:

> [At first] it reminded me of JP [Boston's Jamaica Plain] in the early '90s. It was very much that sort of feel like a town that has good bones, you know, like all of the right stuff in the right places and a sort of graveness that reminded me of the pre-gentrification Jamaica Plain when it was really artist and gay folk, and you know there was just sort of a sense of possibility. I really saw that in Greenfield. It really felt to me like that JP I had loved back in the day when we walked safety patrols in the neighborhood for the crime watch, although it's not nearly that pricey here. So I liked Greenfield. I liked that there was . . . I could see the possibility that [the kids] might be able to ride their bikes to

the Y or you know to the library and do those sorts of things. . . . So I like the *town-ness*.

These narratives emphasize both Greenfield's grit *and* its "good bones." Many appreciate the comingling of indicators of the city's past and future and their sense of Greenfield as on the cusp of the next thing.[39]

Given this taste for grit and for the "up and coming," many, especially recent arrivals, relish the contrasts between Greenfield and highly gentrified Northampton. One said, "I just kind of got over the hipster, young feel of Northampton and . . . I just liked how Greenfield felt a lot more authentic." For many, Greenfield's "authenticity" rests on its minimal affluence and limited materialism: "[In Northampton] it's like 'This is my little box,' you know, 'Stay out of my little box.'" Relatedly, some celebrate the fact that Greenfield's LBQ residents are not as wealthy or at least not as materialistic as Northampton lesbians, although over and again LBQ migrants suggest that this distinction came as a welcome surprise; that is, prior to moving they had not anticipated such variation amongst LBQ residents within the Valley. Liz, a woman in her fifties, cherishes the fact that Greenfield is *not* Northampton and hopes it will stay that way:

> I really don't care about lesbian marriage. . . . I don't want to get married. . . . There are other things we could be protesting about! But I'm a very jaded lesbian. . . . You've probably heard these stories. . . . "Gay people have assimilated so much and the whole marriage thing and people having children." And that's nice. I'm not against that and I think it's great and don't misunderstand me but I think it's like, you know you watch a show like The *L Word* and it's like all these beautiful lesbians, they all make tons of money. . . . You know that ain't what it was like when I was growing up, you know? . . . And it isn't even really like that for a lot of people now. . . . There's just been so much assimilation.

When I asked, "Do you see [beautiful lesbians with tons of money] in Greenfield?" she replied, "No, Greenfield's actually pretty, it seems pretty normal in a way. No, I don't see rich, beautiful lesbians much in Greenfield. . . . But Greenfield's kind of cool actually." In this sense, she celebrates Greenfield for being "outside" of dominant scripts about contemporary LBQ politics and believes that Northampton (like the glittery version of Los Angeles at the center of the *L Word*) occupies the opposite end of this spectrum. This reflects and supports a broader ethos about Greenfield as a place to applaud for its humble return to the basics—to food, family, farm, and community; what Liz describes as "pretty normal."

Yet many imply that "normalcy" is pleasurable *because* change is afoot. Those who have lived in Greenfield long enough to remember an earlier city (generally since the 1990s or before) are less nostalgic. A doctor explained that a decade ago she was hesitant to accept a job offer in Greenfield:

> I just didn't want to spend my time driving so we decided to move up here. I felt really despondent moving to Greenfield. . . . [Ten years ago] to me Greenfield was like this kind of working-class town. There wasn't any politics. There wasn't any culture. There was nothing. Like I never came here. Why would you go to Greenfield when there's Northampton and Amherst and all that going on? . . . And then they fought off Walmart that year and so I was very impressed. That was the first time I thought anything positive about Greenfield.

She now has a much more positive view of Greenfield, which she describes as "about to pop." Indeed, she works to rebuff any threats to revitalization, expressing concern that Walmart might try yet again to establish itself in Greenfield: "I'm very worried that Greenfield is going to change in a very negative way when they build this Walmart. I'm afraid it's going to destroy the downtown. . . . You know they've renovated several buildings down on Bank Row and there's all kinds of little funky things going on. There's a lot of local energy and projects and art and business being produced." Logan offers a similar narrative of welcome transformation. She recalled the "old" days:

> They put a planter on the bench in front of the co-op because of the undesirable people sitting out there and I think at some point a woman was soliciting her services. . . . [It's] a crazy thing because you know that bench is totally open now and people sit on it all the time. . . . Things were like [different]. I mean there was no People's Pint. This [the LBQ-owned sandwich shop in which I interviewed her] was the Corner Cupboard. So the only business that was like-minded in my mind was the co-op. You know it's like you could have cheeseburger chowder at Famous Bills or go to Herm's for like a burger . . . and when you talk to people from that era who went to boarding school around here and they can come to Greenfield and they would just be like 'ugh.'

Yet, she is careful to differentiate herself from those who said "ugh" about Greenfield, essentially celebrating her ability to recognize a diamond in the rough. Even in rough-around-the-edges Greenfield, she recognized kindred spirits (primarily straight): "There was this bunch of people. . . . They were young and hip and kind of had the same [progressive] values . . . and so I could feel that there was a kinship."

Some worry that Greenfield may lose its "normalcy" and "values" by becoming more upscale and status oriented. Twenty-something newcomers articulated this anxiety:

> Some of the shops, the little shops in Greenfield have kind of been changing pretty frequently and we have like the new my gosh the "supreme-fueled-coffee" where the rich people in Greenfield will buy a $4 cup of coffee and sip it slowly. It's like come on. So it's kind of like what's up with this coffee place? It's just kind of a warning sign of where Greenfield is headed and we're like, "Oh no."

Their anxiety is not just about gentrification per se. Like Liz, they also worry about the kind of LBQ residents that gentrification will call out: they present an image of a status-oriented individual who may not share the back-to-the-roots ethos that many newcomers find provides a common foundation in their interactions with heterosexual residents. Above all else, their anxiety reveals their confidence in Greenfield's continued evolution, as well as a lack of clarity about whether that evolution is for the better or for the worse.

Logan offers yet another account for why she and other LBQ residents should be cautious about upscaling. She suggests that Greenfield increasingly welcomes LBQ individuals in part because, as a result of historic economic decline, it *must*. That is, in her view heterosexual residents regard LBQ individuals as productively repopulating postindustrial Greenfield. Referring to a large billboard near a major exit ramp off of Interstate 91, she said: "When you drive into Greenfield it says 'Everyone's Hometown,' which I think is because the people who grew up here left and don't want it to be their hometown. So they are weirdly welcoming to [us]." Beyond the billboard, Chamber of Commerce literature emphasizes, "When we say that there's something for everyone, we do mean everyone." She does not think that the economic origins of this receptivity make it insincere. She feels appreciated and proud of the role that she and other LBQ residents have played in "improving" the city: "It's really nice. I really think they're just so happy. You know, I regularly have people come in and say, 'Thank you . . . for opening a [business].'" Indeed, she appreciates a growing sense of belonging, embodied by a local bank that helped support her small business. She suggests that overt homophobia is receding:

> You know, I always said that I felt like a strong sense of homophobia around here. . . . Like the women at Foster's stared at me and at Stop and Shop and one time somebody was really rude to me at Friendly's. But for the most part,

this is so cheesy but, for the most part, I really feel like since Ellen [Degeneres came out], I think she just took it really mainstream and I think people have been really okay with it.

In the broader narrative of Greenfield that she offers, she presents "grit" as becoming more attractive over time and gestures to specific conditions—namely, declining homophobia and a revitalizing commercial center—that allow her to express nostalgia for an earlier and less LBQ-hospitable Greenfield. Here, nostalgia is not, as it is in Ithaca, for bygone lesbian community, but, instead, for an earlier, grittier Greenfield.

Echoing others, she worries about the potential scale of this change; that it may go too far. Why is this? After all, she once wondered why she did not live in a place with a larger LBQ population and in which she felt more accepted. "[I used to ask myself:] Why would I live somewhere like this? Isn't that so weird?" She worries Greenfield will ultimately become a place in which she is not at home (like Northampton). That is, she wishes to parse increasing acceptance (which she welcomes) from gentrification:

Orange [a neighboring city] reminds me a lot of what Greenfield felt like in 1996. . . . I was just talking to somebody about how I love the authenticity . . . there. Like there's just zero pretention, there's no hipness and it's a very sweet little town and I really enjoy it. And when you meet somebody who's, you know, out there they're there only because either they want to be or they sort of fell into it but both are very authentic and it's not about like "oh this is up and coming." Like no one is talking about Orange being up and coming the way they are with Greenfield.[40]

When I asked her why she worried about Greenfield being "up and coming," she said, "I love a lost cause and there was a long time I thought Greenfield was a lost cause. . . . I mean I don't want to like romanticize [poverty]." In almost the same breath she said, as if to illustrate the degree to which Greenfield has emerged from its lost-cause state, "I don't even think Northampton has as many gay owned restaurants as we do." She said,

I went to boarding school with somebody who grew up in this town and we're always like on Facebook like talking back and forth and she's like, "I can't believe you would not want to leave Greenfield. I couldn't wait to leave Greenfield." And I'm always like, "Greenfield's cool now." You know, I mean I always tell people that the only reason I ever leave Greenfield is like to drive to Sunderland and do yoga. . . . As soon as there's [her desired yoga studio] in Greenfield I will like never leave.

Logan knows she is not alone in finding Greenfield to be "cool now." She reports a constant, "tiny trickle" of LBQ individuals from Northampton, which contributes to the changes she notes. She at once welcomes this and worries that Greenfield might unintentionally become Northampton.

While there is much one might parse from Logan's fascination with Greenfield's "lost-cause" qualities, what I wish to highlight is the constancy of her attention to transformation. For Logan, to talk about Greenfield is to talk about a changing place; not a place that has neatly transformed from gritty to gentrified, but a place that is characterized by alteration itself. Indeed, Logan and others seem somewhat uncertain of precisely what has changed, as well as about the pace and upper limits of its changes. They suggest that Greenfield is more upscale, but still underdeveloped (indeed, many expressed fear that Walmart might still destroy downtown). They indicate that Greenfield is increasingly accepting of LBQ residents but not without homophobia. It is gritty but not as "authentic" as other towns. They also express uncertainty about how or if indicators of Greenfield's commercial upscaling relate to its growing LBQ population. One woman noted that a group of LBQ business owners had concluded, "It must just be a fluke that there are so many lesbian business owners in Greenfield."

If LBQ residents are not entirely certain about what is transforming, why all this talk of change? By charting how Greenfield is changing, they chart how place is changing *them* and demonstrate the degree to which they frame Greenfield as in flux. They are at once telling a story about a move from cheeseburger chowder to $4 coffee and from the "Big Gay Brunch" to a "*Back to the Future* town"; from a city that called out lesbian-feminist identities and ties and dependence on Northampton to a more autonomous city— one that is marked by abundance and acceptance and narratives of the city as up and coming and a cultural destination in its own right—that cultivates post-identity politics and ambient community.

To be sure, Greenfield has experienced economic and demographic shifts, but so, too have the other cities that this book features (in Portland, for instance, gentrification is charging full steam ahead, particularly, post-2010, in the Munjoy Hill neighborhood where many LBQ individuals lived).[41] Portland residents frequently volunteered commentary about the gentrification unfolding around them, of which they understood themselves to be a part. Indeed, in recent years housing prices rose in Portland, and the city's main commercial district witnessed the arrival of several high-profile restaurants, such as Duckfat, a restaurant serving fries cooked in, as the name suggests, duck fat. If Greenfield is home to $4 coffee, Portland is increasingly a place of $13 sandwiches and $7.50 milkshakes. A similar argument could be made about San Luis Obispo, with its swiftly increasing property values and an influx of high-end chains.

Why, then, do Greenfield's LBQ residents so emphasize change? Cultural, political and geographic proximity to Northampton—Greenfield's measuring stick—produces a heightened sense of change and, in turn, a particularly responsive or swiftly evolving LBQ identity.[42] In this sense, while we might think of all of the sites as cars moving on tracks, for Greenfield residents having Northampton on the horizon makes a sense of motion especially acute. Thus, Greenfield epitomizes the way that place is at once real and imagined—it is commercial turnover, increasing numbers of college-educated residents, the growing proportion of lesbian couples *and* narratives of change and progress; both material and symbolic facets of place are consequential for LBQ identities and ties.[43] In addition, it underlines the adaptability of sexual identities, as migrants, new and old, arrange and rearrange a sense of sexual personhood in relation to their evolving city.

Conclusion

Greenfield is a bellwether for several lessons at the heart of this book about how places shape identities and ties. Specifically, it sheds light on what is and is *not* at work in shaping identity culture. We learn, for instance, that chain migration—the movement to a city of one woman, informed by the movement of another before her and so on—does not neatly account for the emergence of newcomers' post-identity-politics orientation. If it did, we would expect that newcomers or members of the newer migration cohort would be more like Jo and others like her in their approach (i.e., lesbian feminists with strong ties to and identification with Northampton). Moreover, we would *not* expect lesbian feminist longtimers to report that their own ties and, to a lesser degree, their identities are shifting as Greenfield changes. Nor would chain migration account for the presence of a few very recent arrivals in the Greenfield area who seem to embrace and perform an identity politics, such as by organizing a Pride run and hosting LBQ gatherings in their backyard (if my findings are any indication, we can anticipate that once embedded in the Greenfield context their self-understanding and ties will shift away from identity politics toward integration).[44] Greenfield's story is not one of a neat chain migration of migrants with inside knowledge of local identities. As in the other sites, newcomers report arriving in Greenfield with one approach to their identity, only to find that it takes new shape as they build a life in a new city.

From Greenfield we also learn that LBQ migrants' identities and ties do not respond to an enduring, static sense of "place character" rooted in a defining historic event (Molotch et al. 2000). Instead, place conditions are dynamic and help to produce an evolving sense of city "character." In turn, this changed city character is consequential for how new migrants relate to neighbors, heterosexual and otherwise, and, ultimately, how they think about themselves. Greenfield is, increasingly, a cultural and economic destination in its own right, and with this the local identity culture has also shifted. This underlines the power of place to set parameters for self-understanding and ties. It also reminds that places change, taking "character" and reputation with them as well.[45]

Greenfield also instructs that cities do not exist in vacuums. We, perhaps especially those of us with the mobility and privilege to voluntarily relocate, come into frequent contact with other places. A proximate city like Northampton can serve as an identity and community resource for some and can also allow for the coexistence of lesbian feminist (among an older migration cohort) and post-identity-politics cultures (among a newer migration cohort).[46] Beyond serving as a practical resource (for identities and networks), a nearby place that residents bestow with symbolic meaning can influence how they perceive their own city, and not just via conflict or competition, but also via meaningful, positive engagement.[47] However, and crucially, we see that this influence is not one-way: Greenfield itself directs Northampton's influence. Even moderate changes in Greenfield's economic fortunes, the robustness of narratives about city progress, and the degree to which LBQ residents feel accepted, influence the degree to which they align with Northampton and turn to it for fun, friendship, and even work and school.

Given what Greenfield reveals about how identity cultures and ties respond to local conditions, we should not anticipate that in twenty years or even two, Portland's LBQ population will rely on hyphenated identities, or that San Luis Obispo will always possess a stalwart lesbian community. When local conditions change, identities and ties change, too. Sexual identities are not enshrined in time or place; they are responsive social identities that take form via context-specific interaction.[48] It is to the question of precisely how city features shape these interactions, and, ultimately, self-understanding, that the next and final chapter turns.

FIVE

How Places Make Us

We have seen evidence of the many ways that cities nurture distinctive identity cultures in each of the first four chapters. We have seen, for instance, how in Portland modest feelings of abundance and acceptance, combined with narratives of the city, and its lesbian, bisexual, and/or queer (LBQ) population, as constituting a cultural and intellectual frontier, encouraged Sam to identify as stone butch and polyamorous and to organize her social life around those identities. Yet a broader, comparative perspective—built from the individual cities and the words of their residents but reaching beyond and between them—brings the sources of that variation into sharper relief. This chapter offers an extended comparison across all four of our cities in order to elucidate the larger patterns at work in the creation of identity cultures.

Let's start with the things that *don't* explain how places make us. In the course of our explorations, we have already discarded a number of plausible explanations, both for the constancy of identities across demographic and friendship groups within cities, and for the differences in identity cultures across the cities. We have learned that marked differences in the demographic traits of LBQ residents between the cities—such as those related to race or generation or class—cannot account for the existence of distinctive identity cultures.[1] We have also learned that chain migration, or the intentional seeking of existing identity cultures, cannot explain our puzzle. Because the cities share many characteristics, the chapters also demonstrate the fallacy of assuming that some singular city characteristic drives differences in identity culture, such as the distance between it and a larger city, or whether our city possesses a college or university, or whether it supports a particular type of LBQ organization.[2]

If these explanations fail, where do we go next? What explains why LBQ residents—who share many traits and reside in four similar cities—approach sexual identity and difference in such distinctive ways? Why does Jo, a white, professional long-time resident of Greenfield, identify as lesbian feminist, while Jan, a white, professional longtime resident of Ithaca who is almost exactly the same age as Jo, told me that she prefers to identify as queer and that "sometimes you can take sisterhood and shove it"? Likewise, why did Jen, an androgynous twenty-two-year-old white woman in Ithaca, tell me that she "doesn't really identify," while a white woman of the same age who lives in San Luis Obispo—and who even dresses and styles her hair very much like Jen—identifies as "lesbian"?

I have found that three reasons in particular apply to all our cities and I suspect, to most cities. In the pages that follow I map how LBQ identity cultures respond to three dimensions of city ecology, which we have encountered throughout this book. Of course, there are many dimensions of city ecology, but these three are of outsized influence in directing local sexual identity cultures. The first dimension of local ecology is "abundance and acceptance," which refers to the amount of LBQ residents who live in an area relative to the total population, and how they are dispersed across the metro area; these population numbers, in turn, are inextricably linked to their sense of safety, as well as the city's indicators of acceptance. The second is "place narratives," which refers to the stories a city tells about who it is—via billboards, Chamber of Commerce fliers, newspaper articles, and everyday conversation. The third, which partially emerges from and reproduces the others, is the city's "socioscape." That is, the ways that residents experience the community around them, and especially the LBQ population. That is, the residents' perspectives on the demographic, social, and cultural traits of the residents of their city, and especially those of the LBQ population.[3] Almost as important as each of these three dimensions individually is the fact that they work in tandem, and that the relative importance of each varies by city and changes over time.[4]

Below, I turn to the ways that the LBQ migrants I spoke with accounted for their own city-specific identities. As I spoke with people in city after city, I found myself returning to the same question: why are they not more aware of how they are shaped by the place they live? I now realize that this question is applicable to every one of us: I think that, more often than not, we are all largely unaware of the ways place shapes identity. That lack of awareness, as we'll see, makes sense: it is obvious to all of us that New York is different from Los Angeles—that nearly every city has some kind of distinct identity. But we tend to think of those distinctions between one place and the next as the result of categorical differences. Mapping how cities shape identities, the task at the center of this chapter, not only solves the puzzle at the heart of this book but also advances a new, more sensitive and specific approach to place; an approach that calls scholars and LBQ migrants alike to seriously consider the influence of even subtle differences in city ecology on self and group.

False Assumptions

Until now, we have immersed ourselves in a collage of city-specific orientations to sexual identity and difference. Given the vibrancy of their differences, it is surprising that LBQ residents are largely unaware of the place-specificity of their identity. To be sure, some hints of awareness bubble up both in individual anecdotes and pop culture. A 2013 blog post detailed the divided "breeding habits" of lesbians in the northern and southern sections of Brooklyn's Park Slope, suggesting that lesbian identities and practices vary within Brooklyn's most notorious LBQ neighborhood, with a certain "breed" of lesbian inhabiting one end of the neighborhood and another breed the other.[5] Similarly, several women I spoke with in SLO joked about "LA lesbians," implying that they, like Los Angeles itself, are uniquely focused on each other's affluence and wardrobe.[6]

References to Los Angeles were not the only statements I heard of how identities vary by place. As the reader may recall, a Greenfield woman said that in her previous town, an upscale suburb of New York City, she could not be her "true" self: "There was one [self] that got up and went to work but then on weekends I went into New York to play." After moving to Greenfield, despite this earlier way of identifying—as a sometimes closeted lesbian-identified woman—in a New York suburb, she felt quite at home with the post-identity-politics orientation she adopted. Likewise, a woman mused that she did not identify as "butch" until moving to Portland, Maine, despite years spent living in the larger and more diverse lesbian communities of San Francisco and Chicago. Here and elsewhere, the people I spoke with not only reference place-specific identities, but also how identity evolves with our zip code. But across more than 170 formal interviews and many other informal conversations these were the exceptions that prove the rule.

Furthermore, if overt references to identity as place specific are rare, rarer still are explanations for why identities vary by place. Again, there were a few exceptions: a handful of my informants offered offhand accounts for city-specific identities. A Portlander spoke at length about how her identity orientation is more intellectual and political than it was in Denver, suggesting that this is because the LBQ community in Denver revolves around which bar you go to. She further suggested that in Denver, LBQ community is bar based because "Denver is the bar capital of America," implying that LBQ identities take shape in response to this particular indicator of city economy and culture: the number of bars per capita.[7] Also evoking Denver, an Ithaca woman proposed that her identity would likely change on moving to Denver because there would be fewer lesbians there, gesturing to the possibility that the scale of a city's lesbian population is influential for identity. Greenfield, not surprisingly, was the only city where more than one or two residents offered these details. Several Greenfield residents imply that Northampton's affluence, abundance of lesbian households, and longstanding general emphasis on identity (both class and sexual) produces an "old fashioned" identity politics that contrasts with that which they find in Greenfield.

But that's it. Except for the dozen or so people mentioned above, my informants all told me that the notion of identity as place specific did not occur to them until after they moved to their current place of residence and, in the context of an interview, had the opportunity to reflect on their moves and how they have changed over time (of course, I never asked residents if their identities changed with their moves—after all, the thought did not occur to me until years into the research; I, did, however, ask them how long they had identified as they identify now—as a way of asking about "coming out"— and this sometimes invited reflection on how one's identity changed on moving). Many describe this as an after-the-fact discovery, and no one I spoke with described it as having driven their decision to move. Indeed, many are quite surprised, and some are even disappointed, by the identity cultures they uncover in their new place of residence.[8]

Why might this be true? Why do some have a vague sense of the place specificity of identity but do not pair this with serious inquiry into place-specific identities before relocating? After all, most of us weigh numerous factors before moving somewhere, from the price of housing to the quality of schools. Doesn't it stand to reason that we would also inquire about something as essential as identity? Apparently, no. I see a few reasons that explain this seeming oddity.

First, despite some cognizance of the place specificity of identities, for the most part LBQ individuals, like most of us, assume that variations in identity comes from elsewhere: from demographic, regional, or other categorical differences, such as whether a city is rich or poor, big or small.[9] Thus, if you are moving from Boulder to Portland, it is easy to assume that the lesbian community you find there will be similar. This assumption obscures the possibility that identity will feel different even if you move to a similar city that possesses a demographically similar LBQ population. If we attribute identity variation to categorical differences, there is little reason to expect identities to take novel shape in Portland, compared with what happens in Ithaca, for instance.

Second, few propose that they adopt entirely new identities in each place. Few shift from "straight" to "lesbian"; instead, on moving and without intending to do so one might transition from thinking of oneself as "lesbian" to framing oneself as "butch-lesbian" or "post-lesbian." That is, we rarely become entirely new people on moving, but, instead, we "do" and feel who we are—lesbian or bisexual or butch—in markedly new ways in a new city. Together, the fact that cities typically call out new arrangements or frames for the self, rather than wholesale reinvention, and that we tend to turn to categorical explanations for place-based identity differences (turning, for instance, to whether a place is urban or rural, rich or poor), help to account for underdeveloped awareness of how places shape identities.

The fact that our four cities call out distinctive identity arrangements, rather than altogether disparate visions of the sexual self, is also important for the task at hand. After all, as the first four chapters lay bare, the difference in identity culture between one city and the next is not always extreme; while the identity culture of each place is novel, there are some common attributes. Indeed, when we look across all four cities a pattern emerges, with the identity culture of each place falling into loose pairs, aligning on opposite ends of a spectrum (see fig. 5.1; note: all figures and tables appear at the end of the chapter). Two sites (San Luis Obispo and Portland) fall closer to the "identity politics" end, and the two others (Greenfield and Ithaca) are closer to "post-identity politics."

San Luis Obispo and Portland, on the former end of that spectrum, as we know, share a number of key features: commitment to naming one's identity, identifying with others who share that identity, and organizing one's social life around that commonality. Residents of each city are comfortable with the notion of "essential" and life-defining identities; they readily embrace identity labels, articulate a sense of shared fate, and rarely articulate an "integrationist" ideology. Their sports teams are not open to all, as they more often are in the other two sites, nor their gay bars or their gay, lesbian, bisexual, transgender, and queer (GLBTQ) nightclub events. In other words, while San Luis Obispo and Portland possess indisputably distinct sexual identity cultures, at the core of each is an embrace of identity politics and the belief that sexual identity is life defining. In contrast, LBQ women in Ithaca and, to a lesser degree, in Greenfield (those composing the now-majority cohort of integrationists) celebrate integration with heterosexuals and disavow the centrality of sexuality for self-identity. They are also less universally supportive of gay marriage than are San Luis and Portland residents, and much less comfortable with identity labels. In short, they fall closer to a post-identity-politics orientation, with Ithaca informants closely adhering to this end of the identity spectrum.

If the cities' identity cultures are distinctive and place specific, why call our attention to these patterns? One reason is that recognition of these common elements may mute awareness of the place specificity of identities for those on the ground (who, unlike this ethnographer, have not explicitly tasked themselves with thinking across cities). I also highlight them because identifying the places of overlap in the identity cultures of the sites, and especially of their loose pairing on ends of a spectrum, encourages consideration of why each possesses a novel identity, as well as of why identity cultures are not *entirely* idiosyncratic. Why do the sites cluster (however loosely) on ends of a spectrum? Why aren't the cultures that compose each cluster more closely aligned? In short, recognizing that the cities' identity cultures are not entirely idiosyncratic aids our effort to uncover the source of city-specific identities and signals the import of simultaneously explaining areas of difference *and* synergy.

How Cities Shape Identities

We began this book by reckoning with other ways of explaining the differences in LBQ identities I encountered in these four cities. Each of these—demographic differences, purposive or chain migration, and local organizations—seemed, at least initially, to be plausible. Yet upon further exploration, all of them failed (see table 5.1). If identity cultures do not emerge from these, what is their source? From my inductive process that eliminated the above plausible explanations, as well as from the confirmations offered by informants' words and my fieldwork observations, an alternate understanding of why identities vary by city emerges: namely, that the cities, themselves, drive variation. Cities shape how we interact with our neighbors and, ultimately, our sexual identities.

But how and why do cities matter? How do cities hold such sway over how we understand the most intimate aspects of our identity? It is tempting to assume that such variation in identity cultures can be attributed to a particular feature that is specific to a city, such as whether a city houses a liberal college, or whether the city has been involved in state-level efforts to ban same-sex marriage.[10] Indeed, I spent nearly two years doing just that. Triangulating interview narratives, observations, and census and other demographic and geographic data on these four cities, I considered more than two dozen dimensions of city ecology—from city economic traits to historic events—of plausible influence (see figs. 5.2 and 5.3; tables 5.1–5.8).[11] But each of these eventually fell apart. For instance, the expectation that the presence of a large population of young LBQ residents discourages a post-identity-politics orientation splintered when I realized that of the four cities two that are home to very different identity cultures—San Luis Obispo and Ithaca—also have the lowest median age. Likewise, I briefly wondered if having a large population of LBQ migrants from a big city encouraged adoption of post-identity politics, but this crumbled when I considered Portland—which, despite its identity-politics orientation, attracts many migrants from Boston, New York, and other big cities. Ultimately, I found that rather than taking shape in relationship to specific or singular elements, LBQ identities respond to the combination of three dimensions of city ecology. These particular dimensions are especially relevant, both individually and in combination, to shaping how residents interact with one another and how they think about themselves: abundance and acceptance, place narratives, and socioscape.[12]

These multiple dimensions reflect how many of us, and certainly the LBQ individuals I spoke with, experience—sometimes consciously, oftentimes unconsciously—the places in which we live: as compilations of ecological attributes that together provide a sense of local "character."[13] For instance, when my informants report that their identity changed after moving, they never credit a specific element. Instead, they posit that identities respond to a general sense of what makes their city distinctive, such as Portland's "cutting edge" atmosphere, which is, itself, a product of multiple, contemporaneous features.

Recognizing this common way of seeing the relationship between place and identity helps us with the task at hand. First, it redirects us from the work of unearthing some precise or singular source of city character to the question of how that character communicates itself to and is meaningful for residents. Moreover, if isolatable ecological attributes and the categorical memberships that they imply—such as whether a city is southern or western, progressive or conservative—do not alone direct identities, then our primary question is not *which* place elements are meaningful for identity, but, rather, *how* places shape identity. Or, to phrase it differently, we can stop looking for some essential and singular key to solve this puzzle, and instead explore the (multiple) mechanisms by which cities direct both how we understand ourselves, and how we understand the group(s) to which we belong.[14]

Abundance and Acceptance

The sense of safety and acceptance that an individual feels, as well as the numbers and distribution of LBQ individuals across a metro area, play a foundational role for identity culture, serving a vital orienting function that casts LBQ residents either toward or away from identity politics. For brevity's sake, let's call this dimension "abundance and acceptance." Its importance becomes especially apparent when considering the question of why the sites cluster into two loose groups on an identity spectrum, with San Luis Obispo and Portland on the identity-politics end and Ithaca and Greenfield on the opposite, integrationist end.

As box stores proliferate and architectural trends are mimicked to maximize profit, many places around the world can feel like facsimiles of other places. Despite that facsimile quality, no one is going to confuse SLO with Portland or think that Greenfield and Ithaca are the same. For reasons that extend far beyond the obvious differences in climate and landscape, the cities simply look and sound distinct. Take the differences between San Luis Obispo and Portland as an example. During the monthly Art After Dark event in San Luis Obispo, late-model pickups playing country music cruise downtown, CALPOLY students in designer clothes move in and out of boutiques and bars, homeless youth with a "hippie" aesthetic ask for change outside the Apple Store, and baby boomers exit the leafy patio behind Linnaea's Café to stand shoulder to shoulder at the Museum of Art with neatly attired middle-aged couples—some of whom have traveled from the Central Valley for a weekend at their second home or a seaside hotel. At a parallel event in Portland, a chain of young "punks" perform a sidewalk circus, pushing past tourists and residents in flannel and fleece. At the city's several independent galleries, urbane Salt Institute for Documentary Studies students mingle beside twenty-something baristas, second-home owners who have come in for the evening from coastal villages, University of Southern Maine faculty, and New York weekenders. Even from this short glance, the differences are clear. Portland has more fleece and gray hair, less skin, a more audacious public sphere (can you imagine a punk circus on the sidewalks of San Luis Obispo?), a more urban disposition, and a higher proportion of independent businesses vis-à-vis its region. In turn, San Luis Obispo has more flip-flops, expensive bikes, board shorts, high-end chain stores, and fine wine.[15]

Nonetheless, the cities share a defining set of ecological traits. In both San Luis Obispo and Portland, LBQ residents express concern for their safety (more so in San Luis Obispo than in Portland, but in both sites nearly all told me that they did not feel entirely at ease). Each has a lower proportion of affirming religious institutions than the other cities (although it is important to note that the proportion in Ithaca is relatively comparable—one of many examples of how the differences between the cities on the two ends of the spectrum are not always stark). According to the census, and abundantly supported by residents' informal counts, each possesses a less substantial proportion of lesbian-couple households than do Ithaca or Greenfield, with more evenly matched proportions of lesbian- and gay-couple households than those other two cities. Both are in states that held and lost a marriage referendum in the six years while I was conducting fieldwork. Finally, in each, LBQ residents concentrate in neighboring suburbs in higher proportions than in the city proper, and they articulate a corresponding patchwork-quilt LBQ geography; across the metro area as a whole, there are parts in which they are quite comfortable and experience an abundance of LBQ individuals, but in others they feel more isolated and less at ease.[16] As we saw in chapter 4, one Portland woman differentiates between "good" and "bad" Portland. She described her (then) relatively ungentrified neighborhood, which is home to many working-class white residents, as constituting "a bad part of town"—in contrast to the more gentrified and LBQ-friendly Munjoy Hill and West End. She offered an example of why she considered her neighborhood to be "bad": "We were out next to this fence kissing and making out and . . . this dude came out from next door with a bat and tried to beat us up . . . screaming, 'My kids are watching, you fucking faggots . . . dykes.'" She considered it lucky that neighbors eventually intervened and that she and her partner were not physically harmed.

As we have also learned, LBQ residents of both Portland and San Luis Obispo express feelings of "outsiderness"; of having moved to a relatively hospitable city but of not feeling entirely safe or welcome.[17] For instance, a Portland woman stated that she feels "safe," but then clarified: "For the most part I do [feel safe]. Yeah. [But] I almost felt safer in New York. . . . There have been a lot of times . . . I've been walking home alone at 2:00 [a.m.] and there's just like no one on the street and it's kind of foggy." Likewise, a San Luis Obispo–area woman recounted both fear-inducing harassment in her neighborhood and the relief of encountering a sympathetic police officer.

LBQ residents of Portland and San Luis Obispo reside in places they believe to be "safe enough." For instance, the Portland woman threatened with a bat says that "there's always somebody there to stop it . . . because even when that bat stuff happened . . . by the time we ran in the house, there were already people out there like yelling at that dude and like calling the cops." But these are still places in which daily conditions prohibit them from forgetting about their sexuality, and thus overtly define them in relation to those who do and do not share their identity. No surprise, then, that identity-based culture and community abounds—a sense of "outside togetherness" in which informants take comfort but also pleasure.[18]

In contrast, residents in Ithaca—and, to a lesser degree, Greenfield—propose that the sense of safety and acceptance they feel make possible a departure from identity politics and enable "insiderness." A Greenfield newcomer we met in chapter 4 reflects on why her ties are not based on sexual identity: "Certainly a number of friends are [LBQ], but that's not why primarily we connect. . . . Which is nice, because for me at least it's been really nice that we connect through activities. . . . The orientation of people isn't at the top of the list of what's important. It's not one of those 'I'm gay you're gay we should be friends.' You're friends because you're friends." When I asked why, she said, "To me it's a reflection of more openness and acceptance within the community because earlier when I lived in Boston I very strongly identified with a lesbian community because I felt like I *had* to. I had to for safety, and I'm glad that I don't have to here." Likewise, a recent migrant to Ithaca described her adjustment to the degree to which Ithacans de-emphasize sexual identity: "My daughter's wondering where the rainbow flags are and where the men dressed as women are. . . . Gay Pride was very important to our family in [LA] and . . . those things are very different [in Ithaca]. . . . So [in Ithaca] it isn't so separate, which is what I think I always hoped for. That's part of why I wanted to be here. . . . I think that what we traded in was being separate."

Moreover, LBQ residents of Ithaca and Greenfield do not appear to be concentrated in particular parts of the city, nor do they articulate the sense that this is necessary. In contrast to the sense of scarcity that many in San Luis Obispo and some in Portland express, they describe an abundance of LBQ residents. Crucially, as we learned in the Greenfield and Ithaca chapters, they report that the local LBQ population includes candidates for and holders of elected positions. One, who has lived in large US cities, said that "you go out and see a zillion lesbians . . . you have never seen before." This preponderance of lesbians, she suggests, is a well-established fact (a "fact" that may be rooted in the legacy of women's and LGBQ collectives near both Ithaca and Greenfield). A thirty-four-year-old social worker said, "Here everywhere you go you see lesbians. Like I'm going to get a massage today by a lesbian. My chiropractor's a lesbian. Everywhere you go, they're just there." A twenty-five-year-old emphasized the significance of out elected officials in Ithaca and added: "The police are obviously here to protect us, which I have never found to be the case anywhere else." A Greenfield mother and teacher suggested that she rarely goes to the Farmers Market without encountering new lesbians. Moreover, in Ithaca and Greenfield residents report that LBQ residents live "everywhere." In both cities this includes neighboring hill towns (in one, outside of Greenfield, LBQ residents hold monthly potlucks) and many neighborhoods.

Residents' observations regarding the breadth and distribution of LBQ individuals reflect census and other indicators, as well as local histories. Greenfield and Ithaca are seats of counties that, as of 2000, had the second and third highest proportion of lesbian couples in the nation.[19] Each has a notably higher proportion of lesbian than gay couples, a legacy of LGBTQ land or communes, and, according to LBQ residents, at least one elected LBQ official in each city.[20] Finally, each possesses businesses owned or co-owned by openly LBQ residents. For instance, in 2016 Greenfield's small downtown had at least five LBQ-owned restaurants and in recent years had as many as seven (see table 5.9).

As these figures and informants' words suggest, abundance and acceptance serve a crucial orienting function for sexual identity cultures, positioning a collective compass toward or away from integration and identity politics. The proportion of LBQ households (independently and relative to that of gay men), the degree of their dispersion across a metro area, experiences of safety and hospitability (e.g., the number of affirming religious institutions, recent marriage votes, the nomination and/or election of LBQ candidates), and the presence or absence of an established tradition of LBQ place ownership and place claiming (as indicated by women's and LGBTQ land and LBQ small business ownership), position LBQ residents relative to a sense of "outside-togetherness" that engenders emphasis on sexuality as an enduring trait and a source of inimitable common ground. Some conditions encourage the "outside togetherness" found in San Luis Obispo and Portland, whereas the opposite conditions encourage the sense of "insiderness" found in Ithaca and among newcomers to Greenfield that encourages emphasis on integration and a rejection of traditional identity politics.

Put differently, if we wanted to create a post-identity-politics environment in which LBQ residents celebrate integration, we would want a large and highly visible LBQ population—one that outnumbers gay men—anchored by LBQ-owned establishments and LBQ elected officials, and dispersed across neighborhoods and even surrounding villages. We would also want a city in which LBQ residents experience a sense of safety and belonging, buoyed by markers of acceptance, such as the presence of affirming religious institutions and a sense of an enduring local LBQ legacy, perhaps marked by stories of extant women's and LBQ collectives or lesbian bookstores. We might also predict that these conditions are more likely to be found in places, like Greenfield and Ithaca, that contain or are proximate to multiple longstanding and prominent educational institutions and in places that have cultivated progressive movements (beyond those that directly pertain to LBQ populations), such as Greenfield and Ithaca's natural and organic foods movements and history of environmental advocacy.[21]

Looking across the cities it becomes apparent that LBQ residents are quite sensitive to signals of abundance and acceptance. After all, neither San Luis Obispo nor Portland is a particularly inhospitable place to be LBQ, nor are Greenfield and Ithaca markedly more welcoming. All four cities are places to which many informants relocated anticipating safety and acceptance. This underlines how subtle differences in a city's ecology can influence cultures; the difference, for instance, of having 24 percent of religious institutions be affirming (San Luis Obispo) versus 43 percent (Greenfield), and of lesbian couples composing 15.93 percent of unmarried households (Greenfield) versus 9.3 percent (Portland) (Bureau of the Census 2010). Cumulatively, these differences in abundance and acceptance powerfully direct identities toward or away from identity politics. Next, though, I underline how abundance and acceptance work with other facets of local ecology to direct sexual identity cultures.

Place Narratives

Having tackled the question of why the sites pair in their orientations to identity politics, this section addresses an opposite but closely related question: why aren't all integrationist or identity-politics cultures identical? Why, in San Luis Obispo, do residents "do" identity politics by emphasizing lesbian identities, whereas in Portland they emphasize hybridity and hyphenation? While acceptance and numbers direct identity cultures toward or away from "outside togetherness" and the identity politics it cultivates, they do not alone cast sexual identity culture. Place narratives—or the stories locals tell about where they live—that residents encounter and advance are also instrumental.[22]

There are three paths via which place narratives influence identity culture. Most powerfully, narratives provide models of who and how one should be in the local context. This becomes especially apparent when we consider the source of the differences between the San Luis Obispo and Portland brands of identity politics. Narratives also shape or intervene in residents' interpolation of what Harvey Molotch (2002) proposes we think of as the "hard features" of place or facts and figures; in Ithaca, for instance, narratives that present the city as a harmonious bubble encourage LBQ individuals' disavowal of experiences of fear and exclusion. In this sense, narratives can exacerbate, mitigate, or even obfuscate the influence of other local conditions, particularly those related to abundance and acceptance. Finally, models of the appropriate local resident and lifestyle are embedded not only in talk of the place where one lives but also in talk of other places. This is particularly apparent in Greenfield, where many frequently evoke neighboring North-ampton as a crucial point of contrast to Greenfield.

The first path—narrative influence—is especially apparent when we consider why identity politics takes different form in San Luis Obispo and Port-land.[23] LBQ residents present Portland as cutting edge, quirky, and hard-scrabble: "I say that it's surprising. I say that there's a lot of young, beautiful, cool interesting people here that you wouldn't expect to find in Maine. It's kind of off the beaten path." Another echoes this: "The ocean and the brick streets . . . the architecture, which doesn't seem to fit together but which I really like nonetheless . . . I enjoy the quirks." They portray Portland as a desirable alternative to larger cities: "I say that Portland is like a mini–Park Slope. . . . I'll say, 'Think of a bigger JP,'" a reference to Boston's Jamaica Plain neighborhood. Another agrees: "I used to live in Brooklyn and it reminds me a lot of Brooklyn in terms of sort of having cute shops and a lot of diversity." They present Portland as a site of urbanity and creativity, offering parallel narratives about the city and its residents. One describes Portland's East End as peopled by LBQ residents who are "just really creative and young. . . . The feeling over here is almost bohemian." Here, they touch on architecture and landscape, but especially emphasize Portland's (urbane) social character.

In contrast, San Luis Obispo narratives highlight the (nonurban) land-scape. One boasts that she lives in "Camelot"; a couple describes it as "Mid-dle Earth." Habitually, informants emphasize the natural over the social: "the nature and the weather"; "being by the ocean, the fresh air"; "it is just pure beauty . . . it's the water, its mountains . . . the air."

Crucially, they rarely draw parallels between San Luis Obispo and other California cities; they present their city as a refuge from the Central Valley, other rural locales, and conservative Western cities, but not as a formida-ble lefty haven. One said: "San Luis is more conservative than some of the other areas. . . . It's not akin to the [Central] Valley, which is more solidly conservative. It's sort of a blend between coastal liberal and conservative." Despite acknowledgment of this (mild) conservatism, beyond advocating for gay marriage, few seek to transform the area. San Luis Obispo, they sug-gest, is a place one comes to *be*—to pause for the view atop a mountain or to find a quiet life among retirees in a mobile home park—not to innovate or transform.

The details of these LBQ place narratives parallel the ways each city has marketed and branded itself.[24] City narratives present San Luis Obispo as an escape. The Chamber of Commerce's website[25]—devoted to encouraging tourism—proclaims San Luis "the happiest city in America" (borrowing the claim from a 2010 book) and notes many activities one can engage in: "Hiking, Biking, Beaches, Farmers Markets, Wine Tasting, Shopping, Relaxing."[26] But it and related websites also presents San Luis and its "laidback" environs as a place of welcome *in*activity: of vineyards, beaches, and spas in which one "unwind[s] from the stresses of life" and sips "worries away."[27] San Luis Obispo, with its idyllic weather, galleries, hiking, and nearby beaches, is presented as an even-keeled alternative to other coastal cities. A 2011 *USA Today* article encapsulates this, noting that its acronym, "appropriately, is SLO. Or as locals call it: Slo Town" (Clark 2011).

In contrast, while Portland's Chamber of Commerce and its official tourism site promote the city as a tourist destination and a "top city to live" (Forbes 2009), it is presented as anything but slow or an escape. Rather, it is "the economic engine of Maine" and "the hub of business activity in Maine."[28] Moreover, "Portland's natural deep water port rivals Boston, New York and Philadelphia. . . . With its growing airport, discount airlines, frequent buses and daily train service . . . Portland, Maine is fast becoming *the* place to live and work."[29] Thus, Portland presents itself as a place of natural charm, culture, and culinary delight, but also as an economic engine with a rising creative profile. This mirrors how Portland informants cast themselves, as innovators and identity entrepreneurs, and contrasts with San Luis Obispo residents who present themselves as having accomplished the work of self-discovery and now seek the "good life" in a place of quiet and beauty.

Few people, gay or straight, would believe that their identities have been shaped by a local tourism website. I point out this connection not to say that websites or tourist slogans directly make us, but rather to show how narratives about the character of the city where we live, which slogans and websites partially capture and propel, influence how we think about our own character, as individuals and as members of a group. That is, these narratives, partially bolstered by the bumper stickers and website slogans that they inform, help to shape how LBQ residents fashion their identity politics, with Portlanders approaching identity as a personal project and opportunity for self-expression, and San Luis Obispo residents presenting it as a fact to be acknowledged and incorporated, not played with or displayed.

Differences in the degree to which narratives cast each city as a "gay" place and, more generally, as hospitable to LBQ individuals, also fuel these different approaches to identity politics. While San Luis Obispo websites present the area as "accepting," Portland's tourism site devotes an entire section to LGBTQ visitors, proclaiming that, "Portland's lesbian, gay, bisexual, transgender and questioning roots go back . . . waaaay back."[30] Indeed, one site *incorrectly* states that Portland, Maine, is "#3 in the country in terms of per capita lesbian couples."[31] In this sense, Portland takes steps unmatched by San Luis Obispo to present itself as a "gay mecca" (ibid). Lest this narrative seem to contradict informants' lukewarm sense of acceptance, its boosterism contrasts with Ithaca and Greenfield's quiet confidence with regard to hospitability; in 2007 *The Advocate* (Caldwell 2007) listed Ithaca as one of the "Best Places to Live," and locals boast that Greenfield is a short drive from "Lesbianville, USA."[32]

These narrative differences parallel differences in how LBQ residents and others interpret the many things that San Luis Obispo and Portland share in common, from a booming tourism industry to excellent (though not internationally famous) educational institutions, and from a moderate sense of hospitability to (relative to the other two cities) a lower proportion of lesbian couples. While tourism bureaus, the Chamber, magazines, and books present each as tourist destinations in which hospitability to LBQs cannot go without saying, there are important narrative differences, too—with San Luis Obispo presented as a low-key alternative to coastal, urban centers, and Portland presented as a rising regional contender and innovator. In sum, both cities present themselves as beautiful and semiremote, but one (Portland) promotes the city's remove—their "frontier"—as a stage or opportunity from which to speak to other cities, while the other (San Luis) is presented as an idyllic respite from everywhere else. The sites' sexual identity cultures mirror these broader narrative patterns, with Portland's LBQ residents emphasizing creative, cutting-edge identity politics, and San Luis Obispo residents emphasizing a more traditional version thereof. These subtle narrative differences contribute to areas of dissimilarity in their identity cultures, and partially explain how and why abundance and acceptance start, but don't finish, the task of explaining overlap and discord in city identity cultures.

Place narratives do not just provide a model of who to be or how to live, they also instruct residents on how to interpret or weigh other dimensions of city ecology. All narratives, in one way or another, instruct their listeners. After all, such is the most basic function of a story, to tell us how to live in this world. But their instructional purpose becomes especially clear when we consider how place narratives influence how residents interpolate indicators of abundance and acceptance. This second path is especially apparent in Ithaca. There, informants' narratives about the city as safe haven are inaccurate, on two counts: they do not coincide with FBI hate crime data or with informants' own experiences. First, residents overestimate the degree to which Ithaca is free of crime related to sexual identity.[33] With the exception of one woman who described being physically threatened by a former partner and her family, residents initially and seemingly instinctively responded to a question about safety by stating that they are *entirely* safe and without fear. However, when pressed, some acknowledge how their experiences contradict this. Specifically, when I followed a "sense of safety" question with one about experiences of violence, harassment, or discrimination, they often admitted that they had, in fact, experienced these things. One recounted teenagers forcing her car off the road while taunting her for the bumper stickers that outed her. Several recalled being harassed on the street outside an LBQ-owned bar.[34] Ithacans are also "wrong" in their oft-stated mantra that Ithaca is, as the ubiquitous bumper sticker says, "ten square miles surrounded by reality."

Yet Ithacans are not alone. LBQ residents in all of these cities experience their own as a bastion of tolerance, and in none of the sites do crime statistics bear this out. Each experiences *higher* rates of reported sexual orientation and other hate crimes than their respective counties or states.[35]

What is the source of mismatch between stories women tell about the degree to which they are safe and accepted, and data thereon? Narratives about place—in Ithaca a narrative best embodied by the slogan that Ithaca is "ten square miles surrounded by reality"—inform interpolation of the local ecology. In Ithaca's case, this narrative and a closely relatedly one about Ithaca as one of the "best college towns" in America, with attendant assumptions about tolerance and progressive politics, discourages residents from paying attention to moments in which Ithaca is not the safe "bubble" of "integration" residents (and the Chamber of Commerce) wish it to be.[36] Indeed, place narratives are so influential that, despite a wide variety of experiences with violence and harassment in Ithaca, initial responses to my safety questions—with only that one exception—were uniformly positive; place narratives encourage a uniform sensibility about self and local experience (despite, for instance, moments when crowds have witnessed harassment of LBQ residents outside of Felicia's on State Street in downtown Ithaca). Thus, abundance and acceptance certainly influence identity cultures, but place narratives also intervene as these cultures are being formed and shape how informants interpret features of city ecology related to abundance and acceptance.

Finally, narratives about *other* places are also influential. In each city, the narratives I heard referenced both near and distant places (e.g., how Brooklyn and Boston are disparate from Ithaca or Portland); in all cities, talk of other places bolsters narratives about how one's own city is special. However, stories about another place are particularly evident and influential in Greenfield. There, residents encounter and extend competing narratives about Greenfield and neighboring Northampton. As we have already seen, these dual narratives help to produce Greenfield's bifurcated identity culture.

Some present Greenfield as an extension of Northampton, evoking their shared Pioneer Valley. One woman said, "I was interested in the area because I knew about Northampton, you know, the 'Provincetown of the West.' . . . I just knew that there were a lot of lesbians in the Pioneer Valley [and that] the people of that persuasion called it the Happy Valley." Notably, this woman does not differentiate between the northern and southern portions of the Valley, where Greenfield and Northampton sit, respectively. Another echoes this, emphasizing traits that connect disparate parts of the Valley: "This area is called Happy Valley. . . . There's a lot of ex-hippies who live here, people who are disfranchised one way or another—either through economics or education or orientation or politics. . . . [We] form a body." In this narrative, Greenfield and Northampton also "clump together" to form a single "Happy Valley."

An alternate narrative distinguishes Greenfield from Northampton; yet here, too, Northampton plays a defining role. The chef whom we met in chapter 4 suggests (sounding like Ithacans) that identity in Greenfield, contra Northampton, is formulated around interests and lifestyle:

When you're in Northampton and you work in a restaurant everybody's like, "Well, what else do you do?" Like you must be a student or an artist or something and I wasn't and I liked how [in Greenfield] everyone was like, "What are you growing this year?" You know, like, "Do you have any extra seedlings?" Like everybody talks about their gardens and how they're brewing beer in the bathroom, and I really liked the fact that people were settled here in Greenfield and doing interesting things.

Those, like the woman above, who emphasize general distinctions between Greenfield and Northampton use talk of Northampton to underline what is distinctive about Greenfield residents' orientation to sexuality. Recall the woman who says that Greenfield's LBQ residents, in contrast to those in Northampton, were "sort of just doing their thing and lesbian wasn't the focus." Likewise, the woman who celebrates the absence of "rich, beautiful" lesbians in Greenfield—a group she associates with Northampton. In this narrative, Greenfield is the anti-Northampton: a down to earth, nature-centered place in which sexual identity is ancillary. Instead, a generalized lifestyle flourishes, rooted in, for instance, what one cooks, grows, or brews, and what one believes defines the self.

These dual narratives—Greenfield as a northern extension of Northampton and Greenfield as humble, less identity-driven alternative to Northampton—help to carve space for dual identity cultures, as we have seen. With more recent migrants, who are more apt to articulate integrationist tendencies, emphasizing Greenfield's distinction from Northampton, and long-standing residents, who tend to adhere to an identity-politics framework, emphasizing synergies between Greenfield and Northampton.

Thus, via three overlapping paths—providing a script for who one should be and how one should live in a place, intervening in the effects of other place elements and facilitating a sense of the local constructed in contradistinction to other places (and people)—LBQ migrants encounter and extend scripts about the "character" of their new place of residence and the kind of self that belongs there. Over and again, residents interpret place narratives as meaningful for sexual identity, translating them into narratives about the "appropriate" way to be LBQ in their hometown. As a result, narrative differences extend the heterogeneity of contemporary LBQ identities; even if two cities were perfectly matched in terms of abundance and acceptance, city-specific narratives would cast each place's identity culture in a distinct fashion, in part by directing interpolation of abundance and acceptance. Thus, as long as we continue to tell novel stories about the cities in which we live, and about how they are different than other places, we can anticipate the place-specific recasting of the self.

Socioscape

This section more directly engages something that all of us do when we move to a new place: we seek and interpret evidence of the local ecology, particularly about its social dimensions.[37] As we have seen, our LBQ residents, as migrants and as members of a minority, are shaped by abundance and acceptance and city narratives. However, an additional feature of the local ecology is also of moderate influence: the "socioscape," a broad and sometimes abstract concept that encompasses the demographic, social, and cultural characteristics of city residents, particularly of LBQ residents.[38]

Most of us, on moving, seek to learn what we can about our new neighbors: what they do for work and fun, how long they've lived in the city, and the kinds of people with whom they socialize. For their part, LBQ migrants seek evidence about their neighbors, but especially about other LBQ residents. They quickly develop a sense of the demographic features, life histories, and cultural orientations of other people like them—including their orientation to sexual identity and difference.

Because LBQ newcomers are attentive to the cultural orientations of the existing LBQ population in that place, the identity culture and other dimensions of city ecology constitute a positive feedback loop. An identity culture takes basic shape in response to abundance and acceptance and place narratives, but, once established, the city that newcomers encounter is marked by, among other things, that identity culture. In this sense, even though other features of the local ecology give basic and initial form to identity culture, LBQ migrants come to contribute to the broader city "character" and partially constitute the social world in which these newcomers soon find themselves enmeshed. From the case of Greenfield, and the recent shift in identity culture there, we know that identity culture does not automatically replicate or independently renew itself; if it did, Greenfield's LBQ residents, new and old, would only identify as lesbian feminist. But that is not the full story; the pages below explore how identity culture, and, more substantially, LBQ demographic and social traits, are neither passive.

As they make a home for themselves in their new city, LBQ newcomers are particularly attentive to certain traits, such as the paths that other migrants have taken to their new city, as well as their educational backgrounds. These traits of the LBQ population do not directly or independently shape identity culture; if they did, we would expect the demographic profiles of LBQ residents of each city to be far more distinctive than they actually are. Yet neither are these traits irrelevant. Together with place narratives, then, a city's particular stew of population traits—which is inextricably linked to stories that LBQ residents convey to one another about who they are—encourage city-specific responses to shared ecological conditions (such as, in the case of San Luis Obispo and Portland, a restrained sense of belonging). Furthermore, place narratives also shape the meaning and weight of specific LBQ population traits; for instance, residents of most of the cities are, on average, unusually highly educated and many have attended high-status schools— but in Portland this looms especially large in the stories LBQ residents convey about themselves. The influence of LBQ demographics, and how they are interpreted in and through broader place narratives, reveal themselves when we return to the question of why Portland and San Luis Obispo are home to distinctive brands of identity politics.

There are subtle differences between the demographic profiles and life histories of the Portland and San Luis Obispo residents with whom I spoke. Those in San Luis Obispo are less highly educated and have attended fewer "top" schools than those in Portland (see figs. 5.2 and 5.3). In addition, a higher proportion of Portland informants have lived in large cities, maintaining ties to those large cities via friends, family, and work. These differences provide residents in Portland and in SLO with distinct sets of resources as they encounter similar ecological conditions (as we have seen, a dispersed and moderately sized LBQ population, and an uneven sense of abundance and acceptance). In other words, these demographic profiles and life histories do not (independently) tip residents toward or away from identity politics, but they do contribute to each city's distinctive vein of identity politics.

In Portland, more than in any other site, LBQ residents told me eagerly that the LBQ population—young, creative, and urbane—mirrors and complements city character. That connection between a place and its people heightens the perceived significance of these collective traits for their identity culture. Many in Portland present the city as a place that LBQ individuals seek in order to create a particular kind of life. In turn, they partially attribute the city's "edgy," "creative," and "quirky" character to the LBQ residents who have come here to seek this kind of life. One suggests that Portlanders move from urban centers for novel opportunities: "I know people who have moved from the other Portland [Oregon], and people who have moved from Boston." Portland is thus seen as an urbane alternative to bigger or more well-established gay and lesbian centers—Boston, New York, or Northampton—other places that Portlanders see as at least as hospitable, if not more so, to LBQ populations. One said: "A lot of people I've met recently have actually moved from New York City. . . . They just end up loving it here and winding up here. And in a lot of ways this place . . . is similar to Brooklyn." Another states why she prefers Portland to Boston: "I lived on Mission Hill. I lived in the Back Bay . . . and I spent a lot of time in Jamaica Plain. . . . [Boston] maintains a very closed scope of seeing, I think." Cumulatively, they present Portland not as a place one "lands," but, instead, as a city sought for reasons related to but also extending beyond sexuality; a fecund and cutting-edge city worthy of migration from major metropolises. This is a way of talking about Portland, but it is also a way of communicating the basic "character" of LBQ residents. Here, residents present their LBQ neighbors, like the city, as urbane and edgy, as agents of creativity.

For their part, with the exception of a few who report having sought landscape and outdoor activities, San Luis Obispo residents suggest that lifestyle concerns did not drive their moves. Instead, they report relocating to be near aging parents, or to attend the local community college, or for work. A musician was drawn by desire, at middle age, to live near her parents: "My folks lived down in Southern California and they moved up here." Another retired to San Luis Obispo to care for her father, and yet another for a job at CALPOLY. In this manner they told me that San Luis Obispo's cultural attributes *permit* their moves, and many celebrate the city as a hospitable alternative to California's Central Valley, but few identify these features as primary, motivating forces for their relocation.

Experiences and narratives about relocation relate to broader ways of framing the collective traits of a given LBQ population; for instance, there are close parallels between how residents frame their residential and educational paths. LBQ residents of San Luis Obispo, as we have seen, present themselves as practical people. They present degrees, like residential choices, as utilitarian. One said that after beginning her studies at a large public university she rethought her major to better align with career opportunities: "I changed my major to criminal justice, and was thinking of [being] either [a] lawyer or cop." Another explained how divorce and coming out encouraged her to adopt a pragmatic approach to education:

> I went to a college [that] at the time was one of the top ten colleges in the country for schools of its size. . . . It was a really good school. And . . . at the time I thought I was going to go on to be a clinical psychologist, but that's another seven years down the road and in the meantime I had met a guy who was in the military and was sent to Vietnam and I wound up with two little kids and then divorced and the kids had gotten used to eating. . . . They're funny about that. And so I wound up digging up an eight hundred square foot vegetable garden, poaching deer, and going back to nursing school.

Over and again, San Luis Obispo residents present educational, residential, and other life choices, like identities, as inevitable. That impulse informs how they "do" identity politics.

In contrast, Portland residents frequently emphasize how schools, like residential choices, influence lifestyle. Indeed, many emphasize specific institutions they attended: selective liberal arts colleges with lefty reputations such as Hampshire, Oberlin, and Sarah Lawrence; women's colleges such as Smith, Barnard, and Mount Holyoke; other elite Northeastern institutions, such as Harvard, Brown, Princeton, Swarthmore, and Bates. Many frame this bundle of well-known schools as a vital source of knowledge about queer politics and identities, and credit the collective educational backgrounds of the city's LBQ population with helping to constitute the intellectual character of identity talk in Portland. Paralleling narratives about why they've moved to Portland, these LBQ residents credit college with shaping their approach to life; one said of her school, "It was really formative." An Oberlin grad said, "I went to the multicultural resource center a lot and hung out with the LGBTQ coordinator. . . . [I] was friends with people who had politicized queer identities"; she brings the conversations she had at Oberlin to the table in Portland—even if her interpolation of herself as a sexual person has shifted since moving to Maine. Residents present such colleges and universities, like Portland itself, as arenas for identity play: "[I] saw Hampshire and said, 'Oh my God, here's all these freaky people, I have to go here.'" Their embrace of intellectual play alongside identity, and of seminar-style debate encountered at such schools, contributes to the Portland brand of identity politics.[39]

How exactly does a newcomer encounter manifestations of socioscape? How does she learn that her neighbors are intellectual and creative or, alternately, think of themselves as matter of fact or practical? In short: because she is told, again and again, in ways large and small, implicit and explicit, one way or another in nearly every encounter with LBQ residents. Take one of the many examples we have explored: at a potluck for "older" San Luis Obispo lesbians, a newcomer was presented with the life histories of local residents and gained an understanding of how those residents frame their histories. She also came face to face with residents' articulation of a central tenet of the identity culture: the notion of sexuality as an innate and immutable fact of life. At the dinner, a longer-term resident mentioned an article on sexualities. Using herself as evidence, she argued that sexual identity is innate and rooted in biology ("I thought [heterosexuality] was a matter of practice. I practiced and practiced. It is not"). The newcomer countered that socialization shapes gender and sexuality. The rest of the women gently disagreed, drawing on their own stories, until the newcomer abandoned her position. This moment is a small one, the kind of interaction many of us experience in one way or another all the time; rarely do we consider the significance of such moments for our sense of identity. Yet this moment captures a key path by which socioscape is communicated by old residents and thus regenerated for new residents: via presentation of the character of the local LBQ population, including their identity culture, to a newcomer. Here, she learned that several had been married to men, that most had encountered theories of socialization in college classrooms, and that local residents are in the habit of reading learned and lefty publications, such as the *New York Times* and the *New Yorker*, and discussing their content. Moreover, she walked away mindful of the dominance of *lesbian* identity in particular in San Luis Obispo and of residents' confidence in the notion of sexual identity as innate and life defining.

Think about how that exchange might have unfolded in a room populated by Portlanders. For instance, that potluck debate would, ultimately, have arrived at a similar conclusion: that sexual identity is innate and life defining. Yet the path to get to that point would have doubtless been different: in a room full of Portland residents, gender identity and hybridity and hyphenation would have been front and center, and the conversation might have included overt references to theories encountered in college or university texts and classroom debates. That hypothetical difference helps us further envision how the backgrounds of LBQ residents subtly influence the contours of their identity cultures.

Some LBQ residents are aware that such interactions communicate identity culture, however unintentionally, to newcomers and others. In fact, some articulate misgivings about instances when they feel they serve as ambassadors of an identity culture and, as a result, influence newcomers. For instance, a gender-queer resident I spoke with laments the amount of integration they see in Ithaca, but nonetheless instructs newcomers to read the absence of a lesbian bookstore or community center as signs of integration rather than as intolerance. The organizers of the Portland Dyke March are self-conscious about the prominent role of femme-identified women on the planning committee and about their decision, at one of the first marches, to distribute "femme" stickers to those they so identified. In each case, they realized, too late, that they were representing, and encouraging, one particular identity culture. Self-consciousness about their role as ambassadors of an established culture reveals their sense that such interactions and representations are, indeed, consequential; that these seemingly small moments do indeed influence how another resident might think about herself. Indeed, the above evidence of quick adoption suggests that this sense of influence is well founded; identity cultures inevitably take shape in relation to local context and are constantly created and renewed via narrative and interaction, particularly that triggered by newcomers' arrival.

The influence of extant identity culture on migrants is most apparent in the words of those who complain about the constraints of the identity culture of their new home, even as they adopt it. Take, for instance, the Ithaca mother who moved seeking integration, but who remained nostalgic for the identity politics she had found elsewhere. Or, also in Ithaca, residents who told me that they initially misread indicators of the abundant LBQ population—such as the ubiquity of softball teams, a lesbian-owned bar, and the legacy of a women's bookstore—as promising an identity-politics emphasis. For her part, a Portland woman expressed misgivings about the local emphasis on microidentities, yet spoke of her "beautiful femme" partner. Narratives don't always center on disappointment, although they are particularly apparent in the words of the disappointed; those who feel somewhat apart from an identity culture are often the best able to describe it.[40] Other times, narratives emphasize surprise, such as a migrant from San Francisco who anticipated, incorrectly, that in "less gay" San Luis Obispo her lesbian identity would be on the backburner. Above all else, these examples demonstrate newcomers' awareness of the existence of a city-specific identity culture and, in some cases, their sense of the inevitability of adoption thereof.

Thus, residents' collective demographic, social, and cultural traits provide resources they use as they assemble local identities. Such traits are interpolated in and through local place narratives and the more general, but closely related, sense of city "character."[41] That is, residents do not speak of demographic facts and figures, such as median years of education or the proportion of LBQ individuals once married to men. Instead, they emphasize their perceptions of how place and person meet; just as place narratives influence a sense of safety in Ithaca, residents interpret LBQ population traits via broad narratives about place. This underlines how they experience LBQ groups as place-specific, as well as their sense that LBQ residents are at once constituted by *and* constitutive of city "character." Put differently, the young, creative, and highly educated Portland LBQ resident contributes to Portland's social profile—but she also thinks of herself as young, creative, and highly educated because she lives in a place that thinks of itself as possessing those traits.

One thing that stands out in the narratives of LBQ residents is a consistent presentation of their city's LBQ population as relatively homogeneous; with the exception of Greenfield, residents emphasize being a part of a place-wide cohort, and downplay the presence of multiple and distinct cohorts within their city, which are shaped by generation or interests or other traits.[42] This sense of a monolithic LBQ body—highly educated, urbane, and edgy in Portland; utilitarian and family oriented in San Luis Obispo—reinforces the influence of the dominant identity culture; opportunities for identity variation are limited when one does not select among cohorts, but, instead, encounters a dominant orientation and sees that residents are bound together by common demographics and life histories.[43]

The role of socioscape, of course, has a circular dimension: I have argued that sexual identity cultures respond to dimensions of city ecology and that one of these dimensions is the LBQ population itself.[44] While this may seem inelegant, or even tautological, it accurately captures how informants experience city ecology on the ground and day by day: as something that dominates them but that they also shape, even if only subtly (e.g., via their collective traits); as something that is both enduring *and* evolving. These residents are both reacting to and engaging in the formation of local ecology, or what Jack Halberstam (2005) terms "queer place-making"

(6). That engagement, again, is both circular and multiple: these residents understand self- and group identity to be made or shaped by place, but also recognize their social group and its identity culture as partially constitutive of that place.[45] I encountered this circularity across each city I examined, and though I initially resisted it, I now believe it is every bit as important as more straightforward aspects like abundance and acceptance and narratives. I propose that city ecology is not merely an independent variable, shaping identities, but something that LBQ residents, as a group, influence.

This instructs us to approach city ecology as at once constituting, and constituted—and not only once, in the past, by a defining event or decision, but over and again, yesterday and today—as LBQ residents with degrees from elite schools take to the streets of Portland's downtown for their annual Dyke March and as fifty- and sixty-year-old lesbian-identified women approach the back door of a bank outside of San Luis Obispo, potluck dishes in hand.[46] Where LBQ residents meet and with whom they gather is a product of their city, but as any newcomer quickly realizes, such residents are also, quite literally, part of that cityscape. In this sense, "cityscape" and "socioscape" blur and blend, becoming, together, a responsive and evolving city ecology.

Conclusion

The comparative discussion of this chapter, I hope, has built on our ongoing investigation of how and why the local matters. Here we have seen how a city's concatenation of ecological dimensions create the social environment that LBQ migrants encounter on moving there, and how—in accordance with those features—they adjust their relation to local heterosexuals, to other LBQ individuals, and, ultimately, to their own sexual identity.

This chapter offers lessons that extend beyond the puzzle at hand. One, it calls us to reconsider traditional ways of thinking about "place" and cities. We have seen that categorical and quantitative ecological differences are not the only influence. Identity cultures respond to subtle differences in city ecology, including a combination of mutually constitutive facts (e.g., the proportion of lesbian couples) and scripts (e.g., place narratives), or what Harvey Molotch terms "hard features" and "soft factors" (2002). Recognizing that essential combination helps us avoid reductive assumptions. If we try to understand cities and their distinctions as defined by discrete attributes, events, or narratives, or as belonging in discrete categories, we miss the degree to which these individual attributes assemble into a more complex and influential ecology, as well as how residents are at once shaped by and constitutive of place. Cities are per capita income, roads and bridges, and city council politics; cities are also the stories we tell about these and every other facet of city life, as well as the people who hear and tell these stories.

This chapter absorbs the lessons of each individual city and then goes even further in upending the premise that categorical differences drive identity variation. Most of us are in the habit of thinking of cities as belonging in one box or another, perhaps no more so than when we think about gay, lesbian, bisexual, transgender, queer, and intersex (GLBTQI) individuals and the places they live. However, our thinking about place and identity should not stop there; the world is not neatly divisible into spaces in which GLBTQI populations are shunned and other spaces where they are embraced; into spaces where we congregate and others spaces that we flee. Conversely, this book has highlighted substantial variation in identity cultures within four cities that, in the popular imagination, look quite similar to each other, standing together as bastions of tolerance and progressive politics. This instructs that identities do not just respond to whether one lives in a red or blue state or in the country or a big city; they respond to more subtle differences in what it feels like to LBQ in a place. Moreover, as we have also seen, LBQ identities take shape not only in relation to a particular measure like the relative degree of tolerance or acceptance but also in response to more general ecological dimensions, such as broad-reaching narratives about what kind of a place a city is.

Thus, we have here modeled a holistic approach to cities by including the traits, identities, and narratives of the study population in our conception of "ecology," and by suggesting that the weight and role of each can fluctuate, depending on the city, and are context dependent. This challenges the notion that we ought to evaluate the impact of individual ecological traits or sets thereof on population outcomes and other dependent variables.[47] That assumption is often reductive. At what point do outcomes *become* a part of place or otherwise impact "independent" variables? Are the health, or education levels, or identities of a given population products of ecology or producers thereof? Moreover, ecological conditions do not just influence actors; actors help to constitute that ecology, over and again through their presence, and through their interactions with the many other components of that ecology. In sum, this book reveals city ecologies that are evolving, idiosyncratic, dynamic, and best approached holistically.

Are all identities responsive to city ecology? While a definitive answer requires further investigation, the resounding patterns this chapter uncovers suggest that we can anticipate that abundance and acceptance, narratives, and socioscape are broadly consequential. A sense of scarcity and insecurity likely encourages an identity-politics, or "outside togetherness," orientation across a range of populations and places. It is also likely that minority groups' identities are especially sensitive to ecological conditions; those who are numerically in the minority, and especially those who experience social, cultural, and political marginalization are presumably, by necessity, more attentive to city ecology than other, more status-secure groups. If a person's place on the "inside" is insecure, it is little surprise that one will busy oneself with the work of carefully assessing local conditions—including city demographic traits and especially the traits of other members of the group of which one is a part.

However, I have also underlined how different dimensions of ecology—for example, narratives, abundance, and socioscape—interact, creating idiosyncratic, local responses to conditions also present in other cities. Those idiosyncrasies caution us against the easy assumption that a certain threshold of safety, or a certain type of narrative, will function predictably across all cities, while nonetheless suggesting that the ecological dimensions that this chapter identifies are of broad consequence, perhaps especially for migrants and minority groups who rely on being closely attentive to local conditions.

How do some cities generate an ecology that lends itself to the post-identity politics found in Ithaca and Greenfield, while cities like Portland and San Luis Obispo generate identity politics? This chapter has not offered an extended discussion of how, for instance, Portland became Portland or Ithaca became Ithaca. However, as a thought experiment we can consider the underlying conditions required to create a city ecology generative of identity politics, like that found in San Luis Obispo and Portland. For instance, to encourage identity politics among LBQ residents we might cultivate the presence of gay men, perhaps via the development of the type of arts scene and expansive commercial opportunities present in the two cities. We could also develop only a single major college or university, with other high-profile private and public colleges and universities located in other parts of the state. We might also draw tourists to the locale, and rely on the moderate politics of the broader county to discourage high profile activism on behalf of progressive causes and to limit overt displays of acceptance by institutions that heterosexuals dominate. Of course, the first residents of San Luis Obispo and Portland did not do any of those things, or at least didn't do any of these things intentionally. They did not set out to cultivate cities with ecological conditions that would encourage identity politics. Rather than exploring intention, I gesture to the many accidents of history and the many discrete choices—political and social and economic alike—that, together, create the places we know today. Those historical accidents make Ithaca a place with more "affirming" religious institutions, and a higher proportion of lesbian couple households, than San Luis Obispo; a whole other series of accidents, similarly, attract more gay men to Portland than to Greenfield.[48]

In closing, this chapter demonstrates the value of careful consideration of city ecology. The lessons it offers may be extended as we grapple with, among other things, heterogeneity in politics, community dynamics, gender, and race. Identities shape movements, migration, organizations, ties, and interactions, and the notion of places as productive of identity should be urgently integrated into how we think about these identity-related topics.[49] Going forward we ought to devote far greater attention to how and why places matter, and to further consideration of culture as a product not only of the group, region, or nation but also of specific locales.

Sexual Identity as Life-defining   Sexual Identity as Ancillary/Value Integration

<-->

+ San Luis Obispo   + Portland   +Greenfield   +Ithaca

5.1. Visual approximation of attitudes, by site, to identity politics and integrationist approaches to sexual identity.

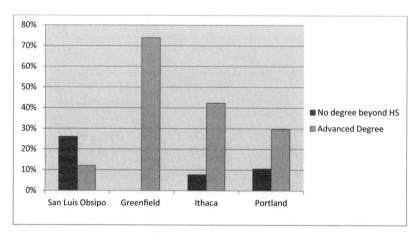

5.2. Respondents' educational characteristics by site. Educational characteristics are from respondent surveys and interviews.

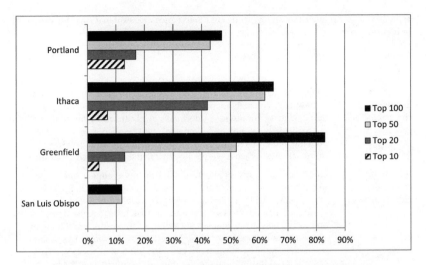

5.3. Prestige of respondents' undergraduate and graduate educational institutions. Educational characteristics are from respondent surveys and interviews; institutional prestige is from *US News and World Report* 2012 ranking of national universities and liberal arts colleges.

Table 5.1. Why do identities vary by study city? Select "negative explanations" for variation in identities by site

Possible explanation	Reason for elimination
Informants' demographic characteristics	Differences across the cities in terms of informants' race, age, and education are minimal. Where differences exist, they stop short of explaining variation in identity. For instance, informants in all sites are highly educated, but particularly so in Ithaca, Greenfield, and, to a slightly lesser degree, Portland. Moreover, many residents of Ithaca and Portland have degrees from high-prestige schools—yet identity orientations in each are distinct.
Informants' economic characteristics	One difference worthy of attention is informants' economic traits, namely, Ithaca informants' apparent affluence relative to informants in San Luis Obispo, Greenfield, and Portland. For three reasons this difference is less substantial than numbers seem to indicate. First, Ithaca's respondent population is internally heterogeneous, including a few wealthy individuals and many with quite modest incomes. Second, across site differences in social position are minimized when one considers informants' mean years of education and institutional prestige. Ithaca, Greenfield, and Portland possess notably highly educated LBQ populations (e.g., Ithaca and Portland respondents' mean years of education are 15.8 and 16.3, respectively). Moreover, Portland respondents attended particularly elite schools; 12 percent of Portland respondents who attended college or university enrolled at a top-ten school (according to 2012 *US News and World Report*). More than 21 percent attended a college or university ranked between eleven and twenty-five, and 7 percent attended one ranked between twenty-six and thirty-five. Third, respondents' median home values are higher in Portland than in the other sites.
Ethnographer's role/identity	Nearly constant across site/solo ethnographer.
Lesbian generations	Residents in each site are age diverse, and local identities span age/generational differences. Moreover, sites with lower median age (Ithaca and San Luis Obispo) or higher proportions of LBQ residents aged fifty years or above (in sample) (Greenfield and San Luis) nonetheless have quite distinct identity cultures.
Migratory networks	Many LBQ residents in each site, particularly in Ithaca, Greenfield, and Portland, have lived in the same large cities and even in the same neighborhoods in those cities (e.g., Boston's Jamaica Plain and Brooklyn's Park Slope). Nearly all report that they were surprised by the identity culture of their new home.

Note: "Negative explanations" is from Katz (1982); the phrase is not intended to suggest that the above explanations altogether fail, but rather that in isolation they are insufficient explanations for variation in identities across sites.

Table 5.2. Economic and demographic characteristics of the research sites

City	Type	Population	Median family income, $	Per capita income, $	Population below poverty level, %	Median home value, $	Female same-sex unmarried partner households, % of total households	Male same-sex unmarried partner households, % of total households	Female same-sex unmarried partner households, % of total unmarried partner households	Male same-sex unmarried partner households, % of total unmarried partner household
Ithaca	College town; long-standing enclave	30,014	63,367	16,041	44.4	165,100	1.028	.4035	14.97	5.87
San Luis Obispo	College town; emerging enclave	45,119	71,864	24,638	33.2	589,100	.297	.349	4.64	5.46
Greenfield[a]	Emerging enclave	17,456	59,074	24,892	16.4	190,400	1.566	.395	15.93	4.02
Portland	Long-standing enclave	66,194	65,125	28,754	18.3	239,200	.980	.716	9.31	6.81

Note: With the following exceptions, data are from the Bureau of the Census (2010): Economic/Housing Characteristics for Portland City from American Community Survey (ACS) 2010 one-year estimates; Economic/Housing Characteristics from all other cities from ACS five-year estimates (ACS 2005–9).
[a]Greenfield Town City, MA, for Same-Sex Characteristics and Population 2010 Census 100% Data: Greenfield Town, Franklin County, MA, Fact Sheet ACS five-year estimates for Economic and Housing Characteristics (ACS 2005–9).

Table 5.3. Representative place elements examined

	Ithaca	San Luis Obispo	Greenfield	Portland
Dominant regional lesbian enclave	Yes	No	No	Yes
State gay-marriage referendum lost during fieldwork	No	Yes	No	Yes
Affirming religious institutions, %	27.5	24	43	23
Greater proportion of lesbian couple households than gay male couple households	Yes	No	Yes	Yes, but by small margin
LBQ women's perceptions of safety	Highest of sites	Moderate/Low	High	Moderate
Dominant educational institution	Yes	Yes, but tourism, vine-yards, and agriculture also play large roles	No	Yes, but tourism and seaport also play large roles
Informants report publicly visible LBQ elected official or candidate	Yes	No	Yes	Yes
Proximity to major city (by car)	4+ hours	3.5+ hours	2 hours	2 hours
Region	Northeast	West Coast	New England	New England

	College town	College town, coastal and wine country tourist destination, agriculture	Former factory town	Fishing port, tourist destination, college town
Place category				
Migration patterns	Migrants from New York, Boston, San Francisco, etc., as well as from rural New York and other locales	Migrants from Las Vegas, Los Angeles, Central Valley, etc.	Migrants from Northampton, New York, Boston, rural New England, etc.	Migrants from rural Maine, Boston, New York, San Francisco, etc.
Registered Republicans, % (in city and county, respectively)	11.23 and 24.48	30.3 and 40.17	9.93 and 9.84	15 and 25.048
Population size	30,014	45,119	17,456	66,194
Legacy of nearby Women's Land or GLBT Commune(s)	Yes	No	Yes	Not in immediate area
Presence of airport	Yes	Yes	No	Yes

Note: Population size from 2010 census (Bureau of the Census 2010). Political party affiliation is from the Secretaries of State and Boards of Election websites for the state in which each city is located and based on state records from October or November 2010. See http://www.sec.state.ma.us/ele/ele10/enrollment_count _regdt_10132010.pdf; http://www.maine.gov/sos/cec/elec/data/20101102r-e-active.pdf; http://www.elections.ny-gov/NYSBOE/enrollment/county/county_nov10.pdf; http://elections.cdn.sos.ca.gov/ror/ror-pages/15day-prim-10/county.pdf; http://elections.cdn.sos.ca.gov/ror/ror-pages/15day-prim-10/political-sub.pdf; and https:// www.elections.ny.gov/nysboe/Enrollment/election%20district/2010/November/TompkinsED_nov10.pdf. The proportion of affirming religious institutions was calcu- lated by using the Yellow Pages online database to identify the universe of religious institutions in each study city. Religious institutions were deemed "affirming and welcoming" if they explicitly mention that they are LGBTQ friendly on their website.

Table 5.4. Hate crime rates (2007–10) by site, county, and state

	Sexual orientation hate crimes per 10,000 people	Hate crimes per 10,000 people
San Luis Obispo	0.35	1.60
San Luis County	0.19	0.27
California	0.07	0.32
Portland	0.36	1.10
Cumberland County	0.21	0.48
Maine	0.14	0.47
Greenfield	0.40	0.85
Franklin County	0.10	0.39
Massachusetts	0.11	0.49
Ithaca	0.34	1.25
Tompkins County	0.10	0.43
New York	0.05	0.31

Note: Federal Bureau of Investigation (2007–10).

Table 5.5. Informants' economic characteristics by site

Site	Personal income	Household income	Home purchase price	Estimated assessed home value at time of interview
Ithaca	61,063	107,400	187,938	254,267
San Luis Obispo	34,605	39,305	166,000	278,000
Portland	38,790	54,815	238,636	303,900
Greenfield	42,499	60,042	182,285	212,885

Note: Figures are based on data informants provided on surveys and in interviews. Amounts shown are mean dollars.

Table 5.6. Distribution of selected industries

	Educational services and health care and social assistance, %	Retail trade, %	Arts, entertainment, recreation, accommodation, food services, %
Portland	28.3	13.2	11.4
Greenfield	30.6	12.1	9.8
Ithaca	57.7	5.4	10.1
San Luis Obispo	22.6	14.1	16.4

Note: Data are from ACS (2006–10).

Table 5.7. Selected city occupational categories by research site

	Management, business, science and arts, %	Sales and office, %	Service, %
Portland	43.1	23.9	18.6
Greenfield	35.5	24.1	19.7
Ithaca	54.5	21.3	17.1
San Luis Obispo	38.9	28.2	21.4

Note: Data are from ACS (2006–10).

Table 5.8. Select "negative explanations" for *how* cities influence sexual identity cultures

Place category	All are small cities and county seats. All have a college or university, although Greenfield stands out by having only a two-year community college. Two sites with very distinct identity cultures, Ithaca and San Luis Obispo, are prototypical "college towns."
Distance from major city	Both Ithaca and San Luis Obispo are approximately four hours from a major city (complicating attempts to use this to explain differences in identity across these sites), while Portland is 2 hours from Boston and 4+ hours from New York.
Presence or absence of dominant local university	Three sites possess at least one four-year college or university; Greenfield possesses a community college.
City and county level demographics	In all sites: predominantly white and highly educated.
Dominant regional lesbian enclave	Both Ithaca and Portland are dominant regional lesbian enclaves, yet their identity cultures are quite distinct.
Region	Ithaca, Portland, and Greenfield are in the Northeast.
Political party affiliation	San Luis Obispo stands out from the other sites, with a higher proportion of Republicans. However, party affiliation does not offer an across-the-board explanation, as Portland and Ithaca, with their similar populations but very distinct identity cultures, have comparable proportions of Republicans at the city and county levels.
Occupations and industry	Distribution of major occupations and industries is relatively comparable across the sites, with the exception of Ithaca where the industry category "education, health care, social services" is larger than in the other sites. This, of course, cannot account for variation across the three additional sites.

Note: "Negative explanations" is from Katz (1982); the phrase is not intended to suggest that the above explanations altogether fail, but rather that in isolation they are insufficient explanations for variation in identities across sites.

Table 5.9. Place elements associated with identity-politics and integrationist orientations

Identity-politics orientation (San Luis Obispo and Portland)	Integrationist orientation (Ithaca and, increasingly, Greenfield)
Marriage referendum lost during period of study	History of women's or LGBQ land or collectives
LBQ population dispersion across metro areas and pockets of concentration within city	High rates of small business ownership by LBQ residents
Lower proportion of lesbian couple households (relative to other sites)	High rate accepting/welcoming religious institutions
Lower proportion of lesbian than gay male couples	Population concentration in study city (proper)
Report reduced sense of safety	Higher proportion of lesbian than gay male couples
Lower rate of accepting/welcoming religious institutions	Notably high proportions of female same-sex households Residents report LBQ elected officials Report heightened sense of safety

CONCLUSION

We live in a fascinating and contradictory moment. Much of American culture has taken vast strides in awareness about and acceptance of people who live outside the sexual norm. Indeed, the very idea that there is a "norm," or what that normal might consist of, has been troubled. And in the wake of all that change has come a tendency to define what the new normal is. A 2016 *New York Magazine* feature on the theorist Judith Butler proposes that all young people today approach gender as performance; the article's tagline reads, "It is Judith Butler's World."[1] Much like claims that all LGBTQI individuals have exited the closet, or that everyone these days is "post-gay," the article proposes that we, collectively, have embraced a common understanding about sexuality and gender—or, at least, that the next generation of adults have embraced Butler's vision. And thus, the implication goes, our cultural understanding is on a clear trajectory.[2] Gender is performance; identity is a series of costumes that we take on and off. That's all there is to it.

Beyond all else, I hope that this book unsteadies the notion that there is any universal, or even general, way of approaching sexuality (same with gender).[3] As we have seen again and again, we may live in a globalized world, but we cannot ignore the profound role that the world outside our door plays. The local filters the influence of shared cultural signposts and even lends them novel significance and meaning. This is true even in an era in which a theorist like Butler serves as a touch point for many, and especially for those who share the traits of the many people with whom I spoke—most of whom are middle and upper-middle class, white, and highly educated— and when, at the click of a button, any of us can access articles and books and blog posts and online discussions about gender performance or any other trending concept. It is easy to feel like we are all speaking the same language. We are not. A dyke in Portland might display Butler's *Gender Trouble* on her table during an interview, but in San Luis Obispo the book and its concepts are off the table, literally and figuratively.

How Places Make Us is far from alone in recognizing the multiplicity of ways we experience sexual difference and conceptualize the sexual self; I am delighted to stand with a growing number of authors and theorists when I argue against the notion that we all embrace gender as performance, celebrate gay marriage, or are "post-mo."[4] However, the book's attention to sexual identity cultures as city specific—and its exploration of the local orientations to sexual identity and difference—sets it apart from other related arguments, both scholarly and popular. Typically, both media coverage and academic analysis attributes the heterogeneity or novelty of identities either to the small group or institution that is being discussed and, most commonly, to categories of place or person; more often than not, your sexual identity is shaped, so the thinking goes, by whether you are African American or Latino, Southern or Northern, male or female. Take, for instance, a 2014 *New York Times* op-ed that opines that "The equality divide that we face is no longer between red and blue states, but between urban and rural America" (House 2014). Here, in an effort to complicate notions of a single "gay experience," the author offers a different simplification, and clusters together all rural and all urban experiences.

This book highlights the risks of looking past the tremendous variation *within* urban and rural America, and even within the same region—and for that matter, even within the same state. It is a banal truism that gays like living in big cities. The corresponding presupposition—that LBQ individuals are ill at ease in America's smaller places—sounds absurd to the Greenfield lesbian who delights in her place alongside heterosexual men at a rural wild game dinner.[5] Likewise, the notion of cities as uniformly embracing of sexual diversity rings hollow to LBQ residents who have experienced violence and harassment in Portland, Maine.

At its core, this book tells a story of personal malleability. At first glance, the concept itself is not surprising. After all, we live in a cultural moment that emphasizes self-improvement, calls for relentless actualization, and lauds the intentional crafting of the self.[6] But this book is not about self-evolution as we usually think about it. On the contrary, the LBQ residents I spoke with told me again and again of transformation that is involuntary.[7] This is a story not of the practiced shaping of the self or of the body as performance, but about our exquisite, though often ignored, sensitivity to our environment; it is a story about the unintentional and unplanned remolding of the self in relation to one's surroundings.[8]

Imagine that we took the lesbians of San Luis Obispo and deposited them in Ithaca. This book's findings suggest that, despite the lesbian identities they nourished in San Luis Obispo, they would not—as dominant ways of thinking would presuppose—turn Ithaca "lavender." Instead, if we were willing to wait a few months and certainly if we returned after a few years, we would see their identities take new shape in response to their new city; if the experiences documented throughout this book are any indication, a new sensibility about sexual identity will announce itself among these newcomers. In time, our Ithaca transplants would identify as lesbian no longer, embracing a post-identity-politics orientation and celebrating "ambient community" with heterosexual neighbors at the Farmers Market and on the trails around Ithaca's famed gorges. Likewise, if we took Ithaca's LBQ residents, with all their celebration of post-identity politics, and instructed them to set up household in San Luis Obispo, we could anticipate that something very different—a lesbian identity politics—would gradually take root. In the context of California's Central Coast, they would find themselves drawn to lesbian-only potlucks, bonfires, and dances, and to a corresponding way of thinking about the self, first and foremost, as lesbian.

Toward a Differentiated Social Geography of Identity

I remember, as a teenager growing up in Massachusetts, some classmates quipping that living in Northampton or Provincetown could "turn" you gay. I have no desire to repeat such absurdities. I am not suggesting that cities make us gay or straight, just as it is unlikely that a city alone would change one's political orientation from staunchly conservative to staunchly progressive. What I am proposing is, on the surface, far less earth shattering. We do not become entirely new people on moving. Instead, we feel who we are in a new way; mirroring Judith Butler, we might even say that we "do" who we are in a new way.[9] Thus, the *kind* of LBQ individual one is, or the type of progressive activist one is, will shift on moving in or out of Northampton or Provincetown or anywhere else.

But on a deeper level, another facet of my findings is, in fact, quite radical: the finding that subtle differences in city ecology are so consequential for self-understanding. It is no surprise that we are shaped by our environment; if not, the nature versus nurture debate would have been solved a long time ago. Yet it is surprising to consider that the streets on which we spend our days shape a matter as intimate as our sexual identity. That the most personal of questions—"Who am I?"—is in fact answered collectively, by the ecology of the city in which we live. In other words, it is true that we are not entirely plastic; we cannot be easily moved from one end of the political spectrum to the other, or from one end of the Kinsey scale to the other. Yet this book reveals that we are, nonetheless, acutely sensitive to our environs. Our most private selves are, in fact, deeply social and stunningly responsive to what is around us: to abundance and acceptance, narratives, and socioscape. This book thus serves as a call for a differentiated social geography of sexual identities; we must recognize, and we must further investigate, how cities shape whom we desire and how we desire them, as well as the sense we make of that desire (or of its absence).

Perhaps more radical yet is the degree to which I propose that cities call identity into being. Others, writing on similar themes, have shown the ways that other facets of life—usually referring to contextual factors unrelated to place, such as epoch, age, or race—impact identity.[10] These other factors are, of course, important: identity is nothing if not a stew, a messy combination of numerous ingredients. The problem is that these arguments imply that identity already exists before or outside of place. This book provides an alternate view. While places may not be responsible for whether we desire someone of the same or of the opposite sex, they play a crucial role in determining the meaning we ascribe to who we are, providing a particular, localized sensibility for characterizing one's self and directing how we compose ourselves in relation to others. The implication of this is far-reaching. Without place-derived meaning and interaction there is little being, there is little *is*: ultimately, there is little identity at all. After all, I am not myself until I think about what it means to be "me," and the meaning of "me" only emerges in relation to others, through interaction and dialogue. This book reminds that (despite the increasing amount of time we spend in virtual realities and virtual communities) most of those interactions and conversations are local and that they always unfold in place.[11] In this sense, identity becomes salient, or becomes fully formed, only in and through place; it is nearly impossible to imagine identity or self that is *un*placed. In this sense, places truly make us, even if they don't alter our DNA or obliterate our earlier histories, for there is no identity without geography.

This is not to say that all cultural material is originally, or inherently, local. Instead, this book reveals how place, via interaction and dialogue, renders that material locally resonant. That is, we bring to the places we live lessons and patterns that have been cultivated (both by ourselves and by others) in other places and contexts—whether spending a weekend at Michigan Womyn's Music Festival or two years living in Williamsburg, or reading the poems of Audre Lorde, or watching a season of the *L Word*. And yet, places structure the sense we make of that material, and even which of that material we ultimately integrate into our sense of self. Differences in city ecology explain why, for instance, LBQ residents of Portland and Ithaca can attend Michigan or watch the same television show, imbibing these shared cultural images and messages, and still experience and understand their sexuality in very different ways.

Imagine that we each view our identity through a kaleidoscope. Much of the material inside of it—the individual, colorful components that ultimately come to form the single image that fills our vision—comes from other places and contexts: from one's hometown, from college, from national debates about same-sex marriage, from the pulpit of a church, from the pages of a novel. This book demonstrates how cities function as the body of that kaleidoscope—lens, tube, and mirrors—and as such how they ultimately determine how we experience the cultural material we, individually and collectively, contain. In other words, cities give structure and meaning to the cultural components we carry with us, discretely and together. It is a city that determines when and how the kaleidoscope turns, shifting its contents—as that city's ecology evolves—to create a new vision. The longer we live in a given place, the more that city produces some of the material that constitutes that vision, and, as our city changes, so, too, do the mechanisms that make sense of that material for us.

By evoking a kaleidoscope I do not mean to suggest that identities are merely composed of disaggregated parts; on this point I break with Judith Butler and many other queer theorists (e.g., Scott 1997; Martin 1994).[12] I do not believe identity is entirely fractured or constantly shifting, just as I also don't believe that identity is fixed, singular, or strictly "authentic." After all, these pages reveal as much about shared identity orientations within each city as they do about variation across them. Cities provide an organizing structure for the cultural stuff we unpack when we move to a new place, as well as for all the material we accumulate—from inside and outside the city— once we settle in. Places reassemble this cultural stuff, bringing them into harmony with local conditions, thus providing structure and meaning for our identities. In some places, the structure and meaning that a city lends will look more like a "queer politics" than in others, but in no two cities will that politics—queer or otherwise—appear the same, just as no two kaleidoscopes present identical visual assemblages.

Can we anticipate that all social groups will experience similarly place-responsive identities? For years, I thought that was impossible and assumed that as groups of people we were far too varied to be swayed in the same ways by a given place. Yet the more time I spent in these four cities, the more I was convinced that this is the case; as social creatures we are highly attentive to even subtle features of our surroundings, such as abundance and acceptance, narratives, and socioscape. I also long wondered whether sexual minorities might be especially sensitive to city ecology. After all, sexuality inhabits and even partially structures very intimate dimensions of our lives. And yet, when we stop to think about it we can recognize that all kinds of social identities, such as those that relate to race, gender, and class, also shape very intimate parts of our lives, such as whom we partner with (e.g., the race and class characteristics of our partners), and how we display and think about our bodies. However, the degree of our attentiveness may not be constant. More than any of the more obvious aspects of ourselves, our vulnerability heightens sensitivity to place—whether that vulnerability arises from marginalization related to whom we desire, life stage, economic position, immigration status, or simply from being new to a city. Take life stage as an example. An adolescent, for instance, navigating the sometimes-rocky transition from childhood to adulthood, might be especially sensitive to city ecology, becoming one teenager in Syracuse and another in Albany.[13] Likewise, a retiree experiencing newfound physical limitations and shifting networks as she ages might approach retirement in a different way, and assign different meaning to that life stage, in Asheville than in Charlottesville. For the retiree, subtle differences in ease of mobility, related to city infrastructure, or in the proportion of city institutions that provide services for the elderly, may structure the degree to which they are integrated into their environs and, relatedly, the degree to which one thinks of oneself as "elderly" or "retired."

And, as I have mentioned throughout the book, there are likely direct parallels between the experiences of sexual and racial and ethnic minorities. After all, we have every reason to believe that racial and ethnic minorities will be at least as sensitive to abundance and acceptance, place narratives, and socioscape as the LBQ migrants this book features.[14] This book's findings suggest that Sacramento and Fresno will produce different orientations to Latino identities, just as Chicago and Milwaukee will produce different orientations to African American identities.[15]

Is there reason to believe that LBQ identities will be more malleable than the identities of other social groups? Some propose, for instance, that women's sexuality is more fluid than men's, with more women than men identifying as bisexual.[16] This implicitly raises the question of whether the identities of gay men—or of any other man, for that matter—are equally place sensitive. Given the degree to which categorical traits, such as generation, class, and race, fail to explain the identity differences this book uncovers, we ought to be skeptical about such suppositions. If the LBQ residents

I studied possess traits that make them more likely than other groups to adapt to city ecology I suspect that they are traits that they likely share, as I have already suggested, with racial minorities, as well as with many others at particular junctures, such as with adolescents and the elderly. In other words, if anything makes them attentive to city ecology it is not something as narrow as same-sex attraction or even gender. Instead, it is the more general experience of social marginalization, belonging to a population group that constitutes a numerical minority (at least in the local context) and migrant status (that is, the fact that they are nonnatives). These traits, individually and especially in concert, likely heighten sensitivity to city ecology, fueling identity adaptability. But, to be clear, while I suspect that these traits might make LBQ residents and others who share them particularly sensitive to city ecology, I anticipate that all of us respond to local conditions; that places, to varying degrees, make all of us. I imagine that some of us have noticed this. While we like to chuckle that all "hipsters" or bankers look alike, most of us, on reflection, can recognize that the Brooklyn hipster and the Manhattan banker comes in slightly different form than her counterparts in San Francisco and Miami.

It is my hope that this book provides a model for future inquires into how cities shape a variety of social identities. Indeed, much of what sets this book apart from other accounts of the malleable self is its identification of city ecology, and specific dimensions thereof, as productive of cultural differences.[17] Following the revelations offered by our four cities, we no longer need to attribute variation in identity to just broad, and ultimately unsatisfying, categorical differences, whether differences in social status or type of locale.[18] And neither do the specific ecological attributes that produce identity differences need to remain in a "black box."[19] The ecological features that are consequential for, say, adolescent identities might be slightly different than those that shape LBQ identities, but this book provides a model for identifying the ecological sources of identity, and of culture more generally, for any group of people.

Why Cities?

Why is it that the particular conditions of a city are so meaningful for identity cultures? Why do those I spoke with take more of their identity cues from the city in which they live, as opposed to from region, state, or neighborhood? Why does the city play such a vital organizing role in shaping how we relate to those around us and therefore to ourselves?[20] After all, this book tells a story of surprising identity heterogeneity—across cities—and, at the same time, of notably closely aligned identity orientations within each city, despite the fact that the individuals I spoke with live in disparate neighborhoods, belong to different local organizations, and are of a variety of ages and inhabit many walks of life.[21]

Part of the answer rests in the fact that contemporary lives, especially those of the mobile, professional individuals I studied, typically extend beyond one's specific block or neighborhood. One might live in South Portland, but work downtown. Alternately, one might live in San Luis Obispo, but travel to an adjacent town for work. Or, one might reside in a semirural stretch of Greenfield or Ithaca, but shop and socialize downtown. In this sense, our identities do not just respond to our neighborhood, because our interactions span multiple parts of the city and even the metro area.[22]

Second, while we are sure to encounter neighborhood narratives, reputations, and identities, these often are less prominent than metropolitan narratives, reputations, and identities. After all, the reputation of a neighborhood and even more so the identity and the narrative of that neighborhood, are often less resonant outside the local context than a city's reputation.[23] Moreover, if one is a citizen not only of one's residential neighborhood but also of the other parts of a city in which one works, socializes, votes, and consumes, then a broad city reputation will serve as a crucial touchstone. Indeed, informants generally had more to say about the broad identity and reputation of their city than of their neighborhood.[24]

For LBQ residents, like all of us, certain institutions reinforce our identification with the city as a whole, such as city newspapers, governments, cultural institutions, festivals (like Ithaca Festival), markets (like the Farmers Markets where many gather in each city), and, in some places, citywide Pride or Dyke March celebrations.[25] These narratives, identities, institutions, and traditions attune us to the city, and we identify the city as a whole as our crucial point of reference. In turn, this encourages the LBQ migrant to consider the city's conditions as a means to evaluate the crucial mechanisms that we've identified as particularly essential: their sense of abundance and acceptance, place narratives, and socioscape.

One additional factor encourages LBQ residents' attention to the cities where they live: municipal government and everything from its elections to its policies. LBQ residents of the four cities frequently reference the degree to which their sense of acceptance (or lack thereof) and more general sense of city "character" rest on the elections for and policies of that city's government. These range from an effort to block Walmart in Greenfield, nondiscrimination initiatives, and, in two cities, the election of out-LBQ individuals to local office. Moreover, in Portland and San Luis Obispo, where marriage referenda occurred while I was conducting research, informants cited municipal results (often holding them up against state results). Here, the city—as an official political entity—calls attention to itself.[26] Together, via these influences, the city serves as umbrella to the smaller scenes that compose it; those who meet for tea at Portland's North Star Café on Munjoy Hill and those who prefer to spend the evening downtown dancing at Styxx nonetheless find themselves talking and thinking about sexual identity and difference in the same overarching mode.

This does not mean that region, state, neighborhood, and even block do not constitute part of the material in our kaleidoscope. Instead, it signals the degree to which we continue to call the cities where we live, however big or small, "home"—regardless of whether we were born there or how much we might disagree with some of what takes place there. Cities remain a crucial point of reference and source of identification, and, in turn, they powerfully inform residents' identities. In other words, cities matter for identities in large part because we have decided, collectively, that, in much more general terms, they matter. They are also of influence—more so than region or state—because so many of our interactions are inherently local; while most of us, especially those of us who are middle and upper-middle class, are not confined to our block or neighborhood, many of the interactions that communicate the "character" of the place we live and that ultimately shape how we think about ourselves take place within the cities we call home rather than in the broader territory of our states and regions.[27] This book suggests that, at least for LBQ residents, the power of the city cannot be overlooked, and that we ought to cultivate a more robust sociology of the city—not just of the broad regions or of the individual neighborhoods that constitute the larger places where so many of us live.[28]

The Persistence of LBQ Identities and Enclaves

Stepping away for a moment from the question of why cities matter, this book counters several points of mounting popular concern. Most centrally it offsets the notion that place distinction is fading and the concurrent lament that place is becoming homogeneous, that every city looks more and more like every other city. From the vantage point of our cities, that notion—even though it is repeated by some of my informants—rings untrue. Instead, even cities that from afar appear to be very similar are different enough to produce quite varied sexual identity cultures. To be sure, the cities this book features are home to chains and to increasingly ubiquitous methods of upscaling, from architectural styles to specific types of cuisine.[29] However, even among the ever-present Starbucks, the inevitable brick oven pizzeria, and innumerable farm shares, distinctive local cultures flourish.

The book also counters a parallel cynicism, which purports that people, like places, are more and more the same. The logic goes that in an increasingly wired and commercial world, the distinctions between each of us—like those of the places where we live—are diminishing; that we have lost or are losing our local voices and distinctive affect, whether the bullish Boston driver or the indifferent New York pedestrian. In this book's chapters we find, instead, the persistence of distinctive cultural repertoires and of inimitable human characters. We might, as social creatures, mirror one another, but this book demonstrates how those who live around us serve as our primary models and reference points and how this habit of modeling ourselves on our neighbors ultimately helps to ensure that our cities continue to produce unique social characters; though counterintuitive, our reliance on the people around us as models for ourselves guarantees the heterogeneity that so many of us value.

The book also counters concern about the perseverance of contemporary LGBTQI spaces and identities, and especially the worry about how the spaces and identities of LBQ individuals are disappearing. We live in an era in which academics, and many others, vacillate between the celebration of cultural advances that have enabled the supposed decline of gay-identity politics and nostalgia for earlier, identity-driven ways of understanding the self and engaging with one another.[30] With marriage equality now federal law, and among the increasingly visible presence of out LGBTQI individuals, it seems that an increasing number of LGBTQI Americans no longer approach their sexuality via an identity-politics framework; sexual identity is less and less regarded as a source of common ground and a basis for collective action.[31] That we even have the freedom to abandon identity politics is a remarkable achievement; at the same time, many LBQ individuals feel that they have lost a valued camaraderie and connection that identity politics fueled. We long for gay bars and lesbian enclaves, even as we celebrate the freedom to move beyond them.[32]

This book outlines the errors underlying some of these anxieties, largely because they rest on assumptions about the ubiquity of a retreat from identity politics. As we have seen again and again in these pages, identity politics have not perished, even if they are no longer ubiquitous and even if there is no singular identity politics. Indeed, if identity-politics orientations flourish in San Luis Obispo and Portland, then they must also be alive and well in many other places, particularly those that are less embracing of LGBTQI individuals than our four cities. Indeed, if identity politics live on in two coastal cities with progressive reputations and state universities, they can flourish almost anywhere.

Of course, there is a less optimistic way to read this persistence, which is to say that identity politics persists because—even in places that we generally hold up as beacons of acceptance—the embrace of LBQ residents is, at best, inconsistent. It is safe to say that these cities were not beacons at all on the evening when a transgender activist was beaten in the street, when a neighbor threatened two kissing women with a bat, or when a man screamed homophobic obscenities at a retiree. These reports of harassment and violence from San Luis Obispo and Portland, and to a lesser degree from Ithaca and Greenfield, call for subtle reorganization of the mental maps of LBQ-friendly spaces that many of us carry around, as well as of internal clocks that anticipate our neat temporal progression away from identity politics. Even today, even in the kinds of spaces we tend to think of as "safe" for LBQ residents, acceptance can be inconsistent and tenuous, and city ecology sometimes calls out identity politics.[33]

Some may, however, simultaneously read the persistence of identity politics in San Luis Obispo and Portland in a more hopeful manner: as the intentional maintenance of a valued connection. After all, identity politics provides a way of thinking about the self and engaging with one another that was crucial in fueling the movements that ultimately altered the conditions that made identity politics a source of survival in the first place.[34] We have encountered the words of LBQ residents of Ithaca and Greenfield who mourn the loss of lesbian bars, women's bookstores, and, more generally, lesbian-only networks.[35] But at the same time, this book contests, at least partially, their certainty that these things are entirely out of reach; the emblems of identity politics, and those who nurture it, persist in some cities—even if their ubiquity has waned in their own hometowns. Some will no doubt lament the persistence of identity politics and dismiss it as outmoded. But others will welcome the evidence of its persistence and embrace the value that emerges in the feeling of difference from those who do not share your sexuality and the feeling of inimitable common ground with those who do.

Closely linked to this anxiety about declining identity politics is pessimism about the future of LGBTQI residential concentrations, otherwise known as gayborhoods. Many fear the disappearance of places like Manhattan's Chelsea, Brooklyn's Park Slope, Chicago's Boystown, and cities like West Hollywood. The argument goes that conditions purportedly transforming identity politics also reduce the need for LGBTQI individuals to concentrate together in their own demarcated neighborhoods. Newspaper articles and other reports featuring LGBTQI residents conquering the suburbs, or those who have moved back to their small hometown, spouse and children in tow, abound.[36]

In contrast, this book demonstrates that LGBTQI concentrations persist; that even a relatively privileged set of individuals—who have the resources that might enable their "blending" in any number of neighborhoods—continue to choose to move to places that possess high proportions of female same-sex couples. We continue to take comfort and pleasure in the company of others who share with us a defining trait, and we continue to move to cities where we believe we will have a better than average chance of being accepted for who we are (even if the particulars of "who we are" shifts upon arrival).

The book sheds light, in particular, on the lesbian version of the gay-borhood or the lesbian enclave. The continued residential concentrations of LBQ residents that this book documents is especially notable given longstanding cynicism within the academy about whether the "lesbian enclave" has ever existed, with some arguing that lesbians simply do not or cannot (for financial reasons) establish residential concentrations.[37] I hope to have countered both that longstanding cynicism and more recent anxiety that—to the degree that they ever existed—lesbian enclaves are fading.[38] Indeed, this project demonstrates that lesbian enclaves endure (two, Greenfield and Ithaca, have existed for several decades), and that they even continue to grow and emerge. It is quite plausible that we have missed this, given our disproportionate attention to the central city enclaves that have historically been most popular with gay men—particularly those who are white and affluent.[39] I propose that the Ithacas and Greenfields of the world have been flying below the radar, largely because of inattention to LBQ women within the media, in other forms of popular culture, and in the academy, and because so much of our attention focuses on neighborhoods within big cities—rather than the small cities that the residents with whom I spoke call home. This missed recognition may have fed our cynicism about the decline of lesbian population concentrations and about the loss of GLBTQI enclaves more generally.

Even more prolific than concern about the lost lesbian enclave is anxiety about sites of LBQ congregation. Within and beyond the academy there is much concern about, for instance, the loss of the "lesbian bar." On a stage in New York City, while serving on a panel on gentrification, I mentioned an article on the closure of San Francisco's last remaining lesbian bar. The crowd, mostly composed of heterosexuals, let out a cry of shock and dismay. While the prototypical lesbian bar—a more or less LBQ-only space that advertises itself as such—cannot be found in any of the study cities, visible and relatively accessible opportunities for LBQ congregation nonetheless persist in at least three of the four cities. Many of these operate as de facto lesbian bars or as alternate venues for romance, politics, friendship, conflict, and everything in between. One might be hard pressed to distinguish between an "official" lesbian bar and Felicia's in Ithaca, especially after a softball game or on a night when a lesbian singer/songwriter performs. On such evenings, LBQ residents occupied nearly every seat in the bar, on the front porch and in the alleyway patio; bodies pressed against one another as thirsty customers jockeyed for the attention of the (mostly LBQ) bartenders. Bonfires, potlucks, formally organized bar nights, dances, dinners, and hikes provide similar opportunities for communion in San Luis Obispo, while the staff at Portland's North Star Café seemed to know nearly everyone's name.

To be sure, these spaces—Felicia's, which did not mark itself as a lesbian bar, the North Star Café, which sought to be a community center for "everyone," and lesbian events advertised via a listserv—are not synonymous with traditional bars and clubs. However, the persistence of these alternate means of communion in these cities underlines how LBQ residents continue to seek one another's company—even in places in which identity politics has fallen by the wayside. Moreover, it underlines the adaptability of this communion: the constant renewal, in concert with changing city ecology, of creative methods for coming together. As one institution closes, another appears or residents begin organizing more informal opportunities to gather. This cautions us against measuring LBQ "community" via the number of demarcated institutions and partially assuages growing anxiety about opportunities for camaraderie in a changing landscape for sexual minorities.

This is not to say that such anxieties are unfounded. It is my guess that such concerns are felt by nearly every gay man and lesbian who is old enough to remember Stonewall, and even many of us who are a decade or two or three younger (I, for instance, will happily indulge anyone who asks in nostalgic tales of Provincetown circa 1997). We miss the certainty that one will discover a sense of common ground based on shared sexual identity—even if the politics and identities that the sense of common ground produces varies by city—regardless of where one lives. We miss having marked or designated space, whether a bar or bookstore. This nostalgia makes good sense in a world in which some LBQ individuals, in places like Ithaca and Greenfield, actively reject sexuality as a basis for identity and congregation. However, this book cautions that this nostalgia is not without risk. Specifically, narratives of loss and nostalgia blanket our recognition of the diversity our ties and the adaptability of our identities; narratives of loss, after all, presume that there is one "we" and one way of interacting—and that we all change together.

Above all else, I hope that this book ushers us away from that reductive way of thinking about identities and communities. If we can escape the nostalgic notion that there was some glorious (or terrible) time in the past, then we can better understand the vast complexity of our lives in the present, and perhaps even begin the work of going back and tracing the heterogeneity of lives lived long ago, too.

Have Places Always Made Us?

Despite the finding that some older ways of identifying, congregating, and concentrating persist in our cities, we must consider the possibility that the identity heterogeneity identified in this book is a product of the moment in which we live—of our era's unprecedentedly broad cultural and political changes. Is it possible that the LBQ residents of these four cities have only been liberated to constitute city-specific identity cultures as a result of shifts that have introduced a queer politics, that have enabled view of sexuality as fluid, and that have made it normal to see identity as an assemblage?[40] Is it plausible that the heterogeneity I have found is only possible in an era in which many of us, gay and straight alike, experience newfound freedom and flexibility, and the license to think about sexuality outside of an identity-politics framework? In the past, would such identity malleability have been impossible?

This book cautions against overconfidence in such conclusions. First, because of a paucity of empirical data on how LBQ individuals in a variety of social settings conceived of themselves in any earlier era, we cannot definitively mark the degree to which identity orientations have changed.[41] Moreover, too few studies of LBQ identities are comparative; thus, it is hard to say how uniform LBQ identity politics actually were across demographic groups and geographic spaces in, say, 1978 or 1984. Moreover, there are simply too few studies of LBQ individuals. Those studies that do exist, like so many studies of GLBTQI individuals, tend to have extrapolated findings from a single group or place to be indicative of broad trends, regardless of how narrow their source. In the 1990s, let's say, were identity politics truly synonymous among gay men and lesbians in Providence and Milwaukee, Memphis and Savannah, and among Latinos and Asian Americans?

More crucially, this book troubles the notion of a singular "identity politics." It reveals that identity is much more multivalent and responsive than notions of a singular script, or a rejection thereof, presuppose. If the cultural material we use to construct self- and group understanding is constitutive of and constituted by place, then orientations to identity politics or any other way of framing sexual identity and difference is always already inherently localized and particular. The power of the local that we have seen throughout this book thus cautions us against the idea of any singular approach driving orientations to sexual identity and difference—now or in the past. Rather, we ought to anticipate that there are, and have always been, localized versions of "identity politics" or "post-identity politics" that take shape in response to city ecology.

The book also reveals that cultural identities are always responsive and innovative—not just in "settled" or "unsettled" times (Swidler 1986) and not just in response to heterosexual scripts, which is why the place we are *now*, the place where one currently resides, is so powerfully influential.[42] Thus, this moment may be one when, on the whole, many experience greater freedom to experiment with and creatively parse identity than those who came before—but we ought to be cautious about temporal accounts of identity transformation, since they call us to disregard the particular and varied and mutable—and, very relatedly, the local—in favor of sweeping patterns. This misses, for instance, how individual cities structure the degree to which residents experience the various options for one's identity and are invited to play with the components of that identity.

Thus, we are left, again and again, with the local. We must inquire into local cultures—past, present, and future—and especially into the city ecologies that generate them. There is no reason to limit our inquiries to LBQ identities, although there is much more to be learned about them and the local contexts that draw them out. How, for instance, do African American LBQ individuals' identities take shape in response to the ecologies of Los Angeles, Atlanta, Oakland, and Memphis? How do those who work behind the counters of Walmart and Target in Green Bay and Louisville understand their class identities differently? By pursuing such questions we will learn as much about how places work and about the unique and evolving character of our cities as we learn about identities. If people in our four cities leave us with any lesson, it is that to understand identities we must understand place—and vice versa. And the lessons this book offers need not only extend to identities; we ought to also pursue, among other things, how places shape politics, community dynamics, organizations, and social movements.[43] In short, this book calls us to devote far greater attention to how and why places matter. We make places, but places also—and far more than we might like to believe—make us.

ACKNOWLEDGMENTS

For helpful feedback on various iterations of this project, I thank Emily Barman, Jean Beaman, Wayne Brekhus, Wendy Cadge, Cati Connell, Andrew Deener, Holly Donovan, Susan Eckstein, Bob Emerson, Corey Fields, Gary Alan Fine, Julian Go, David Grazian, Wendy Griswold, Joe Harris, Johanna Hiitola, Maggie Kusenbach, Noah McClain, Erin Metz McDonnell, Terry McDonnell, Ashley Mears, Amit Nigam, Minna Nikunen, Jon Norman, Sigrun Olafsdottir, Jeffrey Parker, Christi Smith, and Amy Wilkins. Robin Bartram and Lida Maxwell deserve special thanks for reading not only individual chapters or papers but also the entire manuscript. For helpful advice and/or conversations along the way, I thank many wonderful mentors, colleagues, and friends, including, but certainly not limited to, Wendy Griswold, Mary Pattillo, Gary Alan Fine, Al Hunter, Nancy Ammerman, Lane Fenrich, Harel Shapira, and Anne Figert.

I have benefited from generous feedback at a variety of workshops and colloquia, including the following: Northwestern University's Culture and Society Workshop; Five College Women's Studies Research Center; Brandeis Sociology Colloquium; Northwestern University Ethnography Workshop; University of Chicago City, Society, and Space Workshop; UCLA Ethnography Working Group; Boston University Society, Politics and Culture Workshop; Temple University Department of Sociology; University of Notre Dame Sociology Colloquium; Northwestern University Sexual Reputations Mini-Conference; Northeastern University Sociology Colloquium; Notre Dame Culture Workshop; Harvard Culture and Social Analysis Workshop; Great Cities/Ordinary Lives Mini-Conference at the University of Illinois at Chicago; Trinity College Global Urban Experience across Time and Space Symposium; Tufts University Sociology Colloquium; and the MIT Queers in the Built Environment Workshop.

I owe a debt of gratitude to Doug Mitchell and Kyle Wagner for their time and care with the project, and for the very productive reviews that they secured. I am abundantly grateful for the reviewers' careful and thoughtful recommendations. For their own feedback, I am yet again indebted to Bob Emerson and Jack Katz, the editors of the Fieldwork Encounters and Discoveries series. Jack's enthusiasm for the project kept me going as I revised and rethought, and I cannot possibly fully express my appreciation for his keen eye and careful attention to this book. He offered spot-on feedback on everything from argument to evidence to phrasing. For his insights, as well as for his championing of the project from the start, I owe him many, many thanks. For her careful and insightful copyediting, I thank Elissa Park. I am also very grateful for David Lobenstine who, near the end of this endeavor, helped me to refine the chapters. In the process, he reminded me that writing—and even revising—can be a pleasure. For that, as much as for his terrific assistance with this book, I am immensely grateful.

For research assistance, I thank Meaghan Stiman, Megan O'Leary, Taylor Cain, and Pamela Devan. For research support, I thank the Five College Women's Studies Research Center, Loyola University Chicago, and especially Boston University—particularly the Department of Sociology and its Morris Fund. For helping me make time for writing and research, I thank department chairs, first, at Loyola University Chicago, where this project began, and, later, at Boston University: Fred Kniss, Rhys Williams, Nancy Ammerman, and Nazli Kibria.

I am grateful to the following journals for allowing me to build on arguments originally presented in their pages: *American Journal of Sociology*, *Qualitative Sociology*, *Social Problems*, and *Sexualities*. I also thank my coauthor, Jeffrey Parker, for allowing me to extend some of our thinking on sexualities and place reputation in these pages.

For support and distraction, I thank many friends, but especially Liz Titus, Alisa Shor, Emily Sosland, and Amit Nigam. In addition, the following friends and family offered rooms—and sometimes whole houses or apartments— for me to stay in while I was in the field: Katherine Biers, Katherine Lieber, Becky Givan, Jen Sandler, Lauren Faulkner-Duncan, Carol Maxwell, Jocelyn Brown-Saracino, and Cynthia Yackenchick. In Ithaca, many Cornell friends provided practical assistance and happy time away from fieldwork; among these, Cary Howie deserves particular thanks. In Boston, I thank many friends for everything from meals to childcare swaps that helped make the final stages of writing possible, but especially Julie and Chris Ahnallen, Ruth Chaffee, and Lauren Graber.

I owe my family more than I can say. They have helped and supported this project in innumerable ways. Foremost among the gifts that they have shared are the many miles they have traveled to care for my three children so that I could research and write. For this, the most important gift of all, I thank Mike Saracino, Maggie Saracino, Carol Maxwell, Phil Maxwell, Annie Garvey, Jocelyn Brown-Saracino, and Brooke Brown-Saracino. My mother, Pam Brown, deserves particular thanks for the time she has spent with her grandchildren over the last year. We are all better for it, and I am more grateful than I can say.

I dedicate this book to my remarkable partner, Lida Maxwell, who has been with me, and therefore with this book, from the project's inception. Indeed, this book might not exist if she had not given me a reason to move to Ithaca. Not only has she read several iterations of the book; Lida sometimes accompanied me to the field and at times managed our busy family while I conducted research or took time to write. Throughout, Lida made parenting our three small children while doing her own writing, researching, and teaching appear seamless; she somehow manages to consistently fill our home and lives with books, new ideas, delicious food, and much happiness. For that, as much as for the many insights she has shared that have touched these pages, I am more appreciative than I can say.

I am equally grateful for the presence and patience of my three wonderful children, Louisa, Ezra, and Arlo. From infancy, Louisa endured being carted from field site to field site, as well as my frequent travel. When Louisa was two years old, her preschool teacher reported that Louisa had spent part of the morning scribbling on page after page, tossing each aside as soon as she marked it. When asked what she was doing, Louisa said, "Writing chapters. Quickly." Louisa and her delightful brothers, Ezra and Arlo, are beautiful reminders that not all things can or should happen quickly. I thank them for making me leave my desk to pick raspberries, walk in the arboretum, and read stories.

Last but far from least, I thank the terrific individuals who welcomed me into their cities and lives. It was an honor to meet and speak with each of you. It is my greatest hope that this book will allow others to share the distinct pleasure I have had of learning from you and your experiences.

METHODOLOGICAL APPENDIX

The pages that follow expand on the discussion of the study design and methods started in the Introduction. Here I elaborate how I selected cities to study and how I constructed my sample of informants and observational scenes, as well as the benefits and constraints I found in relying on a comparative research design. I conclude by outlining the path forward for future studies of identity and place.

Selecting Cities

This book pursues questions about the character and origin of lesbian, bisexual, and/or queer (LBQ) identities in four small US cities and, closely related, about the nature of LBQ migrants' interactions with heterosexual and LBQ residents. However, originally the book was supposed to be about the role of LBQ residents in gentrifying places; thus, I selected study cities with that goal in mind. Why smaller cities in particular? Two reasons. First, analyses of US census data suggest that the migration of lesbian couple households is disproportionately oriented toward small cities (particularly those with natural amenities, a college or university, and large populations of retirees).[1] Second, studies of the gentrification of smaller cities are too far and few between—as are inquiries into why LBQ individuals move to such places in the first place, and the shape their lives take once there. For these reasons, I wanted to understand how LBQ migrants might participate (or not) in the upscaling of this type of city.

Relying heavily on extant analyses of where LBQ individuals live and on the character of their residential concentrations—both those that analyze recent census data on same-sex households and ethnographies of lesbian "enclaves"—I compiled a list of places in the United States that fit the above profile. There were more than a dozen possibilities. Most were in the northern United States. Many were on a coast, with an especially high concentration in the Northeast. Most had populations that are primarily white.[2]

I sought to study four cities—enough sites to allow me to explore variation (or its absence), but a small enough number that I could manage to collect ethnographic data independently—that varied in terms of their place in the country, cost of living, proximity to a major city, the ratio of lesbian to gay male households, the proportion of lesbian couples, duration of the existing lesbian enclave and of a related reputation as "lesbian friendly," and the spatial concentration patterns within the metro area. I suspected that attributes, such as a city's cost of living and region, would influence gentrification dynamics and outcomes. I anticipated, for instance, that newly forming LBQ enclaves might produce more extreme degrees of commercial and residential clustering than more long-standing enclaves. Thus, I sought two cities with long-standing LBQ populations and two with recently emerging concentrations.

Our current methods for counting and mapping LBQ populations have significant limitations, namely, that broadscale counts of sexual minorities are notoriously inaccurate; thus, I had to select my four cities with only imperfect knowledge of their actual LBQ populations. The only actual counts I had was an "estimated lesbian household population size," as determined by the US census for the first time in 2000 (Bureau of the Census 2000); that figure counts only "lesbian couple households"—excluding all LBQ individuals who do not cohabitate with another woman and including some households that contain two women who are not romantically involved. The lack of more detailed information about LBQ populations was both a hindrance to, but also a motivation for, undertaking the kind of study I intended to launch. Thus, most background research for this book pertained to the dimensions of city ecology to which urban scholars typically attend, and that is accessible from afar, such as population size and demographics, cost of living, patterns of industry and occupation, and political-affiliation figures. I did, however, turn to media coverage and the cities' own promotional materials (e.g., Chamber of Commerce and Visitors' Bureau pamphlets and websites) to confirm or disconfirm that the cities had established or burgeoning "lesbian-friendly" reputations. For instance, newspaper articles and online profiles periodically feature Ithaca and Portland as LBQ-friendly cities. Historical accounts also point to extant women's or gay and lesbian land in or near some cities that possess unusually high proportions of LBQ residents, which I thus used as one indicator of the longevity of a city's LBQ concentration.

After a few months of background research I selected Ithaca. I had lived and worked in Ithaca and had informally contemplated the origins of its substantial LBQ population and the impact thereof for the city. More importantly, Ithaca seemed to embody the image of the prototypical LBQ enclave emerging from recent census analyses: it is a college town with natural amenities and left-leaning politics, and Tompkins County, of which Ithaca is the seat, possesses one of the highest proportions of lesbian-couple households in the nation.[3]

Selection of Ithaca partially guided my choice of additional study cities. For instance, since Ithaca has a long-standing LBQ-friendly reputation, I looked for another college town but one with a more recent concentration of LBQ residents, a city in a different region, and a city with a higher cost of living. Ultimately, this persuaded me to adopt San Luis Obispo as a site that would serve as complement to and "foil" for Ithaca. My aim throughout was to bring cities into conversation with one another.[4]

From the remaining list of candidates, I next selected Greenfield, Massachusetts. At the time of the 2000 census, Franklin County, of which Greenfield is seat, contained the second highest proportion of lesbian households in the country.[5] This affirmed my informal observations, when visiting family in the area, of the increasingly visible presence of LBQ residents in public spaces, such as at the tables outside of the natural foods cooperative, at a nearby restaurant bar, and at the Farmers Market. Also, given its proximity to Northampton, Massachusetts, I was intrigued by the possible gentrification-contagion story that Greenfield might reveal. Did gentrification price LBQ residents out of Northampton and encourage migration to Greenfield? If so, how might migrants to Greenfield approach gentrification and Greenfield itself? Finally, Greenfield shared many attributes with Ithaca; like Ithaca, it is a Northeastern county seat with many natural amenities and a long established progressive political reputation. However, it does not possess a Cornell University or Ithaca College (rather, it is home to the locally esteemed but much less nationally visible Greenfield Community College). Thus, Greenfield provided valuable points of contrast to and correspondence with Ithaca.

As these three sites crystalized I puzzled over the fourth. Should I select a Midwestern or Southern site, expanding my design to include one Northeastern, one New England, one West Coast, and one Midwestern or Southern case? For a time, I sought to include regional variation in the design. However, I struggled to find a Midwestern or Southern site that did not depart substantially from all three of the others on some crucial dimension (beyond region), troubling my ability to hold some facets of the sites "constant." Madison, Wisconsin, for instance, has a much larger population (nearly a quarter million in 2010) than the other study cities. Ann Arbor appeared far too similar to Ithaca (with region as the only major point of departure). Decatur, Georgia, was an intriguing possibility, but its very close proximity to a major city (Atlanta) set it apart from the other sites. Moreover, Decatur was much more racially diverse than nearly all the other cities on my long list of prospective study sites. If I selected one city that departed from the others in this way, I risked limiting my efforts to explain variation in gentrification and other plausible outcomes across cases.

I highlight here only a handful of the cities that I considered and ultimately discarded. (To name a few others, I also considered Asheville, North Carolina, Burlington, Vermont, Portland, Oregon, and Brattleboro, Vermont.) My goal was not to present a holistic or comprehensive portrait of contemporary LBQ lives (this book, as I hope is clear, serves as a reminder of the impossibility of such a task); if comprehensiveness had been my goal, I would have aimed for a much more heterogeneous collection of cities possessing much more heterogeneous LBQ populations. Instead, I sought to document the motivations for and consequences of LBQ migration to a certain type of city. Necessarily this meant focusing on a specific type of city, and, by default, on a pool of LBQ individuals who, demographically speaking, are relatively homogenous; reside in that type of place; and tend to engender gentrification.[6]

After a few months of deliberation, I had to face the reality that, as a single ethnographer, I could not capture all the possible variations of LBQ community in any single design. That acknowledgment guided my selection of Portland, Maine. After learning that South Portland, Maine—a seaside suburb adjacent to Portland proper—contains a quite high proportion of lesbian couples, I began to think about how Portland shared certain attributes with San Luis Obispo that would make it an ideal fourth case. Like San Luis Obispo, Portland's LBQ population concentration is smaller and less established than that of Ithaca and Greenfield. Each metro area possesses a state university and a community college and, compared to Ithaca and Greenfield, a higher cost of living and a lower proportion of registered Democrats. Portland and San Luis Obispo are also alike in that gay-male households slightly outnumber lesbian households, and that lesbian couple households concentrate in highest numbers just outside of the city proper.[7] Moreover, San Luis Obispo and Portland's location on opposite coasts, combined with Portland's status as the most populous city in Maine and closer proximity to a larger city (Boston) provided points of contrast, ultimately affirming my selection of Portland.

In sum, I selected the sites for two primary and partially overlapping reasons. First, I was intrigued by city-specific puzzles that I hoped would address broader questions pertaining to LBQ populations and gentrification. For instance, Ithaca facilitated exploration of how and why LBQ residents concentrate in a city far removed from a major metropolis, while Greenfield permitted examination of why LBQ individuals move from one lesbian enclave (Northampton) to another (Greenfield). More centrally, I chose the four cities because they share certain attributes and in other ways are dissimilar; that combination, I believed would create a richness to my fieldwork and also would enable me to explain whatever dynamics I uncovered. For instance, maybe distance from a large city reduces the likelihood of LBQ-generated gentrification. Perhaps long-standing enclaves attract lesbian feminists who eagerly mark LBQ enclaves or commercial districts, signaling the desirability of the city to certain other politically progressive populations. I aimed to make certain that each city shared a certain attribute (e.g., cost of living or proximity to a major city) with at least one other site and also departed from at least one other site on the same measure.

Of course on recognizing, two-thirds of the way through fieldwork, the existence of place-specific identity cultures, my core research questions, pertaining to the role of LBQ migrants in gentrification, shifted substantially, calling me to shift focus from questions pertaining to migration and gentrification and to attend more closely to questions of identity and networks; I no longer pursued questions about the role of LBQ migration in gentrification processes. In one sense, the months that I spent crafting a design that would allow me to answer questions about gentrification were for naught. However, several choices served me well even as my research questions shifted. Specifically, the degree to which the cities constitute "like cases" or otherwise share many characteristics prohibited relying on categorical explanations—such as a city's region or whether it is in a red or blue state—for the place-specific identities and ties that fieldwork unexpectedly uncovered.[8] Moreover, on the whole, the full sample of LBQ individuals interviewed and observed across the four cities is relatively homogeneous; most are white and possess at least a BA. Yet, within each city there is some heterogeneity, especially in terms of age, income, and duration of residence. These overarching demographic commonalities across cities, and the subtle heterogeneity within each city, permitted me to eliminate many plausible explanations for identity variation I uncovered, significantly deepening the puzzle of why identities and communities varied across cases. Put differently, reliance on multiple sites allowed identity variation to announce itself to me. Without my choice of four varied cities, this might be a book about the dominance of lesbian identity politics or, alternately, of post-identity politics. In other words, as others have before, we might have taken the identity orientation of residents in a single city to be universal or, at least, indicative of a broad trend. Certainly, we would have missed how places shape identities and, even more crucially, how specific features of city ecology are responsible for identity heterogeneity across cities.

Of course, reliance on multiple cities is not without challenges. Most centrally, the use of multiple sites reduces the time one can devote to each study city. Dividing attention has its costs. I sought to limit those costs by deeply embedding myself in each during the primary period of study (roughly three months in Portland, San Luis Obispo, and Ithaca, and more than a year—with stops and starts corresponding with my other academic responsibilities—in Greenfield). To maintain ties to informants, extend my relationships with each city, capture crucial events, and observe change over time, I made multiple return visits to each city for observation and follow-up interviews. I also maintained contact with key informants and followed developments in the field via newspaper articles and listserv discussions. Finally, I collected more interviews—a relatively efficient method for garnering insights about a population and its dynamics—than I might have if I had studied a single site.

To address these limits of comparative research, some rely on a team of ethnographers, typically assigning different ethnographers to different research sites. While that works well in certain instances, in this case working alone was an unexpected necessity. Specifically, conducting research alone in all four cities prevented me from misattributing variation in findings across cities to subtle differences in method, or personality, or demographic traits, among the different ethnographers involved. By working independently, I could be certain that the ethnographer, as research instrument, was not calling out the city-specific differences the data presented; this allowed the differences in city ecology that this book highlights to announce itself as driving identity differences.

Indeed, my awareness of the place specificity of sexual identity began to build and finally crystalized in Portland as I slowly recognized that I was, quite literally, pulling different clothes from my suitcase in each city. In Ithaca and San Luis Obispo, I rarely considered wearing anything other than jeans. Once I got to Portland, those jeans that served me so well simply did not feel right; I found myself in skirts and dresses more than in any of the other cities. This was not a conscious effort to blend; rather—perhaps much like the people I was studying—without knowing it I was taking subtle cues from those around me about who and how to be myself in the local context. Indeed, I only became aware of this subtle self-adjustment when a Portland informant drew attention to my clothes. Sitting in a downtown coffee shop she asked, point blank, "How do you identify?" Before I could answer, she acknowledged what I had subtly felt for weeks—that the people I was studying were scrutinizing my clothes and my presentation of self just as much as I was scrutinizing them. Several years later, I can still hear her voice, as she leaned across the table, saying, "We've noticed that you wear a lot of skirts and dresses and that your hair is chin length, but we're not sure how you identify." Here, clothes I had (literally) carried with me to other cities found themselves pulled out of the closet more than in other places and, crucially, took on new meaning and significance. The ethnographer—and her wardrobe—stayed more or less constant across several years in the field, but the meaning those around her ascribed to themselves and therefore to her varied substantially by city. In Portland, as my informant indicated, the relevant question was not whether I was LBQ, but, instead, the specifics of how I identified, and she called me to recognize how, intentionally or not, I was signaling this microidentity via my wardrobe. Had I only studied Portland or any other single site, I would have missed this insight—about how we reflexively mirror our environs—entirely. Yet, once I recognized it, by the time I completed fieldwork and conducted my final visits to the four study cities, I could anticipate which version of myself felt most comfortable in a given place and throw the "right" clothes for each city in my bag before hitting the road. This is yet another way in which working alone—across four cities—fostered awareness of the source of sexual identity cultures.

Sampling

In total I interviewed just over one hundred seventy individuals, with most interviews lasting between sixty and ninety minutes. I recorded, and later transcribed and coded, each interview; most of the time I chose not to take written notes in order to not interrupt the flow of the conversation. I prioritized interviews with those individuals who had moved to the given city within the last decade, although in each site roughly 10 percent of interviews were with long-standing residents. My sample from each city contains economic, age, gender, racial, and ethnic heterogeneity; I spoke with working- and upper-class individuals alike, with male-to-female and female-to-male transgender informants, and with African American, white, Latino, Native American, and Asian American residents, as well as with some who had emigrated from abroad. However, the bulk of informants identify as female and white, are highly educated, were born in the United States, and hold professional positions.

Before arriving in a city, I distributed calls for participation via a heterogeneous set of institutions, websites, and email lists. On arrival, I turned to public display of flyers in a variety of settings, my participation in a range of scenes, and snowball sampling to cultivate an interview sample; I also reached out to institutions of which I had previously been unaware and redistributed news of the research to institutions, websites, and email lists I had contacted before arriving. This expansive sampling approach prohibited the formation of a narrow pool based on initial informants' friendship, professional, or other networks.

It is important to consider, as some readers no doubt already have, whether the homogeneity of identity orientations within sites results from snowball sampling—from asking informants for referrals to others they know. Narrow reliance on this method would, of course, introduce the possibility that identity cultures vary by small group rather than by city; that I captured the cultures of friendship groups or other networks and not of the larger cities in which they are embedded. However, sampling methods cannot explain the homogeneity of identity orientations within each city. While snowball sampling was a tool I used, recruitment via institutions, public notices, and participant observation ensured that I spoke with a wide variety of residents in each city. Moreover, I always asked informants to connect me with anyone they knew who did not frequent the spaces where I was currently conducting research and with anyone they knew (or just knew of) who was not a part of their friendship and professional networks.[9]

Sampling was expansive in another sense as well. Triangulation—reliance on interviews, extensive ethnographic observations of a variety of scenes, and some analysis of print and other media—indicates that orientations extend beyond my interview sample.[10] It is one thing to hear an informant describe herself in certain terms in the privacy of an interview and another to encounter evidence of those same terms from those I had never interviewed, whether used by strangers in a public scene or by a reporter in print.

While my interview samples are not random or strictly representative, I am nonetheless confident that they account for sizable proportions of LBQ individuals who had moved to each of these cities in the last decade. Why is this the case? Despite the high proportion of lesbian couples relative to other US cities, the LBQ population in each city is fairly small, enabling interviews with and observations of a sizable range of LBQ migrants. In each city, I encountered the same individuals over and again in a variety of places—from marches and performances to hiking trails and the grocery store—which affirmed my sense that, via interviews and observations, I was engaging with a significant cross section of the LBQ population in that city.

Of course, methods for counting this population are quite imperfect, as we know, and thus I cannot be totally certain of the full universe of LBQ individuals in each city. Toward this end, I want to mention an important caveat: my interview and observational data suggest that I came into contact with many of the *publicly engaged* LBQ individuals in each place.[11] By publicly engaged I do not simply mean those who attend community meetings or are a part of activist groups; rather, I mean those who occasionally stop for a coffee in a local café, breeze through a gallery, run or walk on city sidewalks, and otherwise embed themselves in the many possible public dimensions of city life that exists beyond our front door. Of course, when I became mindful that, for instance, not very many LBQ Portlanders over the age of fifty hung out in coffee shops or went to see street theater, I sought out those scenes in which they did appear. Or, when I noted that very few LBQ individuals of color were a part of my Ithaca sample, I began asking informants to send my contact information specifically to such individuals. This purposive sampling, typically near the end of my time in the field, further enhanced sample heterogeneity.

That said, those who choose not to engage in public realms, or who do so very minimally, or who are deeply excluded from the scenes and networks I sampled (such as, I suspect, the very poor), appear in the book in very small numbers. Are their identities the same as others in their city? We cannot be certain, which is why I refer to identity cultures as dominant and not as all encompassing. Of course, as this section details, the scale and range of my sample suggests that I missed only a few of these people; nevertheless, it would be misleading to suggest that my findings reflect attitudes and practices of all LBQ residents in each city.

While my broad sampling of a variety of social groups and organizations was quite intentional, for reasons I specify below, sample heterogeneity ultimately surpassed my expectations and intentions. In Greenfield and Ithaca, as we know, LBQ residents eschewed identity politics, and some were even uncomfortable participating in research that called for LBQ participants; that, not surprisingly, complicated my sampling efforts.[12] While I sought referrals, these requests rarely gained momentum. As a result, I required evolving and wide-ranging recruitment strategies, which inadvertently enhanced sample diversity. Likewise, in Greenfield and Ithaca LBQ residents were just as likely to report ties to heterosexuals as they were to mention other LBQ residents. This propensity made expanding my sample quite difficult, but also reinforced my ultimate argument: I could not rely merely on snowball sampling, and this was further evidence that I was capturing city-specific identity, rather than just stumbling onto LBQ friendship cultures. Relatedly, Portland LBQ residents primarily socialize in small microidentity networks, which constituted very small snowballs; they were nearly always very quickly exhausted. Thus, in Portland, snowball sampling required me to draw from many independent groups—including some who experience themselves as quite separate from any such microidentity networks. For all these reasons, friendship groups cannot account for the identity homogeneity I uncovered in each city.

Sampling, to be clear, was not limited to interviews; I devoted much time in the field to conducting ethnographic observations. In recent years, sociologists have engaged in debate about the relative merit of interview versus observational data.[13] Each of the two core questions that this book pursues—first, about how individuals understand themselves and their residential choices, and, secondly and of equal importance, how individuals interact and engage with one another—calls for distinct methods. Interviews elicit narratives and provide informants with the opportunity for candor and self-reflection; thus, my interviews were crucial to my efforts to answer the first question. Observational data, by providing evidence of interactional dynamics and other behaviors and practices, addressed the second.

At the same time, each method also provides a valuable perspective on that information generated primarily by the other. Interviews allow us to hear the ways that an informant reflects on, and frames, their interactions with others; observation allows us to witness those interactions firsthand and to note any similarities or differences between how people speak about themselves and their ties outside of the scope of the interview (although, admittedly, variation across these contexts was quite minimal—another product of citywide identity cultures and of the pleasure many residents take in their shared sensibility about sexual identity and difference).

There were many moments in the field when I recognized the potential limitations of one method or another. For instance, in Portland, multiple interviewees told me that I should not bother observing an upcoming Pride Dance Party that was to be held on a dock in the harbor, since "no women" or "few women" go there. "It is all men," one woman told me. I was nonetheless curious and wanted to observe as many Pride-related events as possible, so I attended anyway. Despite what informants had said, many women were present. However, the vast majority were not LBQ individuals whom I encountered elsewhere in Portland, leading me to believe that the event— like much of Portland's Pride celebration—drew tourists and residents from other parts of Maine (a hunch that further observation verified). Regardless of the source of the disjuncture between informants' reports of the event and what I observed, I was glad that I had not heeded their advice and thus misrepresented an event by simply recording their account.

Likewise, if I had not conducted interviews, I might have concluded that Ithacans maintain rich and satisfying ties to other LBQ residents, since I frequently observed intragroup interactions. Only via interviews (and the sense of privacy they afford) did a consistent sense of disappointment with the absence of lesbian-only networks—and, closely related, the high value they place on connections to heterosexual neighbors—become fully apparent. Even more broadly, in the privacy of interviews, across all four cities, I uncovered accounts of loneliness, challenging residential choices, and sexual histories that I likely would not have encountered in the public sphere.

Given the import of observational research to my core research questions, I sought to observe a broad range of scenes, from interactions in bars and parks, at dances, private parties, neighborhood meetings, and festivals. Despite great effort to secure access to as many informants, and their scenes, as time would allow, I was not able to control the degree to which observational opportunities were accessible to me. In cities where LBQ congregation is limited (namely, Ithaca and Greenfield), so, too, are opportunities to observe interactions among LBQ individuals.[14]

However, at first I did not recognize how my challenge achieving access related to the local identity culture. For much of my time in Ithaca, for instance, I worried that my methods were somehow responsible for the paucity of LBQ-only scenes I found. I collected observations at a bar and coffee shops popular with LBQ individuals, and I attended several performances of LBQ musicians; these generated important information about the degree to which LBQ residents embed themselves in such scenes. However, I eventually came to recognize that the paucity of invitations I received to such gatherings in Ithaca and Greenfield—in contrast to my ready, abundant access to the same in Portland and San Luis Obispo—spoke more to features of the places I was studying than to my research strategies.

Specifically, I came to recognize that the unevenness of access across sites resulted from different patterns of congregation in each city; LBQ individuals in Greenfield and Ithaca simply gathered in LBQ-only scenes much less frequently than those in the other two cities. Secondly, to the degree that LBQ individuals socialize with one another in Greenfield and Ithaca, many informants express reticence about framing such gatherings and relationships as rooted in shared sexual identity; for this reason, to call an ethnographer studying LBQ enclaves into such occasions was to risk marking them in a way incongruous with the dominant local identity culture.[15] Eventually, I came to recognize that my frustrations in the field pertaining to access provided valuable insight into the character of ties and identities. Indeed, they drew my attention to the variability of identities and ties across cities.

In this sense, it is not a coincidence that the San Luis Obispo and Portland chapters are more akin to traditional ethnographic studies of a population group; in those settings, much more than in the others, informants operated as a bounded population group with a sense of common ground and shared fate. This underlines the utility of approaching uneven data, particularly that resulting from problems of access, not merely as a reflection of the ethnographer or of design, but also as a data source in its own right. Moreover, the absence of data, resulting from scenes we cannot access or that do not exist, is itself instructive and should be recorded and analyzed along with all that we do observe.[16]

Further Explorations of Cities and Identities

There has been much scholarly and popular attention to recent census and Gallup data that allow us to chart, with increasing specificity, the residential patterns of lesbian, gay, bisexual, transgender, queer, and intersex (LGBTQI) communities. One of the most common narratives that results from this recent scholarship highlights the existence of concentrations in "unlikely" places—that is, outside of major cities.[17] Amidst these narratives, we scholars seem to take particular delight in highlighting "surprising" results, such as LGBTQI households in the suburbs and throughout the rural South.[18]

Not surprisingly, we often speculate on the sources of these population concentrations, suggesting, for instance, that with increasing social acceptance the range of geographies available to LGBTQI populations is expanding; that a place like Greenfield might more readily receive LGBTQI populations today than it had in the past. While there may be truth in this, I caution here that given the relative infancy of census data on same-sex households (and the imperfections thereof), combined with the findings of this and earlier studies, it is a mistake to presume that LGBTQI residential concentrations outside of major cities are altogether new.[19] As the longtimers we meet here readily demonstrate, LBQ individuals have made spaces for themselves with and near heterosexuals in a variety of environments for a long time; we do not have data covering a broad enough time span to fully document or understand the degree to which purported movement out of "gayborhoods," or into otherwise smaller cities, suburbs, and rural locales, is new or novel. Even taken alone, the endurance of certain LBQ population concentrations, including some I studied, troubles such accounts.

We also do not have enough systematically collected qualitative data to understand motivations for contemporary LGBTQI migration. This book points to a host of reasons for LGBTQI residence in politically progressive, peri-urban locales that feature various natural amenities. I caution us against the impulse to impute motivations for residence based on census and other survey data without also asking LGBTQI individuals about their moves (if they have, in fact, moved), and without observing them navigate residential choices and, on moving, their daily lives and sense of self and group.

While I call for qualitative inquiries into the origins and dynamics of these settlements, I also caution us against overemphasizing evidence from single sites. As this book demonstrates, it would be a mistake to treat motivations that LBQ individuals articulate about their moves in, say, San Luis Obispo, as representative of broader trends. In addition, we must be mindful of the dearth of historical evidence of LBQ migration and concentration patterns; the presumption that trends are new or novel should be thoroughly tested. The more histories and ethnographies of contemporary LBQ enclaves we can collect, the better. However, as I hope this book makes clear, such inquiries ought to carefully attend to the places in which enclaves are embedded—that is, to city ecology–and in so doing should work to uncover how places and populations inform one another.

I hope that the possibilities offered by this book's methodology entice others to continue our collective exploration. I urge others to investigate the patterns and dynamics of alternate populations and places. In short, this book calls scholars to pursue the complexity and heterogeneity of identities and ties that extend well beyond the type of person and city this book charts. Indeed, we ought to inquire into how places shape the identities and ties of, for instance, white, working-class men in small, Southern towns, stay-at-home mothers in Northeastern suburbs, Latina service workers in a variety of cities, and West Coast first generation university students in college towns. Building on the spirit of this book, such endeavors will surely deepen and broaden not only our portrait of contemporary identities but also our understanding of the how and why—of causes and processes—behind them.

INTRODUCTION

1. In some instances some identifying characteristics of individuals, such as precise occupation or city of origin, have been changed to preserve their anonymity.

2. See Schippers (2016) on polyamory.

3. I suspect that transgender identities are also different in each city. However, the number of trans-identified individuals I formally interviewed was too small to come to any final conclusions.

4. Informants do not conceive of identity as narrowly attached to or emerging from movements, but informants engage with movement narratives (see Mansbridge 1995). The dispositions that characterize identity cultures extend to and influence practices, such as how residents dress, the types of individuals with whom they partner (e.g., relations, romantic, or otherwise, with transgender and/or gender-queer individuals are most frequent in Portland and least in San Luis Obispo), and political and family practices (e.g., whether they promote gay marriage or parent). The book foregrounds dispositions, but the reader will encounter much evidence of behavior throughout, as well. The components of "sexual identity culture" are standard elements scholars turn to when assessing sexual identity (e.g., Gamson 1995; Moon 2012).

5. In this sense, if we take little league baseball as an example, we can imagine that while individual teams might have some novel habits and beliefs, within a city the broader collection of little league baseball players would share a general orientation to baseball and to what it means to play Little League (see Fine 1979).

6. On "place character" and enduring place distinction, see Molotch (2002) and Paulsen (2004).

7. See Zukin (1991) on Disneyfication.

8. See Taylor (2002), Hyra (2008), and Zukin (2010).

9. See Ghaziani (2014), Podmore (2006), and Nash (2013) on the notion of "post-mo" or "post-gay."

10. A key exception is scholarship on "neighborhood effects" that examines how neighborhood conditions influence life chances, quality of life, and other dimensions of personal experience. However, such work stops short of examining how neighborhoods impact identity. See, e.g., Wilson (1996), Sampson, Morenoff, and Gannon-Rowley (2002), Sampson (2012), and Sharkey (2013).

11. I use "identity" to refer to informants' self-understandings (see Brubaker and Cooper 2000), as well as to their sense of how their identity relates to that of the broader group in which they locate themselves. Despite my use of "identity," I concur with Brubaker and Cooper (2000) that thinking of LBQ women as an "identity group" or "community" has hindered our ability to recognize internal differences in self-understanding and orientations to groupness, as well as the sources of such differences (see also Rubin1993). The book operationalizes "sexual identity cultures" as a set of dispositions informants articulate regarding self-identity or description, as well as coming out, integration with heterosexuals, and extant modes of framing sexual identity and difference, such as the dominant agendas of national GLBTQ organizations or current trends in queer theory. This partially overlaps with Hennen's (2008) use of "sexual culture," but focuses primarily on orientations to self- and group-understanding rather than on sexual activity itself, and, especially, understands sexual identity cultures as locally produced, rather than as emerging from broad subcultures or communities that span place. By referring to this set of dispositions as a "sexual identity culture," I turn our attention to identity as practice (Brubaker and Cooper 2000); to how LBQ individuals live, experience, and talk about their self-understanding on the ground, in their daily lives and interactions (Butler 1990, 1993). I also propose that identity cultures are inherently local or place based.

12. See Gates and Ost (2004) and Cooke and Rapino (2007) on female same-sex couples' residential patterns.

13. See Gates and Ost (2004), Cooke and Rapino (2007), Bureau of the Census (2000, 2010), and Fischer, Gee, and Looney (2016).

14. On natural amenities I draw from Cooke and Rapino's (2007) finding that lesbian couple migration is oriented toward small cities with many natural amenities and high proportions of lesbian couples. They, in turn, draw on McGranahan's (1999) measures of natural amenities, which include warm winter, winter sun, temperate summer, low summer humidity, topographic variation, and water area.

15. This is based on the research of Gates and Ost (2004) and Gates (2013).

16. See a 2016 US Treasury Department report on where married lesbian couples reside (Fisher, Gee, and Looney 2016). The report affirms the pattern revealed by the 2000 and 2010 census (Bureau of the Census 2000, 2010)—with female same-sex married couples concentrating in small cities like those featured in this book.

17. On "like cases," see Molotch, Freudenburg, and Paulsen (2000).

18. To supplement information gathered via interviews and observation, I collected survey information from most informants on income, duration of residence, networks, educational history, home value, etc. In instances when survey information was not collected or was only partial, I approximated data from interviews to the best of my ability (e.g., recorded years of education based on the interview transcript).

19. I omit "T" from "LBQ" because the number of transgender individuals I interviewed is so small that it would misrepresent the sample to suggest that I captured anything definitive about patterns of identity among transgender individuals. On transgender identities, see, e.g., Schilt (2010) and Westbrook and Schilt (2004).

20. See Brown-Saracino (2009).

21. See Brown-Saracino (2014).

22. The precise number of LBQ individuals in each site is difficult if not impossible to capture, for the census only counts couples. Moreover, some in two sites eschew identity categories (Ithaca and Greenfield) and in another regard identity as shifting and evolving (Portland). This would complicate any attempt to conduct a precise count

of the LBQ population in a city. That said, my confidence in the breadth of my local samples comes from the realization, via observation and interviews, that I am familiar with many of the LBQ individuals who populate public spaces and whom others mention in interviews. Moreover, I made concerted efforts to reach those who appear less frequently in such spaces and accounts by continuing to post notice of the research throughout my time in each site, as well as by asking informants and organizational contacts to put me in touch with those who less frequently populate the public sphere. These inquiries led me to interviews with those who had just moved to town, quite elderly women (such as one in her eighties), and a handful of residents uncertain about their comfort with being "out."

23. See Kennedy and Davis (1993), Stein (1997), Laumann et al. (2006), and Moore (2011).

24. See, e.g., Hunter (2013), Laumann et al. (2004), Moore (2011), Greene (2014), Faderman (1981), Kennedy and Davis (1993), and Chauncey (1994).

25. See Whittier (1995) and Stein (1997) on feminist and sexual generations.

26. This is not to suggest that there are never instances or places in which generation might play a more determinative role. Imagine, for instance, an LBQ-dominated retirement community. In that context, generation may play a more determinative role than it did in my research sites, which are relatively age heterogeneous. However, this book builds a case for thinking about how even in a retirement community specific features of the local context that relate to place, such as LBQ residents' position in the city in which the retirement community is located, might also play a defining role. That is, this study's findings suggest that, if one studied multiple LBQ retirement communities, variation in identity orientations would likely emerge across locales. Some geographers consider how place and generation may interact to influence sexual identities, e.g., Nash (2013), Smith and Holt (2005), and Meyer (2003, 2007).

27. On sexual minorities who seek residence in places that will support their existing orientation to sexual identity and difference, see Brekhus (2003), Nash (2013), Ghaziani (2014), Gorman-Murray and Waitt (2009).

28. See Hennen (2008) on gay male sexual cultures. See Brekhus (2003) on gay men's movement to the suburbs. See Greene (2014) and Nash (2013) on the particular cultures of GLBTQI spaces.

29. See Brown-Saracino and Parker (2017) on "lesbian-friendly" cities.

30. While not produced by an informant, a blog entry marks distinctions between the identities of women in distinct parts of Park Slope (Jean Kahler, "On the Habits and Habitats of the Breeding Lesbians of South Brooklyn," *Urban Ecology*, January 24, 2013, http://urbanecology.blogspot.com/2013/01/on-breeding-lesbians-of-south-brooklyn.html). See also Lo and Healy (2000) on perceptions of neighborhood-based differences among lesbians in Vancouver.

31. Another details how identities vary by time and place (see Halberstam 2005; Abbott 1997); in the 1990s, she witnessed transgender politics emerge among LBQ women and regards cities such as San Francisco as better incubators than Portland for transgender identities.

32. Some of this surprise likely results from the fact that, when considering a move, LBQ prospective migrants are primarily attentive to the degree to which a place seems LBQ welcoming and to general place narratives. Moreover, most of their preliminary interactions are with heterosexual realtors, landlords, the Chamber of Commerce, etc., and informants' accounts suggest that these individuals rarely convey accurate portraits of the local LBQ identity culture.

33. See Katz (1982) on "negative explanations"; see also Brown-Saracino (2015).
34. On defining traits of and variation among college towns, see Gumprecht (2003, 2010), Lofland and Lofland (1987), and Florida (2012).
35. On nonurban GLBTQ residential concentrations, see Brekhus (2003), Kazyak (2012), Gray (2009), Smith and Holt (2005), and Barton (2012).
36. See Barton (2012).
37. Paulsen (2004) defines place character as "a particular combination of geography, history, economy, demography, politics, organizations, culture, and aesthetics" (245) that, in tandem, lends a locale distinction. See also Molotch (2002).
38. See Brown-Saracino and Parker (2017).
39. Ibid.
40. On the city as actor, see Latour (2005) and Latour and Hermant (2006).
41. The book's core finding builds on and intercedes in two dominant ways of explaining why different individuals and groups articulate distinct cultural tastes and practices. One approach identifies cultures shared by population and interest or taste groups that span geographic divides, from artist-gentrifiers (Lloyd 2006) to opera fanatics (Benzecry 2011), specific professionals (see Abbott 1988), or newcomers (Griswold and Wright 2004). Another approach suggests that cultural differences emerge from small group dynamics, pointing to the distinctive cultures that develop among members of a baseball team (Fine 1987), mushroom collecting club (Fine 1998), New York booksellers (Duneier 1999), Brooklyn men who raise pigeons (Jerolmack 2012), or a place-based ethnic minority group (Gans 1962; Whyte 1943; Kefalas 2003; Small 2004). Moon (2012) documents identity heterogeneity among Jewish Americans at the individual level suggesting that individuals have some freedom to select an identity that best works for them (see also Wilkins 2008; Green 2008; Fields 2016). While each approach affirms the endurance of group culture, they do not explain why LBQ migrants within a city who belong to a range of demographic, taste, friendship and peer groups nonetheless share a common identity culture. Some scholarship on collective identity poses similar questions about the influence of context on identity. See, for instance, Somers and Gibson (1994).
42. On temporal variation in identities, see D'Emilio (1983), Halberstam (1998, 50), Armstrong (2002), Seidman (2002), Podmore (2006), Brown (2008), and Ghaziani (2011). On differences by class, see Faderman (1981), Kennedy and Davis (1993), and Chauncey (1994). On differences by nation, see Carrillo (2002). On differences by global region, see Fernandez-Alemany and Murray (2002). On differences by generation, see Stein (1997) and Nash (2013). On differences by race and ethnicity, see Laumann et al. 2005, Moore (2011), and Greene (2014). On identity variation within a metro area, see Wilkins (2008); and on variation within a city, see Lo and Healy (2000). Despite this scholarship, it is a mistake to regard attention to variation and difference as universal. Halperin's (2012) book *How to Be Gay* suggests that gay men learn to be gay, not that they become a different kind of gay man in each place in which they reside.
43. On how sexual experiences, identities, and practices may vary by racial or ethnic group see, for instance, Laumann et al. (2004), Moore (2011), and Greene (2014).
44. See, e.g., Carrillo and Hoffman (2017) on the elasticity of sexual identity.
45. For more general arguments about how actors experience identity as fluid, see Gamson (1995), Epstein (1987), Seidman (1993), and Diamond (2008).
46. Echoing this, geographers call for research that will "examine queer lives with an eye to the geographic specificities of place" (Myrdahl 2013, 284).

47. See also Robinson (2014) on regional and city identity.
48. See Wilson (1996), Sampson, Morenoff, and Gannon-Rowley (2002), Sampson (2012), Sharkey (2013), and Wodtke, Harding, and Elwert (2011). For reviews of the literature, see also Small (2004) and Paulsen (2004).
49. See Small (2004) and Paulsen (2004) for a discussion of culture's typical exclusion from studies of neighborhood effects.
50. On regional identity, see Hummon (1990), Lacy (2007), Griswold (2008), Griswold (2016), Carr and Kefalas (2010), Robinson (2014), and Griswold and Wohl (2015).
51. On home and identity, see Hummon (1990) and Kusenbach and Paulsen (2013).
52. Just as scholars of regional identity attend to how and why regions remain distinct, those who study "place character" investigate the origins of city and state differences. "Place character" is "a particular combination of geography, history, economy, demography, politics, organizations, culture, and aesthetics" (Paulsen 2004, 245) that lends a locale distinction. Once established, this character distinguishes a place from others with similar attributes, whether geographic or otherwise (it is place character that helps explain why Vermont feels different from New Hampshire, or Santa Barbara from Ventura) (Kaufman and Kaliner 2011; see also Molotch, Freudenburg, and Paulsen 2000; Milligan 2003; Paulsen 2004; and Borer 2008). A series of crucial decisions or occurrences set place character in motion, everything from the placement of a highway to oil drilling patterns (Molotch, Freudenburg, and Paulsen 2002), or state marketing campaigns and the "idio-cultural migration" (Kaufman and Kaliner 2008) they inspire. This approach suggests that place distinction does not merely emerge from major, categorical features, such as region or industry, but, instead, from more minute but ultimately consequential attributes and decisions. While place character scholars demonstrate that place distinctions endure, they stop short of identifying what they *do* or accomplish.
53. Building on recent census data that broadens our map of where gay and lesbian couples reside, some challenge the "metronormative" accounts that emerge from studies of male and white-dominated central city "gayborhoods" (Halberstam 2005). For analyses of where GLBTBQI individuals live, see Gates and Ost (2004), Cooke and Rapino (2007), Collard (1998), Chauncey (1994), McNaron (2007), Sullivan (2005), D'Emilio (2006), Warner (1993), and Ghaziani (2011). On the limits of studying male-dominated central city neighborhoods, see Valentine (2007) and Hunter (2013). They point to differences between urban, rural, and suburban identities, as well as differences by gender (Kazyak 2012), community or subculture (Hennen 2012), nightlife locale (Green 2008), institution, or generation. On geographic identity differences, see Weston (1995), Howard (1999), Bell (2000), Brekhus (2003), Halberstam (2005), Gray (2009), and Kazyak (2011, 2012). On organizational differences, see Gamson (1996), Connell (2012), and Reger (2012). On generational differences, see Whittier (1995), Stein (1997), Nash (2013), Cohler and Hammack (2007), Hammack and Cohler (2011), Herek, Chopp, and Strohl (2007), Bennett (2010), Ghaziani (2011), Russell and Bohan (2005), Seidman (2002), and Sullivan (2005). They also point to identity differences that emerge from or are affirmed by the choice to reside in a particular type of place, such as in a suburb or central city neighborhood (see Brekhus 2003; Ghaziani 2014). However, such research leaves untouched questions about how specific cities, as distinctive, heterogeneous places, influence identity.
54. On geographic identity differences, see Weston (1995), Howard (1999), Bell (2000), Brekhus (2003), Halberstam (2005), Gray (2009), and Kazyak (2011, 2012). On

organizational differences, see Gamson (1996), Connell (2012), and Reger (2012). On generational differences, see Whittier (1994), Stein (1997), Nash (2013), Cohler and Hammack (2007), Hammack and Cohler (2011), Herek, Chopp, and Strohl (2007), Bennett (2010), Ghaziani (2011), Russell and Bohan (2005), Seidman (2002), and Sullivan (2005). Geographers come closest to articulating the puzzle at the heart of this book. Myrdahl (2013) asks how social conservatism and size matter for "queer place-making" (286). Valentine (1993) writes of residents' "perceptions of the sexuality of space" (398), Brown (2008) refers to "indigenous conceptualizations of homosexuality" (1225), and Nash (2013) writes of the place-specificity of certain identity orientations (see also Wei 2007 and Hubbard 2001). However, most such statements remain propositional or, when based on empirical studies, rely on single-site designs, limiting researchers' ability to identify the role of precise place elements in crafting local modes of sexual identification. Thus, while there is an increasing sense—particularly among geographers—that place matters for sexual identities, *how* it matters remains underexplored and largely undocumented.

55. On how categorical attributes of person or place shape identity, see, e.g., Robinson (2014), Carr and Kefalas (2010), Lacy (2007), Barton (2012), and Grey (2009).

56. I quite consciously rely on the term "ties" rather than "community," since the degree to which informants regard their social ties as constitutive of "community" varies by site; in Ithaca, for instance, despite their supportive local connections LBQ migrants decry the absence of "community." In contrast, in San Luis Obispo they celebrate what they present as a seamless "community"—despite the existence of subtle internal factions. Thus, following Suttles (1974) and Hunter (1974), I aim to let my informants tell us what "community" is for them on the ground in the places they live and work; their words and actions present a portrait of what "community" looks and feels like in their cities, and of the role it plays in their lives. For related scholarship, see Roos, Trigg, and Hartman (2006), Romig (2010), Rothenberg (2003), Krieger (1983), and Rothblum (2010).

57. In this sense, this book traces, in Gerald Suttles's (1974) term, "the relationships between communities and their broader social environments" (14).

58. On imagined community, see Anderson ([1991] 2006), Griswold (1992), Rose (1990), and MacGregor (2010).

59. On "bowling alone" and broader claims about the dissolution of civic life, see Putnam (2000).

60. These are among the types of spaces and institutions via which Putnam (2000) and Oldenburg (1989) suggest many once forged ties.

61. On these and related sources of community dissolution, see Oldenburg (1989), Putnam (2000), and Etzioni (1996).

62. On changing nature of social ties, see McPherson, Smith-Lovin, and Brashears (2006).

63. See Gates and Ost (2004). There are crucial exceptions (see, e.g., Brown 2008; Nash and Bain 2007; Muller 2007; Taylor 2004; Valentine 1993a, 1993b, 1995), but few examine more than one city, limiting our ability to accomplish tasks at the heart of this book: to identify broad trends and make causal arguments that span individual locales. In Tiffany Muller Myrdahl's (2013, 284) terms, this book helps to "disrupt the diffusion model" or the notion that one comes out and moves rapidly to the city (see also Brown and Knopp 2006; Cooke and Rapino 2007; Gorman-Murray 2007; Knopp 2004; and Smith and Holt 2005). For analyses of where GLBTBQI individuals live, see Gates and Ost (2004), Cooke and Rapino (2007), Collard (1998), Chauncey

(1994), McNaron (2007), Sullivan (2005), D'Emilio (1983), Warner (1993), and Ghaziani (2011). On the limits of studying male dominated central city neighborhoods, see Valentine (2007) and Hunter (2013).

CHAPTER ONE

1. By "recognizably LBQ" I mean those made recognizable via their interactions with other women and forms of display (e.g., handholding and coparenting, haircuts, and apparel). Later interviews and observations affirmed nearly all these early assumptions.

2. See Faderman (1991) on women's land.

3. This data leaves substantial gaps in our knowledge of LBQ geographies and populations, by, for instance, including some same-sex roommates who are not romantically involved in counts of same-sex couples, and by overlooking some transgender or gender-queer individuals and, most substantially, failing to include noncoupled LGBTQI individuals—a particularly dramatic oversight in a place such as Ithaca that possesses a high proportion of young people (who are less likely to be coupled). On the limits of census counts of LGBTQI individuals, see Gates and Ost (2004), Cooke and Rapino (2007), Anacker and Morrow-Jones (2005), Hayslett and Kayne (2011), Black et al. (2007), Brown and Knopp (2006), and Walther et al. (2010).

4. From Gates and Ost (2004) and Gates (2013).

5. See the *Advocate*, March 13, 2007.

6. See Castells (1983). Popular narratives, including those that my informants proffered, suggest that this is a product of gender discrimination and related gender pay inequity. It also results from processes of self-selection, which likely also relate to gender and sexual identity biases and inequalities (see Tilcsik, Anteby, and Knight 2015).

7. On lesbian-feminist-separatist communities, see Wolf (1979), Stein (1997), Green (1997), and Ettore (1978).

8. On the move away from "lesbian" identities, see Binnie and Valentine (1999, 178) and Podmore (2006).

9. On "post-mo," see Nash (2013). On "post-gay," see Ghaziani (2011).

10. See Brown-Saracino and Parker (2017) on lesbian-friendly reputations.

11. For similar coverage, see Henbest (2008).

12. See Podmore (2006) on rejection of lesbian-feminist separatism.

13. Such accounts raise the question of whether separatism was as dominant as scholarly and popular accounts suggest. Regardless, this book reveals the import of collective memories about a separatist past; it remains a living history.

14. On lesbian friendliness, see Brown-Saracino and Parker (2017).

15. See Brown-Saracino and Parker (2017).

16. On LBQ mothers and the choice to parent, see Mamo (2007).

17. Knopp (2004) suggests that this combination of nostalgia and disappointment with the places queer individuals relocate to "reflects the entirely predictable failure of a plainly utopian imagination that is at the heart of any quest of this nature" (124).

18. See Fischer (1982), Wellman (1988), and Suttles (1974). It is also plausible that ambient community flourishes in Ithaca in part because its relative racial homogeneity reduces instances of racial or ethnic conflict (see Logan and Spitze 1994; Rotolo 2000). Likewise, its relative geographic isolation may encourage mutual dependence. As Brint (2001) suggests, strong ties flourish in contexts that are "geographically and/or socially set apart" and in which there is a "normative climate of mutual tolerance and respect" (18; see also Fischer 1982; Chaskin 1997; Sampson 1988; and Wellman 1988).

19. On sexual identity communities, see D'Emilio (1983).
20. On identity politics, see, for instance, Calhoun (1998), Seidman (1993), and Taylor and Whittier (1992).
21. On lesbian identity politics and social movement community, see Taylor and Whittier (1992).
22. Of course, the ability to choose to emphasize these facets of the self is a privilege that is unequally distributed.
23. On relations among heterogeneous individuals, see Kornblum (1974), Jerolmack (2012), and Anderson (2011). Neither my informant nor I is the first to use the term "ambient community." However, to the best of my knowledge the meaning this chapter assigns it differs from that typically used. The term is most frequently used in scholarship to describe community formed via technology (e.g., Trappeniers et al. 2008).
24. Many—although far from all—of their ties in Ithaca rest (implicitly) on shared racial and class characteristics, but few of my informants regard these identity characteristics as organizing features of their ties in the way they do those that emerge from interactions at a LGBTQI center or a support group for lesbian parents. That is, most (particularly white and middle-class) informants do not "champion" race or class as a "core identity" around which they explicitly construct ties (Seidman 2002, 87). In this sense, most, likely because of the relative racial and class homogeneity of my sample, are relatively unaware of the role of shared racial, ethnic, and class-identity features in the formation of ties. See also White and Guest (2003) on community.
25. See Anderson (2011) on the cosmopolitan canopy.
26. See Wellman (1985) and White and Guest (2003). White and Guest (2003) write of the "transformation" of community as a paradigm for understanding the contours of contemporary urban ties that stands in contrast to the "community lost" perspective. They identify strands of the transformation of community paradigm in scholarship on "liberated" ties, as well as in work on the persistence of community in urban areas (241–42), and use this "transformation" tradition to pose and test several hypotheses about contemporary urban ties. I use "transformation" to refer to the altered mechanisms informants rely on to generate social ties, not to changes in the number or intensity of ties. See also Wellman (1979, 1988), Webber ([1963] 1999), and Calhoun (1998).
27. Notably, this heterogeneity is typically limited to sexual identity, gender, and profession, for the bulk of Ithaca residents are white, and most informants socialized with those with whom they share a class position.
28. See history of Ithaca College at http://www.ithaca.edu/about/history/.
29. This may be a result of heterosexual residents' good will—many of whom observations suggest sincerely embrace queer neighbors. However, the breadth of Ithaca's LBQ population likely makes the "cost" of intolerance high.
30. Notably, preliminary data collected in two other sites suggest that this arithmetic is place specific. For instance, in a more recently emerging lesbian enclave many express desire to live in a place in which the entire population is LBQ.
31. Informants' words suggest that they regard the ghetto much as Seidman (2002) describes the world of "subcultural gays"—that is, one that is "somewhat bounded, if not territorially, then symbolically. They signal their exclusive group identification by somewhat distinctive self-presentational and communicative styles; for example, through dress, language, or hyper-masculine styles for men or butch gender styles for women" (88–89).
32. The bar has since closed.

33. Despite the literature's suggestion that queer individuals seek either the safety of the "ghetto" or assimilation, many seek residence where they can be "out" while also living alongside heterosexual and LBQ individuals. In other words, as Brekhus (2003) found was the case for many suburban gay men, the bulk of informants wish to live where they can integrate into various facets of town life without having to mask their sexual identity. That is, they value integration over and above two alternate paths: assimilation and ghettoization (ibid; see also Gray and Thumma 1997; Seidman 2002, 90). This conflicts with the notion of a complete shift to post-identity or "post-gay" politics (Ghaziani 2011). As Brekhus (2003) richly illustrates, some queer individuals take a middle path between assimilation and ghettoization.

34. On the sites' "lesbian-friendly reputations," see Brown-Saracino and Parker (2017).

35. See Seidman (2002) and Brekhus (2003) on the desire to present the self as multifaceted.

36. On queer individuals' move away from narrow identities see, for instance, Binnie and Valentine (1999), Seidman (2002), Sullivan (2005), Podmore (2006), Ghaziani (2011), and Nash (2013). I use "post-identity politics" rather than "post-gay" (Ghaziani 2011) or "post-mo" (Nash 2013) to capture that informants are not disavowing queerness or their desire to live near other LBQ individuals and where they feel heterosexuals will accept them. Instead, they specifically reject a politics or sense of self primarily oriented around sexual identity and difference. Moreover, their transformation is rooted less in a shift in their relation to heterosexuals or in overt assimilationist practices and more in a shift in how much one sees oneself via the lens of sexual identity and difference. That is, this is not about the blurring of differences between heterosexuals and queer individuals (Sullivan 2005), but, instead, about making those difference less of an organizing feature of one's relations and self- and group understanding.

37. On how sexual identity has taken different shape in different times, see Ettore (1978), Binnie and Valentine (1999, 178), Stein (1997), Seidman (2002), Podmore (2006), and Ghaziani (2011). This is part of why I refer to these individuals under the rubric "post-identity politics" rather than "post-mo" or "post-gay" (see Brown-Saracino 2011), because they are not inherently "post-gay" but are doing "gay" (or lesbian) differently in a different context.

38. Informants in their twenties articulated greater satisfaction with community because they joined queer college and university networks. Likewise, a handful of older women who have lived in Ithaca for several decades expressed satisfaction. Many who articulate a sense of loss are nostalgic for the type of "social movement community" that Taylor and Whittier (1992) outline.

39. One may surmise that this is a product of the topic of study. However, when I posed questions about friendships and networks few informants exhibited the bias expressed with regard to community.

40. On Pride parades, see Bruce (2016).

41. Fischer (1975) and Handlin (1959, 1969) suggest that cultural clashes help sustain and produce subcultural institutions.

42. See Breton (1964) on the role of institutions in maintaining internal subcultural ties.

43. This raises the possibility that, contra Fischer (1975), a "critical mass" of subcultural members can contribute to the breakdown of that subculture and reduce the number of institutions serving members (ibid; see also Rabinowitz, Kim, and Lazerwitz 1992). This research also demonstrates that subcultures do not automatically come into conflict with others (Fischer 1975, 1326). As Fischer predicted that such conflict

would strengthen subcultures, it is plausible that the absence of conflict helps produce integration and the breakdown of formal identity-based organizations and businesses, underlining how ideological orientations shape subcultures' structure and dynamics.

44. I use the term "integrated" because this is how several informants talk of their social life in Ithaca. Moreover, the term "assimilation" implies a performance of self that meets the needs or expectations of a dominant group. LBQ residents of Ithaca suggest that they are able to be a part of the local social fabric without altering self-presentation in order to achieve access.

45. This furthers Brekhus's (2003) argument that identity is place based, since Ithaca women report that their desire for community centers varies across time and place. Indeed, the homogeneity of attitudes about identity among informants extends Brekhus's argument about the mutually constitutive nature of place and personal identity (see also Hummon 1990).

46. Sexual-identity hate crimes are actually higher than average in Ithaca. However, research suggests that hate crime reports—and the labeling of crimes as hate crimes—is more common in atmospheres of tolerance. Moreover, Ithacans report greater feelings of safety and acceptance than those in any other site. See McVeigh, Welch, and Bjarnason (2003), Stotzer (2010), and Meyer (2008).

47. See Esterberg (1997) on exclusions from lesbian community.

48. See Brown-Saracino (2007).

49. On exclusivity and conflict among LBQ individuals, see Esterberg (1997).

50. Indeed, Ithacans struggled to negotiate the inclusion of a researcher into these tight-knit friendship circles (see Brown-Saracino 2014). Despite articulating the existence of such circles, by, for example, describing membership in a tiny group of femme/butch couples, over and again informants hesitated to invite me into their private interactions. There were exceptions, such as an afternoon at a downtown bar, and a karaoke event, when women opened their networks to this and other newcomers, but their frequency paled in comparison to the other sites.

51. This suggests that LBQ Ithacans imagine "lesbian community" to be relatively effortless or automatic, since they do not regard efforts to bring together disparate elements of Ithaca's queer female population as constituting "real" community.

52. This sensibility shares some characteristics with the attributes of the "cosmopolitan canopy" that Anderson (2011) identifies and the "great good place" that Oldenburg (1989) outlines. Specifically, Ithaca informants' articulation of a sense of respect and celebration of their ability to interact with a variety of residents overlaps with Anderson's (2011) description of the canopy as "settings that offer a respite from the lingering tensions of urban life and an opportunity for diverse peoples to come together. Canopies are in essence pluralistic spaces where people engage one another in a spirit of civility, or even comity and goodwill" (xiv), and Oldenburg's (1984) description of the coffee shops and bars that encourage informal, stress-free interaction between heterogeneous individuals. However, in contradistinction to Anderson's canopy and Oldenburg's great good place, a sense of ambient community neither solely rests on public sphere interactions nor is limited to specific spaces within Ithaca; it emerges from interactions and ties forged in private, parochial, and public realms, and a generalized sense of belonging. More generally, a sense of ambient community depends less on respectful interactions among strangers (Anderson 2011), and more on civility and friendship forged in the parochial realm (Hunter 1985; Lofland 1998).

53. Specifically, informants associate their sense of ambient community with qualities that scholars typically assign to community such as a sense of safety, "understanding, emotional support, material aid, and . . . information" (Wellman 1988, 89; see also Rosenthal 1987; Wellman 1985). The factors that produce this sense of "ambient community" share some traits with Brint's (2001) "geographic" community. However, while Brint suggests that geographic communities fall into two groups—predicated on shared activity and beliefs, respectively—this is not a distinction that informants make. Their sense of ambient community rests on a combination of activity- and belief-based geographic associations. Furthermore, because my informants moved in search of community (explicitly in search of identity-based community and, more implicitly, in search of the sense of safety and belonging associated with ambient community), the neat distinction Brint makes between communities predicated on geography and choice do not apply. Likewise, informants suggest that ambient community also crosses the line some draw between communities that meet instrumental and expressive needs (e.g., Guest 2000).

54. This sense of ambient community rests on a "we-feeling" (Cooley 1902; see also Jerolmack 2012) cultivated in small groups organized around shared beliefs, politics, and practices, or a feeling of mutual fate. See Jerolmack (2009) on ties predicted not on "historical and kin-based ties" but on activities (438). The pigeon keepers he studied may be a model of one of the hobby-based groups that contribute to a broader sense of ambient community within one's neighborhood or town.

55. Ambient community shares some attributes with Oldenburg's (1984) "great good place" (1984) and Anderson's (2004, 2011) "cosmopolitan canopy." However, it sometimes rests on intimate ties, is forged beyond the limits of specific institutions, and is not limited to particular times (e.g., an hour in a coffee shop or at a food court). That is, a sense of ambient community emerges from daily routines and interactions—not from departures or breaks therefrom.

56. See Lofland (1998) on the public and parochial realms.

57. The sense of ambient community that Ithacans experience arises from several mutually constitutive features of sociality—features that arise from city ecology. These include feeling accepted by most residents and a closely related sense of belonging in a variety of local settings; friendships with a range of residents (e.g., both straight and gay) that extend beyond spaces of obligatory interaction, like the workplace; and, finally, frequently informal and friendly interactions as one goes about her daily rounds. There is overlap between some facets of the ties that contribute to a sense of ambient community and other community types' attributes, such as the voluntary nature of McKnight's (1987) "community of association," the freedom to forge non-primordial ties under the (expanded) community of limited liability (Janowitz 1952; Hunter and Suttles 1972), reliance on both informal and formal devices for constructing Warren's (1952) "community as social system," the import of informality for Oldenburg's (1984) "great good place," and the role of civility and a sense of belonging in Anderson's (2004, 2011) "cosmopolitan canopy." Therefore it is plausible that attributes of one or more of the above types produce a sense of ambient community. However, there are also key differences between the attributes of the sense of ambient community my informants highlight and those scholars associate with the above. For instance, the community of association's primary purpose is to provide social and healthcare for its members, the community of limited liability has firm boundaries (Hunter and Suttles 1972, 58), relies heavily on formal institutions (primarily

governmental), and produces instrumental ties (Hunter and Suttles 1972, 45; see also Chaskin 1997, 528), and community as social system produces not only positive affective ties but division and conflict (Warren 1963, 160). Finally, "ownership" may derive not only from living in a place but also from habitual visits (Greene 2014).

58. See Anderson (2011) on role of a sense of "ownership" in creating a civil public sphere.

59. On bars as a source of social support for sexual minorities, see Kennedy and Davis (1993) and Hunter (2010).

60. On identity-based enclave community, see, e.g., Park (1925), Whyte (1943), Gans (1962), Kornblum (1974), Oldenburg (1989), and Anderson (2011).

61. See Lofland (1998) and Hunter (1975) on parochial realm interactions and related social obligations.

62. This is not to suggest that institutions are not involved in ambient community. Mary, for instance, specified that Alcoholics Anonymous serves an important social function in her life. She also mentioned the role of other formal institutions, such as college athletics. However, she specified that many of her ties are formed beyond formal institutions, such as through her business and child-rearing. Thus, institutions can contribute to a sense of ambient community, but single dominant institutions, such as a college, church, park, mall, or coffee shop (Oldenburg 1989; Anderson 2004, 2011), are not the central organizing force.

63. For exceptions, see Jerolmack (2009) and Anderson (2011).

64. On how marginalization increases attention to the quality and character of social ties, see Anderson (2011).

65. On the pleasure of a sense of belonging, see Howe (2001).

66. See Chaskin (1997, 533).

67. Of Ithaca's population, 16.5 percent falls below the federal poverty level (ACS 2009–13).

68. On community as necessarily bounded, see Suttles (1979).

69. See Anderson (2004) on the cosmopolitan canopy, which is rooted in specific spaces. Anderson suggests that the cosmopolitan canopy depends on one's ability to be open with distinct others—even about potentially fraught subjects. My informants' desire to color over tension and violence suggests that a sense of ambient community relies at least as much on tacit silence as open conversation. Furthermore, Anderson regards the canopy as refuge from the city, whereas my informants present Ithaca as refuge from society. Likewise, Jerolmack (2009) demonstrates how a shop connects disparate men, emphasizing the import of a local institution for the construction of boundary-spanning ties. See also Bell (2007) and Oldenburg (1984) on social relations in commercial venues.

70. This suggests that if queer women expressed outrage about encountering homophobia, this might threaten their sense of ambient community by disrupting a tacit sense of unity.

71. For exceptions, see Guest (2000), Logan and Spitze (1994), and Hunter (1975).

72. On place-based ties, see Oldenburg (1984), Jerolmack (2009), and Anderson (2004, 2011).

73. For exceptions, see Kornblum (1946), Oldenburg (1984), Anderson (2004, 2011), and Jerolmack (2009).

74. On place-based LBQ ties, see Taylor and Rupp (1993), Esterberg (1997), and Gray (2009, 27).

CHAPTER TWO

1. See Buettner (2011) on San Luis Obispo and happiness.

2. See Seidman (2002), Knopp and Brown (2006), Podmore (2006), Ghaziani (2011, 2014), Schulman (2013), Moon (2012), Brown-Saracino (2011), Kennedy and Davis (1993), D'Emilio (1996), Krieger (1982), and Valentine (2000).

3. This challenges notions of generation and class as reliable sources of variation in LBQ identities and, most substantially, gestures to how places shape social identities (see Whittier 1995; Reger 2012, Stein 1997; Kennedy and Davis 1993). I alternate between "women" and "residents" throughout the chapter because, to the best of my knowledge, I encountered only female-identified LBQ individuals in San Luis Obispo.

4. On identity community, see D'Emilio (1983), Krieger (1983), Sampson (1988), Anderson (1990), Fischer (1975), Suttles (1974), Wirth (1938), Armstrong (2002), Esterberg (1997), and Rubin (1993).

5. On the role of formal institutions in community, especially for LGBTQ populations, see D'Emilio (1983). See also Hunter (1975), di Leonardo (1998), and Brown-Saracino (2009).

6. The chapter also presents a portrait of a community that marries real-world and online interaction, detailing how online and off-line interaction play mutually supportive roles in creating and sustaining frequent, inclusive social interaction. On how the Internet shapes social ties, see Rheingold (1993), Driskell and Lyon (2002), Wellman and Gulia (1999), Hampton and Wellman (2003), Mesch and Levanon (2003), and Wellman (2001).

7. How do I know this? Because this is not just about how these women talk about themselves in public or to one another; it is how they spoke about themselves with me—in the context of interviews in which they were often strikingly candid (e.g., acknowledging infidelities and sexual violence). Moreover, this way of thinking about the self seems to guide behavior, from the very private (e.g., as far as I can tell fewer anticipated future romantic relationships with men or gender-queer individuals than in the other cities) to the very public (e.g., they act with their feet by surrounding themselves with other lesbians).

8. On generational differences, see Esterberg (1997), Whittier (1995), Stein (1997), and Reger (2012). On "post-gay" identities, see Ghaziani (2011); see also Seidman (2002), Brown-Saracino (2011), Podmore (2006), and Moon (2012).

9. This suggests that how we know, with certainty, that cities shape identities will vary by city. In the case of San Luis Obispo this becomes clear via two analytic techniques: (1) comparing identities in SLO to identities in other sites and (2) comparing city conditions. In other instances, this can also be partially gleaned by attending to residents' accounts of what it is like to live in their city, as well as their more explicit discussion of how their ties have changed with their moves.

10. See Griswold (2016) on regional identities.

11. See Foucault (1977) and Weeks (1986).

12. On recognition of the fluidity and heterogeneity of contemporary identities, see Ghaziani (2011), Moon (2012), Schulman (2013), and Podmore (2006).

13. On the notion of identity as evolving, see Podmore (2006) and Moon (2012).

14. However, see Reger (2012) and Guenther (2010) on unexpected heterogeneity of feminist identities.

15. See "Gay Marriage Ban: A Tale of Two Votes," *Los Angeles Times*, November 4, 2008 (http://www.latimes.com/local/la-2008election-california-results-htmlstory.html);

Josh Friedman and Karen Velie, "Democrats Losing Membership in SLO County," CalCoastNews.com, May 18, 2015 (https://calcoastnews.com/2015/05/democrats -losing-membership-in-slo-county/#sthash.UgAzajN9.dpbs); and California Secretary of State, Elections and Voter Information, Report of Registration, October 20, 2008 (http://elections.cdn.sos.ca.gov/ror/ror-pages/15day-presgen-08/county.pdf).

16. On other experiences of being LBQ in California, see Howe (2001) and Hurewitz (2007).
17. On the politics of being "out," see Seidman (2002) and Sedgwick (1990).
18. See Bureau of the Census (2000 and 2010) and Fisher, Gee, and Looney (2016).
19. See Brown-Saracino (2014).
20. On identity politics as protective, see D'Emilio (1983), Seidman (2002), and Armstrong (2002).
21. See Van Maanen (1991, 32) and Brown-Saracino (2014).
22. See Bureau of the Census (2000, 2010).
23. Ibid.
24. On lesbian bars, see Nestle (1997), Podmore (2006), Chamberland (1993), Faderman (1991), Kennedy and Davis (1993), Skeggs (1999), Retter (1997), Hayslett and Kane (2011), and Hutson (2010).
25. On the role of local institutions for identity groups, see Breton (1964), Castells (1983), Gray and Thumma (1997), and Suttles (1974).
26. On culturally homogeneous LBQ networks, see Esterberg (1997) and Taylor and Rupp (1993).
27. See Fine (1987) and Wilkins (2008) on small-group culture.
28. See Esterberg (1997) on exclusion of those who depart from dominant lesbian identity in her site, such as women of color and working-class lesbians. See also Green (1997) and Valentine and Skelton (2003).
29. See Winfrey (2011) and Buettner (2011). As we have seen, they also speak of San Luis Obispo—albeit less readily—as less than embracing of LBQ women, and the sense of threat this produces also encourages a discourse about local lesbian community as a refuge from imperfect conditions, a Camelot within a less than perfect Camelot.
30. On community as a site of conflict, see Gans (1962), Taylor and Rupp (1993), Esterberg (1997), and Wolf (1979).
31. On notions of "how to be gay," see Halperin (2012) and Seidman (2002).
32. See, e.g., Barton's (2012) account of Bible Belt gays.
33. See Laumann et al. (2004) and Barton (2012). See also D'Emilio (1983), Whittier (1995), Faderman (1991), and Stein (1997).
34. See D'Emilio (1983), Epstein (1987), Ghaziani (2011), Kazyak (2011, 2012), Gray (2009), and Barton (2012).
35. This relates to a broader pattern—in the academy and popular culture—of overstating the homogeneity of LBGQT orientations, identities, and attitudes (Halberstam 2005; Valentine 2007; Gray 2009).
36. On the idea of lesbian community, see Esterberg (1997), Krieger (1982), Levine (1979), and Barnhart (1975).
37. See Reger (2012) and Suttles (1974) on how place shapes social experiences.
38. See Coser (1956).
39. See Reger (2012) on the role of a sense of scarcity in shaping political orientations.
40. On the "who and when" of identity-driven lives, see Janowitz (1952), Kornblum (1976), Kennedy and Davis (1993), Gray and Thumma (1997), and Pritchard, Morgan, and Sedgley (2002).

41. See Podmore (2006) and Ghaziani (2011) on post-gay.
42. On the role of and liberation from demarcated locale, see Valentine (2000) and Millward (2007).
43. On how shared cultural spaces foster identity, see Castells (1983), Kennedy and Davis (1994), and Gans (1962).

CHAPTER THREE

1. South Portland actually contains the highest proportion of female same-sex couples in the Portland metro area (Bureau of the Census 2000, 2010).
2. Scholars debate the degree to which gender and sexuality should be treated separately. See Weeks (1986) on isolating them and Schilt and Westbrook (2009) on approaching them as inseparable.
3. See Armstrong (2002) and Moon (2012).
4. On sexual fluidity, especially among women, see Diamond (2008), Esterberg (1997), Rust (1993), and Golden (2006).
5. The Femme Show is not based in Portland, but they regularly perform there, and this performance included Portland collaborators, and an after party revealed friendships between Boston-based performers and Portland residents.
6. This narrative contrasts with the dominant narrative for understanding how social identities move through space—from sophisticated or edgy urban centers to smaller places (e.g., Castells 1983; Fischer 1975). Many in Portland, even those who have lived in larger metropolises, such as Boston, New York, and San Francisco, regard Portland as an "identity frontier" or site of innovation.
7. See Brown-Saracino and Ghaziani (2009) on Dyke March.
8. See Deleuze and Guattari (1987) on identity as amalgamation.
9. On the culture and history of femme identity, see Nestle (1997).
10. Indeed, scholarship would predict this; see, e.g., Whittier (1995) and Stein (1997).
11. For documentation of and further discussion of educational traits by site, see chap. 5.
12. See Lees (2003) on Portland's gentrification.
13. Of course, it is difficult to know whether these women would have volunteered this information had they not been familiar with my earlier scholarship on gentrification (Brown-Saracino 2004, 2007, 2009, 2010). In some instances, my informants' tone and manner seemed to imply that they had familiarized themselves with my faculty website/bio before our meeting and that this may have encouraged their discursive attention to gentrification. However, I do not believe this entirely accounts for their words, as gentrification was also discussed in the public contexts that I observed.
14. As Suttles (1974) instructs, "Community identities, no less than personal ones, should find their reflection in the looking-glass self" (53). On how shared identity produces community, see Polletta and Jasper (2001), Taylor and Whittier (1992), Taylor (1989), Anderson (1990), Fischer (1975), Suttles (1974), and Wirth (1938). And on looking-glass communities, see Sampson (2012).
15. On how community scale shapes ties, see Wirth (1938) and Tönnies (1887).
16. See Wirth (1938) and Tönnies (1887) on the relation between population size and community character.
17. See Rust (2000) on LGBTQI umbrella community.
18. The hearing was held at the Augusta Civic Center. See Judy Harrison, "Thousands Fill Same-Sex Marriage Hearing in Augusta," BDN Maine, April 22, 2009 (http://bangor dailynews.com/2009/04/22/politics/thousands-fill-samesex-marriage-hearing-in -augusta/).

19. In Suttles's (1974) words again, in the context of neighborhood-based communities, "residential groups are defined in contradistinction to one another. . . . [They] gain their identity by their most apparent differences from one another" (51). See, e.g., Wirth (1938) and Park (1925). Portland social dynamics suggest that this is not just true of residential, neighborhood-based groups of the kind Suttles (1974) and the Chicago School before him sketched—but also of population or identity groups within a metro area.

20. See Bureau of the Census (2010).

21. See Steve Mistler, "Census: Little Change in Maine Poverty Rate, Median Income," *Portland Press Herald*, September 19, 2014 (http://www.pressherald.com/2014/09/19/census-little-change-in-maine-poverty-rate-median-income/).

22. See Bureau of the Census (2000, 2010).

23. See Forstie (2011) on the closure of a lesbian bar.

24. Occasionally, women reported conflict with gay men—such as a physical altercation between a group of LBQ women and a male go-go dancer working at a nightclub. The woman who told me about the altercation reported that the bar's response to the dancer's aggression left her and her LBQ friends feeling unwelcome in the (typically male-dominated) space.

25. The generally successful navigation of microidentities and umbrella identities and communities provides evidence of what Cohen (1997) describes as the "radical potential" of queer politics.

26. On similar dynamics, see Suttles (1974, 41).

27. Affinity community ties could be described as "egocentric, constantly changing, and different from the point of view of each member" (Suttles 1974, 55), and following the "expanded community of limited liability" serve as "a mosaic of partially overlapping communities" (Hunter and Suttles 1972, 59). Yet, affinity community is not as spatially limited or organized as the expanded community of limited liability (ibid.), nor does it rest on the primordial communities captured by the Chicago School (Wirth 1938).

28. Rowley (2014) defines a "community of affinity" as a social group based on a "shared and common interest among members living throughout the urban area" (5), and I rely on this definition. See also Smart and Klein (2013), Friedman (1983), White (2005), and Mosse (1979).

29. On the role of physical separation in producing community cohesion (and other effects), see Buell (1980) and Ruiz-Tagle (2013).

30. According to Suttles (1974), "The most elemental grouping of his coresidents is usually a network of acquaintances who have been selected primarily because they are known from shared conditions of residence and the common usage of local facilities" (55).

31. Many moved because they or a partner (current or former) originated in Maine or have family in Maine. A small handful grew up in Portland itself. Many concluded that Portland is the most opportune place in the state of Maine for establishing affinity ties and simultaneously finding a large population of LBQ individuals. A business owner said: "I have some family in the area. I was living in Minneapolis and in my mid-twenties decided that I didn't want to set down roots so far away from [home]. . . . I'm from Vermont." Another said: "It was time to move out of New York City and my family was here. I mean I grew up in Maine." Their firsthand knowledge gave them confidence about the existence and strength of affinity communities, but despite their familiarity with Portland, the existence of microidentity communities

and even the breadth and strength of the LBQ umbrella community came, for most, as a surprise.

32. See Brown-Saracino and Parker (2017).

33. As Somers (1993) writes, "It is through narrativity that we come to know, understand, and make sense of the social world, and through which we constitute our social identities" (83).

34. See www.visitportland.com.

35. See, e.g., *Travel + Leisure* (http://www.travelandleisure.com/slideshows/so-youre-a -little-weird-the-20-quirkiest-cities-in-america/7); *Forbes* (forbes.com); and *Parenting* (Parenting.com).

36. See Routhier 2012.

37. Ibid.

38. This section of my account of identities and ties in Portland necessarily focuses more on informants' words and accounts than on my own independent observations. There are two reasons for this. First, when observing my informants and others whom I knew to be LBQ in public spaces, I sometimes strongly suspected that those with whom they were socializing—at a park, on the Eastern Promenade, at a Cape Elizabeth beach, over beer in a pub, in the checkout line at Whole Foods—were heterosexual. However, without speaking with their conversation partners or finding an opportunity to ask informants (sometimes I did, sometimes not) "what is the sexual identity of the guy I saw you talking with at Planet Fitness last week?" it was nearly impossible for me to confirm my suspicions. Second, affinity community interactions seem to primarily fall into two camps: (1) fleeting, informal interactions such as with a fellow volunteer or parent in a grocery store aisle or in passing at a gallery, or (2) work-based or private-sphere interactions with coworkers, family members, or members of political or support groups, such as Alcoholics Anonymous (AA). The fleetingness of the first set of affinity interactions exacerbated the awkwardness of grilling residents about their friends' sexual identity, and the second set remained largely outside the purview of my observations. Why was the second set outside the purview of my observations? This, too, instructs about the character of affinity communities in Portland. Generally speaking, my Portland observations were myriad and varied and my access to private scenes—parties and other social gatherings, games, small-group interactions in public spaces, etc.—in Portland far exceeded that in Ithaca and Greenfield. Yet, with only a handful of exceptions—such as the bonfire at the first social gathering I observed in Portland—the scenes I observed were LBQ dominated. This is not a matter over-sampling scenes in which LBQ individuals appear without heterosexual compatriots. Instead, it is because many affinity ties operate in a separate sphere: the family holiday attended *before* exchanging gifts with one's "gay family"; the heterosexual men with whom a butch woman enjoys bantering at the car dealership where she works, but with whom she rarely socializes after 5 p.m.; or the very private exchanges in an AA meeting. This is to suggest that, as many eloquently stated, many informants' affinity ties are episodic or tertiary, limited to a weekly playgroup or organizing sessions, at least when compared to those forged with other LBQ individuals, especially those with whom one shares a microidentity. In this sense, affinity ties are somewhat less intimate than ties to LBQ individuals *or* are *quite* intimate (e.g., one's family or AA) but not as integrated into daily, public interactions and spaces as are informants' ties to LBQ individuals.

39. See Bernstein and Taylor (2013) on attitudes about same-sex marriage.

40. On the notion of a push for "homonormativity," see Duggan (2002).

41. We also encounter a very vibrant and public LBQ life outside the "gayborhoods" in which many imagine such scenes to concentrate (Ghaziani 2014). This does not, however, strictly mean the expansion of such scenes beyond the confines of such spaces (in the face of gentrification and integration), since cities like Portland have long nurtured LBQ populations and their institutions.

42. On Dyke March, see Currans (2012) and Kates and Belk (2001).

43. On the totem, see Durkheim ([1897] 1997).

44. On the retreat from traditional identity politics, see Podmore (2006), Ghaziani (2011, 2014), and Brown-Saracino (2011).

45. See Brekhus (2003), Gray (2009), Barton (2012), Nash and Gorman-Murray (2014), and Browne and Bakshi (2011). See also Hennen (2008) on dispersed sexual cultures.

46. This underlines the import of studying scenes and groups across a city to capture constant elements, as well as the utility of studying multiple places so that intercity variation might reveal itself. Reliance on multiple sites also provides reliefs against which one can measure the significance of intracity variation.

CHAPTER FOUR

1. On concentrations of female same-sex couples in the Northampton area, see Gates and Ost (2004) and Forsyth (1997a and 1997b).

2. For a few years the group had gathered for a weekly "Big Gay Brunch" at an LBQ-owned restaurant. After the restaurant closed, some relied on a (now defunct) listserv to keep the brunch alive.

3. On "lesbian bed death," see Iasenza (2002).

4. For arguments about differences in identity based on age, class, and other characteristics, see Faderman (1981), Kennedy and Davis (1993), Carrillo (2002), Stein (1997), Laumann et al. (2004), and Moore (2011).

5. See Molotch, Freudenburg, and Paulsen (2000), Suttles (1974), Kaufman and Kaliner (2011), and Levitt (2015).

6. This same dynamic—affiliation with a larger, neighboring city—might inure identity cultures in some suburbs from directly or rapidly responding to local ecological changes. We can also imagine that a resident of Ithaca who weekends in New York City (as some academics do) may be slower to adapt to changing local context.

7. On the constancy of neighborhood and metropolitan change, see Park (1925).

8. See Bureau of the Census (2000) and ACS 2010–14 (estimates) on increases in the percentage of residents with a BA or higher and in Greenfield's median household income. Controlling for inflation, there is a steady increase in median income in the city during this period.

9. See Shores (2014) and http://wilsonsdepartmentstore.com/.

10. On the Arts Block, see Davis (2010).

11. On the fate of this building, see Davis and Haddad (1994), Watt (1997), Collins (1997), and Ferguson (1997).

12. More than one-third of Greenfield residents are employed in management, business, science, and arts organizations; a little over 24 percent in sales and office occupations, and, finally, nearly 20 percent in service jobs (ACS 2006–10). Just under one-third of industries in Greenfield are in the education, health care, and social-assistance fields, 12.1 percent retail trade, and 9.1 arts, entertainment, recreation, accommodation, and food services (ibid).

13. On the longevity of Franklin County's LBQ population, see Forsyth (1997a and 1997b).

14. See Forsyth (1997a and 1997b).
15. On the Pioneer Valley as "Happy Valley," see Kirkey and Forsyth (2001), and Rogers and Rogers (2007).
16. Of course, in all the sites LBQ individuals reference the impact of other places on their own identities and lives. In San Luis Obispo, for instance, they take pride in the vitality of their lesbian community vis-à-vis that of Santa Barbara, and in Portland and Ithaca informants readily note parallels and points of departure from the dynamics of lesbian population concentrations in Boston and Brooklyn. And in all sites (although much less so in San Luis than in other places), LBQ individuals speak of Northampton. That is, at least for these mostly white, mostly middle-class, mobile, and female individuals it is tantamount to "The Castro"—simultaneously home-land and otherworldly/mystical (see Howe 2001). Given Northampton's prominence across the sites, it is little wonder that Greenfield's immigrants wrestle with what their simultaneous proximity to and distance from Northampton means about them and their group—particularly in a moment when many actors in Greenfield, some LBQ, are taking steps toward establishing an economic and cultural profile that is closer to Northampton's than Greenfield has had in the past.
17. For scholarship on "geographic community," see Brint (2001) and Flaherty and Brown (2010).
18. Indeed, the same event was staged in Portland, but there it was much less reflective of and productive of the local identity culture. However, this nonetheless reminds that cultural elements—even performances—cut across the study cities, but that what residents "do" with those elements varies greatly.
19. On contra dancing in Greenfield, see Reynolds (2014).
20. See Small (2004) on how memory and neighborhood frames shape approaches to community.
21. Jo's account, together with similar accounts by other longtimers and set against the backdrop of the disjuncture between their orientations to identity and that of newer arrivals, gesture to the import of an extant cultural narrative about place or group for the perpetuation of a longstanding identity culture—even in the face of local trans-formations, such as upscaling and the growing presence of other LBQ individuals (Small 2004). However, the homogeneity of identity orientations in the other sites that have witnessed their own changes reminds that the power of extant narratives is greatest under certain conditions—such as, in Greenfield's case, with a proximate place (and symbol)—Northampton—available for narrative maintenance.
22. On lesbian-feminist identities, see Stein (1997).
23. See also Podmore (2006), Binnie and Valentine (1999, 178), Ettore (1978), Knopp (2004), and Ghaziani (2011, 2014).
24. See Duggan (2002) on increasing efforts to achieve and perform "homonormativity."
25. Town of Greenfield website (http://greenfield-ma.gov/).
26. Franklin County Chamber of Commerce website (http://franklincc.org/tourism-home and http://franklincc.org/eat).
27. This implies different approaches to or ways of "doing" homonormativity (see Dug-gan 2002).
28. On LBQ attitudes regarding same-sex marriages (and marriage more generally), see Smart (2008), Lannutti (2005), Green (2010), Harding (2008), Bernstein and Taylor (2013), Hull and Ortyl (2013), and Greene (2014).
29. It is difficult to assess how close her ideal proportion of lesbians is to the actual number of LBQ residents, as the US census and recent US Department of Treasury

data only count lesbian-couple households—this misses uncoupled individuals (in census data) and unmarried couples (in Treasury data). See Bui (2016).

30. See Williams (1973) and Griswold (1992).
31. See, e.g., http://franklincc.org/tourism-home.
32. See also Brown-Saracino (2007).
33. See Anderson (2011) on role of a sense of "ownership" in creating a civil public sphere.
34. See Gates and Ost (2004) and Forsyth (1997a and 1997b).
35. See Small (2004) on the impact of narratives about a city's past. On place narratives, see also Wynn (2011) and Breen (1996).
36. See Hyra (2008) on urban renewal—new and old.
37. Since 1980, Greenfield has experienced steady increases in the proportion of residents with a BA or higher—from 13.1 percent in 1980 to 27 percent in 2013 (Bureau of the Census 1980 and ACS 2009–13)—as well as, controlling for inflation, in median household income (ibid).
38. On gentrifiers' taste for "grit," see Lloyd (2006).
39. See Tavory and Eliasoph (2013) on futures and anticipation.
40. The 2009–13 ACS estimates actually suggest that poverty levels are slightly higher in Greenfield than in Orange and that Greenfield's median income is only slightly higher than Orange's (ACS 2009–13).
41. Data from the 2000 and 2010 census (Bureau of the Census 2000, 2010) and ACS (2005–9, 2010) suggest that the median value of owner-occupied housing in Portland nearly doubled between the two decades and that the percentage of residents with a BA degree or higher increased by more than 8 percent in the same period. Median household income increased by roughly ten thousand dollars.
42. In other words, it permits identity heterogeneity and transformation unparalleled in the other sites, despite the fact that *all* the sites are dynamic and have certainly experienced change preceding and during the course of study (after all, this should not surprise as the Chicago School instructed a century ago that change is a central fact and dynamic of cities). See, e.g., Burgess (1925) and McKenzie (1925).
43. On the influence of material and symbolic facets of place, see Molotch (2002) and Small (2004).
44. For now, suffice it to say that, given their appreciation for an identity-politics orientation and ties centered thereon, a crystal clear understanding of Greenfield's increasingly dominant post-identity-politics orientation might have dissuaded their move. But move they nonetheless did (from a major West Coast city), drawn by affordability, land, views, and proximity to regional cities, or so the stories others tell about these newcomers suggest.
45. On place reputations and sexualities, see Brown-Saracino and Parker (2017).
46. On Northampton's reputation as a bastion for lesbians, see Forsyth (1997a and 1997b), Kirkey and Forsyth (2001), and Hemmings (1997, 2002).
47. On how cultural perceptions influence experience of place and community, see Hunter (1974), Suttles (1974), and Park (1925).
48. On responsive social identities, see Wilkins (2008).

CHAPTER FIVE

1. The sites' demographic profiles are relatively similar. On the whole, differences are minor and/or fail to align with areas of identity overlap and discord. All the sites possess predominantly white populations. Median family income is relatively compa-

rable, ranging from $59,074 in Greenfield to $71,864 in San Luis Obispo. San Luis Obispo stands out in terms of median home value, followed by Portland where the median home value is somewhat higher than in Greenfield and Ithaca. Poverty rates are highest in two sites possessing a particularly large student population: Ithaca and San Luis Obispo. Yet, identity cultures in the two places are nearly opposed—or at least on opposite ends of our spectrum. Finally, while there is marked variation in the median age of residents (from 22.4 years in Ithaca to 42.6 years in Greenfield), this does not seem to predict identity culture. For instance, San Luis's median age (26.5 years) comes closest to that of Ithaca, yet the sites' cultures are quite distinct. In sum, citywide demographic traits related to race, income, home values, and age (see table 5.2) do not, in isolation, direct identity cultures in the study sites.

2. Despite the identity differences across the four study sites, each possesses a higher education institution. Three (all but Greenfield) possess a four-year institution. Three (all but Ithaca) possess a community college. Ithaca and San Luis each house prominent, highly visible institutions: California Polytechnic Institute (in San Luis Obispo) and Cornell and Ithaca College (in Ithaca). Thus, it is not the presence or absence of colleges and universities that directs the identity differences I have uncovered. Moreover, two sites, Ithaca and San Luis Obispo, are approximately four hours from a major city, whereas Portland and Greenfield are each within two hours of Boston, and three to four from New York. These coupled differences in distance from major city are in contradistinction to the clustering of sites in terms of residents' general orientations to identity politics and integration. That is, one of two sites at greatest distance (four hours or so) from a major city sports post-identity politics, while the other is home to a vibrant, lesbian identity politics.

3. This analytic process closely mirrors the elimination of "a limited set of alternative causal statements" recommended by John Stuart Mill (Savolainen 1994, 1218; see also Skocpol and Sommer 1980 and Skocpol 1984) and used most prominently in recent decades by Skocpol (1984) and other comparative historical scholars. Following Skocpol and others, the goal is not to use the elimination of "alternative causal statements" to isolate a definitive, general cause, but, instead, to identify and rule out explanations that fail to explain outcomes in the cases at hand (Savolainen 1994, 1219).

4. On facets of place working in tandem, see Cuba and Hummon (1993).

5. See Jean Kahler, "On the Habits and Habitats of the Breeding Lesbians of South Brooklyn," *Urban Ecology* (blog), January 23, 2013, http://urbanecology.blogspot.com /2013/01/on-breeding-lesbians-of-south-brooklyn.html. See also Rothenberg (1995).

6. On Los Angeles lesbians and talk thereof, see Moore (2006), Stein (1989), and Faderman and Timmons (2006).

7. Indeed, in 2012 and 2007 Denver sported slightly more bars per ten thousand residents than did other urban US areas of a similar size, such as Boston and Seattle (Economic Census, NAICS Code 7224, "Drinking Places," 2012 and 2007, https:// www.census.gov/econ/isp/sampler.php?naicscode=7224&naicslevel=4).

8. See Brown-Saracino and Parker (2017).

9. On queer identities as "assemblage," see Deleuze and Guattari (1987).

10. How do we know this? If a place element plays a determinative role—e.g., hate crime rates and city demographics—we would anticipate that, to the degree that an element is shared across sites, identities in those sites would align. However, as I've demonstrated, despite their markedly distinct identity cultures, Ithaca and San Luis's sexual identity hate crime rates are comparable. Likewise, Greenfield and Portland have the

lowest cost of living but distinct cultures. Second, if specific, isolated dimensions of city ecology drive differences, given their identity variation one would predict that the sites' population and place elements would be markedly disparate. Instead, sites that share many elements have dissimilar cultures. In sum, the absence of a consistent relationship across sites between a single (or narrow set of) place elements and identity culture casts doubt on the notion of a determinative relation between easily isolated place elements and identity.

11. A handful of expectations, drawn from literature on cities and identities, informed the city elements I considered. For instance, I suspected that high rates of sexual orientation hate crimes might encourage emphasis on a common sexual identity formulated in response to a tangible "other" (see Reger 2012). Relatedly, I anticipated that a determinative event or policy decision, such as the establishment of a university or 1970s women's land (acreage settled by feminists and typically designated as "women only" or for women and children only), would conjure place character and thereby identity outcomes. I also considered the influence of local marketing campaigns and demographic traits (see Hummon 1990; Florida 2002; Molotch 2002; Paulsen 2004; Kaufman and Kaliner 2011; Reger 2012; Guenther 2010). Finally, informants' narratives about the motivations for their residential choices and about local life encouraged inclusion of a few additional elements, such as occupational trends and proximity to major cities (Paulsen 2004). Ultimately, this process revealed that, *in isolation*, these individual dimensions of city ecology fail to explain why identity cultures vary. This process was aided by recognition of variation in identity culture by site, as well as areas of overlap in the sites' identity cultures: San Luis and Portland's identity-politics orientations, and integrationism in Ithaca and, to a lesser degree, in Greenfield. What features of the cities produce differences *and* commonalities in their identity cultures?

12. On how place elements work together to shape city life, see Molotch, Freudenburg, and Paulsen (2000).

13. See Molotch, Freudenburg, and Paulsen (2000) and Paulsen (2004). Paulsen (2004) defines "place character" as "a particular combination of geography, history, economy, demography, politics, organizations, culture, and aesthetics" (245). Building on this, Hinze (2013) explores how neighborhood identification influences immigrants' orientations to integration in Berlin. Internal variation among informants within Hinze's two sites and differences in place attributes across them limit her ability to isolate the specific mechanisms by which place influences attitudes and identities. However, she makes vital strides in demonstrating neighborhood-level interpolation of social position and in outlining how groups incorporate neighborhood identity in their sense of self (see also Kasinitz et al. 2009).

14. One might anticipate that political party affiliation rates in a city might influence identity cultures. However, differences between three of the sites in terms of party affiliation are not stark, and stop short of explaining areas of identity correspondence and divergence across the cities. With 29.8 percent of voters registered as Republican, San Luis stands apart from the other sites. While Ithaca and Greenfield possess nearly identical proportions of Republicans (10 and 11 percent, respectively), Portland follows closely with 14.9 percent Republican. Thus, party affiliation does not independently dictate identity culture.

15. The independent business figure is from Civic Economics, which ranks Portland fourth in New England for independent businesses; San Luis does not make their list of the top ten regional independent cities (http://nebula.wsimg.com/0513e3c

38824cf9fbeb7fb7f1ed76c51?AccessKeyId=8E410A17553441C49302&disposition
=0&alloworigin=1). As tables 5.6 and 5.7 demonstrate, the distribution of resident
occupations across two dominant categories is relatively constant across the sites
(ACS 2006–10: see specifically 2010 publication year). Ithaca stands out from the
other sites in the distribution of industries, with its emphasis on educational services, health care, and social assistance. This might contribute to differences between
Ithaca's identity culture and that of the other sites, but the distribution of industries
and occupations cannot account for differences between the other sites, as well as for
areas of identity overlap in Ithaca and Greenfield. Thus, identity culture differences
do not narrowly emerge from differences in city industry and occupational patterns.

16. See Bureau of the Census (2010).
17. See Reger (2012).
18. See Reger (2012) for a similar argument with regard to gender, feminism, and city, as
    well as institutional context.
19. See Gates and Ost (2004, 29).
20. In neither site was women's or LGBTQ land located within the city proper, but in-
    stead within a half-hour drive. Despite this distance, LBQ women regularly evoke this
    land as an indicator of the endurance of their enclave. Population figures are from
    Bureau of the Census (2000, 2010).
21. See, e.g., the Moosewood in Ithaca, and, in Greenfield, the longstanding Organic
    Foods Production Association. See also Small (2004) for a similar thought experiment.
22. On how neighborhood reputation influences a third identity, associated with neigh-
    borhood, see Hinze (2013).
23. On narrative frames and identity, see Hunt, Benford, and Snow (1994) and Polletta
    (1998).
24. See Greenberg (2008) on place branding.
25. San Luis Obispo Chamber of Commerce website (visitslo.com).
26. See Buettner (2010) on San Luis Obispo and happiness.
27. See San Luis Obispo County website (sanluisobispocounty.com).
28. See Portland Area Chamber of Commerce website (http://www.portlandregion.com).
29. Ibid.
30. San Luis Chamber of Commerce website (visitslo.com).
31. See "Learn Our History: Chronology of a Gay-Friendly City," Greater Portland, Maine
    (http://www.visitportland.com/gay-lesbian-history.aspx.). In fact, Gates and Smith
    (2001) find that Portland, Maine, has the third highest proportion of lesbian *and*
    gay couple households in the United States. However, at the 2000 census (Bureau of
    Census 2000) gay-male couples outnumbered female same-sex household couples
    in Portland.
32. On Northampton as "Lesbianville," see Forsyth (1997a and 1997b).
33. According to FBI data for 2007–10 (https://ucr.fbi.gov/hate-crime), which maps until
    the major period of study, only a marginal difference exists between the sites in terms
    of sexual orientation hate crime rates (see table 5.4). In addition, all possess hate
    crime rates—both sexual identity and others—that are higher than that of the sur-
    rounding county and state (this may be a product of higher reporting rates in places
    in which sexual minorities feel comfortable approaching law enforcement to report
    hate crime incidences). This complicates the notion that substantial differences in
    hate crime rates, in isolation, direct identity culture. That is, my cases suggest that
    looking at hate crime rates is not enough to predict identity culture outcomes.

34. This mismatch between reported sense of safety and experiences of violence or harassment was, to a lesser degree, echoed in Greenfield. In contrast, residents of San Luis Obispo and Portland readily acknowledged moments of fear, discomfort, harassment, and violence. In Portland, at least, a recent and highly visible beating of a transgender (male-to-female) individual in Munjoy Hill, a neighborhood popular with LBQ women, may have heightened informants' sense of fear.

35. It is plausible that in more "tolerant" places residents are more apt to report hate crimes, and/or that places with higher proportions of queer individuals—particularly publicly out and visible queer individuals—may experience more sexual orientation hate crimes. See McVeigh, Welch, and Bjarnason (2003), Stotzer (2010), and Meyer (2008).

36. See, e.g., Peter Jacobs, "12 Reasons Why Ithaca, New York Is the Best College Town in America, *Business Insider*, October 7, 2014 (http://www.businessinsider.com/ithaca-is-the-best-college-town-in-america-2014-10).

37. Both to a researcher and in interactions with others (observed by researcher).

38. Others also use the phrase "socioscape." See, e.g., Carrington (2002) and Sivakumar (2000).

39. However, schools do not direct identity cultures, since we would expect the identity cultures of Greenfield and Portland to be more closely aligned. For instance, each attracts graduates of women's colleges and progressive, alternative colleges, such as Hampshire.

40. Those deeply in the hold of the local identity culture less readily offer accounts of the local culture, instead primarily articulating its key elements in the course of describing self- and group identity.

41. See Molotch, Freudenburg, and Paulsen (2000) and Paulsen (2004) on place character.

42. On identity cohorts, see Whittier (1995), Reger (2012), Small (2004), and Wherry (2011).

43. Apparent change in Greenfield's identity culture indicates that, as with the other mechanisms, the socioscape isn't determinative or unwavering; if it were, we would anticipate that newcomers would constantly replicate the identity-politics orientation of earlier migrants. Part of why extant identity culture and other features of the socioscape related to the LBQ population may play a nondirective or more indirect role is because LBQ residents constitute a small minority of the population; LBQ migrants much more frequently encounter other dimensions of place, such as broad place narratives and a general sense of numbers and acceptance.

44. On city population as a dimension of place, see Hinze (2013).

45. Following Molotch, Freudenburg, and Paulsen (2000), we might also reasonably anticipate that dimensions of identity "character" become codified into tradition, such that we come to anticipate an arrangement of identity elements—religious traditions, culinary practices, or family arrangements—among Irish Americans in Boston and a distinct arrangement of elements among Irish Americans in New York.

46. On city ecology as evolving and as impacted by study populations, see Sharkey (2013) and Hinze (2013).

47. Recent scholarship on neighborhood effects challenges this straightforward relationship (e.g., Sharkey 2013; Wodtke, Harding and Elwert 2011), primarily by exploring neighborhood effects across generations (and therefore sometimes also across neighborhoods). See also Wilson (1996), Sampson, Morenoff, and Gannon-Rowley (2002), and Sampson (2012).

48. See Molotch, Freudenburg, and Paulsen (2000) for groundbreaking work on the origins of place "character." On the origins of place difference or distinction, see also Paulsen (2004), Milligan (2003), Borer (2008), and Silver, Clark, and Yanez (2010).

49. On how identities shape movements, see Guenther (2010) and Reger (2012).

CONCLUSION

1. Molly Fischer, "Think Gender Is Performance? You Have Judith Butler to Thank for That," *New York Magazine*, June 13, 2016, http://nymag.com/thecut/2016/06/judith -butler-c-v-r.html#.

2. On sexuality trajectories, see Seidman (2002), Ghaziani (2011), and Podmore (2006).

3. On the fallacy of assuming a singular approach to sexualities, see Brown-Saracino (2015) and Ferreira and Browne (2015).

4. This book shares a spirit of inquiry with scholarship that maps, according to Green (2008) "the structures of collective sexual life" (25) and work that traces how relatively bounded groups of individuals reinvent and create culture (Fine 1987; Hennen 2008). However, the answer it provides—about the sources of sexual variation and overlap—gestures to meso-level sources for the structuration of sexual social life, rather than that at the level of the individual, small group, or institution. It also stands with recent inquiries into how categories of person and place shape identities and experiences of being GLBTQI (see Brekhus 2003; Laumann et al. 2004; Kazyak 2011, 2012; Barton 2012; Gray 2009; Podmore 2006; Herring 2010; Weston 1995; Howard 1999; Bell 2000; Brekhus 2003; Halberstam 2005; Stein 1997; Carrillo and Fontdevila 2014; Hunter, Guerrero, and Cohen 2010; Tongson 2005). For scholarship on identity variation within a metro area, see Wilkins (2008); on variation within a city, see Lo and Healy (2000). For discussion of the limits of categorical explanations, see Ferreira and Browne (2015, 2).

5. On LGBTQ individuals in smaller places, see, e.g., Gray (2009) and Tongson (2005).

6. See Aschoff (2015) on self-actualization discourses. On how categories of place influence other types of identities, see Hummon (1990), Lacy (2007), Carr and Kefalas (2010), and Robinson (2014). On identity and space as "mutually constitutive," see Nash (2013). See also Hubbard (2006) and Browne and Bakshi (2011).

7. Green (2008, 2013) presupposes much choice in selecting sexual scenes. For instance, he writes, "Contemporary actors have access to diverse sexual milieu such that they may choose individual partners and sexual scenes on the basis of remarkably rarified preference structures, sexual and otherwise" (2014, 11). See also Somers (1993), Hennen (2008), and Golden (2006).

8. This bears some relation to arguments about racial fluidity. However, in contrast to most such arguments this book outlines how identification is not a choice, as well as how social position is contextual—with very specific features of context—or city ecology—shaping identities (Rockquemore and Arend 2002; Saperstein and Penner 2012; Brown, Hitlin, and Elder 2006). For research on the fluidity of sexual identities, which tends to attribute fluidity to epoch or gender, see Gamson (1995), Epstein (1987), Seidman (1993), and Diamond (2008).

9. See Butler (1990).

10. See, e.g., Whitlow and Ould (2015) on how other factors shape identities.

11. See Fine (2012) on "local publics." See also Donovan (2016), Plummer (1982), Humphreys (1970), and Simon and Gagnon (2011) on sexualities and interaction.

12. Contemporary queer theory is focused less on identity and more on debating the

antisocial thesis and the problem of "homo-nationalism." See Edelman (2004), Muñoz (2009), and Puar (2007).

13. See Gonzales et al. (1996) and Harding (2003) on neighborhood effects and adolescence.

14. Might racial minorities experience a different city than their white counterparts, in part because the spaces to which they have ready access and/or in which they experience a sense of acceptance are further delimited—beyond those of other sexual minorities (see Thorpe 1996; Lane 2015; Hunter 2013; Greene 2014; Edelman 2011)? This is plausible, although my African American, Latino, and Asian informants rarely indicate that this is the case. This possibility ought to be explored in more racially diverse metropolitan areas.

15. Moreover, if we wish to understand how, for instance, racial and LBQ identities are mutually constituted in space, we will want to avoid an analysis that presupposes that the meaning and significance of racial or other identities will be constant across city contexts. Instead, while patterns exist across units of geography, we must anticipate localized racial and other identities, and thus that they will intersect with LBQ identities in novel ways in each city.

16. See, e.g., Diamond (2008).

17. The malleability this book documents should not be misinterpreted as suggesting that sexual identity can be consciously manipulated, such as via conversion therapy. The type of change that occurs here happens much less consciously and in response to much more subtle influences. There is no reason to believe that identity would be equally malleable in the face of overt and unwelcomed efforts to transform one's sexual desire; that kind of effort relies on a very distinct set of mechanisms than those charted in these pages.

18. Green (2008) identifies "eroticized schemas related to race, class, gender, age, and nationality, among others" (25)—yet the identity cultures I have identified largely crosscuts these types of differences within each city, troubling categorical explanations for differences in identity schemas.

19. On the "black box," see Small (2004).

20. Speaking generally, I use "city" loosely here. After all, while the places I studied are all technically cities, they are also relatively small and range in size. Despite these differences in population size, they are each at the center of the social world of smaller, surrounding locales. This means, in some ways, that we might expect some remote rural towns that are not official "cities" to be of similar influence–as well as outlying suburbs that do not have immediate access to the city center. I fully expect that such suburbs and rural areas—places that do not have an obvious larger municipality to turn to for facets of social life—also "make" their residents. Put differently, the broader argument of this book is that *places* make us; that meso-level units of geography, many of which constitute "cities," are particularly influential—for reasons discussed herein.

21. See Hayslett and Kayne (2011) on distribution of lesbian and gay households by neighborhood.

22. Those informants who reside in small towns or suburbs adjacent to and oriented around a bigger city may nonetheless affiliate themselves with the bigger city and therefore respond to its character and dynamics.

23. See Brown-Saracino and Parker (2017).

24. This might be less true in larger metropolitan areas. In New York City, for instance, once might identify and take identity cues from Brooklyn, Queens, or Manhattan,

and not just from New York City. However, this book predicts that boroughs will remain much more influential than the smaller neighborhoods that compose them (e.g., Chelsea or Harlem).

25. On Dyke March, see Currans (2012) and Kates and Belk (2001).

26. This, of course, stands in contrast to the work of Green (2008) and Hennen (2008), which identifies distinct "sexual fields" and "sexual cultures" within cities. See also Lo and Healy (2000).

27. On the enduring power of regional identities, see Griswold (2008, 2016).

28. See, for instance, Sampson (2012). It is plausible that city, rather than neighborhood, may be especially relevant for those—like LBQ residents—whose population numbers in any neighborhood—even in the lesbian enclave—are relatively small. This, together with the relative economic privilege of most of those I studied, prohibits their social world from being limited to the neighborhood. However, other than those who are intensely socially isolated, such as some poor racial minorities, most contemporary adults live in social worlds that extend beyond the neighborhood.

29. On Disneyfication, see Zukin (1996).

30. See D'Emilio (1983) on identity politics and community.

31. On shared identity as a basis for collective action, see Nash (2013), Cresswell (2010), McDowell (1999), and Massey (1994).

32. In 2016 a musical "Lost Lesbian Bars of New Orleans" premiered. See Natalie Zarrelli, "The Los Lesbian Bars of New Orleans," *Atlas Obscura*, September 14, 2016 (http://www.atlasobscura.com/articles/the-lost-lesbian-bars-of-new-orleans).

33. Krieger (1982) writes that lesbian population concentrations "provide a haven or home in a hostile or distrusting outside world. They lend support" (91). See also Valentine (1993, 240), Wolf (1979), and Barnhart (1975).

34. On sexual identity politics and movements, see D'Emilio (1983).

35. On lesbian bars, see Nestle (1997), Podmore (2006), Chamberland (1993), Faderman (1991), Kennedy and Davis (1993), Skeggs (1999), Retter (1999), Hayslett and Kane (2011), and Hutson (2010).

36. For scholarship and other reports on GLBTQ movement to the suburbs and other "nontraditional" locales, see Berger (2012), Gates and Newport (2013), Gates (2006, 2007), Ghaziani (2014), Parker (2009), Swan (2014) Brekhus (2003), Kirkey and Forsyth (2001), Bell and Valentine (1995), Smith and Holt (2005), Browne and Bakshi (2011), Weston (1995), and Kramer (1995). See discussion of "cultural archipelagos" in Ghaziani (2014).

37. See Castells (1983), but see counterevidence in Wolf (1979), Krieger (1983), Forsyth (1997a and 1997b), Esterberg (1997), Levine (1979), Barnhart (1975), Green (1997), Kantsa (2002), Lockard (1985), Millward (2007), Nestle (1997), Podmore (2001), Pritchard, Morgan, and Sedgley (2002), Retter (1997), Rothenberg (2003), Stein (1997), and Valentine (1997, 2000).

38. See, e.g., Podmore (2006).

39. For criticisms of this narrow approach, see Berlant (1997), Tongson (2011), and Halberstam (2005).

40. See Deleuze and Guattari (1987) on assemblage.

41. See Cleves (2014) for an account that, on my read, implicitly reveals how place permitted a different frame for a same-sex relationship—in colonial New England.

42. See Swidler (1986) on settled and unsettled times; and see Butler (1990) on scripts and counterscripts.

43. On how identities shape movements, see Guenther (2010) and Reger (2012).

METHODOLOGICAL APPENDIX

1. See Gates and Ost (2004) and Cooke and Rapino (2007).

2. See Gates and Ost (2004) and Cooke and Rapino (2007).

3. See Gates and Ost (2004). See also Gumprecht (2003, 2010) and Lofland and Lofland (1987).

4. A personal connection also initially encouraged me to take notice of San Luis Obispo's place on my list of plausible sites. At the time, family members resided in Los Osos, a quiet town adjacent to San Luis Obispo. To get to their home I passed a nondescript shopping plaza that contains a bookstore with a loyal LBQ clientele. I wondered about the place of this bookshop in this sleepy coastal town, which is home to many retirees and the dramatic Montana de Oro State Park, with its inland peaks and ocean side cliffs. Census data from 2000 (Bureau of the Census 2000) confirmed that Los Osos possessed a higher than average proportion of lesbian households, and this number increased between 2000 and 2010. As I began to seriously contemplate fieldwork, a preliminary visit to the Gay and Lesbian Alliance Center in San Luis Obispo and a few early interviews and observational opportunities pointed me away from Los Osos to San Luis Obispo proper, because LBQ individuals on the ground suggested that, while lesbian couples might concentrate in highest proportion in Los Osos, LBQ singletons—whom the census does not count (unless sharing a residence with another woman)—were scattered throughout the San Luis Obispo area, concentrating especially in San Luis Obispo proper. More importantly, LBQ social life was unmistakably centered in San Luis Obispo: at its GALA Center, Farmers Market, bars, and dances. LBQ residents of towns such as Los Osos socialized in and very much identify with the city of San Luis Obispo. Once my attention turned to San Luis Obispo, its utility as a useful reflection of (college town approximately four hours from the nearest major city) and counterpart to Ithaca (higher home prices, lower proportion of LBQ women, newly emerging status as an enclave, and location on the West Coast) was undeniable. Thus, while I ultimately selected San Luis Obispo as a site, as with the other sites I devoted attention to proximate towns, including, in San Luis Obispo's case, Los Osos.

5. See Gates and Ost (2004). Gates (2013) reports that Franklin County remains third of US counties in its proportion of female same-sex households.

6. The relative homogeneity of the sample allows us to uncover not only heterogeneous sexual identities but also racial, professional, and class identities. On diverse "white" identities, see Hughey (2010). On heterogeneous racial identities, see Fields (2016).

7. See Bureau of the Census (2000).

8. On "like cases," see Molotch, Freudenburg, and Paulsen (2000) and Kaufman and Kaliner (2011).

9. See Brown-Saracino (2009).

10. As I have discussed elsewhere in the book, I collected survey information from most informants on income, duration of residence, networks, educational history, home value, etc. In instances when survey information was not collected or was incomplete, I approximated data from interviews to the best of my ability (e.g., recorded years of education based on interview transcript). The survey results parallel trends identified via interviews and observation.

11. See Annacker and Morrow-Jones (2005), Hayslett and Kane (2011), and Black et al. (2007) on the limitations of census data on same-sex couples. See also Brown-Saracino (2009) on studying publicly engaged individuals.

12. See Brown-Saracino (2014).
13. For an example of this debate, see Jerolmack and Khan (2014) and Lamont and Swidler (2014).
14. However, in all four cities, opportunities for observing LBQ individuals in the general life of the city were abundant. From such observations I can speak to the nearly constant presence of out LBQ individuals in a variety of spheres of city life, from meetings to festivals, from performances to store aisles. This breadth provides vital information about their place in local public life, but it is not the window into LBQ individuals' engagement with one another (to the degree that it occurs) that I also sought.
15. See Brown-Saracino (2014).
16. Ibid.
17. On residence in these "unlikely" places, see, e.g., Leonhardt (2015) and Newport and Gates (2015).
18. For scholarship and other reports on GLBTQ movement to the suburbs and other "nontraditional" locales, see Berger (2012), Gates and Newport (2013), Gates (2006, 2007), Ghaziani (2014), Parker (2009), and Swan (2014).
19. For earlier accounts of lesbian enclaves, see, e.g., Ettore (1978), Faderman (1991), Krieger (1982), Barnhart (1975), and Wolf (1979). On imperfections of census counts of LBQ individuals, see, e.g., Annacker and Morrow-Jones (2005), Hayslett and Kane (2011), and Black et al. (2007).

REFERENCES

Abbott, Andrew. 1988. *The System of Professions: An Essay on the Division of Expert Labor.* Chicago: University of Chicago Press.

———. 1997. "Of Time and Space: The Contemporary Relevance of the Chicago School." *Social Forces* 75 (4): 1149–82.

Abrahamson, Mark. 1996. *Urban Enclaves: Identity and Place in America.* New York: St. Martin's Press.

Adler, Sy, and Johanna Brenner. 2005. "Gender and Space: Lesbians and Gay Men in the City." In *The Urban Sociology Reader,* edited by Jan Lin and Christopher Mele, 200–207. New York: Routledge.

Alkon, Alison H., and Michael Traugot. 2006. "Place Matters, But How? Rural Identity, Environmental Decision Making, and the Social Construction of Place." *City & Community* 7 (2): 97–112.

American Community Survey (ACS). 2005–9. *ACS Five-Year Estimates.* Washington, DC: US Census Bureau's ACS Office.

———. 2006–10. *ACS Five-Year Estimates.* Washington, DC: US Census Bureau's ACS Office.

———. 2007–11. *ACS Five-Year Estimates.* Washington, DC: US Census Bureau's ACS Office.

———. 2009–13. *ACS Five-Year Estimates.* Washington, DC: US Census Bureau's ACS Office.

———. 2010–14. *ACS Five-Year Estimates.* Washington, DC: US Census Bureau's ACS Office.

Anacker, Katrin B., and Hazel A. Morrow-Jones. 2005. "Neighborhood Factors Associated with Same-Sex Households in U.S. Cities." *Urban Geography* 26 (5): 385–409.

Anderson, Benedict. (1991) 2006. *Imagined Communities: Reflections on the Origin and Spread of Nationalism.* New York: Verso Books.

Anderson, Elijah. 1990. *Streetwise: Race, Class, and Change in an Urban Community.* Chicago: University of Chicago Press.

———. 2004. "The Cosmopolitan Canopy." *ANNALS of the American Academy of Political and Social Science* 595 (1): 14–31.

———. 2011. *The Cosmopolitan Canopy: Race and Civility in Everyday Life.* New York: W. W. Norton.

Armstrong, Elizabeth. 2002. *Forging Gay Identities: Organizing Sexuality in San Francisco, 1950–1994.* Chicago: University of Chicago Press.

Aschoff, Nicole. 2015. *The New Prophets of Capital.* New York: Verso Books.

Barnhart, Elizabeth. 1975. "Friends and Lovers in a Counterculture Community." In *Old*

Family/New Family, edited by Nona Glazer-Malbin, 90–115. New York: Van Nostrand Press.

Barton, Bernadette. 2012. *Pray the Gay Away*. New York: New York University Press.

Beggs John, Valeria A. Haines, and Jeanne S. Hurlbert. 1996. "Revisiting the Rural-Urban Contrast: Personal Networks in Nonmetropolitan and Metropolitan Settings." *Rural Sociology* 61 (2): 306–25.

Bell, David. 2000. "Eroticizing the Rural." In *De-Centering Sexualities: Politics and Representations beyond the Metropolis*, edited by Richard Philips, 83–101. London: Routledge.

———. 2007. "The Hospitable City: Social Relations in Commercial Spaces." *Progress in Human Geography* 31 (1): 7–22.

Bell, David, Jon Binnie, Julia Cream, and Gill Valentine. 1994. "All Hyped Up and No Place to Go." *Gender, Place & Culture* 1 (1): 31–47.

Bell, David, and Mark Jayne. 2006. *Small Cities: Urban Experience Beyond the Metropolis*. London: Routledge.

Bell, Michael M. 1994. *Childerley: Nature and Morality in a Country Village*. Chicago: University of Chicago Press.

———. 1997. "The Ghosts of Place." *Theory and Society* 26 (6): 813–36.

Bell, David, and Gill Valentine, eds. 1995. *Mapping Desire: Geographies of Sexualities*. New York: Routledge.

Bellah, Robert N., Richard Madsen, William M. Sullivan, Ann Swidler, and Steven M. Tipton. 1985. *Habits of the Heart: Individualism in American Life*. Berkley: University of California Press.

Bennett, Jeffrey A. 2010. "Queer Teenagers and the Mediation of Utopian Catastrophe." *Critical Studies in Media Communication* 27 (5): 455–76.

Benzecry, Claudio. 2011. *The Opera Fanatic: Ethnography of an Obsession*. Chicago: University of Chicago Press.

Berger, Carolyn. 2012. "Why Some Lesbian Couples Are Moving to the Suburbs." *It's Conceivable*. http://itsconceivablenow.com/2012/02/22/lesbian-couples-moving-suburbs/.

Berlant, Lauren Gail. 1997. *The Queen of America Goes to Washington City: Essays on Sex and Citizenship*. Durham: Duke University Press.

Bernstein, Mary. 1997. "Celebration and Suppression: The Strategic Uses of Identity by the Gay and Lesbian Movement." *American Journal of Sociology* 103 (3): 531–65.

———. 2005. "Identity Politics." *Annual Review of Sociology* 31:47–74.

Bernstein, Mary, and Verta Taylor, eds. 2013. *The Marrying Kind?: Debating Same-Sex Marriage within the Lesbian and Gay Movement*. Minneapolis: University Of Minnesota Press.

Binder, Amy, and Kate Wood. 2013. *Becoming Right: How Campuses Shape Young Conservatives*. Princeton: Princeton University Press

Binnie, Jon, and Gill Valentine. 1999. "Geographies of Sexuality—A Review of Progress." *Progress in Human Geography* 23 (2): 175–87.

Black, Dan, Gary Gates, Seth Sanders, and Lowell Taylor. 2000. "Demographics of the Gay and Lesbian Population in the United States: Evidence from Available Systematic Data Sources." *Demography* 37 (2): 139–54.

———. 2007. "The Measurement of Same-Sex Unmarried Partner Couples in the 2000 U.S. Census." *California Center for Population Research*. http://escholarship.org/uc/item/72r1q94b.

Borer, Michael. 2006. "The Location of Culture: The Urban Culturalist Perspective." *City & Community* 5 (2): 173–97.

———. 2008. *Faithful to Fenway: Believing in Boston, Baseball, and America's Most Beloved Ballpark*. New York: New York University Press.

Breen, T. H. 1996. *Imagining the Past: East Hampton Histories*. Reading: Addison-Wesley Publishing Company.

Brekhus, Wayne. 2003. *Peacocks, Chameleons, Centaurs: Gay Suburbia and the Grammar of Social Identity*. Chicago: University of Chicago Press.

Breton, Raymond. 1964. "Institutional Completeness of Ethnic Communities and the Personal Relations of Immigrants." *American Journal of Sociology* 70 (2): 193–205.

Brint, Steven. 2001. "Gemeinschaft Revisited: A Critique and Reconstruction of the Community Concept." *Sociological Theory* 19 (1): 1–23.

Brown, Gavin. 2008. "Urban (Homo)sexualities: Ordinary Cities and Ordinary Sexualities." *Geography Compass* 2 (4): 1215–31.

———. 2006. "Cosmopolitan Camouflage: (Post-) Gay Space in Spitalfields, East London." In *Cosmopolitan Urbanism*, edited by Jon Binnie, Julian Holloway, Steve Millington, and Craig Young, 130–45. London: Routledge.

Brown, J. S., S. Hitlin, and G. H. Elder. 2006. "The Greater Complexity of Lived Race: An Extension of Harris and Sim." *Social Science Quarterly* 87:411–31.

Brown, Michael, and Larry Knopp. 2006. "Places or Polygons? Governmentality, Scale, and the Census in the Gay and Lesbian Atlas." *Population, Space and Place* 12 (4): 223–42.

Brown-Saracino, Japonica. 2004. "Social Preservationists and the Quest for Authentic Community." *City & Community* 3 (2): 135–56.

———. 2006. "Social Preservation: The Quest for Authentic People, Place and Community." PhD dissertation, Northwestern University.

———. 2007 "Virtuous Marginality: Social Preservationists and the Selection of the Old-timer." *Theory and Society* 36 (5): 437–68.

———. 2008. "LGBTI in Community and Urban Sociology: New Directions for Our Subfield." *Community and Urban Sociology Newsletter* Fall/Winter.

———. 2009. *A Neighborhood That Never Changes: Gentrification, Social Preservation and the Search for Authenticity*. Chicago: University of Chicago Press.

———. 2010. *The Gentrification Debates: A Reader*. London: Routledge.

———. 2011. "From the Lesbian Ghetto to Ambient Community: The Perceived Costs and Benefits of Integration for Community." *Social Problems* 58 (3): 361–88.

———. 2014. "From Methodological Stumbles to Substantive Insights: Gaining Ethnographic Access in Queer Communities." *Qualitative Sociology* 37 (1): 43–68.

———. 2015. "How Places Shape Identity: The Origins of Distinctive LBQ Identities in Four Small U.S. Cities." *American Journal of Sociology* 121 (1): 1–63.

Brown-Saracino, Japonica, and Amin Ghaziani. 2009. "The Constraints of Culture: Evidence from the Chicago Dyke March." *Cultural Sociology* 3 (1): 51–75.

Brown-Saracino, Japonica, and Jeffrey Nathaniel Parker. 2017. "'What is Up with My Sisters? Where are You?' The Origins and Consequences of Lesbian-Friendly Place Reputations for LBQ Migrants." *Sexualities* (February 17). doi:10.1177/1363460716658407.

Browne, Kath, and Leela Bakshi. 2011. "We Are Here to Party? Lesbian, Gay, Bisexual and Trans Leisurescapes beyond Commercial Gay Scenes." *Leisure Studies* 30 (2): 179–96.

Brubaker, Rogers, and Frederick Cooper. 2000. "Beyond 'Identity.'" *Theory and Society* 29:1–47.

Bruch, Elizabeth E., and Robert D. Mare. 2006. "Neighborhood Choice and Neighborhood Change." *American Journal of Sociology* 112 (3): 667–709.

Bruce, Katherine McFarland. 2016. *Pride Parades: How a Parade Changed the World*. New York: New York University Press.

Brunt, Lodewijk. 2001. "Into the Community." In *Handbook of Ethnography*, edited by Paul

Atkinson, Sara Delamont, Amanda Coffey, John Lofland, and Lyn H. Lofland, 80–91. London: Sage.

Bryant, Antony, and Kathy Charmaz. 2007. "Introduction: Grounded Theory Research: Methods and Practice." In *The SAGE Handbook of Grounded Theory*, edited by Antony Bryant and Kathy Charmaz, 1–29. Thousand Oaks: Sage Publications.

Buell, Emmett H. 1980. "Busing and the Defended Neighborhood South Boston, 1974–1977." *Urban Affairs Review* 16 (2): 161–88.

Buettner, Dan. 2010. *Thrive Finding Happiness the Blue Zones Way*. Washington, DC: National Geographic.

Bui, Quoctrung. 2016. "The Most Detailed Map of Gay Marriage in America." *New York Times*: The Upshot. September 12. http://www.nytimes.com/2016/09/13/upshot/the -most-detailed-map-of-gay-marriage-in-america.html.

Bureau of the Census. 1980. *US Census*. Washington, DC: Bureau of the Census.

——. 2000. *US Census*. Washington, DC: Bureau of the Census.

——. 2010. *US Census*. Washington, DC: Bureau of the Census.

Burgess, Ernest. 1925. "The Growth of the City: An Introduction to a Research Project." In *The City: Suggestions for Investigation of Human Behavior in the Urban Environment*, edited by Robert E. Park and Ernest W. Burgess, 47–62. Chicago: University of Chicago Press

Butler, Judith. 1990. *Gender Trouble*. New York: Routledge.

——. 1993. *Bodies That Matter: On the Discursive Limits of Sex*. New York: Routledge.

Caldwell, John. 2007. "Where We Live," March 27. *The Advocate* 982.

Calhoun, Craig. 1998. "Community without Propinquity Revisited: Communications Technology and the Transformation of the Urban Public Sphere." *Sociological Inquiry* 68 (3): 373–97.

Carey, Benedict. 2005. "Straight Gay or Lying? Bisexuality Revisited." *New York Times*. July 5. http://www.nytimes.com/2005/07/05/health/straight-gay-or-lying-bisexuality -revisited.html?_r=0.

Carr, Patrick J., and Maria J. Kefalas. 2010. *Hollowing Out the Middle: The Rural Brain Drain and What it Means for America*. Boston: Beacon Press.

Carrillo, Héctor. 2002. *The Night is Young: Sexuality in Mexico in the Time of AIDS*. Chicago: University of Chicago Press.

Carrillo, Héctor, and Amanda Hoffman. 2017. " 'Straight with a Pinch of Bi': The Construction of Heterosexuality As an Elastic Category Among Adult US Men." *Sexualities* (February 8). doi:1363460716678561.

Carrillo, Héctor, and Jorge Fontdevila. 2014. "Border Crossings and Shifting Sexualities among Mexican Gay Immigrant Men: Beyond Monolithic Conceptions." *Sexualities* 17 (8): 919–38.

Carrington, Victoria. 2002. *New Times, New Families*. New York: Springer.

Castells, Manuel. 1983. *The City and the Grassroots: A Cross-Cultural Theory of Urban Social Movements*. Berkeley: University of California Press.

Chamberland, Line. 1993. "Remembering Lesbian Bars: Montréal, 1955–1975." In *Gay Studies from the French Cultures: Voices from France, Belgium, Brazil, Canada and the Netherlands*, edited by Rommel Mendès-Leite and Pierre-Olivier de Busscher, 231–69. Binghamton: Harrington Park Press.

Chaskin, Robert. 1997. "Perspectives on Neighborhood and Community: A Review of the Literature." *Social Service Review* 71 (4): 521–47.

Chauncey, George. 1994. *Gay New York: Gender, Urban Culture, and the Making of the Gay Male World, 1890–1940*. New York: Basic Books.

Clark, Jayne. 2011. "San Luis Obispo: It's the Happiest Place in the USA." *USA Today*, April 8. http://usatoday30.usatoday.com/LIFE/usaedition/2011-04-08-happytown08_st_U.htm.

Clarke, Adele. 2003. "Situational Analyses: Grounded Theory Mapping after the Postmodern Turn." *Symbolic Interaction* 26 (4): 553–76.

Cleves, Rachel Hope. 2014. *Charity and Sylvia: A Same-Sex Marriage in Early America*. New York: Oxford University Press.

Cohen, Cathy. 1997. "Punks, Bulldaggers and Welfare Queens: The Radical Potential of Queer Politics." *GLQ: A Journal of Lesbian and Gay* Studies 3:437–66.

Cohler, Bertram J., and Phillip L. Hammack. 2007. "The Psychological World of the Gay Teenager: Social Change, Narrative, and "Normality." *Journal of Youth Adolescence* 36: 47–59.

Collard, James. 1998. "Leaving the Gay Ghetto." *Newsweek* 132 (7): 53.

Collins, Chris. 1997. "GTD Owner Ready To Sell, But Town Won't Make Offer." *The Recorder*. July 29.

Connell, Catherine. 2012. "Dangerous Disclosures." *Sexuality Research and Social Policy* 9 (2): 168–77.

———. 2014. *School's Out: Gay and Lesbian Teachers in the Classroom*. Berkeley: University of California Press.

Cooke, Thomas J., and Melanie Rapino. 2007. "The Migration of Partnered Gays and Lesbians between 1995 and 2000." *Professional Geographer* 59 (3): 285–97.

Cooley, Charles H. 1902. *Social Organization: A Study of the Larger Mind*. New York: Charles Scribner's Sons.

Coser, Lewis A. 1956. *Functions of Social Conflict*. New York: Simon and Schuster.

Cresswell, Tim. 2010. "Towards a Politics of Mobility." *Environment and Planning D: Society and Space* 28 (1): 17–31.

Cuba, Lee J. 1987. *Identity and Community on the Alaskan Frontier*. Philadelphia: Temple University Press

Cuba, Lee J., and David M. Hummon. 1993. "A Place to Call Home: Identification with Dwelling, Community, and Region." *Sociological Quarterly* 34 (1): 111–31.

Currans, Elizabeth. 2012. "Claiming Deviance and Honoring Community: Creating Resistant Spaces in U.S. Dyke Marches." *Feminist Formations* 24 (1): 73–101.

D'Emilio, John. 1983. *Sexual Politics, Sexual Communities*. Chicago: University of Chicago Press.

Davila, Arlene. 2004. *Barrio Dreams: Puerto Ricans, Latinos, and the Neoliberal City*. Berkeley: University of California Press.

Davis, Richie, and Russell G. Haddad. 1994. "The Frenchman Who Hopes To 'Create Something Dynamic' in Downtown Greenfield Is a Man 'Full of Ideas,' Says a Woman Who Knows Him Well, and Warned that Someone Else Needs To Bring Those Dreams Down to Earth." *The Recorder*. February 22.

Davis, Whitney. 2010. *Queer Beauty: Sexuality and Aesthetics from Winckelmann to Freud and Beyond*. New York: Columbia University Press.

Deener, Andrew. 2012. *Venice: A Contested Bohemia in Los Angeles*. Chicago: University of Chicago Press.

Deleuze, Gilles, and Felix Guattari. 1987. *A Thousand Plateaus*. Minneapolis: University of Minnesota Press.

di Leonardo, Micaela. 1998. *Exotics at Home: Anthropologies, Others, American Modernity*. Chicago: University of Chicago Press.

Diamond, Lisa. 2008. *Sexual Fluidity: Understanding Women's Love and Desire*. Cambridge: Harvard University Press.

Donovan, Holly. 2016. *Believing, Belonging, and Boundary-Work: Sexuality in Interaction.* PhD dissertation, Boston University.

Driskell, Robyn B., and Larry Lyon. 2002. "Are Virtual Communities True Communities: Examining the Environments and Elements of Community." *City & Community* 1 (4): 373–90.

Duck, Steve, and Roxane Cohen Silver. 1990. *Personal Relationships and Social Support.* London: Sage.

Duggan, Lisa. 2002. "The New Homonormativity: The Sexual Politics of Neoliberalism." In *Materializing Democracy: Toward a Revitalized Cultural Politics*, edited by Russ Castronovo and Dana Nelson, 175–94. Durham: Duke University Press.

Duneier, Mitchell. 1999. *Sidewalk.* New York: Farrar, Straus, and Giroux.

Durkheim, Emile. (1897) 1997. *Suicide.* Edited by J. A. Spaulding and G. Simpson. New York: Free Press.

Edelman, Elijah Adiv. 2011 "This Area Has Been Declared a Prostitution Free Zone": Discursive Formations of Space, the State, and Trans 'Sex Worker' Bodies." *Journal of Homosexuality* 58 (6–7): 848–64.

Edelman, Lee. *No Future: Queer Theory and the Death Drive.* Durham: Duke University Press, 2004.

Elwood, Sarah A. 2000. "Lesbian Living Spaces: Multiple Meanings of Home." In *From Nowhere to Everywhere: Lesbian Geographies*, edited by Gill Valentine, 11–28. New York: Harrington Park Press.

Epstein, Steven. 1987. "Gay Politics, Ethnic Identity: The Limits of Social Constructionism." *Socialist Review* 93:9–54.

Erickcek, George, and Hannah McKinney. 2004. "Small Cities Blues: Looking for Growth Factors in Small and Medium-Sized Cities." Upjohn Institute Staff Working Paper No. 04-100. Kalamazoo: W. E. Upjohn Institute for Employment Research.

Esterberg, Kristin. 1997. *Lesbian and Bisexual Identities: Constructing Communities, Constructing Selves.* Philadelphia: Temple University Press.

Ettore, Elizabeth M. 1978. "Women, Urban Social Movements and the Lesbian Ghetto." *International Journal of Urban and Regional Research* 2 (3): 499–520.

Etzioni, Amitai. 1996. "The Responsive Community: A Communitarian Perspective." *American Sociological Review* 61 (1): 1–11.

Faderman, Lillian. 1981. *Surpassing the Love of Men: Romantic Friendship and Love Between Women from the Renaissance to the Present.* New York: HarperCollins.

———. 1991. *Odd Girls and Twilight Lovers: A History of Lesbian Life in Twentieth-Century America.* New York: Columbia University Press.

Faderman, Lillian, and Stuart Timmons. 2006. *Gay L.A.: A History of Sexual Outlaws, Power Politics, and Lipstick Lesbians.* New York: Basic Books.

Faiman-Silva, Sandra. 2004. *The Courage to Connect: Sexuality, Citizenship, and Community in Provincetown.* Urbana: University of Illinois Press.

Federal Bureau of Investigation. 2007–10. *Uniform Crime Reporting.* https://ucr.fbi.gov/hate-crime.

Ferguson, Deena. 1997. "GTD Is Almost in Town's Hands." *The Recorder.* September 24.

Fernandez-Alemany, Manuel, and Stephen O. Murray. 2002. *Heterogender Homosexuality in Honduras.* Lincoln: Writers Club Press.

Ferreira, Eduarda, and Kath Browne. 2015. *Lesbian Geographies: Gender, Place and Power.* Surrey: Ashgate Publishing

Fields, Corey. 2016. *Black Elephants in the Room: The Unexpected Politics of African American Republicans.* Berkeley: University of California Press.

Fine, Gary Alan. 1979. "Small Groups and Culture Creation: The Idioculture of Little League Baseball Teams." *American Sociological Review* 44 (5): 733–45.

———. 1987. *With the Boys: Little League Baseball and Preadolescent Culture*. Chicago: University of Chicago Press.

———. 1998. *Morel Tales: The Culture of Mushrooming*. Cambridge: Harvard University Press.

———. 2003. "Towards a Peopled Ethnography." *Ethnography* 4:41–60.

———. 2010. "The Sociology of the Local: Action and Its Publics." *Sociological Theory* 28 (4): 355–76.

———. 2012. *Tiny Publics: A Theory of Group Culture and Action*. New York: Russell Sage Foundation.

Fine, Gary Alan, and Sherryl Kleinman. 1979. "Rethinking Subculture: An Interactionist Analysis." *American Journal of Sociology* 85 (1): 1–20.

Finke, Roger, Avery M. Guest, and Rodney Stark. 1996. "Mobilizing Local Religious Markets: Religious Pluralism in the Empire State, 1855 to 1865." *American Sociological Review* 61 (3): 203–18.

Firey, Walter. 1945. "Sentiment and Symbolism as Ecological Variables." *American Sociological Review* 10 (2): 140–48.

Fischer, Claude S. 1975. "Toward a Subcultural Theory of Urbanism." *American Journal of Sociology* 80:1319–41.

———. 1982. *To Dwell among Friends: Personal Networks in Town and City*. Chicago: University of Chicago Press.

———. 2005. "The Subcultural Theory of Urbanism: A Twentieth Year Assessment." *American Journal of Sociology* 101 (3): 543–77.

Fischer, Molly. 2016. "Think Gender Is Performance? You Have Judith Butler to Thank for That." *New York Magazine*, June 13. http://nymag.com/thecut/2016/06/judith-butler-c-v-r.html#.

Fisher, Robin, Geof Gee, and Adam Looney. 2016. "Joint Filing by Same-Sex Couples after Windsor: Characteristics of Married Tax Filers in 2013 and 2014." Department of the Treasury: Office of Tax Analysis Working Paper 108. https://www.treasury.gov/resource-center/tax-policy/tax-analysis/Documents/WP-108.pdf.

Flaherty, Jeremy, and Ralph B. Brown. 2010. "A Multilevel Systemic Model of Community Attachment: Assessing the Relative Importance of the Community and Individual Levels." *American Journal of Sociology* 116 (2): 503–42.

Florida, Richard L. 2002. *The Rise of the Creative Class*. New York: Basic Books.

———. 2003. "Cities and the Creative Class." *City and Community* 1 (2): 3–19.

———. 2012. *The Rise of the Creative Class: Revisited*. New York: Basic Books.

Florida, Richard L., and Gary Gates. 2001. *Technology and Tolerance: The Importance of Diversity to High-Technology Growth*. Washington, DC: Brookings Institution, Center on Urban and Metropolitan Policy.

Foucault, Michel. 1977. *Discipline and Punish*. New York: Pantheon.

Forstie, Claire. 2011. "So Much More than a Bar: The Shifting Meanings of Lesbian Identity at Sisters, a Local Bar." MA thesis, University of Southern Maine.

Forsyth, Ann. 1997a. "Noho: Upscaling Main Street on the Metropolitan Edge." *Urban Geography* 18 (7): 622–52.

———. 1997b. "'Out' in the Valley." *International Journal of Urban and Regional Research* 21 (1): 38–62.

———. 2001. "Sexuality and Space: Nonconformist Populations and Planning Practice." *Journal of Planning Literature* 15 (3): 339–58.

Friedman, Maurice S. 1983. *The Confirmation of Otherness, in Family, Community, and Society*. New York: Pilgrim Press.

Gamson, Joshua. 1995. "Must Identity Movements Self-Destruct? A Queer Dilemma." *Social Problems* 42:390–406.

———. 1996. "The Organizaional Shaping of Collective Identity: The Case of Lesbian and Gay Film in New York." *Sociological Forum* 11 (2): 231–61.

Gans, Herb. 1962. *The Urban Villagers: Group and Class in the Life of Italian-Americans*. New York: Free Press.

———. 1967. *The Levittowners*. New York: Columbia University Press.

Gates, Gary. 2006. "Same-Sex Couples and the Gay, Lesbian, Bisexual Population: New Estimates from the American Community Survey." Los Angeles: Williams Institute, UCLA School of Law.

———. 2007. "Geographic Trends among Same-Sex Couples in the US Census and the American Community Survey." Los Angeles: Williams Institute, UCLA School of Law.

———. 2013. "Geography of the LGBT Population." In *International Handbook of the Demography of Sexuality*, edited by Amanda Baumie, 229–42. New York: Springer.

Gates, Gary, and Frank Newport. 2013. "Gallup Special Report: New Estimates of the LGBT Population in the United States." Los Angeles: Williams Institute, UCLA School of Law.

Gates, Gary, and Jason Ost. 2004. *The Gay and Lesbian Atlas*. Washington, DC: Urban Institute Press.

Gates, Gary J., and David M. Smith. 2001. "Gay and Lesbian Families in the United States: Same-Sex Unmarried Partner Households: A Preliminary Analysis of 2000 United States Census Data." August 22. Washington, DC: Human Rights Campaign. http://files.eric.ed.gov/fulltext/ED457285.pdf.

Ghaziani, Amin. 2011. "Post-Gay Collective Identity Construction." *Social Problems* 58 (1): 99–125.

———. 2014. *There Goes the Gayborhood?* Princeton: Princeton University Press.

Ghaziani, Amin, and Delia Baldassarri. 2011. "Cultural Anchors and the Organization of Differences A Multi-Method Analysis of LGBT Marches on Washington." *American Sociological Review* 76 (2): 179–206.

Golden, Carla. 2006. "What's In A Name? Sexual Self-Identification Among Women." In *The Lives Of Lesbians, Gays, And Bisexuals: Children To Adults*, edited by Ritch C. Savin-Williams and Kenneth M. Cohen, 229–49. Fort Worth: Harcourt Brace.

Gondolf, Ed. 1980. "Institution/Neighborhood Interface: A Clash of Two Cultures." *Journal of the Community Development Society* 11 (2): 19–37.

Gonzales, Nancy A., Ana Mari Cauce, Ruth J. Friedman, and Craig A. Mason. 1996. "Family, Peer, and Neighborhood Influences on Academic Achievement among African-American Adolescents: One-Year Prospective Effects." *American Journal of Community Psychology* 24 (3): 365–87.

Gorman-Murray, Andrew. 2007. "Reconfiguring Domestic Values: Meanings of Home for Gay Men and Lesbians." *Housing, Theory and Society* 24 (3): 229–46.

Gorman-Murray, Andrew, and Gordon Waitt. 2009. "Queer-Friendly Neighbourhoods: Interrogating Social Cohesion Across Sexual Difference in Two Australian Neighbourhoods." *Environment and Planning* 41 (12): 2855–73.

Granovetter, Mark S. 1973. "The Strength of Weak Ties." *American Journal of Sociology* 78 (6): 1360.

Gray, Edward R., and Scott L. Thumma. 1997. "The Gospel Hour: Liminality, Identity, and Religion in a Gay Bar." In *Contemporary American Religion: An Ethnographic Reader*, edited by Penny Edgell Becker and Nancy L. Eisland, 79–98. Walnut Creek: AltaMira Press.

Gray, Mary. 2009. *Out in the Country: Youth, Media, and Queer Visibility in Rural America.* New York: New York University Press.

Green, Adam Isaiah. 2008. "The Social Organization of Desire: The Sexual Fields Approach." *Sociological Theory* 26 (1): 25–50.

———. 2010. "Queer Unions: Same-Sex Spouses Marrying Tradition and Innovation." *Canadian Journal of Sociology* 35 (3): 399–436.

———. 2013. "Debating Same-Sex Marriage: Lesbian and Gay Spouses Speak to the Literature." In *The Marrying Kind?: Debating Same-Sex Marriage within the Lesbian and Gay Movement,* edited by Mary Bernstein and Verta Taylor, 375–405. Minneapolis: University Minnesota Press.

Green, Sarah F. 1997. *Urban Amazons: Lesbian Feminism and Beyond in the Gender, Sexuality and Identity Battles of London.* London: Palgrave MacMillan.

Greenberg, Miriam. 2008. *Branding New York: How a City in Crisis Was Sold to the World.* New York: Routledge.

Greene, Theodore. 2014. "Gay Neighborhoods and the Rights of the Vicarious Citizen." *City & Community* 13 (20): 99–118.

Griswold, Wendy. 1986. *Renaissance Revivals: City Comedy and Revenge Tragedy in the London Theater, 1576–1980.* Chicago: University of Chicago Press.

———. 1992. "The Writing on the Mud Wall: Nigerian Novels and the Imaginary Village." *American Sociological Review* 57 (6): 709–24.

———. 2008. *Regionalism and the Reading Class.* Chicago: University of Chicago Press.

———. 2016. *American Guides: The Federal Writers' Project and the Casting of American Culture.* Chicago: University of Chicago Press.

Griswold, Wendy, and Hannah Wohl. 2015. "Evangelists of Culture: One Book Programs and the Agents who Define Literature, Shape Tastes, and Reproduce Regionalism." *Poetics* 50:96–109.

Griswold, Wendy, and Nathan Wright. 2004. "Cowbird, Locals, and the Dynamic Endurance of Regionalism." *American Journal of Sociology* 109 (6): 1411–51.

Gubrium, Jaber F., and James A. Holstein. 1997. *The New Language of Qualitative Method.* New York: Oxford University Press.

Guenther, Katja M. 2010. *Making Their Place: Feminism after Socialism in East Germany.* Stanford: Stanford University Press.

Guest, Avery M. 2000. "The Mediate Community: The Nature of Local and Extralocal Ties Within the Metropolis." *Urban Affairs Review* 35 (50): 603–27.

———. 2010. *Making their Place: Feminism After Socialism in East Germany.* Stanford: Stanford University Press.

Guest, Avery M., Jane Cover, Ross L. Matsueda, and Charis Kubrin. 2006. "Neighborhood Context and Neighboring Ties." *City & Community* 5 (4): 363–85.

Gumprecht, Blake. 2003. "The American College Town." *Geographical Review* 93 (1): 51–80.

———. 2010. *The American College Town.* Amherst: University of Massachusetts Press.

Habermas, Jurgen. (1962) 1989. *The Structural Transformation of the Public Sphere.* Translated by Thomas Burger. Cambridge: MIT Press.

Halberstam, Judith. 1998. *Female Masculinity.* Durham: Duke University Press

———. 2005. *In a Queer Time and Place: Transgender Bodies, Subcultural Lives.* New York: New York University Press.

Halperin, David. 2012. *How To Be Gay.* Cambridge: Belknap Press.

Hammack, Phillip, and Bertram J. Cohler. 2011. "Narrative, Identity, and the Politics of Exclusion: Social Change and the Gay and Lesbian Life Course." *Sexuality Research and Social Policy* 8:162–82.

Hampton, Keith, and Barry Wellman. 2003. "Neighboring in Netville: How the Internet Supports Community and Social Capital in a Wired Suburb." *City & Community* 2 (4): 277–311.

Handlin, Oscar. 1959. *The Uprooted.* New York: Grosset & Dunlop.

———. 1969. *Boston's Immigrants.* New York: Atheneum.

Harding, David J. 2003. "Counterfactual Models of Neighborhood Effects: The Effect of Neighborhood Poverty on Dropping Out and Teenage Pregnancy." *American Journal of Sociology* 109 (3): 676–719.

Harding, Rosie. 2008. "Recognizing (and Resisting) Regulation: Attitudes to the Introduction of Civil Partnership." *Sexualities* 11 (6): 740–60.

Harris, David R. 1999. "'Property Values Drop When Blacks Move In, Because': Racial and Socioeconomic Determinants of Neighborhood Desirability." *American Sociological Review* 64:461–79.

Haynes, Bruce D. 2001. *Red Lines, Black Spaces: The Politics of Race and Space in a Black Middle-Class Suburb.* New Haven: Yale University Press.

Hayslett, Karen L., and Melinda D. Kane. 2011. "'Out' in Columbus: A Geospatial Analysis of the Neighborhood-Level Distribution of Gay and Lesbian Households." *City & Community* 10 (2): 131–56.

Hemmings, Claire. 1997. "From Landmarks to Spaces: Mapping the Territory of a Bisexual Genealogy." In *Queers in Space: Communities, Public Places, Sites of Resistance,* edited by Yolanda Retter, Anne-Marie Bouthillette, and Gordon Brent Ingram, 147–62. Seattle: Bay Press.

———. 2002. *Bisexual Spaces: A Geography of Sexuality and Gender.* New York: Routledge.

Henbest, Danielle. 2008. "County Study Finds Many Underemployed." *Ithaca Times.* July 2. http://www.ithaca.com/news/local_news/county-study-finds-many-underemployed/article_c6f9f1ed-e8f2-5995-8cd5-d2af05abb941.html.

Henderson, Vernon. 1997. "Medium Sized Cities." *Regional Science and Urban Economics* 27:583–612.

Hennen, Peter. 2008. *Faeries, Bears, and Leathermen: Men in Community Queering the Masculine.* Chicago: University of Chicago Press.

Herek, Gregory M., Regina Chopp, and Darryl Strohl. 2007. "Sexual Stigma: Putting Sexual Minority Issues in Context." In *The Health of Sexual Minorities: Public Health Perspectives on Lesbian, Gay, Bisexual and Transgendered Populations,* edited by Ilan H. Myer and Mary E. Northridge, 171–208. New York: Springer.

Herring, Scott. 2010. *Another Country: Queer Anti-Urbanism.* New York: New York University Press.

Hinze, Annika M. 2013. *Turkish Berlin: Integration Policy and Urban Space.* Minneapolis: University of Minnesota Press.

Howard, John. 1999. *Men Like That: A Southern Queer History.* Chicago: University of Chicago Press.

Howe, Alyssa Cymene. 2001. "Queer Pilgrimage: The San Francisco Homeland and Identity Tourism." *Cultural Anthropology* 16 (1): 35–61.

Hsieh, Chang-tseh, and Ben-chieh Liu. 1983. "The Pursuance of Better Quality of Life: In the Long Run, Better Quality of Social Life Is the Most Important Factor in Migration" *American Journal of Economics and Sociology* 42 (4): 431–40.

Hubbard, Phil. 2001. "Sex Zones: Intimacy, Citizenship, and Public Space." *Sexualities* 4 (1): 51–71.

———. 2006. "Out of Touch and Out of Time? The Contemporary Policing of Sex Work."

In *Sex Work Now*, edited by Rosie Campbell and Maggie O'Neill, 1–32. Cullompton: Willan Publishing.

Hughey, Matthew W. 2010. "The (Dis) Similarities of White Racial Identities: The Conceptual Framework of 'Hegemonic Whiteness.'" *Ethnic and Racial Studies* 33 (8): 1289–309.

Hull, Kathleen, and Timothy Ortyl. 2013. "Same-Sex Marriage and Constituent Perceptions of the LGBT Rights Movement." In *The Marrying Kind?: Debating Same-Sex Marriage within the Lesbian and Gay Movement*, edited by Mary Bernstein and Verta Taylor, 67–102. Minneapolis: University of Minnesota Press.

Hummon, David. 1990. *Commonplaces: Community Ideology and Identity in American Culture*. Albany: New York State University Press.

Humphreys, Laud. 1970. *Tearoom Trade: Impersonal Sex in Public Places*. Rutgers: Transaction Publishers.

Hunt, Scott A., Robert D. Benford, and David A. Snow. 1994. "Identity Fields: Framing Processes and the Social Construction of Movement Identities." In *New Social Movements: From Ideology to Identity*, edited by Joseph R. Hank, Gusfield Enrique, and Johnston Larana, 185–208. Philadelphia: Temple University Press.

Hunter, Albert. 1975. "The Loss Of Community: An Empirical Test Through Replication." *American Sociological Review* 40 (5): 537–52.

Hunter, Albert, and Gerald D. Suttles. 1972. "The Expanding Community Of Limited Liability." In *The Social Construction Of Communities*, edited by Gerald D. Suttles, 44–81. Chicago: University of Chicago Press.

Hunter, Marcus Anthony. 2013. *Black Citymakers: How The Philadelphia Negro Changed Urban America*. New York: Oxford University Press.

Hunter, Marcus Anthony. 2010. "All the Gays Are White and All the Blacks Are Straight: Black Gay Men, Identity, and Community." *Sexuality Research and Social Policy* 7 (2): 81–92.

Hunter, Marcus Anthony, Marissa Guerrero, and Cathy J. Cohen. 2010. "Black Youth Sexuality: Established Paradigms and New Approaches." In *Black Sexualities: Probing Powers, Passions, Practices, and Policies*, edited by Juan Battle and Sandra Barnes, 377–400. New Brunswick: Rutgers University Press.

Hurewitz, Daniel. 2007. *Bohemian Los Angeles: And the Making of Modern Politics*. Berkeley: University of California Press.

Hutson, David J. 2010. "Standing OUT/Fitting IN: Identity, Appearance, and Authenticity in Gay and Lesbian Communities." *Symbolic Interaction* 33 (2): 213–33.

Hyra, Derek. 2008. *The New Urban Renewal: The Economic Transformation of Harlem and Bronzeville*. Chicago: University of Chicago Press.

Iasenza, Suzanne. 2002. "Beyond 'Lesbian Bed Death.'" *Journal of Lesbian Studies* 6 (1): 111–20.

Irvine, Janice. 1994. *Sexual Cultures and the Construction of Adolescent Identities*. Philadelphia: Temple University Press.

Jackson, John L. 2001. *Harlemworld: Doing Race and Class in Contemporary Black America*. Chicago: University of Chicago Press.

Jacobs, Jane. 1961. *The Death and Life of Great American Cities*. New York: Random House.

———. 1993. "The City Unbound: Qualitative Approaches to the City." *Urban Studies* 30 (4–5): 827–48.

Janowitz, Morris. 1952. *The Community Press in an Urban Setting*. Glencoe: Free Press.

Jerolmack, Colin. 2009. "Primary Groups and Cosmopolitan Ties: The Rooftop Pigeon Flyers of New York City." *Ethnography* 10 (4): 435–57.

―――. 2012. *Global Pigeon*. Chicago: University of Chicago Press.

Jerolmack, Colin, and Shamus Khan. 2014. "Talk Is Cheap Ethnography and the Attitudinal Fallacy." *Sociological Methods & Research* 43 (1): 1–12.

Kantsa, Venetia. 2002. "'Certain Places Have Different Energy': Spatial Transformations in Eresos, Lesvos." *GLQ* 8 (1): 35–55.

Kasinitz, Philip, Mary Waters, John Mollenkopf, and Jennifer Holdaway. 2009. *Inheriting the City: The Children of Immigrants Come of Age*. New York: Russell Sage.

Kates, Steven M., and Russell W. Belk. 2001. "The Meanings of Lesbian and Gay Pride Day Resistance through Consumption and Resistance to Consumption." *Journal of Contemporary Ethnography* 30 (4): 392–429.

Katz, Jack. 1982. *Poor People's Lawyers in Transition*. New Brunswick: Rutgers University Press.

―――. 2001. "From How to Why: On Luminous Description and Causal Inference in Ethnography (Part I)." *Ethnography* 2 (4): 443–73.

Katz, James E., and Ronald E. Rice. 2002. *Social Consequences of Internet Use: Access, Involvement, and Interaction*. Cambridge: MIT Press.

Kaufman, Jason, and Matthew Kaliner. 2011. "The Re-Accomplishment of Place in Twentieth Century Vermont and New Hampshire: History Repeats Itself, Until It Doesn't." *Theory & Society* 40 (2): 119–54.

Kazyak, Emily. 2011. "Disrupting Cultural Selves: Constructing Gay and Lesbian Identities in Rural Locales." *Qualitative Sociology* 34 (4): 561–81.

―――. 2012. "Midwest or Lesbian? Gender, Rurality, and Sexuality." *Gender & Society* 26 (6): 825–48.

Kefalas, Maria. 2003. *Working-Class Heroes: Protecting Home, Community, and Nation in a Chicago Neighborhood*. Berkeley: University of California Press.

Kennedy, Elizabeth, and Madeline D. Davis. 1993. *Boots of Leather, Slippers of Gold: The History of a Lesbian Community*. New York: Routledge.

Kirkey, Kenneth, and Ann Forsyth. 2001. "Men in the Valley: Gay Male Life on the Suburban-Rural Fringe." *Journal of Rural Studies* 17 (4): 421–41.

Knopp, Larry. 2004. "Ontologies of Place, Placelessness, and Movement: Queer Quests For Identity and Their Impacts on Contemporary Geographic Thought." *Gender, Place, and Culture: A Journal of Feminist Geography* 11 (1): 121–34.

Knopp, Lawrence. 1990. "Some Theoretical Implications of Gay Involvement in an Urban Land Market." *Political Geography Quarterly* 9 (4): 337–52.

―――. 1997. "Gentrification and Gay Neighborhood Formation in New Orleans." In *Homo Economics: Capitalism, Community, And Lesbian And Gay Life*, edited by Amy Gluckman and Betsy Reed, 45–59. New York: Routledge.

Kornblum, William. 1974. *Blue Collar Community*. Chicago: University of Chicago Press.

Krahulik, Karen. 2005. *Provincetown: From Pilgrim Landing to Gay Resort*. New York: New York University Press.

Kramer, Jerry Lee. 1995. "Bachelor Farmers and Spinsters: Gay and Lesbian Identities and Communities in Rural North Dakota." In *Mapping Desire: Geographies of Sexualities*, edited by David Bell and Gill Valentine, 182–94. New York: Routledge.

Krieger, Susan L. 1982. "Lesbian Identity and Community: Recent Social Science Literature." *Signs* 9 (1): 91–108.

―――. 1983. *The Mirror Dance: Identity in a Women's Community*. Philadelphia: Temple University Press.

Kusenbach, M., and K. Paulsen, eds. 2013. *Home: International Perspectives on Culture, Identity, and Belonging*. Frankfurt am Main: Peter Lang Academic Publishing.

Lacy, Karyn. 2007. *Blue-Chip Black: Race, Class, and Status in the New Black Middle Class*. Berkeley: University of California Press.

Lamont, Michèle. 2000. *The Dignity of Working Men: Morality and the Boundaries of Race, Class, and Immigration*. Cambridge: Harvard University Press.

Lamont, Michèle, and Ann Swidler. 2014. "Methodological Pluralism and the Possibilities and Limits of Interviewing." *Qualitative Sociology* 37 (2): 153–71.

Lane, Nikki. 2015. "All the Lesbians Are White, All the Villages Are Gay, but Some of Us Are Brave: Intersectionality, Belonging, and Black Queer Women's Scene Space in Washington, DC." In *Lesbian Geographies: Gender, Place, and Power*, edited by Kath Browne and Eduarda Ferreira, 219–42. London: Routledge.

Lannutti, Pamela J. 2005. "For Better or Worse: Exploring the Meanings of Same-Sex Marriage within the Lesbian, Gay, Bisexual and Transgendered Community." *Journal of Social and Personal Relationships* 22 (1): 5–18.

Latour, Bruno. 2005. *Reassembling the Social: An Introduction to Actor-Network-Theory*. Oxford University Press.

Latour, Bruno, and Emile Hermant. 2006. *Paris: Invisible City*. Translated by Liz Carey-Libbrecht. Paris: Institut Synthelabo.

Laumann, Edward O., Stephen Ellingson, Jenna Mahay, Anthony Paik, and Yoosik Youm. 2004. *The Sexual Organization of the City*. Chicago: University of Chicago Press.

Lauria, Mickey, and Lawrence Knopp. 1985. "Toward an Analysis of the Role of Gay Communities in the Urban Renaissance." *Urban Geography* 6 (2): 152–69.

Lees, Loretta. 2003. "The Ambivalence of Diversity and the Politics of Urban Renaissance: The Case of Youth in Downtown Portland, Maine." *International Journal of Urban and Regional Research* 27 (3): 613–34.

Levine, Martin P. 1979. "Gay Ghetto." *Journal of Homosexuality* 79 (4): 363–78.

Levitt, Peggy. 2015. *Artifacts and Allegiances: How Museums Put the Nation and the World on Display*. Berkeley: University of California Press.

Levy, Ariel. 2009. "Lesbian Nation." *New Yorker*. March 2. http://www.newyorker.com/magazine/2009/03/02/lesbian-nation.

Lewin, Ellen. 1996. *Out in the Field: Reflections of Gay and Lesbian Anthropologists*. Urbana: University of Illinois Press.

Lichterman, Paul. 1999. "Talking Identity In The Public Sphere: Broad Visions And Small Spaces In Sexual Identity Politics." *Theory & Society* 28 (1): 101–41.

Lloyd, Richard. 2006. *Neo-Bohemia: Art and Commerce in the Post-Industrial City*. New York: Routledge.

Lo, Jenny, and Theresa Healy. 2000. "Flagrantly Flaunting It? Contesting Perceptions of Locational Identity among Urban Vancouver Lesbians." In *From Nowhere to Everywhere*, edited by Gill Valentine, 29–44. New York: Huntington Park Press.

Lockard, Denyse. 1985. "The Lesbian Community: An Anthropological Approach." *Journal of Homosexuality* 11 (3–4): 83–95.

Lofland, John, and Lyn H. Lofland. 1987. "Lime Politics: The Selectively Progressive Ethos of Davis, California." *Research in Political Sociology* 3:245–68.

Lofland, Lyn. 1998. *The Public Realm: Exploring the City's Quintessential Social Territory*. New York: Aldine de Gruyter.

Logan, John, and Glenna Spitze. 1994. "Family Neighbors." *American Journal of Sociology* 100 (2): 453–76.

MacGregor, Lyn C. 2010. *Habits of the Heartland: Small-Town Life in Modern America*. Ithaca: Cornell University Press.

Mamo, Laura. 2007. *Queering Reproduction: Achieving Pregnancy in the Age of Technoscience.* Durham: Duke University Press.

Mansbridge, Jane. 1995. "What is the Feminist Movement?" In *Feminist Organizations: Harvest of the New Women's Movement,* edited by Myra Marx Ferree and Patricia Yancey Martin, 27–35. Philadelphia: Temple University Press.

Martin, Biddy. 1994. "Sexualities without Genders and Other Queer Utopias." *diacritics* 24 (2/3): 104–21.

Massey, Doreen. 1994. *Space, Place and Gender.* Cambridge: Polity.

McDowell, Linda. 1999. *Gender, Place and Identity: Understanding Feminist Geographies.* Minneapolis: University of Minnesota Press, Minneapolis.

McGranahan, David A. 1999. *Natural Amenities Drive Rural Population Change.* Agricultural Economic Report No. 781 (AER-781). October. Washington, DC: United States Department of Agriculture, Economic Research Service.

McKenzie, Roderick. 1925. "The Ecological Approach to the Study of Human Community." In *The City: Suggestions for Investigation of Human Behavior in the Urban Environment,* edited by Robert E. Park and Ernest W. Burgess, 63–79. Chicago: University of Chicago Press.

McKnight, John L. 1987. "Regenerating Community." *Social Policy* (Winter): 54–58.

McNaron, Toni A. H. 2007. "Post-Lesbian? Not Yet." *Journal of Lesbian Studies* 11 (1–2): 145–51.

McPherson, Miller, Lynn Smith-Lovin, and Matthew E. Brashears. 2006. "Social Isolation in America: Changes in Core Discussion Networks over Two Decades." *American Sociological Review* 71 (3): 353–75.

McVeigh, Rory, Michael R. Welch, and Thoroddur Bjarnason. 2003. "Hate Crime Reporting as a Successful Social Movement Outcome." *American Sociological Review* 68 (6): 843–67.

Mesch, Gustavo S., and Yael Levanon. 2003. "Community Networking and Locally-Based Social Ties in Two Suburban Localities." *City & Community* 2 (4): 335–51.

Meyer, Doug. 2008. "Interpreting and Experiencing Anti-Queer Violence: Race, Class, and Gender Differences among LGBT Hate Crime Victims." *Race, Gender & Class* 15 (3–4): 262–82.

Meyer, Ilan H. 2003. "Prejudice, Social Stress, and Mental Health in Lesbian, Gay and Bisexual Populations: Conceptual Issues and Research." *Psychological Bulletin* 129 (5): 674–97.

———. 2007. "Prejudice and Discrimination as Social Stressors." In *The Health of Sexual Minorities: Public Health Perspectives on Gay, Lesbian, Transgendered Populations,* edited by Ilan Meyer and Mary Northridge, 242–67. New York: Springer.

Milligan, Melinda. 2003. "Displacement and Identity Discontinuity: The Role of Nostalgia in Establishing New Identity Categories." *Symbolic Interaction* 26 (3): 381–403.

Millward, Liz. 2007. "New Xenaland: Lesbian Place Making, the Xenaverse, and Aotearoa New Zealand." *Gender, Place & Culture: A Journal of Feminist Geography* 14 (4): 427–43.

Molotch, Harvey. 2002. "Place in Product." *International Journal of Urban and Regional Research* 26 (4): 665–88.

Molotch, Harvey, William Freudenburg, and Krista Paulsen. 2000. "History Repeats Itself, but How? City Character, Urban Tradition, and the Accomplishment of Place." *American Sociological Review* 65 (6): 791–823.

Monti, Daniel, Colleen Butler, Alexandra Curley, Kirsten Tilney, and Melissa Weiner. 2003. "Private Lives and Public Worlds: Changes in Americans' Social Ties and Civic Attachments in Late-20th Century America." *City and Community* 2 (2): 143–63.

Moon, Dawne. 2012. "Who Am I and Who Are We? Conflicting Narratives of Collective Selfhood in Stigmatized Groups." *American Journal of Sociology* 117 (5): 1336–79.

Moore, Mignon R. 2006. "Lipstick or Timberlands? Meanings of Gender Presentation in Black Lesbian Communities." *Signs* 32 (1): 113–39.

———. 2011. *Invisible Families: Gay Identities, Relationships and Motherhood among Black Women*. Berkeley: University of California Press.

Mosse, George L. 1979. "National Cemeteries and National Revival: The Cult of the Fallen Soldiers in Germany." *Journal of Contemporary History* 14 (1): 1–20.

Muller, Tiffany. 2007. "Lesbian Community in WNBA Spaces." *Social & Cultural Geography* 8 (1): 9–28.

Muñoz, José Esteban. 2009. *Cruising Utopia: The Then and There of Queer Futurity*. New York: New York University Press.

Myrdahl, Tiffany Muller. 2013. "Ordinary (Small) Cities and LGBQ Lives." *ACME: An International EJournal for Critical Geographies* 12 (2): 279–304.

Nash, Catherine J. 2013. "The Age of the 'Post-Mo'? Toronto's Gay Village and a New Generation." *Geoforum* 49:243–52.

Nash, Catherine J., and Alison Bain. 2007. " 'Reclaiming Raunch': Spatializing Queer Identities at Toronto Women's Bathhouse Events." *Social and Cultural Geography* 8 (1): 16–42.

Nash, Catherine J., and Andrew Gorman-Murray. 2014. "LGBT Neighbourhoods and 'New Mobilities': Towards Understanding Transformations in Sexual and Gendered Urban Landscapes." *International Journal of Urban and Regional Research* 38 (3): 756–72.

Nestle, Joan. 1997. "Restrictions and Reclamation: Lesbian Bars and Beaches on the 1950s." In *Queers in Space: Communities, Public Places, Sites of Resistance*, edited by Gordon Brent Ingram, Anne-Marie Bouthillette, and Yolanda Retter, 61–68. Seattle: Bay Press.

Newton, Esther. 1993. *Cherry Grove, Fire Island: Sixty Years in America's First Gay and Lesbian Town*. Boston: Beacon Press.

Nichols Clark, T. 2004. *The City as an Entertainment Machine*. Amsterdam: Jai/Elsevier.

Norman, Jon. 2013. *Small Cities USA: Growth, Diversity, and Inequality*. New Brunswick: Rutgers University Press.

O'Malley, Greenburg Zack. 2009. "America's Most Livable Cities." *Forbes*. April 1. http://www.forbes.com/2009/04/01/cities-city-ten-lifestyle-real-estate-livable-cities.html.

Olcott, Mike. 2011. "Making Noise: Meet the Burlesque 'Dishes.'" *Portland Press Herald*. March 24.

Oldenburg, Ray. 1989. *The Great Good Place: Cafes, Coffee Shops, Bookstores, Bars, Hair Salons, and Other Hangouts at the Heart of a Community*. New York: Marlowe & Company.

Park, Robert E. 1925. *The City: Suggestions for the Study of Human Nature in the Urban Environment*. Chicago: University of Chicago Press.

Parker, Jeffrey. 2009. "Negotiating the Space between Avant-garde and 'Hip Enough': Businesses and Commercial Gentrification in Wicker Park." Master's thesis, University of Chicago.

Parker, Lonnae O'Neal. 2009. Same-Sex Couples Make Themselves at Home in Welcoming Prince George's Suburbs. *Washington Post*. June 29. http://www.washingtonpost.com/wp-dyn/content/article/2009/06/28/AR2009062802467.html.

Paulsen, Krista. 2004. "Making Character Concrete: Empirical Strategies for Studying Place Distinction." *City & Community* 3 (3): 243–62.

Plummer, Ken. 1982. "Symbolic Interactionism and Sexual Conduct: An Emergent Perspective." In *Human Sexual Relations*, edited by Mike Brake, 223–41. New York: Pantheon Books.

Podmore, Julie A. 2001. "Lesbians in the Crowd: Gender, Sexuality and Visibility along Montréal's Boul. St-Laurent." *Gender, Place & Culture* 8 (4): 333–55.

———. 2006. "Gone 'Underground'? Lesbian Visibility and the Consolidation of Queer Space in Montréal." *Social & Cultural Geography* 7 (4): 595–625.

Polletta, Francesca. 1998. "Contending Stories: Narrative in Social Movements." *Qualitative Sociology* 21 (4): 419–46.

Polletta, Francesca, and James M. Jasper. 2001. "Collective Identity and Social Movements." *Annual Review of Sociology* 27:283–305.

Pritchard, Annette, Nigel Morgan, and Diane Sedgley. 2002. "In Search of Lesbian Space? The Experience of Manchester's Gay Village." *Leisure Studies* 21:105–23.

Puar, Jasbir K. 2007. *Terrorist Assemblages: Homonationalism in Queer Times*. Durham: Duke University Press.

Pulido, Laura. 1996. "Development Of The 'People Of Color' Identity in the Environmental Movement of the Southwestern United States." *Socialist Review* 26 (3–4): 145–80.

Putnam, Robert D. 2000. *Bowling Alone: The Collapse and Revival of American Community*. New York: Simon & Schuster.

Rabinowitz, Jonathan, Israel Kim, and Bernard Lazerwitz. 1992. "Metropolitan Size and Participation in Religion-Ethnic Communities." *Journal for the Scientific Study of Religion* 31 (3): 339–45.

Rainville, David. 2014. "Courthouse Construction Underway, Night and Day." *Greenfield Recorder*. November 19. http://infoweb.newsbank.com/resources/doc/nb/news/151B7BFD219B16A0?p=NewsBank.

Rambo, Eric, and Elaine Chan. 1990. "Text, Structure, and Action in Cultural Sociology: A Commentary on 'Positive Objectivity' in Wuthnow and Archer." *Theory and Society* 19 (5): 635–48.

Reger, Jo. 2012. *Everywhere and Nowhere: U.S. Feminist Communities in the 21st Century*. New York: Oxford University Press.

Retter, Yolanda. 1997. "Lesbian Spaces in Los Angeles, 1970–90." In *Queers in Space: Communities, Public Places, Sites of Resistance*, edited by Yolanda Retter, Anne-Marie Bouthillette, and Gordon Brent Ingram, 325–37. Seattle: Bay Press

Reynolds, Beth. 2014. "Up and Down the Contra Line." *The Recorder*. November 28. http://infoweb.newsbank.com/resources/doc/nb/news/151E718CEE797218?p=NewsBank.

Rheingold, Howard. 1993. *The Virtual Community: Homesteading on the Electronic Frontier*. Cambridge: MIT Press.

Riis, Jacob. 1971. *How the Other Half Lives: Studies Among the Tenements of New York*. Penguin Books.

Robinson, Zandria F. 2014. *This Ain't Chicago: Race, Class, and Regional Identity in the Post-Soul South*. Chapel Hill: University of North Carolina Press Books.

Rockquemore, Kerry Ann, and Patricia Arend. 2002. "Opting for White: Choice, Fluidity, and Racial Identity Construction in Post Civil-Rights America." *Race & Society* 5 (1): 49–64.

Rogers, Barbara, and Stillman Rogers. 2007. *Massachusetts Off the Beaten Path*. Lanham: Globe Pequot Press.

Romig, Kevin. 2010. "Community and Social Capital in Upper-Income Neighborhoods: An Investigation in Metropolitan Phoenix." *Urban Geography* 31 (8): 1065–79.

Roos, Patricia A., Mary K. Trigg, and Mary S. Hartman. 2006. "Changing Families/Changing Communities." *Community, Work & Family* 9 (2): 197–224.

Rose, Gillian. 1990. "Imagining Poplar in the 1920s: Contested Concepts of Community." *Journal of Historical Geography* 16 (4): 425–37.

Rosenthal, Carolyn. 1987. "Aging and Intergenerational Relations in Canada." In *Aging in Canada*, edited by Victor W. Marshall, 311–42. Toronto: Fitzhenry & Whiteside.

Rothblum, Esther. 2010. "Where Is the 'Women's Community?' Voices of Lesbian, Bisexual, and Queer Women and Heterosexual Sisters." *Feminism & Psychology* 20 (4): 454–72.

Rothenberg, Tamar. 1995. " 'And She Told Two Friends:' Lesbians Creating Urban Social Space." In *Mapping Desire: Geographies of Sexuality*, edited by David Bell and Gill Valentine, 150–65. New York: Routledge.

Rotolo, Thomas. 2000. "Town Heterogeneity and Affiliation: A Multilevel Analysis of Voluntary Association Membership." *Sociological Perspectives* 43 (2): 271–89.

Routhier, Ray. 2012. "Portland Excels at Making the List." *Portland Press Herald*. August 13.

Rowley, Rex J. 2014. "Multidimensional Community and the Las Vegas Experience." *GeoJournal* 80 (3): 1–18.

Rubin, Gayle. 1993. "Thinking Sex: Notes for a Radical Theory of the Politics of Sexuality." In *Lesbian and Gay Studies Reader*, edited by Henry Abelove, Michele Aina Barale, and David Halperin, 3–44. London: Routledge.

Ruiz-Tagle, Javier. 2013. "A Theory of Socio-Spatial Integration: Problems, Policies and Concepts from a US Perspective." *International Journal of Urban and Regional Research* 37 (2): 388–408.

Russell, G. M., and J. S. Bohan. 2005. "The Gay Generation Gap: Communicating Across the LGBT Generational Divide." *Institute for Gay and Lesbian Strategic Studies* 8 (1): 1–8.

Rust, Paula C. 1993. " 'Coming Out' In The Age Of Social Constructionism: Sexual Identity Formation among Lesbian and Bisexual Women." *Gender & Society* 7 (1): 50–77.

———. 2000. "Make Me a Map." *Journal of Bisexuality* 1 (2–3): 47–108.

Ryle, Robyn R., and Robert V. Robinson. 2006. "Ideology, Moral Cosmology, and Community in the United States." *City and Community* 5 (1): 53–69.

Sampson, Robert J. 1988. "Local Friendship Ties and Community Attachment in Mass Society: A Multilevel Systemic Model." *American Sociological Review* 53 (5): 766–79.

———. 2012. *Great American City: Chicago and the Enduring Neighborhood Effect*. Chicago: University of Chicago Press.

Sampson, Robert J, Jeffrey D. Morenoff, and Thomas Gannon-Rowley. 2002. "Assessing 'Neighborhood Effects': Social Processes and New Directions in Research." *Annual Review of Sociology* 28:443–78.

Saperstein, Aliya, and Andrew M. Penner. 2012. "Racial Fluidity and Inequality in the United States." *American Journal of Sociology* 118 (3): 676–727.

Savolainen, Jukka. 1994. "The Rationality of Drawing Big Conclusions Based on Small Samples: In Defense of Mill's Methods." *Social Forces* 72 (4): 1217–24.

Schilt, Kristen. 2010. *Just One of the Guys?: Transgender Men and the Persistence of Gender Inequality*. Chicago: University of Chicago Press.

Schilt, Kristen, and Laurel Westbrook. 2009. "Doing Gender, Doing Heteronormativity 'Gender Normals', Transgender People, and the Social Maintenance of Heterosexuality." *Gender & Society* 23 (4): 440–64.

Schippers, Mimi. 2016. *Beyond Monogamy: Polyamory and the Future of Polyqueer Sexualities*. New York: New York University Press.

Schmalenbach, Herman. 1961. "The Sociological Category of Communion." *Theories of Society* 1:331–47.

Schulman, Michael. 2013. "Generation LBGTQIA." *New York Times* (Fashion & Style). January 10, p. E1.

Scott, Joan W. "The Evidence of Experience." *Critical Inquiry* 17 (4): 773–97.

Sedgwick, Eve. 1990. *Epistemology of the Closet*. Berkeley: University of California Press.

———. 2003. *Touching Feeling: Affect, Pedagogy, Performativity*. Durham: Duke University Press.

Seidman, Steven. 1993. "Identity and Politics in a Postmodern Gay Culture." In *Fear of a Queer Planet*, edited by Michael Warner, 105–42. Minneapolis: University of Minnesota Press.

———. 2002. *Beyond the Closet: The Transformation of Gay and Lesbian Life*. New York: Routledge.

Sennett, Richard. 1977. *The Fall of Public Man*. New York: Knopf.

Sharkey, Patrick. 2013. *Stuck in Place: Urban Neighborhoods and the End of Progress toward Racial Equality*. Chicago: University of Chicago Press.

Shores, Chris. 2014. "In Turbulent Tenure, Susan Hollins, as Superintendent, Helped Stabilize Greenfield Schools." *Greenfield Recorder*. June 29. http://infoweb.newsbank.com /resources/doc/nb/news/14EC557C12F689B8?p=NewsBank.

Sibalis, Michael. 2004. "Urban Space and Homosexuality: The Example of the Marais, Paris' 'Gay Ghetto.'" *Urban Studies* 41 (9): 1739–58.

Silver, Daniel, Terry Nichols Clark, and Clemente Jesus Navarro Yannez. 2010. "Scenes: Social Context in an Age of Contingency." *Social Forces* 88 (5): 2293–324.

Simmel, Georg. 1971. "The Metropolis and Metropolitan Life." In *Georg Simmel: On Individualism and Social Forms*, edited by Donald N. Levine, 324–39. Chicago: University of Chicago Press.

Simon, William, and John Gagnon. 2011. *Sexual Conduct: The Social Sources of Human Sexuality*. Rutgers: Transaction Publishers.

Sivakumar, Chitra. 2000. "Inner-City Socioscape." *Economic and Political Weekly* 25 (38): 16–22.

Skeggs, Bev. 1999. "Matter Out Of Place: Visibility And Sexualities In Leisure Spaces." *Leisure Studies* 18 (3): 213–32.

Skocpol, Theda. 1984. *Vision and Method in Historical Sociology*. New York: Cambridge University Press.

Skocpol, Theda, and Margaret Somers. 1980. "The Uses of Comparative History in Macrosocial Inquiry." *Comparative Studies in Society and History* 22 (2): 174–97.

Small, Mario. 2004. *Villa Victoria: The Transformation of Social Capital in a Boston Barrio*. Chicago: University of Chicago Press.

Smart, Carol. 2008. "'Can I Be Bridesmaid?' Combining the Personal and Political in Same-Sex Weddings." *Sexualities* 11 (6): 761–76.

Smart, Michael J., and Nicholas J. Klein. 2013. "Neighborhoods of Affinity." *Journal of the American Planning Association* 79 (2): 110–24.

Smith, Darren P., and Louise Holt. 2005. "'Lesbian Migrants in the Gentrified Valley' and 'Other' Geographies of Rural Gentrification." *Journal of Rural Studies* 21 (3): 313–22.

Smith, David M. and Gary J. Gates. 2001. *Gay and Lesbian Families in the United States: Same-Sex Unmarried Partner Households: A Preliminary Analysis of 2000 United States Census Data*. Washington, DC: Human Rights Campaign.

Somers, Margaret R. 1993. "Citizenship and the Place of the Public Sphere: Law, Community, and Political Culture in the Transition to Democracy." *American Sociological Review* 58 (5): 587–620.

Somers, Margaret R., and Gloria D. Gibson. 1994. "Reclaiming the Epistemological 'Other': Narrative and the Social Construction of Identity." In *Social Theory and the Politics of Identity*, edited by Craig Calhoun, 39–99. Cambridge: Blackwell.

South, Scott J., and Kyle D. Crowder. 1998. "Avenues and Barriers to Residential Mobility among Single Mothers." *Journal of Marriage and the Family* 60 (4): 866–77.

South, Scott J., and Glenn D. Deane. 1993. "Race and Residential Mobility: Individual Determinants and Structural Constraints." *Social Forces* 72 (1): 147–67.

Spear, Alden, Jr. 1974. "Residential Satisfaction as an Intervening Variable in Residential Mobility." *Demography* 11 (2): 173–88.

Stack, Carol. 1974. *All Our Kin*. New York: Random House.

Stein, Arlene. 1989. All Dressed Up, But No Place to Go? Style Wars and the New Lesbianism." *Out/look* 1 (4): 34–44.

———. 1997. *Sex and Sensibility: Stories of a Lesbian Generation*. Berkeley: University of California Press.

Stein, Maurice Robert. 1960. *The Eclipse of Community: An Interpretation of American Studies*. Princeton: Princeton University Press.

Stotzer, Rebecca L. 2010. "Sexual Orientation-Based Hate Crimes on Campus: The Impact of Policy on Reporting Rates." *Sexuality Research and Social Policy* 7 (3): 147–54.

Sullivan, Andrew. 2005. "The End of Gay Culture." *New Republic*. October 23, 16–21.

Suttles, Gerald D. 1968. *The Social Order of the Slum: Ethnicity and Territory in the Inner City*. Chicago: University of Chicago Press.

———. 1974. *The Social Construction of Communities*. Chicago: University of Chicago Press.

Swan, Rachel. 2014. "Pride of Place: As the Nation's Gay Districts Grow More Affluent, Lesbians are Migrating to the 'Burbs." *San Francisco Weekly*. June 25. http://www.sfweekly.com/news/pride-of-place-as-the-nations-gay-districts-grow-more-affluent-lesbians-are-migrating-to-the-burbs/.

Swidler, Ann. 1986. "Culture in Action: Symbols and Strategies." *American Sociological Review* 51 (2): 273–86.

Tavory, Iddo, and Nina Eliasoph. 2013. "Coordinating Futures: Toward a Theory of Anticipation." *American Journal of Sociology* 118 (4): 908–42.

Taylor, Monique. 2002. *Harlem: Between Heaven and Hell*. Minneapolis: University of Minnesota Press.

Taylor, Verta. 1989. "Social Movement Continuity: The Women's Movement in Abeyance." *American Sociological Review* 54 (5): 761–75.

Taylor, Verta, and Leila Rupp. 1993. "Women's Culture and Lesbian Feminist Activism: A Reconsideration of Cultural Feminism." *Signs: Journal of Women in Culture and Society* 19:32–61.

Taylor, Verta, and Nancy E. Whittier. 1992. "Collective Identity in Social Movement Communities." In *Frontiers in Social Movement Theory*, edited by Aldon. D. Morris and Carol McClurg Mueller, 104–29. New Haven: Yale University Press.

———. 1999. "Collective Identity in Social Movement Communities." In *Waves of Protest: Social Movements Since the Sixties*, edited by Victoria Johnson and Jo Freeman, 169–88. Lanham: Rowan & Littlefield.

Taylor, Yvette. 2004. "Negotiation and Navigation—An Exploration of the Spaces/Places of Working-Class Lesbians." *Sociological Research Online* 9 (1). http://socresonline.org.uk/9/1/taylor.html.

Thorpe, Rochelle. 1996. "'A House Where Queers Go': African-American Lesbian Nightlife in Detroit, 1940–1975. In *Inventing Lesbian Cultures in America*, edited by E. Lewin, 40–61. Boston: Beacon Press.

Tilcsik, András, Michel Anteby, and Carly Knight. 2015. "Concealable Stigma and Occupational Segregation: Toward a Theory of Gay and Lesbian Occupations." *Administrative Science Quarterly* 60 (3): 446–81.

Tongson, Karen. 2011. *Relocations: Queer Suburban Imaginaries*. New York: New York University Press.

—. 2005. Metronormativity and Gay Globalization. In *Quer durch die Geisteswissenschaften: Perspektiven der Queer Theory*, edited by Elahe Haschemi Tekani and Beatrice Micahelis, 40–53. Berlin: Querverlag.

Tönnies, F. (1887) 1963. *Community and Society [Gemeinschaft and Gesellschaft]*. Translated and edited by Charles P. Lumis. New York: Harper & Row.

Trappeniers, Lieven, Marc Godon, Laurence Claeys, Oliver Martinot, and Emmanuel Marilly. 2008. "Cross-Media Experiences: Ambient Community Interactions in the City." *Bell Labs Technical Journal* 13 (2): 5–11.

Valentine, Gill. 1993a. "Hetero-Sexing Space: Lesbian Perceptions and Experiences of Everyday Spaces." *Environment and Planning D—Society and Space* 9 (3): 395–413.

—. 1993b. "Negotiating and Managing Multiple Sexual Identities: Lesbian Time-Space Strategies." *Transactions of the Institute of British Geographers* 18 (2): 237–48.

—. 1995. "Out and About: Geographies of Lesbian Landscapes." *International Journal of Urban and Regional Research* 19 (1): 96–111.

—. 1997. "Making Space: Lesbian Separatist Communities in the United States." In *Contested Countryside Cultures: Otherness, Marginalisation and Rurality*, edited by Paul Cloke and Jo Little, 105–17. London: Routledge.

—. 2000. *From Nowhere to Everywhere: Lesbian Geographies*. New York: Harrington Park Press.

—. 2007. "Theorizing and Researching Intersectionality: A Challenge for Feminist Geography." *Professional Geographer* 59 (1): 10–21.

Valentine, Gill, and Tracey Skelton. 2003. "Finding Oneself, Losing Oneself: The Lesbian and Gay 'Scene' as a Paradoxical Space." *International Journal of Urban and Regional Research* 27 (4): 849–66.

Van Maanen, John. 1991. "Playing Back the Tape: Early Days in the Field." In *Experiencing Fieldwork: An Inside View of Qualitative Research*, edited by William Shaffir and Robert Alan Stebbins, 31–42. Newbury Park: Sage.

Walther, Carol S., Dudley L. Poston Jr., and Yuan Gu. 2010. "Ecological Analyses of Gay Male and Lesbian Partnering in the Metropolitan United States in 2000." *Population Research and Policy Review* 30 (3): 419–48.

Warner, Michael. 1993. *Fear of a Queer Planet: Queer Politics and Social Theory*. Minneapolis: University of Minnesota Press.

Warren, Roland E. 1963. *The Community in America*. Chicago: Rand McNally.

—. 1970. "Toward a Non-Utopian Normative Model of Community." *American Sociological Review* 35 (2): 219–28.

Watt, Katherine. 1997. "Selectmen Approve Uses for $600,000 Block Grant." *The Recorder*. November 14.

Webber, Melvin M. (1963) 1999. "Order in Diversity: Community Without Propinquity." In *American Cities Technology Reader: Wilderness to Wired City*, edited by Gerrylynn K. Roberts, 201–10. New York: Routledge.

Weber, Max. (1922) 1978. *Economy and Society, vol. 1 and 2*. Edited by Guenther Roth and Claus Wittich. Berkeley: University of California Press.

Weeks, Jeffrey. 1986. *Sexuality (Key Ideas)*. New York: Routledge.

Wei, Wei. 2007. "Wandering Men No Longer Wander Around: The Production and Transformation of Local Homosexual Identities in Contemporary Chengdu, China." *Inter-Asia Cultural Studies* 8 (4): 572–88.

Wellman, Barry. 1977. "The Community Question: Intimate Ties in East New York." Research Paper No. 90. Toronto: University of Toronto Centre for Urban and Community Studies.

———. 1979. "The Community Question: The Intimate Networks of East Yorkers." *American Journal of Sociology* 84 (5): 1201–31.

———. 1985. "DomesticWork, PaidWork and NetWork." In *Understanding Personal Relationships*, edited by Steve Duck and Daniel Perlman, 159–91. Chicago: University of Chicago Press.

———. 1988. "The Community Question Reevaluated." In *Power, Community and the City*, edited by Michael Peter Smith, 81–107. Rutgers: Transaction Publishers.

———. 1999. *Networks in the Global Village: Life in Contemporary Communities*. Boulder: Westview Press.

———. 2001. "Physical Place and Cyberplace: The Rise of Personalized Networking." *International Journal of Urban and Regional Research* 25 (2): 227–52.

Wellman, Barry, and Milena Gulia. 1999. "Net Surfers Don't Ride Alone: Virtual Communities as Communities." In *Communities in Cyberspace*, edited by Marc A. Smith and Peter Kollock, 167–94. New York: Routledge

Wellman, Barry, and Barry Leighton. 1979. "Networks, Neighborhoods and Communities: Approaches to the Study of the Community Question." *Urban Affairs Review* 14 (3): 363–90.

Wellman, Barry, and Scot Wortley. 1990. "Different Strokes for Different Folks: Community Ties and Social Support." *American Journal of Sociology* 96 (3): 558–88.

Westbrook, Laurel, and Kristen Schilt. 2014. "Doing Gender, Determining Gender: Transgender People, Gender Panics, and the Maintenance of the Sex/Gender/Sexuality System." *Gender & Society* 28 (1): 32–57.

Weston, Kath. 1995. "Get Thee to a Big City: Sexual Imaginary and the Great Gay Migration." *GLQ* 2 (3): 253–78.

Wherry, Frederick. 2011. *The Philadelphia Barrio: The Arts, Branding, and Neighborhood Transformation*. Chicago: University of Chicago Press.

White, Carol Wayne. 2005. "Religious Scriptors of Human Possibilities and Cultural Transformations." *Iowa Journal of Cultural Studies* 7 (1): 46–62.

White, Katherine J. Curtis, and Avery M. Guest. 2003. "Community Lost or Transformed? Urbanization and Social Ties." *City and Community* 2 (3): 239–59.

Whitlow, Julie, and Patricia Ould. 2015. *Same-Sex Marriage, Context, and Lesbian Identity: Wedded but Not Always a Wife*. Lanham: Lexington Books.

Whittier, Nancy. 1995. *Feminist Generations: The Persistence of the Radical Women's Movement*. Philadelphia: Temple University Press.

Whyte, William Foote. 1943. *Street Corner Society: The Social Structure of an Italian Slum*. Chicago: University of Chicago Press.

Wilkins, Amy C. 2008. *Wannabes, Goths, and Christians: The Boundaries of Sex, Style, and Status*. Chicago: University of Chicago Press.

Wilkinson, Lindsey, and Jennifer Pearson. 2013. "High School Religious Context and Reports of Same-Sex Attraction and Sexual Identity in Young Adulthood." *Social Psychology Quarterly* 76 (2): 180–202.

Williams, Raymond. 1973. *The Country and the City*. London: Oxford University Press.

Wilson, William Julius. 1996. *When Work Disappears: The World of the New Urban Poor*. New York: Knopf.

Winchester, Hilary, and Paul White. 1988. "The Location of Marginalized Groups in the Inner City." *Environment and Planning D: Society and Space* 6 (1): 37–54.

Winfrey, Oprah. 2011. *Happiest City in America: San Luis Obispo*. The Oprah Winfrey Show. January 26. http://www.oprah.com/oprahshow/Happiest-City-in-America-San-Luis-Obispo-Video#.

Wirth, Louis. 1938. "Urbanism as a Way of Life." *American Journal of Sociology* 44 (1): 1–24.

Wodtke, Geoffrey, David J. Harding, and Felix Elwert. 2011. "Neighborhood Effects in Temporal Perspective." *American Sociological Review* 76 (5): 713–36.

Wolf, Deborah Goleman. 1979. *The Lesbian Community.* Berkeley: University of California Press.

Wuthnow, Robert. 1989. *Meaning and Moral Order: Explorations in Cultural Analysis.* Berkeley: University of California Press.

Wynn, Jonathan. *The Tour Guide: Walking and Talking New York.* Chicago: University of Chicago Press.

Zonn, Leo E. 1984. "Decision-Making within a Constrained Population: Residential Choice by Black Urban Households." *Journal of Black Studies* 14 (3): 327–40.

Zukin, Sharon. 1991. *Landscapes of Power: From Detroit to Disney World.* Berkley: University of California Press.

———. 1996. *The Cultures of Cities.* Hoboken: Wiley-Blackwell.

———. 2010. *Naked City: The Death and Life of Authentic Urban Places.* New York: Oxford University Press.

INDEX

abundance and acceptance, 20, 122, 164, 175, 177–79, 193, 237–38, 240; city ecology, 14, 198, 203–8, 223; identity cultures, 20, 207, 212, 214; identity politics, 208; and place, 203–8; place narratives, 15, 208–9, 212

ACT-UP, 117

affinity community, 106, 138, 140–41, 144–47, 282n27, 282n28, 283n38; ambient community, difference between, 137; exclusivity of, 142–43

African Americans, 55–56, 138, 238, 247

ambient community, 18–19, 27–28, 51, 54–57, 82–83, 138, 146, 154, 160, 167, 169, 179–87, 193, 273n18, 276n52, 277n53, 277n55, 278n62, 278n70; affinity community, difference between, 137; city ecology, 52, 277n57; informal ties, 52–53; local ties, 58; and marginalization, 53; post-identity politics, 62–63, 89; shared sexual identity, 53; as term, 274n23; "we-feeling," 277n54

Amherst (Massachusetts), 153, 158–59, 161–62, 176, 190

Anderson, Elijah, 128; cosmopolitan canopy, 276n52, 277n55, 277n57, 278n69

Arabica Coffee, 116

Art After Dark, 204

Asheville (North Carolina), 238

Atlanta (Georgia), 247

Bakersfield (California), 75

Berkeley (California), 22

Bible Belt, 99

Boston (Massachusetts), 1, 3, 51, 108, 155, 159, 181, 203, 206, 210, 212, 216, 242, 281n5, 281n6, 285n16, 287n2, 287n7; Irish Americans in, 290n45; Jamaica Plain, 12, 209

Boston Femme Show, 109

Boulder (Colorado), 78–79, 87, 132, 200

Boys Don't Cry (movie), 177

Brattleboro (Vermont), 159

Brekhus, Wayne, 17, 271n53, 275n33, 276n45

Brint, Steven, 273n18, 277n53

Brooklyn (New York), 212, 216, 239, 285n16; Park Slope, 12–13, 199, 209, 243

Brown, Gavin, 271–72n54

Brubaker, Rogers, 17, 268n11

Buettner, Dan, 61

burlesque, 119

Butch Is a Noun (Bergman), 116

Butch Project, 125

Butler, Judith, 233–35, 237

California, 29, 61, 70–72, 97, 99

California Polytechnic Institute (CALPOLY), 61, 67, 72, 76, 94, 204, 287n2

Cambridge (Massachusetts), 158

Cayuga Heights (New York), 21

Central Coast, 4, 61, 85–86, 98, 235

Central Coast Lesbian Listserv, 62, 65, 86, 91

Central Valley, 70–71, 75–76, 92, 209, 216–17